FILLING THE GAPS OF THE MIDDLE-LENGTH DISCOURSES

VOLUME 1

DR ARIYATHUSHEL ARAHANT

CLEVER FOX PUBLISHING
Chennai, India

Published by CLEVER FOX PUBLISHING 2024
Copyright © Dr Ariyathushel Arahant 2024

All Rights Reserved.
PAPERBACK ISBN: 978-93-67077-90-0
HARDBACK ISBN: 978-93-67076-12-5

This book has been published with all reasonable efforts taken to make the material error-free after the consent of the author. No part of this book shall be used, reproduced in any manner whatsoever without written permission from the author, except in the case of brief quotations embodied in critical articles and reviews.

The Author of this book is solely responsible and liable for its content including but not limited to the views, representations, descriptions, statements, information, opinions and references ["Content"]. The Content of this book shall not constitute or be construed or deemed to reflect the opinion or expression of the Publisher or Editor. Neither the Publisher nor Editor endorse or approve the Content of this book or guarantee the reliability, accuracy or completeness of the Content published herein and do not make any representations or warranties of any kind, express or implied, including but not limited to the implied warranties of merchantability, fitness for a particular purpose. The Publisher and Editor shall not be liable whatsoever for any errors, omissions, whether such errors or omissions result from negligence, accident, or any other cause or claims for loss or damages of any kind, including without limitation, indirect or consequential loss or damage arising out of use, inability to use, or about the reliability, accuracy or sufficiency of the information contained in this book.

Homage to the Supremely Enlightened Buddha!

Certainly, Buddha's Dhamma leads to cessation, Nibbana across stages.
Certainly, Buddha is the knower of all worlds, the highest of the Triple Gem.
Homage to the Supremely Enlightened Buddha!
-Dr Ariyathushel Arahant

Summary of the Practice Leading to Four-fold Nibbana, Sotapanna (Stream Entry):

The practice leading to Nibbana should include multiple aspects that reflect the qualities of the Triple Gem in thoughts as much as possible in daily life and abandoning fetters. This requires within daily life maintaining the mind in the middle way; becoming a good person in all areas of life; and not discriminating against self or others based on social divisions.

It also requires engaging in meritorious activities, maintaining precepts in daily life and engaging in Dhamma activities to facilitate the process of leading to Stream entry and beyond. If you want to experience four-fold Nibbana, you may pay homage to the supremely enlightened Buddha in your thoughts day and night! After that, four-fold Nibbana (universal Dhamma) and universal (Savaka) Sangha! Include noble virtues[1] into your practice of Dhamma and engage in ten wholesome activities, especially work on developing the right view (i.e. give up grasping conventions). This is a summary of the practice leading to Sotapanna (Stream Entry). The practice remains the same for all.

---

[1] Fourth factor of Stream Entry refers to developing noble virtues; noble virtues can be developed by treating others in the manner one would like to be treated, maintain noble precepts (abstain from killing living beings, stealing, sexual misconduct, false speech, backbiting, harsh or abusive speech, useless or meaningless conversation, wrong means of livelihood) , becoming a good person who looks after others as applicable to oneself (it may be looking after friends, family, an employer or employees, ascetics and so forth), and becoming an ethical person who genuinely cares for others and avoids discriminating against others on any grounds is the practice that is helpful in developing noble virtues, a factor of stream entry.

Table of Contents

Preface 9

Chapter 1
Introduction 10

Chapter 2
The Right view: The Four-fold Path and the Practice to Nibbana
.... 12

Chapter 3
Middle Discourses 1: Mūlapariyāyasutta *The Root of All Things* 19

Chapter 4
Middle Discourses 2: Sabbāsavasutta *All the Defilements* 29

Chapter 5
Middle Discourses 3: Dhammadāyādasutta *Heirs in the Teaching* 37

Chapter 6
Middle Discourses 4: Bhayabheravasutta *Fear and Dread* 42

Chapter 7
Middle Discourses 5: Anaṅgaṇasutta *Unblemished* 49

Chapter 8
Middle Discourses 6: Ākaṅkheyyasutta *One Might Wish* 56

Chapter 9
Middle Discourses 7: Vatthasutta *The Simile of the Cloth* 61

Chapter 10
Middle Discourses 8: Sallekhasutta *Self-Effacement* 67

Chapter 11
Middle Discourses 9: Sammādiṭṭhisutta *Right View* 79

Chapter 12
Middle Discourses 10: Mahāsatipaṭṭhānasutta *Discourse on the Applications of Mindfulness* 93

Chapter 13
Middle Discourses 11: Cūḷasīhanādasutta *The Shorter Discourse on the Lion's Roar* 111

Chapter 14
Middle Discourses 12: Mahāsīhanādasutta *The Longer Discourse on the Lion's Roar* 120

Chapter 15
Middle Discourses 13: Mahādukkhakkhandhasutta *The Longer Discourse on the Mass of Suffering* 135

Chapter 16
Middle Discourses 14: Cūḷadukkhakkhandhasutta *The Shorter Discourse on the Mass of Suffering* 146

Chapter 17
Middle Discourses 15: Anumānasutta *Measuring Up* 152

Chapter 18
Middle Discourses 16: Cetokhilasutta *Hard-heartedness* 157

Chapter 19
Middle Discourses 17: Vanapatthasutta *Jungle Thickets* 162

Chapter 20
Middle Discourses 18: Madhupiṇḍikasutta *The Honey-Cake* 166

Chapter 21
Middle Discourses 19: Dvedhāvitakkasutta *Two Kinds of Thought* 173

Chapter 22
Middle Discourses 20: Vitakkasaṇṭhānasutta *How to Stop Thinking* 180

Chapter 23
Middle Discourses 21: Kakacūpamasutta *The Simile of the Saw* 185

Chapter 24
Middle Discourses 22: Alagaddūpamasutta *The Simile of the Cobra* 193

Chapter 25
Middle Discourses 23: Vammikasutta *The Termite Mound* 210

Chapter 26
Middle Discourses 24: Rathavinītasutta *Chariots at the Ready* 213

Chapter 27
Middle Discourses 25: Nivāpasutta *Sowing* 219

Chapter 28
Middle Discourses 26: Pāsarāsisutta *The Noble Quest* 224

Chapter 29
Middle Discourses 27: Cūḷahatthipadopamasutta *The Shorter Simile of the Elephant's Footprint* 239

Chapter 30
Middle Discourses 28: Mahāhatthipadopama Suttaṁ *The Longer Simile of the Elephant's Footprint* 251

Chapter 31
Middle Discourses 29: Mahāsāropamasutta *The Longer Simile of the Heartwood* 259

Chapter 32
Middle Discourses 30: Cūḷasāropamasutta *The Shorter Simile of the Heartwood* 263

Chapter 33
Middle Discourses 31: Cūḷagosiṅgasutta *The Shorter Discourse at Gosiṅga* 270

Chapter 34
Middle Discourses 32: Mahāgosiṅgasutta *The Longer Discourse at Gosiṅga* 275

Chapter 35
Middle Discourses 33: Mahāgopālakasutta *The Longer Discourse on the Cowherd* 280

Chapter 36
Middle Discourses 34: Cūḷagopālakasutta *The Shorter Discourse on the Cowherd* 285

Chapter 37
Middle Discourses 35: Cūḷasaccakasutta *The Shorter Discourse with Saccaka* 288

Chapter 38
Middle Discourses 36: Mahāsaccakasutta *The Longer Discourse with Saccaka* 297

Chapter 39
Middle Discourses 37: Cūḷataṇhāsaṅkhayasutta *The Shorter Discourse on the Ending of Craving* 310

Chapter 40
Middle Discourses 38: Mahātaṇhāsaṅkhaya Sutta *The Greater Discourse on the Complete Elimination of Craving* 314

Chapter 41
  Middle Discourses 39: Mahāassapurasutta *The Longer Discourse at Assapura* 330
Chapter 42
  Middle Discourses 40: Cūḷaassapurasutta *The Shorter Discourse at Assapura* 338
Chapter 43
  Middle Discourses 41: Sāleyyakasutta *The People of Sālā* 343
Chapter 44
  Middle Discourses 42: Verañjakasutta *The People of Verañjā* 349
Chapter 45
  Middle Discourses 43: Mahāvedallasutta *The Great Elaboration*............. 352
Chapter 46
  Middle Discourses 44: Cūḷavedallasutta *The Shorter Elaboration* 361
Chapter 47
  Middle Discourses 45: Cūḷadhammasamādānasutta *The Shorter Discourse on Taking Up Practices* 368
Chapter 48
  Middle Discourses 46: Mahādhammasamādānasutta *The Great Discourse on Taking Up Practices* 372
Chapter 49
  Middle Discourses 47: Vīmaṁsakasutta *The Inquirer* 378
Chapter 50
  Middle Discourses 48: Kosambiyasutta *The Mendicants of Kosambī* 385
Chapter 51
  Middle Discourses 49: Brahmanimantanikasutta *On the Invitation of Divinity* 392
Chapter 52
  Middle Discourses 50: Māratajjanīyasutta *The Condemnation of Māra* 397
Chapter 53
  Middle Discourses 51: Kandarakasutta *With Kandaraka* 402
Chapter 54
  Concluding Remarks... 413

Preface

Pali Canon has been preserved over centuries. Presently, Pali Canon is one of the common sources through which ordinary practitioners who are seeking Buddha's Dhamma are trying to understand Dhamma; four-fold Nibbana.

The Canon in its present format does not contain everything that the Buddha taught and is missing some of the important content. This gap must be filled to open the path for those who are seeking Nibbana. This book provides the missing content in an easy-to-understand way and fills the gap of the Majjhima Nikaya, or Middle Length Discourses of the Buddha, by paving the way for perfection, Arahantship. Due to absence of Arahants, important information regarding the practice leading to Nibbana has been absent over the centuries. Limited understandings of the Canonical content by the ordinary Sangha have made it difficult for ordinary practitioners to gain Nibbana during their lifetimes; a task that is rarely achievable by most wanting to know and learn how to practice the mind to gain cessation.

Some of the most important content as taught by the Buddha are not clearly written down and are missing in the Pali Canon. The missing content that is hidden underneath each discourse are known only by the noble ones. it is the task and responsibility of today's Arahants to open the vision leading to Nibbana for those who aspire Nibbana. Allowing an ordinary practitioner to read and understand the missing content, opening doors to deathless; four-fold Nibbana with supreme respect to our teacher; Supreme Buddha and out of immense respect, and care to fellow spiritual practitioners who seek Nibbana, in this book, I present the in-depth interpretation of each discourse based on what the Buddha said, and what Buddha meant by saying these words of wisdom, path to Nibbana.

Chapter 1

Introduction

Carrying Dhamma through oral transmission over centuries, and limited understanding and misinterpretations of "Tathata/Tathagata" and "Tatagata's Dhamma by the ordinary Sangha particularly through the periods of absence of Arahants, an accurate explanation of four-fold Nibbana *(i.e. Cessation, Nirvana)* is rare. Misinterpreting Dhamma can prevent Nibbana while understanding Dhamma opens up the Noble Path.

A right understanding, a right view, is the first step towards Nibbana. The possibility of developing a noble vision is obstructed by various opinions and interpretations of Nibbana offered by ordinary Sangha.

Dhamma means Sotapanna to Arahant.

Sangha means Sotapanna to Arahant.

Over centuries, despite reading discourses, including the vast majority of those who write books, translate, interpret, and discuss Dhamma, they don't gain Nibbana. Instead, they remain unenlightened due to being unable to develop and grow their vision beyond the existing sources. This is because the vision and understanding of Buddha's Dhamma (Sotapanna to Arahant) among ordinary practitioners remains limited as there is much confusion and many views of Dhamma. The confusion can only be resolved by evaluation and linking it to higher Dhamma with reasoning, a task that only Arahants can do. Yet, without a vision, the Noble Path cannot be developed. Without a vision, one may be lost at a practice and may not gain a fruition. What to practice and what not to practice requires clarification with reasoning.

The noble understanding (view) and Noble Path and Nibbana are linked. Only by following the Noble Path can a person reach Nibbana. The words of the Buddha that provide the path to Nibbana, Buddhahood gained through immeasurable scarifies, and completion of Paramis for the wellbeing of many, the route to escape samsara, and blocking the path by misinterpreting Dhamma can prevent Nibbana for ordinary bhikkhus/spiritual companions and many attendees. Instead, learning to interpreting Dhamma with accuracy and expanding the understanding of Dhamma can aid progress to Nibbana for many.

A person with integrity would not describe a path to Nibbana before at least becoming a Sotapanna (Stream-enterer or Stream Winner). With direct knowledge, I say that Nibbana is four-fold Nibbana (awakening) includes four stages (Stream-enterer, Once-returner, Non-returner and Arahant). Right view of an ordinary person is understanding universally applicable law of karma to a reasonable level. Right view of a Sotapanna is possessing confirmed confidence in the Triple Gem and not grasping in to the first three fetters). The way in which an ordinary person interprets a discourse and understand Nibbana is limited. Instead, noble interpretation can provide you in-depth detail about each discourse in line with four-fold Nibbana. In doing so, this book contributes to filling this gap that has existed through the centuries, clarifying the missing content, pointing out misinterpretations, and attempting to remove the misunderstanding of Nibbana by linking existing sources to higher Dhamma in a way that facilitates readers who are familiar with conventional Dhamma to climb up the ladder to reach Sotapanna and above through developing their vision of Dhamma; Nibbana.

In this book (Volume 1), "Middle Discourses" (MN 1-51) are presented in the same order as it has been presented over centuries in the Pali Canon to facilitate readers who are already familiar with discourses or various other conventional Dhamma knowledge and practices to develop and expand new knowledge leading to Sotapanna to Arahant. In this way, those who have already developed a vision of conventional Dhamma, which is a preliminary Dhamma, get an opportunity to expand their vision to reach a noble vision and to follow through the Noble Path based on the noble vision.

Chapter 2

The Right View: The Four-fold Path & the Practice to Nibbana

There are only four kinds of Buddha's disciples (Sotapanna to Arahant). Nibbana is a mental state. The path that Buddha wanted to open for people who are suffering has been kept open not just for one category of people (ritual, division, tradition, lifestyle) but for all.

Nibbana is a universal happening. One cannot receive monkhood from others. However, one can receive monkhood from self by letting go of grasping self-views and conventions (and ten fetters across four-fold Nibbana), developing wisdom similar to that of Buddha (hence why take refuge in the universal Buddha, universal Dhamma, and universal Sangha) and blending with the universal ways. When you want to practice the Noble Path, you want to make sure you don't train yourself to a practice of grasping conventional Dhamma, such as rituals and divisions, as they are preliminary practices. This is because just as streams of water turn to rivers, and rivers meet and unite with the sea, all those who follow conventional Dhamma become the same when they meet universal Dhamma; Nibbana, Sotapanna to Arahant.

Some drops of water, with the aid of other drops of water, make it to the sea. Similarly, among the Sangha, only a few make it to the four-fold Nibbana. Yet, the training a person develops during the present birth (and samsara) will aid those who don't make it immediately to four-fold Nibbana to get to the end purpose over time.

Words and concepts are social constructs. They are things that are made as real by convention or collective agreement among people in society. Social constructs reflect shared ideas or perceptions that only exist because people in a group or society accept that they do. The word enlightenment, a social construct, is used by various people in various ways. For example, in the post-Buddha period (after Buddhaparinirvana), it is most common to hear about the word Dhamma and enlightenment as "one flash enlightenment that's different to four-fold Nibbana originally taught by the Buddha. Such different versions of Dhamma and distorted versions of practices of Dhamma created by ordinary Sangha have made a split in the universal Dhamma: four-fold Nibbana. The new version of enlightenment, "one flash enlightenment," such as being just here and now, just being Awareness, and remaining as the Awareness or Consciousness (Atman/Self), are all relatively easily done if you know how - including jhana practices. However, that is not what is meant by BODHI/AWAKENING, to experience Cessation within genuine Buddha's Dhamma (four-fold Nibbana). This explains how look-alike dhamma has prevented the practice that leads to four-fold Nibbana for those who aspire to Nibbana through Buddha's Dhamma.

A person who aspires to Nibbana could potentially constantly strive to purify their mind, grasping conventions to reach four-fold Nibbana. The purpose of taking precepts, meditation, and offerings is simply to reduce the desire for worldly life, a person's interpretation of worldly life based on conventions.

You may support all Sangha in fulfilling their training without considering the differences and divisions seen from a conventional perspective. Drops of water that reach their destination unite in the sea (Cessation, Nibbana). In other words, irrespective of conventional background and the route taken to reach Buddhahood (Supreme Buddha, private Buddha, Noble Sangha route), those who reach Buddhahood experience cessation in the same way as they end their samsara.

By refuge in the Triple Gem, you can find refugeeing self across four-fold Nibbana.

Intentional actions are karma and Dhamma. Given that, a person's intentional actions (not actions alone as one can act with various intentions) are karma and Dhamma, finding the Triple Gem through an appearance or an action alone can be a difficult task for another person, especially because an ordinary person cannot read another person's intentional actions. Instead, ordinary people may comprehend the Triple Gem through words of wisdom.

The subject matter and the content related to four-fold Nibbana should be explained as universally applicable Dhamma that happens at a random occasion shaped by one's karma and merits by whoever explains.

Dhamma has been carried by one person after another (Sangha) over centuries. Dhamma carried by ordinary Sangha doesn't allow you to reach its final destination, which is the four-fold Nibbana. Even when they had not gained Nibbana, even when Arahants are rare, there had been great many ordinary Sangha over centuries who had taught you the basics. Ordinary Sangha from various traditions, divisions, and lifestyles seen from conventional backgrounds had taught you the basics with great effort and dedication. They had lived a basic life and provided you an opportunity to learn the basics, which was all they knew of

Dhamma. Most of them had been honest as they had declared they had not gained Nibbana. Their aspiration was that even when they failed to gain Nibbana, you should develop further and gain Nibbana for yourself, which was a sacrifice on their behalf. If you've followed various divisions, traditions, and lifestyles taught to you by a great many ordinary Sangha over centuries and have learned the basics from them, the greatest respect you can give them (and to the Buddha and Dhamma) is to fulfill the training, gain a higher knowledge of Dhamma) four-fold Nibbana. You could make use of preliminary Dhamma that is taught to you by ordinary Sangha over centuries to link it to the Noble Path. Sangha is not a person but a community that represents the same purpose - the path to Nibbana. With few exceptions, all written books of Dhamma were written by conventional Sangha who have a limited understanding of Nibbana. For example, if we were to talk about some of the oldest sources and existing books, the discourses given in the Pali Canon usually begin with "Thus, I heard" and not "Thus, I know". The Bodicaryavatara (A Guide To the Bodhisattva Way Of Life) is an ancient text written by Shantideva in 7oo CE, and emerging from his comments, it is clear that he is devoted to Buddha and the enlightened disciples of Buddha but he does not claim that he has gained Nibbana before writing the book and asserts he has no concern for the welfare of others but he writes the book to help him in training to gain Nibbana. The Mūlamadhyamakakārikā written by Nāgārjuna (ca. 150 C.E.), the author does not claim that he has gained Nibbana or that his work will help one gain Nibbana or abandon suffering. He does not directly talk about four-fold Nibbana but talk about doctrine of dependent origination based on what he understands as the teachings of Buddha. In another book, Visuddimagga (Path of Purification) written by Buddhaghosa does not claim that the author gained Nibbana before his writings, and for example, kasina-meditation departs from the practice leading to Nibbana.

> "We are monks by convention, not monks through liberation. In the beginning we establish conventions like this, but if a person merely ordains, this doesn't mean he overcomes defilements."
>
> - "A Taste of Freedom" by Ajahn Chah

By acknowledging the good intentions of all authors of dhamma books for preserving Dhamma in its conventional formats as exist today, it is simply for the benefit of those who seek Nibbana, there is a need of us to discuss missing points, misinterpretations, and misunderstandings of Buddha's Dhamma; four-fold Nibbana. What is true is that unless one gains Nibbana, one cannot explain the training path that leads to Nibbana. An incomplete understanding of Dhamma, merely trying to explain Dhamma written by ordinary Sangha based on books, can prevent people from reaching Nibbana. This is because higher Dhamma knowledge (Sotapanna to Arahant) among ordinary Sangha is limited. Throughout history, you can see most people who take Suttas as the words of Buddha depend on writings, translations, interpretations, and discussions of Suttas done by ordinary Sangha and commentaries that are written by ordinary Sangha with a limited knowledge of Nibbana. Among discourses, certain aspects of the full discourse have been dropped and are missing. It is not possible for those who have not experienced Nibbana to instruct another person to gain Nibbana. That is not to say that such bhikkhus/spiritual companions are superior, inferior or the same as others as a person, as every person is precious as a person. Yet, when they misinterpret, such acts of misinterpretation are inappropriate, unwholesome, and not the right thing to do for the sake of many.

A limited knowledge among the vast majority makes them tangled with limited vision, which can prevent noble vision. Instead, by expanding a limited vision and linking existing sources to a noble vision, one can develop the Noble Path. Without knowing what to practice and what not to practice reaching Nibbana, practitioners can sometimes engage in various practices that don't lead them to gain Nibbana. Things that are not important in the Noble Path are conventions and external factors. Thus, conventions should simply be used to understand four-fold Nibbana and to let go of grasping to conventions in the middle way.

When translating the Pali Canon, most people interpret and translate word to word without knowing the wider context. Translating word to word is a limited way, which can generate a limited interpretation or meaning from words. Words can mean anything, and the same words can mean many things. For example, bhikkhu means someone who has abandoned fetters (Sotapanna to Arahant), yet common people think and understand the word bhikkhu as someone who follows a ritualistic lifestyle. Instead, if you know the context out of which words emerge as only Arahants know, they can interpret beyond word-to-word translating, linking words to the whole scenario: four-fold Nibbana. The direct experience of Nibbana and triple knowledge allow an Arahant to know the context that happened and the content that was told as interpreted by the Buddha. Precise interpretation provided under each discourse in this book can allow readers to bridge the gap in vision; from ordinary to noble vision and develop the right view leading to four-fold Nibbana.

The right view is the first step towards the Noble Path. What is the right view? Nibbana refers to Sotapanna to Arahant, is a universal happening shaped by karma and merits. Nibbana is not a sila based lifestyle but a wisdom and karma-based path and training. Things such as a person's good health and wisdom can be gained through both universal and conventional ways: previous merits, developing merits, putting efforts into developing self, working hard on tasks, etc. The middle way means simply making use of universal ways and conventions without grasping but giving up grasping to reach cessation. Therefore, jhana practice among ordinary people and the practice of jhana by an Anagami in the training path of four-fold Nibbana differs.

The practice leading to Nibbana is the right view. Right view for an ordinary person is understanding that life is an interaction between the universe and conventions, and universal way of functioning, rhythm (karma) to a reasonable level. A person can only develop the right view based on evidence coming from one's life experience. The universe functions in such a way that, when a person is born, birth brings death, illnesses, losses, gains, falls and rises are part of life, the way of life. The universe function in such a way that seasonal phenomena of winds, rain are a way of its functioning. Universe function in such a way that rice produced from rice-seed, sugary taste from sugarcane or honey, and so on. Universe function in such a way that intentional actions lead to consequences.

Most of those who gained Nibbana don't recall they aspiring to gain such a state, at least during this birth. Nibbana, a happening, at a random time to a random person. Wisdom, merits, and Nibbana are linked. The universal law of karma always applies to all beings. Thus, the practice leading to Nibbana always begins by refuge in Triple Gem. Those who attend Buddha and Arahants will gain higher wisdom, genuine care, and merits that are needed for good things in life and Nibbana.

An ordinary person cannot see samsara due to attachment to limited vision. When your vision is stuck in conventions, you tend to forget universal ways of functioning. Yet, what your eyes cannot see, you can see with wisdom. In this way, wisdom can be developed by developing merits, shaping karma and putting efforts to practicing Dhamma in a way leading to four-fold Nibbana.

One who gains the right understanding or view at the first stage of enlightenment (or who attains the Stream Entry or Sotapanna) is capable in practicing the Noble Eight-fold Path in the correct way. Thus, one who attain the first stage of enlightenment is guaranteed to become an Arahant. For those who wish to attain enlightenment, it will be beneficial to put extra efforts in attaining the first stage of enlightenment.

The key things to remember about Nibbana are that;

1. One's ability to gain Nibbana is shaped by one's merits and one's karma.

2. Nibbana is a natural process just like the birth of beings; it happens on its own time shaped by karmic influence.

3. Nibbana, transformation from an ordinary being to a noble person is a happening that happens to a person irrespective of conventions, what they dress, lifestyle, and whether or not they follow rituals, and irrespective of what ritual they follow.

4. Disciple of Buddha by conventions makes a conventional Sangha, monk by rituals makes a conventional Sangha.

5. Disciple of Buddha by universal making makes a noble Sangha, monk out of rituals and monk out of mental attachment to conventional practices makes a noble Sangha.

6. Path to four-fold Nibbana is universal, and the practice remain the same for all.

7. The Noble Path is about renunciation, giving up the desire for conventions; likes (greed) and dislikes (hate), expectations (delusion) for such things.

8. One does not require giving up sensual desires to become a Sotapanna. This is because sensual desires are given up at the state of an Anagami, a happening, and this makes it practical for most practitioners to practice the Noble Path.

9. What is mutually agreed upon among the people across societies and the conventional dhamma can have various presentations; traditions, divisions rituals, lifestyles based on conventions, etc. Commonly accepted as Buddha's Dhamma is not what is the universally accepted Dhamma; four-fold Nibbana. What is seen commonly seen, conventional Dhamma are preliminary practices that requires developing further to reach universal Dhamma; four-fold Nibbana.

10. Live a life dedicated to wholesome deeds and abandoning mental attachment to conventions are relevant.

11. Four-fold Nibbana is a merit and wisdom-based path. Accumulating merits through both conventional (i.e putting efforts to do wholesome things etc.) and universal ways (refuge in the Triple Gem; those who have given up fetters or constraints will make you give up fetters across four-fold Nibbana in the middle way). This allows you to enhance your wisdom across stages of Nibbana.

12. There are many silas, and, among these silas, are noble precepts; the eight precepts with the right livelihood (The Ajivatthamaka Sila corresponds to the Noble Eightfold Path) are the ones that can help you the most to gain Nibbana.

13. There are many meditations. Among meditations, the most appropriate meditation to gain Sotapanna is reflecting the qualities of the Triple Gem. Those who are unable to do so may try to engage in "chittanupassana" or understanding the causes and analysing thoughts.

14. Among all "Dana", giving Sotapanna to Arahant brings an end to your worldly suffering, it is the "Dana" that Arahants gift to you.

15. Among the laws, certain ways of universal functioning, and one of the orders which operate in the universe is that intentional actions produce corresponding consequences; when you start a practice of reducing clinging to conventions, as a consequence, your mental pain will subside.

Among the laws, certain ways of universal functioning, and one of the orders that operate in the universe is that intentional actions produce corresponding consequences; when you establish a friendship and offer "Dana" (your time, your skills, your friendship, materials, non-materials) to those who have given up mental attachment to ten fetters, as a consequence, your mental attachment to fetters disappears, and your mental pain will subside.

Chapter 3

Middle Discourses 1: Mūlapariyāyasutta

The Root of All Things

The meaning emerging out of this discourse is that the root of all things (mental sufferings) is deluded understanding. By giving up deluded understanding, which means reducing mental attachment, and by developing a noble understanding based on true life experience to reach Sotapanna, you could develop the Noble Path and the right view. Right view can be developed by developing wisdom[2].

Ordinary state is characterized by ongoing cycle of worldly experiences such as sadness, happiness and alike in cycles. Intentional action of a Sotapanna carries Dhamma doing; reduce grasping to conventions, fulfilling responsibilities to others, not worrying too much about bad things in self, others and the world. While you are an ordinary, you may develop a Dhamma doing similar to that of a Sotapanna within your lifestyle.

At Sotapanna and Sakadagami states, one doesn't become a monk created by the universal functioning and karma due to retaining sensual pleasures, instead one remains a very happy householder meaning one who experience joy, and pleasures both in good and bad worldly experiences due to stable understanding; impermanent is worldly experiences, there is no permanent self, and all bad things that happen to self are really not happening to self makes one remain happy all throughout day and night. At Anagami state, one comes to realize one is free from the ill will, and sensual pleasures. Thereafter, at Arahant stage, one does not like or dislike things. Nibbana is not a sila, or meditation-based path instead it is a wisdom and merit based path.

Reducing deluded understanding can be developed slowly within daily life. Understanding self as someone who can retain worldly experiences with stability can make you feel too upset when self and the experiences change following illnesses and changes in friendships and relationships and situations. Thus, in general, ordinary people tend to grasp into worldly experiences day and night;

---

[2] Wisdom can be developed by both conventional and universal ways.

earth, water, fire, air, creatures, gods, progenitor, divinity, universal beauty, abundant fruit, vanquisher, and jhanas including the dimension of infinite space, infinite consciousness, infinite nothingness and so on.

The way to abandon deluded understanding is four-fold Nibbana. For an ordinary person, right view is understanding Nibbana is a universal happening shaped one's karma and merits. Right view of a Stream Winner (Sotapanna) is acceptance of karma.

Deluded understanding can make you experience distress in daily life, and deluded understanding is the reason for excessive greediness (i.e too much likes) and excessive hatred (i.e too much dislikes). Deluded understanding (i.e expectations) comes from the view that you can gain things you want, and you can retain things with stability.

Thinking that it is possible to retain stability in self and worldly experiences, a person may develop a habit of touching worldly experiences too much in mind since birth. Thinking that the things on earth belong to a person, a person may grasp at changing worldly experiences. In this manner, grasping at changing experiences is a common way of thinking since birth. Common ways of thinking include getting attached to worldly experiences. Touching worldly experiences too much in mind is a common way, as is the inability to be satisfied with whatever way one presently has and instead seeking more and more worldly experiences. Thinking that happiness and joy gained out of worldly experiences can last forever, an ordinary person touches the world in mind since birth, liking and disliking worldly experiences too much again and again. As joy and pleasures arise from worldly experiences, liking them too much, a person may expect to experience more and more joys and pleasures through worldly life. Yet, changes happen to joys and pleasures experienced through worldly life; joys can turn into sorrow, and pleasures can turn in to displeasures. Often, it is the same thing you liked the most that produce the most mental pain when it changes. In this manner, based on common ways of thinking, an ordinary person (since birth everyone walks in this path) may initially be baffled and experience disbelief or shock when forced to experience changing worldly experiences in life. Common ways of thinking are founded in social practices. Social practices based on standard ways of thinking teach people to think and behave in certain ways. Based on social learning and conditioning, people learn to associate happiness with winning and sadness with loosing, happiness at birth, and sadness at death. In this manner, since birth, people learn to connect certain things such as winning, gains, birth and the feelings of happiness that cause you to become happy. Similarly, people learn to connect certain things such as loosing, death and the feeling of sadness that cause you to become unhappy based on social learning and conditioning to interpret worldly experiences based on standard ways. Eventually, an association between events and responses is learned. You'll find that many, if not most, of your ways of thinking and actions can be traced back to standard ways of thinking and doing things.

To give up deluded understanding; by understanding (right view), a person can escape deluded thinking. Based on your life experiences, if you understand that conventions and worldly experiences are subject to change, this realization is the first step toward understanding. Then, if you understand that things that begin come to end in worldly life, that is in the natural and universal functioning of all beings. Therefore, you will realize that clinging to changing things leads to experiencing mental pain, which is hard to endure and not worthwhile. This realization is the second step of understanding. Given that things are changing anyway within worldly life, letting go of grasping changing experiences is a wise thing for the wellbeing of yourself and others. This is the third step of understanding. These three steps can help you develop middle mind training. By understanding your personal experience with wisdom, the realization of life experiences, and truth, you can learn to reframe your thinking to accept the truth that is applicable to all; let go of things that are gone (do not grasp them too much in your mind creating stress), focus and attend to things that need attention, look after yourself and others to the best level while they are there. Wisdom is required to think beyond standard ways of thinking.

Wisdom can be developed by developing merits/engaging in meritorious activities, putting efforts etc. blending with both conventional and universal ways. Cultivating your wisdom, so that you know the difference between what you can and can't change, and doing what you can do to resolve things, let go of things that are not possible to change a wise approach to life. Instead, by reducing deluded understanding, a person can attempt to slowly reduce greediness and hatred. It takes time to reduce these things and there are many ways a person can reduce these things.

When you have a limited vision, you don't see beyond. When you look back on your past, you might notice that here were occasions where you did not see things, and that you had a limited vision. Just because you don't see, that does not necessary mean there are things beyond your vision. When your vision is stuck in conventions, you tend to forget universal ways of functioning. Yet, what your eyes cannot see, you can see with wisdom. In this way, wisdom can be developed by developing merits, and engaging in wholesome activities.

"Thus have I heard. On one occasion the Buddha was staying near Ukkaṭṭhā, in the Subhaga Forest at the root of a magnificent sal tree. There the Buddha addressed the spiritual companions, "Companions!"

"Venerable sir," they replied. The Buddha said this:

"Companions, I will teach you the explanation of the root of all things. Listen and apply your minds well, I will speak."

"Yes, sir," they replied. The Buddha said this:

"Take an unlearned ordinary person who has not seen the noble ones[3], and is neither skilled nor trained in the teaching of the noble ones. They've not seen noble persons and are neither skilled nor trained in the teaching of the noble persons. They perceive earth as earth. Having perceived earth as earth, they conceive it to be earth, they conceive it in earth, they conceive it as earth, they conceive that 'earth is mine', they take pleasure in earth. Why is that? Because they haven't completely understood it, I say.

They perceive water as water. Having perceived water as water, they conceive it to be water … Why is that? Because they haven't completely understood it, I say.

They perceive fire as fire. Having perceived fire as fire, they conceive it to be fire … Why is that? Because they haven't completely understood it, I say.

They perceive air as air. Having perceived air as air, they conceive it to be air … Why is that? Because they haven't completely understood it, I say.

They perceive creatures as creatures. Having perceived creatures as creatures, they conceive it to be creatures … Why is that? Because they haven't completely understood it, I say.

They perceive gods as gods. Having perceived gods as gods, they conceive it to be gods … Why is that? Because they haven't completely understood it, I say.

---

[3] The Noble Path can be known only by those who have gained Nibbana. it is easier to misunderstand dhamma leading to four-fold Nibbana. Thus, meeting with Triple Gem means hearing Dhamma from Sotapanna to Arahant and marks an important step for practitioners who are seeking Nibbana and fulfilling merits required for completing Arahantship through the noble Sangha route.

They perceive the Progenitor as the Progenitor. Having perceived the Progenitor as the Progenitor, they conceive it to be the Progenitor … Why is that? Because they haven't completely understood it, I say.

They perceive Brahmā as Brahmā. Having perceived Brahmā as Brahmā, they conceive it to be Brahmā … Why is that? Because they haven't completely understood it, I say.

They perceive those of streaming radiance as those of streaming radiance. Having perceived those of streaming radiance as those of streaming radiance, they conceive it to be those of streaming radiance … Why is that? Because they haven't completely understood it, I say.

They perceive those replete with glory as those replete with glory. Having perceived those replete with glory as those replete with glory, they conceive it to be those replete with glory … Why is that? Because they haven't completely understood it, I say.

They perceive those of abundant fruit as those of abundant fruit. Having perceived those of abundant fruit as those of abundant fruit, they conceive it to be those of abundant fruit … Why is that? Because they haven't completely understood it, I say.

They perceive the Vanquisher as the Vanquisher. Having perceived the Vanquisher as the Vanquisher, they conceive it to be the Vanquisher … Why is that? Because they haven't completely understood it, I say.

They perceive the dimension of infinite space as the dimension of infinite space. Having perceived the dimension of infinite space as the dimension of infinite space, they conceive it to be the dimension of infinite space … Why is that? Because they haven't completely understood it, I say.

They perceive the dimension of infinite consciousness as the dimension of infinite consciousness. Having perceived the dimension of infinite consciousness as the dimension of infinite consciousness, they conceive it to be the dimension of infinite consciousness … Why is that? Because they haven't completely understood it, I say.

They perceive the dimension of nothingness as the dimension of nothingness. Having perceived the dimension of nothingness as the dimension of nothingness, they conceive it to be the dimension of nothingness … Why is that? Because they haven't completely understood it, I say.

They perceive the dimension of neither perception nor non-perception as the dimension of neither perception nor non-perception. Having perceived the dimension of neither perception nor non-perception as the dimension of neither perception nor non-perception, they conceive it to be the dimension of neither perception nor non-perception … Why is that? Because they haven't completely understood it, I say.

They perceive the seen as the seen. Having perceived the seen as the seen, they conceive it to be the seen … Why is that? Because they haven't completely understood it, I say.

They perceive the heard as the heard. Having perceived the heard as the heard, they conceive it to be the heard … Why is that? Because they haven't completely understood it, I say.

They perceive the thought as the thought. Having perceived the thought as the thought, they conceive it to be the thought … Why is that? Because they haven't completely understood it, I say.

They perceive the known as the known. Having perceived the known as the known, they conceive it to be the known … Why is that? Because they haven't completely understood it, I say.

They perceive oneness as oneness. Having perceived oneness as oneness, they conceive it to be oneness … Why is that? Because they haven't completely understood it, I say.

They perceive diversity as diversity. Having perceived diversity as diversity, they conceive it to be diversity … Why is that? Because they haven't completely understood it, I say.

They perceive all as all. Having perceived all as all, they conceive it to be all … Why is that? Because they haven't completely understood it, I say.

They perceive extinguishment as extinguishment. Having perceived extinguishment as extinguishment, they conceive it to be extinguishment, they conceive it in extinguishment, they conceive it as extinguishment, they conceive that 'extinguishment is mine', they take pleasure in extinguishment. Why is that? Because they haven't completely understood it, I say.

An individual who is a trainee (Sotapanna, Sakadagami, Anagami), who hasn't achieved their heart's desire (Nibbana in full; Arahantship), but lives aspiring to the supreme sanctuary from the yoke (Arahantship), directly knows earth as earth. Having directly known earth as earth, let them not conceive it to be earth[4], let them not conceive it in earth, let them not conceive it as earth, let them not conceive that 'earth is mine', let them not take pleasure in earth. Why is that? So that they may completely understand it, I say.

They directly know water … fire … air … creatures … gods … the Progenitor … Brahmā … those of streaming radiance … those replete with glory … those of abundant fruit … the Vanquisher … the dimension of infinite space … the dimension of infinite consciousness … the dimension of nothingness … the dimension of neither perception nor non-perception … the seen … the heard … the thought … the known

---

[4] Reduce desire towards worldly life experience by abandoning the remaining fetters.

… oneness … diversity … all … They directly know extinguishment as extinguishment. Having directly known extinguishment as extinguishment, let them not conceive it to be extinguishment, let them not conceive it in extinguishment, let them not conceive it as extinguishment, let them not conceive that 'extinguishment is mine', let them not take pleasure in extinguishment. Why is that? So that they may completely understand it, I say.

An individual who is an Arahant—with defilements ended, who has completed the spiritual journey, done what had to be done, laid down the burden, achieved their own true goal, utterly ended the fetters of rebirth, and is rightly freed through enlightenment—directly knows earth as earth. Having directly known earth as earth, they do not conceive it to be earth, they do not conceive it in earth, they do not conceive it as earth, they do not conceive that 'earth is mine', they do not take pleasure in earth. Why is that? Because they have completely understood it, I say.

They directly know water … fire … air … creatures … gods … the Progenitor … Brahmā … those of streaming radiance … those replete with glory … those of abundant fruit … the Vanquisher … the dimension of infinite space … the dimension of infinite consciousness … the dimension of nothingness … the dimension of neither perception nor non-perception … the seen … the heard … the thought … the known … oneness … diversity … all … They directly know extinguishment as extinguishment. Having directly known extinguishment as extinguishment, they do not conceive it to be extinguishment, they do not conceive it in extinguishment, they do not conceive it as extinguishment, they do not conceive that 'extinguishment is mine', they do not take pleasure in extinguishment. Why is that? Because they have completely understood it, I say.

An individual who is an Arahant—with defilements ended, who has completed the spiritual journey, done what had to be done, laid down the burden, achieved their own true goal, utterly ended the fetters of rebirth, and is rightly freed through enlightenment—directly knows earth as earth. Having directly known earth as earth, they do not conceive it to be earth, they do not conceive it in earth, they do not conceive it as earth, they do not conceive that 'earth is mine', they do not take pleasure in earth. Why is that? Because they're free of greed due to the ending of greed.

They directly know water … fire … air … creatures … gods … the Progenitor … Brahmā … those of streaming radiance … those replete with glory … those of abundant fruit … the Vanquisher … the dimension of infinite space … the dimension of infinite consciousness … the dimension of nothingness … the dimension of neither perception nor non-perception … the seen … the heard … the thought … the known

... oneness ... diversity ... all ... They directly know extinguishment as extinguishment. Having directly known extinguishment as extinguishment, they do not conceive it to be extinguishment, they do not conceive it in extinguishment, they do not conceive it as extinguishment, they do not conceive that 'extinguishment is mine', they do not take pleasure in extinguishment. Why is that? Because they're free of greed due to the ending of greed.

An individual who is an Arahant —with defilements ended, who has completed the spiritual journey, done what had to be done, laid down the burden, achieved their own true goal, utterly ended the fetters of rebirth, and is rightly freed through enlightenment— directly knows earth as earth. Having directly known earth as earth, they do not conceive it to be earth, they do not conceive it in earth, they do not conceive it as earth, they do not conceive that 'earth is mine', they do not take pleasure in earth. Why is that? Because they're free of hate due to the ending of hate.

They directly know water ... fire ... air ... creatures ... gods ... the Progenitor ... Brahmā ... those of streaming radiance ... those replete with glory ... those of abundant fruit ... the Vanquisher ... the dimension of infinite space ... the dimension of infinite consciousness ... the dimension of nothingness ... the dimension of neither perception nor non-perception ... the seen ... the heard ... the thought ... the known ... oneness ... diversity ... all ... They directly know extinguishment as extinguishment. Having directly known extinguishment as extinguishment, they do not conceive it to be extinguishment, they do not conceive it in extinguishment, they do not conceive it as extinguishment, they do not conceive that 'extinguishment is mine', they do not take pleasure in extinguishment. Why is that? Because they're free of hate due to the ending of hate.

An individual who is an Arahant —with defilements ended, who has completed the spiritual journey, done what had to be done, laid down the burden, achieved their own true goal, utterly ended the fetters of rebirth, and is rightly freed through enlightenment— directly knows earth as earth. Having directly known earth as earth, they do not conceive it to be earth, they do not conceive it in earth, they do not conceive it as earth, they do not conceive that 'earth is mine', they do not take pleasure in earth. Why is that? Because they're free of delusion due to the ending of delusion.

They directly know water ... fire ... air ... creatures ... gods ... the Progenitor ... Brahmā ... those of streaming radiance ... those replete with glory ... those of abundant fruit ... the Vanquisher ... the dimension of infinite space ... the dimension of infinite consciousness ... the dimension of nothingness ... the dimension of neither perception nor non-perception ... the seen ... the heard ... the thought ... the known

... oneness ... diversity ... all ... They directly know extinguishment as extinguishment. Having directly known extinguishment as extinguishment, they do not conceive it to be extinguishment, they do not conceive it in extinguishment, they do not conceive it as extinguishment, they do not conceive that 'extinguishment is mine', they do not take pleasure in extinguishment. Why is that? Because they're free of delusion due to the ending of delusion.

The Realized One, the perfected one, the fully awakened Buddha directly knows earth as earth. Having directly known earth as earth, he does not conceive it to be earth, he does not conceive it in earth, he does not conceive it as earth, he does not conceive that 'earth is mine', he does not take pleasure in earth. Why is that? Because the Realized One has completely understood it to the end, I say.

He directly knows water ... fire ... air ... creatures ... gods ... the Progenitor ... Brahmā ... those of streaming radiance ... those replete with glory ... those of abundant fruit ... the Vanquisher ... the dimension of infinite space ... the dimension of infinite consciousness ... the dimension of nothingness ... the dimension of neither perception nor non-perception ... the seen ... the heard ... the thought ... the known ... oneness ... diversity ... all ... He directly knows extinguishment as extinguishment. Having directly known extinguishment as extinguishment, he does not conceive it to be extinguishment, he does not conceive it in extinguishment, he does not conceive it as extinguishment, he does not conceive that 'extinguishment is mine', he does not take pleasure in extinguishment. Why is that? Because the Realized One has completely understood it to the end, I say.

The Realized One, the perfected one, the fully awakened Buddha directly knows earth as earth. Having directly known earth as earth, he does not conceive it to be earth, he does not conceive it in earth, he does not conceive it as earth, he does not conceive that 'earth is mine', he does not take pleasure in earth. Why is that? Because he has understood that taking pleasure is the root of suffering, and that rebirth comes from continued existence; whoever has come to be gets old and dies. That's why the Realized One—with the ending, fading away, cessation, giving up, and letting go of all cravings—has awakened to the supreme perfect Awakening, I say.

He directly knows water ... fire ... air ... creatures ... gods ... the Progenitor ... Brahmā ... those of streaming radiance ... those replete with glory ... those of abundant fruit ... the Vanquisher ... the dimension of infinite space ... the dimension of infinite consciousness ... the dimension of nothingness ... the dimension of neither perception nor non-perception ... the seen ... the heard ... the thought ... the known ... oneness ... diversity ... all ... He directly knows extinguishment as extinguishment. Having directly known extinguishment as extinguishment, he does not conceive it to be extinguishment, he does not conceive it in extinguishment, he does not conceive it as extinguishment, he does not conceive that 'extinguishment is mine', he does not take pleasure in extinguishment. Why is that? Because he has understood that taking pleasure is the root of suffering, and that rebirth comes from continued existence; whoever has come to be gets old and dies. That's why the Realized One—with the ending, fading away, cessation, giving up, and letting go of all cravings—has awakened to the supreme perfect Awakening, I say."

That is what the Buddha said. But the companions took no pleasure [5]in what the Buddha said."

---

[5] The companions understood what the Buddha said without mental attachment.

Chapter 4

Middle Discourses 2: Sabbāsavasutta

All the Defilements

If Nibbana were a convention, that would be subject to change. Rather, Nibbana brings an end to changing conventions, birth and death, and samsara. If Nibbana could be visible to human eye; it would be easy for everyone to see Nibbana. Yet, because Nibbana lies beyond the limits of human eye, an ordinary wise person can understand Nibbana only through wisdom, and wise words.

Awakening to true life experience, and understanding life experienced based on wisdom, an ordinary person can develop the Noble Path. Nibbana is a wisdom and merits based path. A person may born with certain wisdom that can grow over time, and when certain people hear wise words, they get to understand Nibbana. Yet, for others, even if they hear wise words, the words do not make much sense. In this manner, Nibbana opens up only for those who are wise through a wisdom gained through one's own merit in Samsara. By further developing merits and wisdom, a person can train to reach Nibbana.

Many techniques may be adopted to give up defilements and purify from conventions. First, by applying reasoning, you can learn to give up defilements and purify from grasping to conventions. Unless one gains Nibbana, one cannot know what Nibbana is or explain it to another with accuracy. Limited explanations of Nibbana can limit your potential for gaining Nibbana. Therefore, practitioners who seek Nibbana should approach one who claims to have gained Nibbana.

Those who merely attempt to understand Dhamma based on books written by ordinary Sangha can go wrong in their practice, and those who don't apply reasoning but are merely accepting what they are being told by others can go wrong in their practice, so that they do not get to experience Nibbana despite their years of Dhamma practice.

Those who are not able to comprehend who is noble and who is not; those who are unable to comprehend what is noble Dhamma and what is not; those who are unable to comprehend what practice leads to cessation and what does not; those who do not understand Triple Gem; and those who think they know Triple Gem but it is not the true Triple Gem are all running a far shore and are practicing in a way that does not lead to cessation. Instead, they are practicing growing defilement, grasping self-view and conventions, because they are unable to comprehend based on their own wisdom, a wisdom a person gains due to pervious karma. Their potential to gain Nibbana can be prevented.

At times, practicing Dhamma itself can make you grow various views. if you begin to grasp conventions, rituals, lifestyles, traditions, and so on, including permanent existence. Was I in the past? Will I be in the future? If you worry too much about the past and are too anxious about the future, and if you feel burning within, take a moment and reflect on what caused you to feel burned within. You feel burned inside because you desire[6] your past and future. You desire, because you have experienced pleasures in worldly life, which makes you naturally want to experience such worldly pleasures. Yet, worldly life is not only pleasure but also displeasure. By ignoring true life experiences that reveal to you that worldly life is both ups and downs, if you desire only pleasures, something that is not possible to experience, and if you tend to get attached into your thoughts, you are likely to be more affected and consumed by your own thoughts. When you get attached into your thoughts and into earthy experiences, you tend to experience distress. Instead, by applying reasoning and by understanding worldly life, you can learn to reduce getting attached to into your own thoughts and applying reasoning to understand life experiences within daily life is a constant practice that an ordinary person can do to reduce distress.

By grasping to views, and views of cosmos; for example, "cloud is in me", "cosmos is me" and "I am cosmos", these views that make you strengthen self-view. Instead of grasping or refusing to interconnect between self and the nature and beings in the middle way, applying wisdom to reflect that each person experiences mental distress within your own thoughts; a reasonable way to understand yourself.

The practice of applying restraint alone without a right view will not allow you to enter the Noble Path. Restraint when you understand is impermanent, and when you experience pain and are aware and that you understand mental pain is hard to bear, that understanding will help you to reduce desires (likes, dislikes). Instead of focusing on the external environment and others, a person can develop the noble practice by taking self as a self-responsibility. You may apply a technique

---

[6] Desire meaning greediness (likes), hatred(dislikes), delusion (expectations based on mental attachment).

of restraint to give up some defilements. You may set your own rules. For example, you may decide to refrain from getting excessively worried about your worldly experiences even though others worry about such things. Once you deepen your understanding about your life experience, that understanding cannot be undone but can only be replaced by a higher understanding of Nibbana. "Defilement given up" by using as discussed in this discourse is mainly applicable to Anagamis; they may engage in taking food simply for survival, and so on. Defilement given up to endure discomforts of life when practicing Dhamma, minority ways. There may be some who, when you practice Dhamma (meaning training the mind to understand beyond ordinary ways "against the current ways of thinking and doing" (patisotagamini[7]), may neglect you, misunderstand you, and you may have to tolerate such experiences with patience for giving priority to Dhamma. Giving priority to Dhamma is what makes you a noble person, a noble monk.

Those who tolerate worldly experiences; pleasant, neutral and unpleasant experiences for the sake of Dhamma can expect to grow in Dhamma. Dhamma means developing the right view and reducing mental attachment across stages. If, for some reason, instead of reducing attachment, you develop more attachment to Dhamma, that will obstruct you from developing the Noble Path. Dhamma is simply for reducing mental pain coming from worldly experiences but not for grasping.

Even for the sake of survival, if you expect money, materials, and honor through Dhamma, and you cause harm to self or others, such intentions will obstruct you from purifying self-view and conventions, and mental pain that comes along with views. Instead, if you try constantly to purify yourself, if you can maintain pure intentions of not selling or dividing universal Dhamma for the benefit of self and many, such intentions will help you abandon self-view. One who gives priority to Dhamma gives priority to Buddha and vice versa. One who gives priority to Dhamma, and Buddha (vice-versa) is a monk by reducing mental attachment, four-fold Nibbana.

---

[7] To practice noble way of thinking, you have to surpass the majority way of thinking and doing. For example, let's say that in a particular region, the majority of individuals engage in killing living beings, or treating others differently based on conventions (gender, class, nationality, age, education, position) and, for them that is a normal thing to do as accepted within social practices. Instead, a person who aspires inner peace through middle way practice will decide for oneself that, just because others engage in killing living beings or engage in things that are causing distress to others (e.g. Differential treatment towards others), that person does not need to be engaged in doing such things. This allows a practitioner to develop self-responsibility, a self-practice to do good irrespective of what others are doing and saying. In this manner, despite others physical presence (or absence), if you choose to do always good, you can find peace within.

Certain defilements are to be given up by avoiding; you may avoid bad associates, things that are intoxicating and that steal your ability to think straight in daily life, things that reduce your clarity and thinking regarding life experience, unsuitable places, pointless arguments, and things that contradict Dhamma to grow in Dhamma within. An ordinary person may constantly try to purify; reduce grasping to conventions in daily life. There are many techniques. Some defilements can be given up by applying reasoning, and some can be given up by applying restraint. Some constraints are given up by tolerance. Some constraints are given up by avoiding; avoiding bad people, and avoiding harmful substances and habits. By understanding what to give up and what not to give up, you can develop the Noble Path. Grasping to sensuality is given up only by an Anagami. Thus, five precepts are sufficient, and noble precepts (including right living) can aid better to reduce mental attachment in daily life.

"So I have heard. At one time the Buddha was staying near Sāvatthī in Jeta's Grove, Anāthapiṇḍika's monastery. There the Buddha addressed the spiritual saints and practitioners, "spiritual companions!"

"Venerable sir," they replied. The Buddha said this:

"Spiritual companions, I will teach you the explanation of the restraint of all defilements. Listen and apply your mind well, I will speak."

"Yes, sir," they replied. The Buddha said this:

"Spiritual companions, I say that the ending of defilements is for one who knows and sees, not for one who does not know or see. For one who knows and sees what? Rational application of mind and irrational application of mind. You need to be able to think logically and with wisdom, When you apply the mind irrationally, defilements arise, and once arisen they grow. When you apply the mind rationally, defilements don't arise, and those that have already arisen are given up.

Some defilements should be given up by seeing, some by restraint, some by using, some by enduring, some by avoiding, some by dispelling, and some by developing.

1. Defilements Given Up by Seeing

And what are the defilements that should be given up by seeing? Take an unlearned ordinary person who has not seen the noble ones, and is neither skilled nor trained in the teaching of the noble ones. They've not seen true persons, and are neither skilled nor trained in the teaching of the true persons. They don't understand to which things they should apply the mind and to which things they should not apply the mind. So they apply the mind to things they shouldn't and don't apply the mind to things they should. (Those who do not get to meet with noble people, are likely to get lost in a vast number of ordinary views and practices without ever achieving Nibbana).

And what are the things to which they apply the mind but should not? They are the things that, when the mind is applied to them, give rise to unarisen defilements and make arisen defilements grow: the defilements of sensual desire, desire to be reborn, and ignorance. These are the things to which they apply the mind but should not. (They think and do things that increase their mental defilements despite their intent to give up).

And what are the things to which they do not apply the mind but should? They are the things that, when the mind is applied to them, do not give rise to unarisen defilements and give up arisen defilements: the defilements of sensual desire, desire to be reborn, and ignorance. These are the things to which they do not apply the mind but should.

Because of applying the mind to what they should not and not applying the mind to what they should, unarisen defilements arise and arisen defilements grow.

This is how they apply the mind irrationally: 'Did I exist in the past? Did I not exist in the past? What was I in the past? How was I in the past? After being what, what did I become in the past? Will I exist in the future? Will I not exist in the future? What will I be in the future? How will I be in the future? After being what, what will I become in the future?' Or they are undecided about the present thus: 'Am I? Am I not? What am I? How am I? This sentient being—where did it come from? And where will it go?'

When they apply the mind irrationally in this way, one of the following six views arises in them and is taken as a genuine fact. The view: 'My self survives.' The view: 'My self does not survive.' The view: 'I perceive the self with the self.' The view: 'I perceive what is not-self with the self.' The view: 'I perceive the self with what is not-self.' Or they have such a view: 'This self of mine is he, the speaker, the knower who experiences the results of good and bad deeds in all the different realms. This self is permanent, everlasting, eternal, and imperishable, and will last forever and ever.' This is called a misconception, the thicket of views, the desert of views, the twist of views, the dodge of views, the fetter of views. An unlearned ordinary person who is fettered by views is not freed from rebirth, old age, and death, from sorrow, lamentation, pain, sadness, and distress. They're not freed from suffering, I say.

But take a learned noble disciple who has seen the noble ones, and is skilled and trained in the teaching of the noble ones. They've seen noble persons, and are skilled and trained in the teaching of the true persons. They understand to which things they should apply the mind and to which things they should not apply the mind. So they apply the mind to things they should and don't apply the mind to things they shouldn't.

And what are the things to which they don't apply the mind and should not? They are the things that, when the mind is applied to them, give rise to unarisen defilements and make arisen defilements grow: the defilements of sensual desire, desire to be reborn, and ignorance. These are the things to which they don't apply the mind and should not.

And what are the things to which they do apply the mind and should? They are the things that, when the mind is applied to them, do not give rise to unarisen defilements and give up arisen defilements: the defilements of sensual desire, desire to be reborn, and ignorance. These are the things to which they do apply the mind and should.

Because of not applying the mind to what they should not and applying the mind to what they should, unarisen defilements don't arise and arisen defilements are given up.

They rationally apply the mind: 'This is suffering' … 'This is the origin of suffering' … 'This is the cessation of suffering' … 'This is the practice that leads to the cessation of suffering'. And as they do so, they give up three fetters: substantialist view, doubt, and misapprehension of precepts and observances. These are called the defilements that should be given up by seeing.

2. Defilements Given Up by Restraint

And what are the defilements that should be given up by restraint? Take an individual who, reflecting rationally, lives restraining the faculty of the eye. For the distressing and feverish defilements that might arise in someone who lives without restraint of the eye faculty do not arise when there is such restraint. Reflecting rationally, they live restraining the faculty of the ear … the nose … the tongue … the body … the mind. For the distressing and feverish defilements that might arise in someone who lives without restraint of the mind faculty do not arise when there is such restraint.

For the distressing and feverish defilements that might arise in someone who lives without restraint do not arise when there is such restraint. These are called the defilements that should be given up by restraint.

3. Defilements Given Up by Using

And what are the defilements that should be given up by using? Take an individual who, reflecting rationally, makes use of robes: 'Only for the sake of warding off cold and heat; for warding off the touch of flies, mosquitoes, wind, sun, and reptiles; and for covering up the private parts.'

Reflecting rationally, they make use of almsfood: 'Not for fun, indulgence, adornment, or decoration, but only to sustain this body, to avoid harm, and to support spiritual practice. In this way, I shall put an end to old discomfort and not give rise to new discomfort, and I will live blamelessly and at ease.'

Reflecting rationally, they make use of lodgings: 'Only for the sake of warding off cold and heat; for warding off the touch of flies, mosquitoes, wind, sun, and reptiles; to shelter from harsh weather and to enjoy retreat.'

Reflecting rationally, they make use of medicines and supplies for the sick: 'Only for the sake of warding off the pains of illness and to promote good health.'

For the distressing and feverish defilements that might arise in someone who lives without using these things do not arise when they are used. These are called the defilements that should be given up by using.

4. Defilements Given Up by Enduring

And what are the defilements that should be given up by enduring? Take an individual who, reflecting rationally, endures cold, heat, hunger, and thirst. They endure the touch of flies, mosquitoes, wind, sun, and reptiles. They endure rude and unwelcome criticism. And they put up with physical pain—sharp, severe, acute, unpleasant, disagreeable, and life-threatening.

For the distressing and feverish defilements that might arise in someone who lives without enduring these things do not arise when they are endured. These are called the defilements that should be given up by enduring.

5. Defilements Given Up by Avoiding

And what are the defilements that should be given up by avoiding? Take an individual who, reflecting rationally, avoids a wild elephant, a wild horse, a wild ox, a wild dog, a snake, a stump, thorny ground, a pit, a cliff, a swamp, and a sewer. Reflecting rationally, they avoid sitting on inappropriate seats, walking in inappropriate neighborhoods, and mixing with bad friends—whatever sensible spiritual companions would believe to be a bad setting.

For the distressing and feverish defilements that might arise in someone who lives without avoiding these things do not arise when they are avoided. These are called the defilements that should be given up by avoiding.

6. Defilements Given Up by Dispelling

And what are the defilements that should be given up by dispelling? Take an individual who, reflecting rationally, doesn't tolerate a sensual, malicious, or cruel thought that has arisen, but gives it up, gets rid of it, eliminates it, and obliterates it. They don't tolerate any bad, unskillful qualities that have arisen, but give them up, get rid of them, eliminate them, and obliterate them.

For the distressing and feverish defilements that might arise in someone who lives without dispelling these things do not arise when they are dispelled. These are called the defilements that should be given up by dispelling.

7. Defilements Given Up by Developing

And what are the defilements that should be given up by developing? It's when an individual , reflecting rationally, develops the awakening factors of mindfulness, investigation of principles, energy, rapture, tranquility, immersion, and equanimity, which rely on seclusion, fading away, and cessation, and ripen as letting go.

For the distressing and feverish defilements that might arise in someone who lives without developing these things do not arise when they are developed. These are called the defilements that should be given up by developing.

Now, take an individual who, by seeing, has given up the defilements that should be given up by seeing. By restraint, they've given up the defilements that should be given up by restraint. By using, they've given up the defilements that should be given up by using. By enduring, they've given up the defilements that should be given up by enduring. By avoiding, they've given up the defilements that should be given up by avoiding. By dispelling, they've given up the defilements that should be given up by dispelling. By developing, they've given up the defilements that should be given up by developing. They're called a mendicant who lives having restrained all defilements, who has cut off craving, untied the fetters, and by rightly comprehending conceit has made an end of suffering."

That is what the Buddha said. Satisfied, the spiritual saints and practitioners approved what the Buddha said"

Chapter 5

Middle Discourses 3: Dhammadāyādasutta

Heirs in the Teaching

This discourse discusses the importance of not grasping the external appearance and receiving external things related to Buddha such as fame, material profit. However, maintaining the inner qualities of Buddha within and wisdom similar to that of Buddha by gaining four-fold Nibbana is important. Among other things, simply gaining four-fold Nibbana is the best for one who aspires to have peace of mind; Nibbana irrespective of conventions. When you don't give up what you should give up instead you give up things that are not directly related to Nibbana, Nibbana will be far shore for you.

Buddhahood is a state of wisdom, and wisdom to understand beyond conventions is reflected in the mind and thoughts. Buddhahood has three types; Sammasambuddha (Universal Buddha), Pacceka Buddha (private Buddha), Sāvakabuddha (Arahant), and Buddhahood is a state of wisdom.

Wisdom expressed in the words of Buddhas can only be understood by those who are wise. This is because wisdom is subjective; when someone says something, you can only understand what the person says within your understanding, understanding is the manifestation of a thought/thoughts. Those who are wise when they hear wise words, get to see the state of wisdom, Buddhahood. Buddhahood is not a state of convention. The meaning of this discourse is simply to suggest that one should give more priority to developing cessation, Nibbana without being too concerned about the things that are less important and are not directly related to gaining cessation Nibbana, such as a conventional lifestyle, appearance, food that a person consumes, traditions, rituals, etc. In that sense, the number of years you practiced Dhamma bears no fruit if you thought that you were practicing Dhamma, yet you were not practicing Dhamma in the right way to experience four-fold Nibbana. This is because if you truly practice Dhamma, you should truly experience the fruition of Dhamma; four-fold Nibbana.

Giving priority to Dhamma means not grasping conventions, which is what is required in developing the Noble Path. When you don't apply rationality and logic, you will likely develop ignorance. Instead, by applying reasoning and logic, you can grow wisdom to discover yourself and Nibbana. Ideally, one who truly wants to gain Nibbana, and represent Buddha as a disciple should develop higher wisdom and inner qualities similar to that of Buddha.

In the Noble Path, less priority is given to developing external factors or external appearance, and more priority is given to developing inner wisdom and inner qualities, the Noble Path always lies beyond ordinary training ways.

"So I have heard. At one time the Buddha was staying near Sāvatthī in Jeta's Grove, Anāthapiṇḍika's monastery. There the Buddha addressed the spiritual companions, "companions!"

"Venerable sir," they replied. The Buddha said this:

"Companions, be a part of teaching (inherit my teaching, become a Sotapanna to Arahant), not in things of the flesh (not other things). Out of compassion for you, I think, 'How can my disciples become direct disciple; Sotapanna to Arahant (inherit in the teaching), not in things of the flesh (not other things).?'

If you become heirs in things of the flesh, not in the teaching (if you receive other things in my name but do not gain nibbana, Sotapanna to Arahant), that will make you liable to the accusation: 'The Teacher's disciples live as heirs in things of the flesh, not in the teaching.' And it will make me liable to the accusation: 'The Teacher's disciples live as heirs in things of the flesh, not in the teaching.'

If you become heirs in the teaching (Sotapanna to Arahant), not in things of the flesh, that will make you not liable to the accusation: 'The Buddha's disciples live as heirs in the teaching; four-fold nibbana, not in things of the flesh.' And it will make me not liable to the accusation: 'The Buddha's disciples live as heirs in the teaching (Sotapanna to Arahant), not in things of the flesh.'

So, companions, be my heirs in the teaching, four-fold nibbana, not in things of the flesh. Out of compassion for you, I think, 'How can my disciples become heirs in the teaching, not in things of the flesh?'

Suppose that I had eaten and refused more food, being full, and having had as much as I needed. And there was some extra almsfood that was going to be thrown away. Then two companions were to come who were weak with hunger. I'd say to them, 'Companions, I have eaten and refused more food, being full, and having had as much as I need. And there is this extra almsfood that's going to be thrown away. Eat it if you like. Otherwise I'll throw it out where there is little that grows, or drop it into water that has no living creatures.'

Then one of those practitioners thought, 'The Buddha has eaten and refused more food. And he has some extra almsfood that's going to be thrown away. If we don't eat it he'll throw it away. But the Buddha has also said: "Be my heirs in the teaching, not in things of the flesh." And alms food is one of the things of the flesh.

If I eat alms food or if I don't eat, it does not matter but instead of giving priority to eating this alms food, why don't I give priority to the teachings, and practice in away leading to four-fold nibbana?' And that's what they did.

Then the second of those practitioners thought, 'The Buddha has eaten and refused more food. And he has some extra almsfood that's going to be thrown away. If we don't eat it he'll throw it away.

Why don't I eat this alms food, then spend the day and night having got rid of my hunger and weakness? They give more priority to alms food and they give less priority to teachings, four-fold nibbana, and that's what they did.

Even though that person, after eating the almsfood, spent the day and night rid of hunger and weakness, it is the former companion who is more worthy of respect and praise. Why is that? Because four-fold nibbana will help a person to abandon desires by becoming an Arahant; A person who is an Arahant has no desires (no likes, dislikes or expectations), content, self-effacing, unburdensome, and energetic.

So, companions, receive my teachings; Sotapanna to Arahant and not other things (be my heirs in the teaching, not in things of the flesh). Out of compassion for you, I think, 'How can my disciples become heirs in the teaching, Sotapanna to Arahant not in things of the flesh?'"

That is what the Buddha said. When he had spoken, the Holy One got up from his seat and entered his dwelling.

Then soon after the Buddha left, Arahant Sāriputta said to the companions, "Respected, companions!"

"Reverend," they replied. Arahant Sāriputta said this:

"Respected companions, how do the ordinary disciples of the Buddha who lives in seclusion not train in seclusion? And how do they train in seclusion?"

"Respected companions, we would travel a long way to learn the meaning of this statement in the presence of Arahant Sāriputta. May Arahant Sāriputta himself please clarify the meaning of this. The companions will listen and remember it."

"Well then, respected companions, listen and apply your mind well, I will speak."

"Yes, respected sir," they replied. Arahant Sāriputta said this:

"Respected companions, how do the ordinary practitioners who attempt to become the disciples of the Buddha who lives in seclusion not train in seclusion?

The ordinary disciples of a teacher who lives in seclusion do not train in seclusion. They don't give up what the Buddha's path (noble path, inner path) tells them to give up.

They're indulgent and slack, leaders in backsliding, neglecting seclusion. In this case, the senior companions should be criticized on three grounds. 'The person who train to become a disciple of the Buddha who lives in seclusion do not train in seclusion in mind (in the absence or presence of others).' This is the first ground.

'They don't give up what the Buddha's noble path tells them to give up.' This is the second ground. 'They're indulgent and slack, leaders in backsliding, neglecting seclusion.' This is the third ground.

The senior companions should be criticized on these three grounds. In this case, the middle companions and the junior companions should be criticized on the same three grounds. This is how a person who train to become the disciples of the buddha who lives in seclusion do not train in seclusion I mind (in the presence or absence of self, others and the world) .

And how does an ordinary person who train to become the disciples (Sotapanna to Arahant) of the Buddha who lives in seclusion train in seclusion?

An ordinary person who trains to become the disciples of the Buddha (Sotapanna to Arahant) who lives in seclusion train in seclusion. They give up what the Buddha tells them to give up.

They're not indulgent and slack, leaders in backsliding, neglecting seclusion. In this case, the senior companions should be praised on three grounds. 'A person who trains to become the disciples of the buddha who lives in seclusion train in seclusion.' This is the first ground.

'They give up what the Buddha's path (noble path, an inner path) tells them to give up.' This is the second ground. 'They're not indulgent and slack, leaders in backsliding, neglecting seclusion.'

This is the third ground. The senior companions should be praised on these three grounds. In this case, the middle companions and the junior companions should be praised on the same three grounds. This is how a person who train to become the disciples of the buddha who lives in seclusion train in seclusion.

The bad thing here is greed (too much likes) and hate (too much dislikes). There is a middle way of practice; four-fold nibbana for giving up greed and hate at Arahant stage. It gives vision and knowledge, and leads to peace, direct knowledge, awakening, and extinguishment.

And what is that middle way of practice? It is simply this noble eightfold path, that is: right view (nibbana is a wisdom and karma based path), right thought, right speech, right action, right livelihood, right effort, right mindfulness, and right immersion. This is that middle way of practice, which gives vision and knowledge, and leads to peace, direct knowledge, awakening, and extinguishment.

The bad thing here is anger and hostility. … disdain and contempt … jealousy and stinginess … deceit and deviousness … obstinacy and aggression … conceit and arrogance … vanity and negligence. There is a middle way of practice for giving up vanity and negligence. It gives vision and knowledge, and leads to peace, direct knowledge, awakening, and extinguishment.

And what is that middle way of practice? It is simply this noble eightfold path, that is: right view, right thought, right speech, right action, right livelihood, right effort, right mindfulness, and right immersion.

This is that middle way of practice, which gives vision and knowledge, and leads to peace, direct knowledge, awakening, and extinguishment."

This is what Arahant Sāriputta said. Satisfied, the companions approved what Arahant Sāriputta said."

Chapter 6

Middle Discourses 4: Bhayabheravasutta

Fear and Dread

A person who met with Buddha speaks about the challenges faced by spiritual practitioners who attempt to live in forests and similar places. Before gaining Nibbana, Buddha tried the common ways. Buddha lived in dangerous places, such as an isolated forest, trying to practice asceticism based on common ways. Just like Buddha, many others followed similar lifestyles and ascetic practices. Yet, among those who lived in forests and attempted to find a spiritual life, only Buddha became a Buddha and no others. This is because of the completion of paramis in previous births.

Some ascetics who lived in forests similar to Buddha's had minds full of jealousy, stinginess, and bad qualities. In other words, simply by following common ways, not everyone who followed what was typical for those days, such as living in forests and isolated places, managed to develop purification in their intentional actions or give up grasping to conventions. Living in forests or isolation is not necessary for Nibbana. It is not the forest that purifies a person. Otherwise, everyone in the forest or everyone who goes into a forest should be able to purify themselves. Rather, it is the person who can purify their mind whether or not they live in a forest. Thus, the common ways of asceticism were rejected by Buddha. Mental attachment to external things requires giving up. For those who give up mental attachment, any place can be an isolated place.[8]

A person who purifies themself can beautify both self and a surrounding. Having tried common ways and realizing that common ways are limited, Buddha found his own way that goes beyond common ways, leading to Nibbana. Thus, after gaining Nibbana, Buddha rarely lived in isolated places; instead, he lived in crowded places, meeting people and speaking about Dhamma. The point is Dhamma is not found externally in forests. Forest is a mental image in a person's mind. Dhamma should be cultivated within, irrespective of external factors.

---

[8] See Dhp 163: Devadatta's proposed rules that the bhikkhus should live in the forest etc. were rejected by the Buddha. This is because Nibbana is not a sila-based path. Nibbana is a karma and merit-based path.

External factors can only reside within one's thoughts. If an external path were the Noble Path, there would be many who would easily take it over the eternal path to become Nibbana. Yet, the inner path is the Noble Path. It is rare for those who purify internally despite external factors and conventions. Just as one moment connects to another, one thought connects to another thought, linking both past and present as the light of a candle that appears and vanishes, the mental continuum of a person (who has completed Paramis's in previous births) will reach Cessation if the current practice can boost a mind to give up grasping conventions, and engage in wholesome intentions/ deeds.

If an ordinary person strives to do good and avoid bad (for example, reduce grasping conventions, not become too sad, not become too anxious, and so on, not become proud, not treat others differently due to their backgrounds, not using materials, knowledge, or whatever one possesses for the benefit of self alone rather sharing with others in a kind and humble and gentle manner, fulfilling responsibilities towards others, becoming a good person and collecting merits, engaging in wholesome intentional actions/deeds), these actions can help practitioners gain Nibbana. Just as we jump up on earth, we fall back. The law of karma applies to all. Thus, for one who engages in wholesome intentional actions and develops wisdom through wholesome intentional actions blending with the universal rhythm, Nibbana will follow through naturally in line with how the universe functions.

"So I have heard. At one time the Buddha was staying near Sāvatthī in Jeta's Grove, Anāthapiṇḍika's monastery.

Then the brahmin Jānussoṇi went up to the Buddha, and exchanged greetings with him. When the greetings and polite conversation were over, he sat down to one side and said to the Buddha:

"Mister Gotama, those gentlemen who have commenced a spiritual practice; practice of the dhamma out of faith in you have Mister Gotama to lead the way, help them out, and give them encouragement. And those people follow Mister Gotama's example."

"That's so true, brahmin! Everything you say is true, brahmin!"

"But Mister Gotama, remote lodgings in the wilderness and the forest are challenging. It's hard to maintain seclusion and hard to find joy in solitude. The forests seem to rob the mind of a person who isn't immersed in noble concentration (Anagami)."

"That's so true, brahmin! Everything you say is true, brahmin!

Before my awakening—when I was still unawakened but intent on awakening—I too thought, 'Remote lodgings in the wilderness and the forest are challenging. It's hard to maintain seclusion and hard to find joy in solitude. The forests seem to rob the mind of a person who isn't immersed in noble concentration (Anagami).'

Then I thought, 'There are other people (ascetics and spiritual practitioners) with unpurified conduct of body, speech, and mind who frequent remote lodgings in the wilderness and the forest.

Those ascetics and spiritual practitioners summon unskillful fear and dread because of these defects in their conduct. But I don't frequent remote lodgings in the wilderness and the forest with unpurified conduct of body, speech, and mind. My conduct is purified.

I am one of those noble ones who frequent remote lodgings in the wilderness and the forest with purified conduct of body, speech, and mind.' Seeing this purity of conduct in myself I felt even more unruffled about staying in the forest.

Then I thought, 'There are ascetics and spiritual practitioners with unpurified livelihood who frequent remote lodgings in the wilderness and the forest.

Those ascetics and spiritual practitioners summon unskillful fear and dread because of these defects in their livelihood. But I don't frequent remote lodgings in the wilderness and the forest with unpurified livelihood. My livelihood is purified.

I am one of those noble ones who frequent remote lodgings in the wilderness and the forest with purified livelihood.' Seeing this purity of livelihood in myself I felt even more unruffled about staying in the forest.

Then I thought, 'There are ascetics and spiritual practitioners full of desire for sensual pleasures, with acute lust … I am not full of desire …'

'There are ascetics and spiritual practitioners full of ill will, with malicious intentions … I have a heart full of love …'

'There are ascetics and spiritual practitioners overcome with dullness and drowsiness … I am free of dullness and drowsiness …'

'There are ascetics and spiritual practitioners who are restless, with no peace of mind … My mind is peaceful …'

'There are ascetics and spiritual practitioners who are doubting and uncertain … I've gone beyond doubt …'

'There are ascetics and spiritual practitioners who glorify themselves and put others down … I don't glorify myself and put others down …'

'There are ascetics and spiritual practitioners who are cowardly and craven … I don't get startled …'

'There are ascetics and spiritual practitioners who enjoy possessions, honor, and popularity … I have few wishes …'

'There are ascetics and spiritual practitioners who are lazy and lack energy … I am energetic …'

'There are ascetics and spiritual practitioners who are unmindful and lack situational awareness … I am mindful …'

'There are ascetics and spiritual practitioners who lack immersion, with straying minds … I am accomplished in immersion …'

'There are ascetics and spiritual practitioners who are witless and stupid who frequent remote lodgings in the wilderness and the forest. Those ascetics and brahmins summon unskillful fear and dread because of the defects of witlessness and stupidity. But I don't frequent remote lodgings in the wilderness and the forest witless and stupid.

I am accomplished in wisdom. I am one of those noble ones who frequent remote lodgings in the wilderness and the forest accomplished in wisdom.' Seeing this accomplishment of wisdom in myself I felt even more unruffled about staying in the forest.

Then I thought, 'There are certain nights that are recognized as specially portentous: the fourteenth, fifteenth, and eighth of the fortnight. On such nights, why don't I stay in awe-inspiring and hair-raising shrines in parks, forests, and trees?

In such lodgings, hopefully I might see that fear and dread.' Some time later, that's what I did. As I was staying there a deer came by, or a peacock snapped a twig, or the wind rustled the leaves. Then I thought, 'Is this that fear and dread coming?' Then I thought, 'Why do I always meditate expecting that fear to come? Why don't I get rid of that fear and dread just as it comes, while remaining just as I am?' Then that fear and dread came upon me as I was walking.

I didn't stand still or sit down or lie down until I had got rid of that fear and dread while walking. Then that fear and dread came upon me as I was standing. I didn't walk or sit down or lie down until I had got rid of that fear and dread while standing. Then that fear and dread came upon me as I was sitting. I didn't lie down or stand still or walk until I had got rid of that fear and dread while sitting. Then that fear and dread came upon me as

I was lying down. I didn't sit up or stand still or walk until I had got rid of that fear and dread while lying down.

There are some ascetics and spiritual practitioners who perceive that it's day when in fact it's night, or perceive that it's night when in fact it's day. This meditation of theirs is delusional, I say.

I perceive that it's night when in fact it is night, and perceive that it's day when in fact it is day. And if there's anyone of whom it may be rightly said that a being not liable to delusion has arisen in the world for the welfare and happiness of the people, out of sympathy for the world, for the benefit, welfare, and happiness of gods and humans, it's of me that this should be said.

My energy was roused up and unflagging, my mindfulness was established and lucid, my body was tranquil and undisturbed, and my mind was immersed in noble concentration (Anagami).

Quite secluded from sensual pleasures, secluded from unskillful qualities, I entered and remained in the first absorption, which has the rapture and bliss born of seclusion, while placing the mind and keeping it connected. As the placing of the mind and keeping it connected were stilled, I entered and remained in the second absorption, which has the rapture and bliss born of immersion, with internal clarity and mind at one, without placing the mind and keeping it connected.

And with the fading away of rapture, I entered and remained in the third absorption, where I experienced equanimity, mindful and aware, personally experiencing the bliss of which the noble ones declare, 'Equanimous and mindful, one experiences bliss.' With the giving up of pleasure and pain, and the ending of former happiness and sadness, I entered and remained in the fourth absorption, without pleasure or pain, with pure equanimity and mindfulness.

When my mind had become immersed in noble concentration like this—purified, bright, flawless, rid of corruptions, pliable, workable, steady, and imperturbable—I extended it toward recollection of past lives. I recollected many kinds of past lives.

That is: one, two, three, four, five, ten, twenty, thirty, forty, fifty, a hundred, a thousand, a hundred thousand rebirths; many eons of the world contracting, many eons of the world expanding, many eons of the world contracting and expanding. I remembered: 'There, I was named this, my clan was that, I looked like this, and that was my food. This was how I felt pleasure and pain, and that was how my life ended.

When I passed away from that place I was reborn somewhere else. There, too, I was named this, my clan was that, I looked like this, and that was my food. This was how I felt pleasure and pain, and that was how my life ended. When I passed away from that place, I was reborn here.' And so, I recollected my many kinds of past lives, with features and details.

This was the first knowledge, which I achieved in the first watch of the night. Ignorance was destroyed and knowledge arose; darkness was destroyed, and light arose, as happens for a person who is diligent, keen, and resolute.

When my mind had become immersed in noble concentration like this—purified, bright, flawless, rid of corruptions, pliable, workable, steady, and imperturbable—I extended it toward knowledge of the death and rebirth of sentient beings. With clairvoyance that is purified and superhuman, I saw sentient beings passing away and being reborn—inferior and superior, beautiful and ugly, in a good place or a bad place.

I understood how sentient beings are reborn according to their deeds: 'These dear beings did bad things by way of body, speech, and mind. They spoke ill of the noble ones; they had wrong view; and they chose to act out of that wrong view.

When their body breaks up, after death, they're reborn in a place of loss, a bad place, the underworld, hell. These dear beings, however, did good things by way of body, speech, and mind. They never spoke ill of the noble ones; they had right view; and they chose to act out of that right view.

When their body breaks up, after death, they're reborn in a good place, a heavenly realm.' And so, with clairvoyance that is purified and superhuman, I saw sentient beings passing away and being reborn—inferior and superior, beautiful and ugly, in a good place or a bad place. I understood how sentient beings are reborn according to their deeds.

This was the second knowledge, which I achieved in the middle watch of the night. Ignorance was destroyed and knowledge arose; darkness was destroyed, and light arose, as happens for a person who is diligent, keen, and resolute.

When my mind had become immersed in noble concentration like this—purified, bright, flawless, rid of corruptions, pliable, workable, steady, and imperturbable—I extended it toward knowledge of the ending of defilements. I truly understood: 'This is suffering' … 'This is the origin of suffering' … 'This is the cessation of suffering' … 'This is the practice that leads to the cessation of suffering'. I truly understood: 'These are defilements' … 'This is the origin of defilements' … 'This is the cessation of defilements' … 'This is the practice that leads to the cessation of defilements'.

Knowing and seeing like this, my mind was freed from the defilements of sensuality, desire to be reborn, and ignorance. When it was freed, I knew it was freed.

I understood I gained Buddhahood and arahantship: 'Rebirth is ended, the spiritual journey has been completed, what had to be done has been done, there is nothing further for this place.'"

This was the third knowledge, which I achieved in the final watch of the night. Ignorance was destroyed and knowledge arose; darkness was destroyed, and light arose, as happens for a person who is diligent, keen, and resolute.

Brahmin, you might think: 'Perhaps the recluse Gotama is not free of greed, hate, and delusion even today, and that is why he still frequents living in isolation (in the wilderness, the forest etc.).' But you should not see it like this. I see two reasons to live in isolation. I see a happy life for myself in the present, and I have sympathy for future generations."

"Indeed, Mister Gotama has sympathy for future generations, since he is a perfected one, a fully awakened Buddha. Excellent, Mister Gotama! Excellent, Mister Gotama!

As if he were righting the overturned, or revealing the hidden, or pointing out the path to the lost, or lighting a lamp in the dark so people with clear eyes can see what's there, Buddha Gotama has made the universal teaching clear in many ways. I go for refuge to Buddha Gotama, to the universal teaching, and to the universal (noble) Saṅgha. From this day forth, may Buddha Gotama remember me as an ordinary follower who has gone for refuge for life."

Chapter 7

Middle Discourses 5: Anaṅgaṇasutta

Unblemished

Dhamma practice is a self-practice. An ordinary person who aspires to their peace, Nibbana should be able to constantly work on identifying one's own weaknesses and to improve oneself in line with Dhamma. It requires constant effort and putting effort into working on improving self in the middle way, meaning not too hard and not too ignorant but in a comfortable middle way. By recognizing one's own weaknesses, a person can improve themselves. Otherwise, merely by ignoring them, a person will be unlikely to be improving self. For example, a person with a higher degree of ego is unlikely to want to observe their weaknesses. A person may be unwilling to accept their own faults; rather, they want to blame others. By reducing ego and examining one's weaknesses, a person gets a humble opportunity to improve self. In that sense, a person with less ego is likely to make progress on the noble path.

The world is created in one's thoughts. When too many thoughts occupy one's mind, one may experience tiredness and weariness. Removing attachment to thoughts across four-fold Nibbana can bring satisfaction. Samsara is created in one's thoughts, from one thought through to another.

The practice leading to Nibbana requires not getting attached to one's thoughts in daily life, because accepting that there is a self, a world, other things, and others are created in one's thoughts. Thus, by investigating the situation, analyzing an understanding and rectifying weakness in self; thoughts, an ordinary person can make progress on the Noble Path and train to not grasp into conventions; fetters across stages. For those who refuse to accept their own weakness when it's reasonable to do so, Nibbana and the training leading to Nibbana will be far to reach. Those who are able to see their weaknesses and reduce grasp conventions are more likely to make progress on the Noble Path.

"So I have heard. At one time the Buddha was staying near Sāvatthī in Jeta's Grove, Anāthapiṇḍika's monastery. Arahant Sāriputta addressed the spiritual companions: "Respected, spiritual companions!"

"Venerable sir," they replied. Arahant Sāriputta said this:

"Companions, these four people are found in the world. What four? One person with a blemish doesn't truly understand: 'There is a blemish in me.' But another person with a blemish does truly understand: 'There is a blemish in me.'
One person without a blemish doesn't truly understand: 'There is no blemish in me.' But another person without a blemish does truly understand: 'There is no blemish in me.'

In this case, of the two persons with a blemish, the one who doesn't understand is said to be worse, while the one who does understand is better. And of the two persons without a blemish, the one who doesn't understand is said to be worse, while the one who does understand is better."

When he said this, Arahant Mahāmoggallāna said to him:
"What is the cause, Arahant Sāriputta, what is the reason why, of the two persons with a blemish, one is said to be worse and one better?
And what is the cause, what is the reason why, of the two persons without a blemish, one is said to be worse and one better?"

"Respected sirs, take the case of the person who has a blemish and does not understand it. You can expect that they won't generate enthusiasm, make an effort, or rouse up energy to give up that blemish. And they will die with greed, hate, and delusion, blemished, with a corrupted mind. Suppose a bronze dish was brought from a shop or smithy covered with dirt or stains. And the owners neither used it or had it cleaned, but kept it in a dirty place. Over time, wouldn't that bronze dish get even dirtier and more stained?"

"Yes, venerable sir."

"In the same way, take the case of the person who has a blemish and does not understand it. You can expect that … they will die with a corrupted mind.

Take the case of an ordinary person who has a blemish and does understand it. You can expect that they will generate enthusiasm, make an effort, and rouse up energy to give up that blemish. And they will die without greed, hate, and delusion, unblemished, with an uncorrupted mind. Suppose a bronze dish was brought from a shop or smithy covered with dirt or stains. But the owners used it and had it cleaned, and didn't keep it in a dirty place. Over time, wouldn't that bronze dish get cleaner and brighter?"

"Yes, venerable sir."

"In the same way, take the case of the person who has a blemish and does understand it. You can expect that … they will die with an uncorrupted mind.

Take the case of an ordinary person who doesn't have a blemish but does not understand it. You can expect that they will focus on the feature of beauty, and because of that, lust will infect their mind. And they will die with greed, hate, and delusion, blemished, with a corrupted mind. Suppose a bronze dish was brought from a shop or smithy clean and bright. And the owners neither used it or had it cleaned, but kept it in a dirty place. Over time, wouldn't that bronze dish get dirtier and more stained?"

"Yes, venerable sir."

"In the same way, take the case of an ordinary person who has no blemish and does not understand it. You can expect that … they will die with a corrupted mind.

Take the case of the person who doesn't have a blemish and does understand it. You can expect that they won't focus on the feature of beauty, and because of that, lust won't infect their mind. And they will die without greed, hate, and delusion, unblemished, with an uncorrupted mind. Suppose a bronze dish was brought from a shop or smithy clean and bright. And the owners used it and had it cleaned, and didn't keep it in a dirty place. Over time, wouldn't that bronze dish get cleaner and brighter?"

"Yes, venerable sir."

"In the same way, take the case of an ordinary person who doesn't have a blemish and does understand it. You can expect that … they will die with an uncorrupted mind.

This is the cause, this is the reason why, of the two persons with a blemish, one is said to be worse and one better. And this is the cause, this is the reason why, of the two persons without a blemish, one is said to be worse and one better."

"Respected sir, the word 'blemish' is spoken of. But what is 'blemish' a term for?"

"Respected sir, 'blemish' is a term for the spheres of bad, unskillful wishes.
It's possible that someone might wish: 'If I commit an offense, I hope others don't find out!' But it's possible that some other people do find out that that person has committed an offense. Thinking, 'The companions have found out about my offense,' they get angry and bitter. And that anger and that bitterness are both blemishes.

It's possible that some people might wish: 'If I commit an offense, I hope the companions accuse me in private, not in the middle of the Saṅgha.' But it's possible that the companions do accuse that person in the middle of the Saṅgha …

It's possible that some people might wish: 'If I commit an offense, I hope I'm accused by a counterpart, not by someone who is not a counterpart.' But it's possible that someone who is not a counterpart accuses that person …

It's possible that some people might wish: 'Oh, I hope the Teacher will teach the companions by repeatedly questioning me alone, not some other companion.' But it's possible that the Teacher will teach the companions by repeatedly questioning some other practitioners…

It's possible that some people might wish: 'Oh, I hope the companions will enter the village for the meal putting me at the very front, not some other person.' But it's possible that the companions will enter the village for the meal putting some other people at the very front …

It's possible that some people might wish: 'Oh, I hope that I alone get the best seat, the best drink, and the best almsfood in the refectory, not some other person.' But it's possible that some other person gets the best seat, the best drink, and the best almsfood in the refectory …

It's possible that some people might wish: 'I hope that I alone give the verses of appreciation after eating in the refectory, not some other person.' But it's possible that some other person gives the verses of appreciation after eating in the refectory …

It's possible that some people might wish: 'Oh, I hope that I might teach the Dhamma to the ordinary people (ordinary monks, ordinary nuns, ordinary householder men, and ordinary householder women), not some other person.'

But it's possible that some other person teaches the Dhamma …
It's possible that some people might wish: 'Oh, I hope that the companions (ordinary monks, ordinary nuns, ordinary householder men, and ordinary householder women) will honor, respect, revere, and venerate me alone, not some other person.'
But it's possible that some other person is honored, respected, revered, and venerated …

It's possible that some people might wish: 'I hope I get the nicest robes, almsfood, lodgings, and medicines and supplies for the sick, not some other person.'
But it's possible that some other person gets the nicest robes, almsfood, lodgings, and medicines and supplies for the sick …
Thinking, 'Some other companions has got the nicest robes, almsfood, lodgings, and medicines and supplies for the sick', they get angry and bitter. And that anger and that bitterness are both blemishes.
'Blemish' is a term for these spheres of bad, unskillful wishes.

Suppose these spheres of bad, unskillful wishes are seen and heard to be not given up by a person. Even though they live a conventional bhikkhu life style; they dwell in the wilderness, in remote lodgings, eat only almsfood, wander indiscriminately for almsfood, wear rag robes, and wear shabby robes, their spiritual companions don't need to honor, respect, revere, and venerate them.

Why is that?
It's because these spheres of bad, unskillful wishes are seen and heard to be not given up by that ordinary monks.

Suppose a bronze dish was brought from a shop or smithy clean and bright. Then the owners were to prepare it with the carcass of a snake, a dog, or a human, cover it with a bronze lid, and parade it through the marketplace.

When people saw it, they'd say: 'My good man, what is it that you're carrying like a precious treasure?' So they'd open up the lid for people to look inside. But as soon as they saw it, they were filled with loathing, revulsion, and disgust. Not even those who were hungry wanted to eat it, let alone those who had eaten.

In the same way, when these spheres of bad, unskillful wishes are seen and heard to be not given up by a person… their spiritual companions should not honor, respect, revere, and venerate them. Why is that? It's because these spheres of bad, unskillful wishes are seen and heard to be not given up by that person.

Suppose these spheres of bad, unskillful wishes are seen and heard to be given up by a person. Even though they dwell wherever (within a village, city, house, temple etc.), accept donations (invitations to a meal etc.), and wear whatever robes, their spiritual companions should honor, respect, revere, and venerate them.

Why is that? It's because these spheres of bad, unskilful wishes are seen and heard to be given up by that venerable, and trainees can gain merits and develop wisdom. Suppose a bronze dish was brought from a shop or smithy clean and bright.

Then the owners were to prepare it with boiled fine rice with the dark grains picked out and served with many soups and sauces, cover it with a bronze lid, and parade it through the marketplace.

When people saw it, they'd say: 'My good man, what is it that you're carrying like a precious treasure?' So they'd open up the lid for people to look inside. And as soon as they saw it, they were filled with liking, attraction, and relish. Even those who had eaten wanted to eat it, let alone those who were hungry.

In the same way, when these spheres of bad, unskillful wishes are seen and heard to be given up by a person … their spiritual companions should honor, respect, revere, and venerate them, why is that? It's because these spheres of bad, unskillful wishes are seen and heard to be given up by that venerable, and trainees can gain merits and develop wisdom.."

When he said this, Arahant Mahāmoggallāna said to him, "Arahant Sāriputta, a simile springs to mind."
"Then speak as you feel inspired," said Arahant Sāriputta.

"Arahant, at one time I was staying right here in Rājagaha, the Mountainfold. Then I robed up in the morning and, taking my bowl and robe, entered Rājagaha for alms.

Now at that time Samīti of the wainwrights was planing the rim of a chariot wheel.

The Ājīvaka ascetic Paṇḍuputta, who was formerly of the wainwrights, was standing by, and this thought came to his mind: 'Oh, I hope Samīti the wainwright planes out the crooks, bends, and flaws in this rim. Then the rim will be rid of crooks, bends, and flaws, pure, and consolidated in the core.' And Samīti planed out the flaws in the rim just as Paṇḍuputta thought. Then Paṇḍuputta expressed his gladness: 'He planes like he knows my heart with his heart!'

In the same way, there are those faithless people who practice a spiritual life not out of faith but to earn a livelihood, make gains.
They're devious, deceitful, and sneaky. They're restless, insolent, fickle, scurrilous, and loose-tongued. They do not guard their sense doors or eat in moderation, and they are not committed to their spiritual practice, wakefulness; four-fold nibbana.
They don't care about the spiritual life in their hearts but pretend to care, and they don't keenly respect the training. They're indulgent and slack, leaders in backsliding, neglecting seclusion, lazy, and lacking energy. They're unmindful, lacking situational awareness and immersion, with straying minds, witless and stupid. Arahant Sāriputta planes their faults with this exposition of the teaching as if he knows my heart with his heart!

But there are those faithless people who practice a spiritual life out of faith. They're not devious, deceitful, and sneaky. They're not restless, insolent, fickle, scurrilous, and loose-tongued.
They guard their sense doors and eat in moderation, and they are committed to their spiritual practice, wakefulness; four-fold nibbana. They care about the spiritual practice, and keenly respect the training. They're not indulgent or slack, nor are they leaders in backsliding, neglecting seclusion. They're energetic and determined.

They're mindful, with situational awareness, immersion, and unified minds; wise, not stupid. Hearing this exposition of the teaching from Arahant Sāriputta, they drink it up and devour it, as it were.

And in speech and thought they say: 'It's good, sirs, that he draws his spiritual companions away from the unskillful and establishes them in the skillful.'

Suppose there was a woman or man who was young, youthful, and fond of adornments, and had bathed their head.

Presented with a garland of lotuses, jasmine, or liana flowers, they would take them in both hands and place them on the crown of the head.
In the same way, are those faithless people who practice a spiritual life out of faith … say: 'It's good, sirs, that he draws his spiritual companions away from the unskillful and establishes them in the skillful.'" And so, these two spiritual giants agreed with each other's fine words."

Chapter 8

Middle Discourses 6: Ākaṅkheyyasutta

One Might Wish

Not understanding Dhamma through personal experience and not understanding Dhamma in full, based on limited understanding, some ordinary Sangha can misinterpret the meaning of this discourse saying that careful observance of ethical precepts is the foundation of all higher achievements in the spiritual life. It should be corrected; virtues refer to noble virtues, and noble virtues gained by a Sotapanna. As other wise, a reasonable argument would be that those who fail to observe ethical precepts, such as Angulimala[9], or Sarkani,[10] should not have gained Nibbana. The reason those who did not manage to keep sila managed to attain Nibbana is because Nibbana is shaped by one's karma and karma is a complex matter. Just as karma shapes the birth and death of beings, karma shapes the Nibbana of beings.

The direct practice is developing factors of Stream Entry including noble virtues.

Achieving Sotapanna, the basic foundation level of Nibbana leads to higher stages of Nibbana. At higher stages of Nibbana, one gets to develop triple knowledge, knowledge developed because of non-attachment to mind and body allows a person to explore, focus, and understand with wisdom to see beyond human eye, hear beyond human ear and see beyond present time or past based on memory etc.

To develop a deep understanding of the teachings of Buddha leading to Nibbana, there is a need to go beyond ordinary views to gain noble views and go beyond ordinary techniques to train in the noble techniques; in doing so to develop factors of Stream Entry (Sotapanna); abandon fetters and develop a mental state of a stream-enterer.

There are four factors of Stream Entry (Sotapanna), and a person who seeks Nibbana would benefit from developing these factors. The first three factors are

---

[9] Angulimala was a serial killer who later became an Arahant. (See MN 86).

[10] Sarakaani was an alcoholic, but he became a Sotapanna. (See SN 55.24, Sarakaani Sutta)

confirmed confidence in the Triple Gem (i.e., first three factors), and that's how a person can enter the stream by refuging the Triple Gem, cleansing the mind through the Triple Gem to reduce worldly desires, and giving priority to the Triple Gem. The fourth factor is noble virtues.

How can one develop confirmed confidence in Triple Gem?

Confirmed confidence in the Triple Gem[11] can be developed by reflecting on the qualities of the Triple Gem day and night; recollect the Tathagata; 'Supreme Gautama Buddha, the Blessed One is worthy and rightly self-awakened, possess perfect and highest knowledge & noble conduct, well-gone, an expert with regard to the world, excellent trainer for those people fit to be instructed, the Teacher of divine & human beings, fully enlightened, understood the path by himself and explained the path to us, and blessed'; recollect Dhamma; 'The Dhamma is well-explained by the Blessed One, those who practice correctly will get to experience Dhamma immediately, applicable for all times and thus, timeless, others can be invited to practice and see for themselves, inviting verification, pertinent, can be realized by those who are wise enough to see beyond ordinary ways', and recollect noble Sangha; 'The noble Sangha of the Blessed One's are the good in their practice, they have practiced Dhamma in a correct manner, they are systematic in their practice, they have practiced correctly, and skilfully and gained realization across four stages; noble Sangha of the blessed ones are the in- comparable field of merit for the world.'

You should be able to reflect the Triple Gem while walking, standing, sitting, and going about doing other things, and attending to the Triple Gem by giving priority to the Triple Gem in one's mind.

How can one develop noble virtues?

At the beginning of one's practice, before reaching a mind state of a Sotapanna, one may take precepts or monastic rules and thereafter develop a higher understanding of Dhamma across four stages. Before reaching Sotapanna stage, one may purify one's bodily action, verbal action, and mental action by repeatedly reflecting upon them; before conducting any bodily, verbal and mental actions, one may reflect whether such physical, verbal, or mental action one is doing lead to

---

[11] To gain Sotapanna, the most appropriate meditation is reflecting the qualities of the Triple Gem. Alternatively for those who are unable to do so, they may try engage in "chittanupassana" or understanding the causes, and analysing thoughts.

cause pain or harm to self or others, if on reflection, one knows that one's action leads to the affliction of self and others, one should not do such things and engage restraint in the future. On the other hand, if on reflection, if one knows one's physical, verbal and mental actions do not lead to affliction of self and others, one may continue with it, stay joyful and training day and night.

"Thus have I heard. On one occasion the Blessed One was living at Sāvatthī in Jeta's Grove, Anāthapiṇḍika's Park. There he addressed the spiritual companions thus: "Bhikkhus."—"Venerable sir," they replied. The Blessed One said this:

"Spiritual companions, dwell possessed of noble virtue, possessed of the noble virtues of a Sotapanna, initially while you are still an ordinary, you may restrained with the restraint of the five/eight/or Pātimokkha, attempt to purify thoughts; intentional actions and resort, and seeing fear in the slightest fault, train by undertaking the training noble precepts.

"If a person should wish: 'May I be dear and agreeable to my companions in the holy life, respected and esteemed by them,' let him fulfil the noble precepts, be devoted to internal serenity of mind, not neglect meditation, be possessed of insight, and dwell in empty huts (Sotapanna etc.)…

"If a person should wish: 'May I be one to obtain clothing, food, accommodation, and medicinal requisites,' let him fulfil the noble precepts…

"If a person should wish: 'May the services of those whose robes, almsfood, resting place, and medicinal requisites I use bring them great fruit and benefit,' let one fulfils the noble precepts (Sotapanna etc.) …

"If a person should wish: 'When my kinsmen and relatives who have passed away and died remember me with confidence in their minds, may that bring them great fruit and great benefit,' let one fulfils the noble precepts (Sotapanna etc.)…

"If a person should wish: 'May I become a conqueror of discontent and delight, and may discontent not conquer me; may I abide transcending discontent whenever it arises,' let one fulfils the noble precepts (Sotapanna etc.) …

"If a person should wish: 'May I become a conqueror of fear and dread, and may fear and dread not conquer me; may I abide transcending fear and dread whenever they arise,' let one fulfils the noble precepts (Sotapanna etc.) …

"If a person should wish: 'May I become one to obtain at will, without trouble or difficulty, the four jhānas that constitute the higher mind and provide a pleasant abiding here and now,' let one fulfils the noble precepts (Sotapanna etc.)…

"If a person should wish: 'May I contact with the body and abide in those liberations that are peaceful and immaterial, transcending forms,' let one fulfils the noble precepts (Sotapanna etc.)…

"If a person should wish: 'May I, with the destruction of three fetters, become a stream-enterer, no longer subject to perdition, bound for deliverance, headed for enlightenment,' let one fulfils the noble precepts (Sotapanna etc.)…

"If a person should wish: 'May I, with the destruction of three fetters and with the attenuation of lust, hate, and delusion, become a once-returner, returning once to this world to make an end of suffering,' let one fulfils the noble precepts (Sotapanna etc.)…

"If a person should wish: 'May I, with the destruction of the five lower fetters, become due to reappear spontaneously in the Pure Abodes and there attain final Nibbāna, without ever returning from that world,' let one fulfils the noble precepts (Sotapanna etc.)…

"If a person should wish: 'May I wield the various kinds of supernormal power: having been one, may I become many; having been many, may I become one; may I appear and vanish; may I go unhindered through a wall, through an enclosure, through a mountain as though through space; may I dive in and out of the earth as though it were water; may I walk on water without sinking as though it were earth; seated cross-legged, may I travel in space like a bird; with my hand may I touch and stroke the moon and sun so powerful and mighty; may I wield bodily mastery, even as far as the Brahma-world,' let one fulfils the noble precepts (Sotapanna etc.)…

"If a person should wish: 'May I, with the divine ear element, which is purified and surpasses the human, hear both kinds of sounds, the divine and the human, those that are far as well as near,' let one fulfils the noble precepts (Sotapanna etc.)…

"If a person should wish: 'May I understand the minds of other beings, of other persons, having encompassed them with my own mind.

May I understand a mind affected by lust as affected by lust and a mind unaffected by lust as unaffected by lust; may I understand a mind affected by hate as affected by hate and a mind unaffected by hate as unaffected by hate; may I understand a mind affected by delusion as affected by delusion and a mind unaffected by delusion as unaffected by delusion; may I understand a contracted mind as contracted and a distracted mind as distracted; may I understand an exalted mind as exalted and an unexalted mind as unexalted; may I understand a surpassed mind as surpassed and an unsurpassed mind as unsurpassed; may I understand a concentrated mind as concentrated and an unconcentrated mind as unconcentrated; may I understand a liberated mind as liberated and an unliberated mind as unliberated,' let one fulfils the noble precepts (Sotapanna etc.)…

"If a person should wish: 'May I recollect my manifold past lives, that is, one birth, two births… Thus with their aspects and their particulars may I recollect my manifold past lives,' let one fulfils the noble precepts (Sotapanna etc.)…

"If a person should wish: 'May I, with the divine eye, which is purified and surpasses the human, see beings passing away and reappearing, inferior and superior, fair and ugly, fortunate and unfortunate; may I understand how beings pass on according to their actions thus:'… let one fulfils the noble precepts (Sotapanna etc.)…

"If a person should wish: 'May I, by realising for myself with direct knowledge, here and now enter upon and abide in the deliverance of mind and deliverance by wisdom that are taintless with the destruction of the taints,' let him fulfil the noble precepts, be devoted to internal serenity of mind, not neglect reflection, be possessed of insight, and dwell in empty huts.

"So it was with reference to this that it was said: 'Companions, dwell possessed of noble virtue (Sotapanna), possessed of the noble virtues, restrained with the restraint of the noble virtues, perfect in conduct and resort, and seeing fear in the slightest fault, train by undertaking the training noble precepts.'"

That is what the Blessed One said. The companions were satisfied and delighted in the Blessed One's words."

Chapter 9

Middle Discourses 7: Vatthasutta

The Simile of the Cloth

Nibbana is a state of mind. Nibbana is not a state of dress or appearance. When the mind is impure, meaning a mind that grasps into conventions, it can produce mental suffering. When the mind is pure, meaning a mind that gives up grasping to conventions, it can take away your mental pain and produce peace. For example, if you were to get too attached to your thoughts of yourself from a conventional perspective when you experience aging, illness, and losses, it can produce intense suffering for you. Instead, if you reduce getting too attached to your thoughts of yourself from a conventional perspective when you experience aging, illness, and losses, it can produce less suffering for you.

Just as a dirty piece of cloth is dyed in various colors and despite the colors, it remains dirty, when someone's mind is not pure, meaning there is too much attachment to their thoughts, a person who has too many likes, dislikes, for worldly experiences, despite what they wear, where they live, and what language they speak and other external factors, their mind that is clinging to conventions can still produce mental sufferings for them. Thus, learning Dhamma through conventions is a preliminary practice that requires not grasping, so it allows a person to move towards higher learning of Dhamma.

Although Nibbana is a happening, allowing Nibbana to happen and allowing the mind to reach such a state, a person who aspires to Nibbana wants to create a supportive mind state and may want to reduce grasping to conventions. Conventions and external factors alone are not able to purify a mind (dress, appearance, monasteries, forest); these things alone cannot purify a mind that has unwholesome ways of thinking. On the other hand, a person may make a constant and conscious attempt to purify self from grasping conventions. When a mind is purified from grasping conventions, irrespective of dress, lifestyle, location and external factors, a person can extinguish in the process of samsara. Thus, grasping conventions is the ordinary way, and conventional truth is a truth that ordinary people may grasp into. When a person experiences Sotapanna, understanding it's happening beyond conventions, a person gives up grasping to conventions. There are two paths: purifying externally and purifying internally. Purifying internally is the Noble Path; refers to reducing the fetters; self-view and other fetters. Purifying internally is the middle-way training in the mind that can be developed to abandon getting attached to one's thoughts related to desire (i.e. "desire to experience things" and "desire to not experience things") across stages that begin when a person reduces clinging to self-view, rituals, and conventions by understanding the impermanent of conventions in the way how the universe functions.

Conventions allow continuation, and Nibbana allows cessation or cessation to exist from conventions in mind, a way of renunciation based on Buddha's ways. There is a reason why things are as they are. Nibbana ends everything including Dhamma. Thus, to continue Dhamma, conventional Sangha is required. To be precise, a larger number of conventional Sangha and a smaller number of noble Sangha are needed to continue Dhamma, because a noble Sangha can easily build up on the basic teachings shared by the conventional Sangha to reveal the higher Dhamma (Sotapanna to Arahant) to the community of friends (Sangha is a community for the same purpose, Nibbana).

Standard ways of thinking and conventions (words, languages, social practices) encourage people to touch worldly life too much in their minds and to maintain a restricted vision by getting stuck into man-made identities, divisions, systems (political, economic systems), rituals (ways of having a birthday party, graduating, conducting a funeral, becoming a monk based on rituals), and ways of doing things and conventions (language, words, etc.) including the common ordinary ways of thinking. To train to cessation, giving up in mind refers to giving up getting attached to one's thoughts that make up the presence of materials, the world, self-view, and others in one's mind. This is because quitting an ordinary world and conventions are not practical and feasible, as wherever one goes, whether in the forest or in the town, given that the ordinary world we live in is filled with conventions, one only gets to live with conventions. Thus, Buddha's Dhamma (Sotapanna to Arahant) shows how a person can find inner satisfaction while living with conventions in an ordinary world by giving up clinging to such conventions in the person's mind. In other words, whatever material things that are physically present and whatever the world is physically present should not interfere with one's mind. Important it is to understand is that Nibbana is a training in mind, and the reason is because the world is created in one's mind, and self-view and others are created in one's mind and in one's thoughts.

Based on Buddha' Dhamma; Bhikkhu means Sotapanna to Arahant, someone who has given up self-view and the relevant fetters (purity refers to free from grasping to self-view, divisions, traditions, rituals, and conventions etc.). Some spiritual practitioners may think that purity comes from a dress, external appearance, food that a person consumes, a place of accommodating and external factors. Thinking can be right or wrong. Purity in Buddha's path refers to not grasping worldly experiences and conventions in one's thoughts. Nibbana, transformation from an ordinary being to a noble person is a happening that happens to a person irrespective of conventions, what they dress, lifestyle, and whether or not they follow rituals, and irrespective of what ritual they follow.

Misunderstanding Nibbana can prevent Nibbana for many. Understanding Nibbana can open up the practice leading to Nibbana for many. One does not require giving up sensual desires to become a Sotapanna (Sensual desires are given up at the state of an Anagami, a happening), and this makes it practical for most practitioners to practice the Noble Path. One needs to make one's life a Dhamma and take your heart as a witness to your Dhamma practice; make your heart a temple and make your mind a refuge for you by taking refuge in the Triple Gem; those who have given up fetters. A person who aspires to peace should learn to give priority to Dhamma in life; taking Dhamma as the guide, a person who attempts to do good will not be bothered or disturbed by what others think and say. The self knows the best about the self. For example, a person who puts all their efforts into doing good and avoiding bad can be free from self-blame, blaming others and the world. One who purifies from the self-view and conventions while recalling to universal Buddha's endless qualities and the qualities of the universal Dhamma and universal Savaka Sangha (and by attending to Triple Gem) will eventually come to experience Nibbana in the shortest possible time.

"So I have heard. At one time the Buddha was staying near Sāvatthī in Jeta's Grove, Anāthapiṇḍika's monastery. There the Buddha addressed the spiritual companions, "Companions!"

"Venerable sir," they replied. The Buddha said this:

"Suppose, companions, there was a cloth that was dirty and soiled. No matter what dye the dyer applied—whether blue or yellow or red or magenta—it would look poorly dyed and impure in color.

Why is that? Because of the impurity of the cloth.

In the same way, when the mind is corrupt, a bad destiny is to be expected. Suppose there was a cloth that was pure and clean. No matter what dye the dyer applied—whether blue or yellow or red or magenta—it would look well dyed and pure in color. Why is that? Because of the purity of the cloth.

In the same way, when the mind isn't corrupt, a good destiny is to be expected.

And what are the corruptions of the mind?

Covetousness and immoral greed, ill will, anger, acrimony, disdain, contempt, jealousy, stinginess, deceit, deviousness, obstinacy, aggression, conceit, arrogance, vanity, and negligence are corruptions of the mind.

A person who understands that covetousness and immoral greed are corruptions of the mind gives them up. A person who understands that ill will … negligence is a corruption of the mind gives it up.

When they have understood these corruptions of the mind for what they are, and have given them up, they have experiential confidence in the universal Buddha: 'That Blessed One is perfected, a fully awakened Buddha, accomplished in knowledge and conduct, holy, knower of the world, supreme guide for those who wish to train, teacher of gods and humans, awakened, blessed.'

They have experiential confidence in the teachings, universal Dhamma; (Sotapanna to Arahant): 'The teaching is well explained by the Buddha—apparent in the present life, immediately effective, inviting inspection, relevant, so that sensible people can know it for themselves.'

They have experiential confidence in the universal (Savaka) Saṅgha: 'The noble Saṅgha of the Buddha's disciples is practicing the way that's good, direct, systematic, and proper. It consists of the four pairs (i.e Sotapanna to Arahant), the eight individuals. This is the noble Saṅgha of the Buddha's disciples that is worthy of offerings dedicated to the gods, worthy of hospitality, worthy of a religious donation, worthy of greeting with joined palms, and is the supreme field of merit for the world.'

When a person has discarded, eliminated, released, given up, and relinquished to this extent by becoming a Sotapanna, thinking, 'I have experiential confidence in the Buddha … the teaching (four-fold Nibbana) … the noble Saṅgha,' they find inspiration in the meaning and the teaching, and find joy connected with the teaching. Thinking: 'I have discarded, eliminated, released, given up, and relinquished to this extent,' they find inspiration in the meaning and the teaching, and find joy connected with the teaching.

When they're joyful, rapture springs up. When the mind is full of rapture, the body becomes tranquil. When the body is tranquil, they feel bliss. And when they're blissful, the mind becomes immersed in noble concentration (attainment of Anagami state).

When a person of such noble ethics, such qualities, and such wisdom eats boiled fine rice with the dark grains picked out and served with many soups and sauces, that is no obstacle for them. Compare with cloth that is dirty and soiled; it can be made pure and clean by pure water. Or unrefined gold, which can be made pure and bright by a forge. In the same way, when a person of noble ethics, noble qualities, and noble wisdom (Sotapanna to Arahant) eats boiled fine rice with the dark grains picked out and served with many soups and sauces, that is no obstacle for them.

They possess loving kindness day and night and spreading a heart full of love to one direction, and to the second, and to the third, and to the fourth. In the same way above, below, across, everywhere, all around, they spread a heart full of love to the whole world—abundant, expansive, limitless, free of enmity and ill will.

They possess loving kindness day and night and spreading a heart full of compassion to one direction, and to the second, and to the third, and to the fourth. In the same way above, below, across, everywhere, all around, they spread a heart full of compassion to the whole world—abundant, expansive, limitless, free of enmity and ill will.

They possess loving kindness day and night and spreading a heart full of rejoicing to one direction, and to the second, and to the third, and to the fourth. In the same way above, below, across, everywhere, all around, they spread a heart full of rejoicing to the whole world—abundant, expansive, limitless, free of enmity and ill will.

They possess loving kindness day and night and spreading a heart full of equanimity to one direction, and to the second, and to the third, and to the fourth. In the same way above, below, across, everywhere, all around, they spread a heart full of equanimity to the whole world—abundant, expansive, limitless, free of enmity and ill will.

They understand: 'There is this, there is what is worse than this, there is what is better than this, and there is an escape beyond the scope of perception.'

Knowing and seeing like this, their mind is freed from the defilements of sensuality, desire to be reborn, and ignorance. When they're freed, they know they're freed (attainment of Arahantship).

They understand: 'Rebirth is ended, the spiritual journey has been completed, what had to be done has been done, there is nothing further for this place.' This is called a person who is bathed with the inner bathing."

Now at that time the brahmin Bhāradvāja of Sundarikā was sitting not far from the Buddha. He said to the Buddha, "But does Mister Gotama go to the river Bāhuka to bathe?"

"Brahmin, why go to the river Bāhuka? What can the river Bāhuka do?"

"Many people deem that the river Bāhukā leads to a heavenly world and bestows merit. And many people wash off their bad deeds in the river Bāhukā."

Then the Buddha addressed Bhāradvāja of Sundarika in verse:

"The Bāhukā and the Adhikakkā, at Gayā and the Sundarikā too, Sarasvatī and Payāga, and the river Bāhumatī: a fool can constantly plunge into them but it won't purify their dark deeds.

What can the Sundarikā do? What the Payāga or the Bāhukā? They can't cleanse a cruel and criminal person from their bad deeds. For the pure in heart it's always the spring festival or the sabbath. For the pure in heart and clean of deed, their vows will always be fulfilled. It's here alone that you should bathe, brahmin, making yourself a sanctuary for all creatures.

And if you speak no lies, nor harm any living creature, nor steal anything not given, and you're faithful (you have established confidence in the triple gem by becoming a Sotapanna) and not stingy: what's the point of going to Gayā? For any well may be your Gayā!"

When he had spoken, the brahmin Bhāradvāja of Sundarika said to the Buddha, "Excellent, Mister Gotama! Excellent! As if he were righting the overturned, or revealing the hidden, or pointing out the path to the lost, or lighting a lamp in the dark so people with clear eyes can see what's there, Mister Gotama has made the teaching clear in many ways. I go for refuge to Mister Gotama, to the four-fold Nibbana, and to the universal (Savaka) Saṅgha. May I receive the permission to become a noble disciple in Mister Gotama's presence?"

And the brahmin Bhāradvāja of Sundarika received the permission to seek refuge in the triple gem and follow a spiritual path, noble path leading to four-fold Nibbana in the Buddha's presence.

Not long after his following a spiritual path, Respected Bhāradvāja, living alone from worldly experience in mind, withdrawn, diligent, keen, and resolute, soon realized the supreme end stage; Arahant of the spiritual path in this very life. He lived having achieved with his own insight the goal for which people live a spiritual life.

He understood: "Rebirth is ended; the spiritual journey has been completed; what had to be done has been done; there is nothing further for this place." And Arahant Bhāradvāja became one of the perfected Arahant."

Chapter 10

Middle Discourses 8: Sallekhasutta

Self-Effacement

This discourse records an occasion that Buddha explains the difference between ordinary "jhanas" (jhānas or the conscious transformation through practicing "jhanas" or meditation practices [12], as suggest some conventional monks/Sangha in contemporary times and the noble jhanas. For example, jhana practice through conscious concentration was practiced by Prince Siddharta's (before gaining Buddhahood) teachers; Alara kalam and Udakaramaputta. Having tried jhana practice through conscious concentration, knowing it does not lead to Cessation, Nibbana, Prince Siddhartha established his focus on the path that he's known since he was a child. On that occasion, his mind went through jhanas that naturally occur before Arahantship, Buddhahood was gained.

Noble jhanas come to establish naturally in the mind of a practitioner at a random instance once after one completed Anagami state. In Noble Path, jhanas are not developed as consciously developed meditation practice, rather jhanas come to establish naturally in the mind of a practitioner at a random instance once after one completed Anagami state followed by insight of non-self-view gained at the Sotapanna level. It is a happening like birth for beings, and not a conscious process of meditation as the practice that is typically done and seen among ordinary friends/Sangha. Developing concentration alone, as jhanas, with an underlying tendency to clinging to conventions in mind where one maintains peaceful concentrated states of mind are subject to change. One way in which people who seek Nibbana can go wrong is by trying to find the universally created truth in socially created ways.

A Sakadagami will typically experience jhanas after attaining the Anagami stage (with removal of two fetters: sensual desires and ill will) and essentially after removing the three fetters at the Sotapanna stage (i.e self-view, doubts about

---

[12] Without right view, meditation cannot be practiced correctly as Buddha intended, towards liberation from suffering. Suffering will not stop, and remain unstable, if one does not at least start working towards attaining right view. The arising of right view happens under two conditions. Listening to the Dhamma from the voice of an Arahant (who is teaching the four-fold Nibbana) and paying proper attention. The right view is the forerunner of the Noble eightfold Path.

Buddha, Dhamma and Sangha, attachment for rites, and rituals). Noble jhanas or the concentrative state would come under the right concentration, which is the eighth factor in the Noble Eightfold Path, should accompany by the right view, and that is to say, the Noble Path always begins with right understanding of a Sotapanna.

Given that Nibbana happens across four stages, it can be said it is a progressive process. However, each state can happen in an instant or in a few moments of time. For example, Stream-entry happens in a moment of time and may continue through a few moments, but a Stream-enterer is unable to sustain the same thoughts for a longer period of time and retain other fetters. By training the mind to the middle way, one can abandon stress. Nibbana happens on its own time, a natural process.

By abandoning three fetters and developing four factors of Stream-entry, one can gain Stream-entry (Sotapanna).

Direct experience of concentration can make an ordinary person experience jhanas[13].

Understanding life experience with wisdom can make an ordinary person experience four-fold Nibbana.

Concentration without wisdom makes one experience jhanas or meditative experiences. Concentration based on wisdom allows a person to experience higher stages of Nibbana. Buddha has tried many ways, such as extreme asceticism and jhānas through concentration with effort and comforts but didn't find Nibbana in such ways. Rejecting both, Buddha established the middle way.

---

[13] *The Path of Purification* suggests that a person takes a meditation practice, a method called *kasina*, in which one stares at an external object until the image of the object is imprinted in one's mind. Yet, when you develop the idea of impermanence through concentration, when you lose concentration, you will likely lose the idea of impermanence. Besides, impermanence is not merely an idea that you imprint through effort but a life experience. When you understand impermanence through imprint, such an understanding can only be short-lived with an underlying tendency to grasp worldly experiences, and the root cause of suffering (desire; likes, dislikes, expectations=greed, hate, delusion) can still retain within. Instead, when you understand impermanence through life experience, understanding can only be replaced by higher understanding, Sotapanna to Arahant.

Life is an interaction between the universe and conventions. The universe functions in such a manner that people are faced with the ups and downs of life. Ordinary practitioners can develop middle way training by applying the understanding of how the universe functions, the understanding that ups and downs are part of life for everyone, by doing things that are needed and beneficial without too much worrying, by reducing expectations as a way of following Buddha's Dhamma, and by walking towards the Noble Path. This is what is referred to as middle-mind training.

It is universally applicable is that mental pain can be reduced by understanding true life experiences; life has both ups and downs and natural and universal functioning. Mental pain can be reduced by reducing mental attachment to changing worldly experiences within daily life.

The noble way of thinking is not grasping identities that are socially created in mind, because it is meaningless to cling to identities that are changing anyway. Identity views ("*I am young*", "*I am old*", "*I am a monk*", "*I am a singer*", etc.) and social divisions are socially created constructs. What is socially constructed is subject to change. Noble ways of thinking do not divide the earth by grasping (meaning not giving too much value to such things in mind; "*I am from this country*" … "*I am better than...*" etc.) and grasping to self-view in many ways. For someone who thinks that there is no stability in self (self-view), instability in self is unlikely to bring too much mental pain.

To practice noble way of thinking, you have to surpass the majority way of thinking and doing. For example, let's say that in a particular region, the majority of individuals engage in killing living beings, or treating others differently based on conventions (gender, class, nationality, age, education, position) and, for them that is a normal thing to do as accepted within social practices. Instead, a person who aspires inner peace through middle way practice will decide for oneself that, just because others engage in killing living beings or engage in things that are causing distress to others (e.g. differential treatment towards others), that person does not need to be engaged in doing such things. This allows a practitioner to develop self-responsibility, a self-practice to do good irrespective of what others are doing and saying. In this manner, despite others physical presence (or absence), if you choose to do always good, you can find peace within. When you surpass the majority way or common way of thinking and doing, you can find peace and satiation within that is hard to find in common ways.

In conclusion, jhanas are needed to gain the higher stages of enlightenment (Arahantship) but in reality, jhanas are not developed as consciously developed meditation practice, rather jhanas come to establish naturally in the mind of a practitioner at a random instance once after one completed Anagami state followed by insight of non-self-view gained at the Sotapanna level.

"Thus, have I heard. On one occasion the Blessed One was living at Sāvatthī in Jeta's Grove, Anāthapiṇḍika's Park.

Then, when it was evening, Mahā Cunda rose from the resting place and went to the Blessed One. After paying homage to the Blessed One he sat down at one side and said to him:

"Venerable sir, various views arise in the world associated either with doctrines of a self or with doctrines about the world. Now does the abandoning and relinquishing of those views come about in a person who is attending only to the beginning of his training to investigate and reflect on his thoughts?"

"Cunda, as to those various views that arise in the world associated either with doctrines of a self or with doctrines about the world: if the object in relation to which those views arise, which they underlie, and which they are exercised upon is seen as it actually is with proper wisdom thus: 'This is not mine, this I am not, this is not myself,' then the abandoning and relinquishing of those views comes about.

The Eight Attainments

"It is possible here, Cunda, that quite secluded from sensual pleasures (by taking precepts/training rules), secluded from unwholesome states, some ordinary people enter upon and abide in the first jhāna, which is accompanied by applied and sustained thought, with rapture and pleasure born of seclusion. He might think thus: 'I am abiding in effacement.' But it is not these attainments that are called 'effacement' in the Noble One's Discipline: these are called 'pleasant abidings here and now' in the Noble One's Discipline.

"It is possible here that with the stilling of applied and sustained thought, some ordinary people enter upon and abides in the second jhāna, which has self-confidence and singleness of mind without applied and sustained thought, with rapture and pleasure born of concentration. He might think thus: 'I am abiding in effacement.' But…these are called 'pleasant abidings here and now' in the Noble One's Discipline.

"It is possible here that with the fading away as well of rapture, some ordinary people abide in equanimity, and mindful and fully aware, still feeling pleasure with the body, he enters upon and abides in the third jhāna, on account of which noble ones announce: 'He has a pleasant abiding who has equanimity and is mindful.' He might think thus: 'I am abiding in effacement.' But…these are called 'pleasant abidings here and now' in the Noble One's Discipline.

"It is possible here that with the abandoning of pleasure and pain, and with the previous disappearance of joy and grief, some bhikkhu enters upon and abides in the fourth jhāna, which has neither-pain-nor-pleasure and purity of mindfulness due to equanimity. He might think thus: 'I am abiding in effacement.' But it is not these attainments that are called 'effacement' in the Noble One's Discipline: these are called 'pleasant abidings here and now' in the Noble One's Discipline.

"It is possible here that with the complete surmounting of perceptions of form, with the disappearance of perceptions of sensory impact, with non-attention to perceptions of diversity, aware that 'space is infinite,' some bhikkhu enters upon and abides in the base of infinite space. He might think thus: 'I am abiding in effacement.' But it is not these attainments that are called 'effacement' in the Noble One's Discipline: these are called 'peaceful abidings' in the Noble One's Discipline.

"It is possible here that by completely surmounting the base of infinite space, aware that 'consciousness is infinite,' some bhikkhu enters upon and abides in the base of infinite consciousness. He might think thus: 'I am abiding in effacement.' But…these are called 'peaceful abidings' in the Noble One's Discipline.

"It is possible here that by completely surmounting the base of infinite consciousness, aware that 'there is nothing,' some bhikkhu enters upon and abides in the base of nothingness. He might think thus: 'I am abiding in effacement.' But…these are called 'peaceful abidings' in the Noble One's Discipline.

"It is possible here that by completely surmounting the base of nothingness, some bhikkhu enters upon and abides in the base of neither-perception-nor-non-perception. He might think thus: 'I am abiding in effacement.' But these attainments are not called 'effacement' in the Noble One's Discipline: these are called 'peaceful abidings' in the Noble One's Discipline.

Effacement

"Now, Cunda, here effacement should be practised by you:

(1) 'Others will be cruel; we shall not be cruel here': effacement should be practised thus.

(2) 'Others will kill living beings; we shall abstain from killing living beings here': effacement should be practised thus.

(3) 'Others will take what is not given; we shall abstain from taking what is not given here': effacement should be practised thus.

(4) 'Others will be uncelibate; we shall be celibate here': effacement should be practised thus.

(5) 'Others will speak falsehood; we shall abstain from false speech here': effacement should be practised thus.

(6) 'Others will speak maliciously; we shall abstain from malicious speech here': effacement should be practised thus.

(7) 'Others will speak harshly; we shall abstain from harsh speech here': effacement should be practised thus.

(8) 'Others will gossip; we shall abstain from gossip here': effacement should be practised thus.

(9) 'Others will be covetous; we shall be uncovetous here': effacement should be practised thus.

(10) 'Others will have ill will; we shall be without ill will here': effacement should be practised thus.

(11) 'Others will be of wrong view; we shall be of right view here': effacement should be practised thus.

(12) 'Others will be of wrong intention; we shall be of right intention here': effacement should be practised thus.

(13) 'Others will be of wrong speech; we shall be of right speech here': effacement should be practised thus.

(14) 'Others will be of wrong action; we shall be of right action here': effacement should be practised thus.

(15) 'Others will be of wrong livelihood; we shall be of right livelihood here': effacement should be practised thus.

(16) 'Others will be of wrong effort; we shall be of right effort here': effacement should be practised thus.

(17) 'Others will be of wrong mindfulness; we shall be of right mindfulness here': effacement should be practised thus.

(18) 'Others will be of wrong concentration; we shall be of right concentration here': effacement should be practised thus.

(19) 'Others will be of wrong knowledge; we shall be of right knowledge here': effacement should be practised thus.

(20) 'Others will be of wrong deliverance; we shall be of right deliverance here': effacement should be practised thus.

(21) 'Others will be overcome by sloth and torpor; we shall be free from sloth and torpor here': effacement should be practised thus.

(22) 'Others will be restless; we shall not be restless here': effacement should be practised thus.

(23) 'Others will be doubters; we shall go beyond doubt here': effacement should be practised thus.

(24) 'Others will be angry; we shall not be angry here': effacement should be practised thus.

(25) 'Others will be resentful; we shall not be resentful here': effacement should be practised thus.

(26) 'Others will be contemptuous; we shall not be contemptuous here': effacement should be practised thus.

(27) 'Others will be insolent; we shall not be insolent here': effacement should be practised thus.

(28) 'Others will be envious; we shall not be envious here': effacement should be practised thus.

(29) 'Others will be avaricious; we shall not be avaricious here': effacement should be practised thus.

(30) 'Others will be fraudulent; we shall not be fraudulent here': effacement should be practised thus.

(31) 'Others will be deceitful; we shall not be deceitful here': effacement should be practised thus.

(32) 'Others will be obstinate; we shall not be obstinate here': effacement should be practised thus.

(33) 'Others will be arrogant; we shall not be arrogant here': effacement should be practised thus.

(34) 'Others will be difficult to admonish; we shall be easy to admonish here': effacement should be practised thus.

(35) 'Others will have bad friends; we shall have good friends here': effacement should be practised thus.

(36) 'Others will be negligent; we shall be diligent here': effacement should be practised thus.

(37) 'Others will be faithless; we shall be faithful here': effacement should be practised thus.

(38) 'Others will be shameless; we shall be shameful here': effacement should be practised thus.

(39) 'Others will have no fear of wrongdoing; we shall be afraid of wrongdoing here': effacement should be practised thus.

(40) 'Others will be of little learning; we shall be of great learning here': effacement should be practised thus.

(41) 'Others will be lazy; we shall be energetic here': effacement should be practised thus.

(42) 'Others will be unmindful; we shall be established in mindfulness here': effacement should be practised thus.

(43) 'Others will lack wisdom; we shall possess wisdom here': effacement should be practised thus.

(44) 'Others will adhere to their own views, hold on to them tenaciously, and relinquish them with difficulty; we shall not adhere to our own views or hold on to them tenaciously, but shall relinquish them easily': effacement should be practised thus.

Inclination of Mind

"Cunda, I say that even the inclination of mind towards wholesome states is of great benefit, so what should be said of bodily and verbal acts conforming to such a state of mind? Therefore, Cunda:

(1) Mind should be inclined thus: 'Others will be cruel; we shall not be cruel here.'

(2) Mind should be inclined thus: 'Others will kill living beings; we shall abstain from killing living beings here.'

(3–43) Mind should be inclined thus:...

(44) Mind should be inclined thus: 'Others will adhere to their own views, hold on to them tenaciously, and relinquish them with difficulty; we shall not adhere to our own views or hold on to them tenaciously, but shall relinquish them easily.'

Avoidance

"Cunda, suppose there were an uneven path and another even path by which to avoid it; and suppose there were an uneven ford and another even ford by which to avoid it. So too:

(1) A person given to cruelty has non-cruelty by which to avoid it.

(2) One given to killing living beings has abstention from killing living beings by which to avoid it.

(3) One given to taking what is not given has abstention from taking what is not given by which to avoid it.

(4) One given to be uncelibate has celibacy by which to avoid it.

(5) One given to false speech has abstention from false speech by which to avoid it.

(6) One given to malicious speech has abstention from malicious speech by which to avoid it.

(7) One given to harsh speech has abstention from harsh speech by which to avoid it.

(8) One given to gossip has abstention from gossip by which to avoid it.

(9) One given to covetousness has uncovetousness by which to avoid it.

(10) One given to ill will has non-ill will by which to avoid it.

(11) One given to wrong view has right view by which to avoid it.

(12) One given to wrong intention has right intention by which to avoid it.

(13) One given to wrong speech has right speech by which to avoid it.

(14) One given to wrong action has right action by which to avoid it.

(15) One given to wrong livelihood has right livelihood by which to avoid it.

(16) One given to wrong effort has right effort by which to avoid it.

(17) One given to wrong mindfulness has right mindfulness by which to avoid it.

(18) One given to wrong concentration has right concentration by which to avoid it.

(19) One given to wrong knowledge has right knowledge by which to avoid it.

(20) One given to wrong deliverance has right deliverance by which to avoid it.

(21) One given to sloth and torpor has freedom from sloth and torpor by which to avoid it.

(22) One given to restlessness has non-restlessness by which to avoid it.

(23) One given to doubt has the state beyond doubt by which to avoid it.

(24) One given to anger has non-anger by which to avoid it.

(25) One given to resentment has non-resentment by which to avoid it.

(26) One given to contempt has non-contempt by which to avoid it.

(27) One given to insolence has non-insolence by which to avoid it.

(28) One given to envy has non-envy by which to avoid it.

(29) One given to avarice has non-avarice by which to avoid it.

(30) One given to fraud has non-fraud by which to avoid it.

(31) One given to deceit has non-deceit by which to avoid it.

(32) One given to obstinacy has non-obstinacy by which to avoid it.

(33) One given to arrogance has non-arrogance by which to avoid it.

(34) One given to being difficult to admonish has being easy to admonish by which to avoid it.

(35) One given to making bad friends has making good friends by which to avoid it.

(36) One given to negligence has diligence by which to avoid it.

(37) One given to faithlessness has faith by which to avoid it.

(38) One given to shamelessness has shame by which to avoid it.

(39) One given to fearlessness of wrongdoing has fear of wrongdoing by which to avoid it.

(40) One given to little learning has great learning by which to avoid it.

(41) One given to laziness has the arousal of energy by which to avoid it.

(42) One given to unmindfulness has the establishment of mindfulness by which to avoid it.

(43) One given to lack of wisdom has the acquisition of wisdom by which to avoid it.

(44) One given to adhere to his own views, who holds on to them tenaciously and relinquishes them with difficulty, has non-adherence to his own views, not holding on to them tenaciously and relinquishing them easily, by which to avoid it.

The Way Leading Upwards

"Cunda, just as all unwholesome states lead downwards and all wholesome states lead upwards, so too:

(1) A person given to cruelty has non-cruelty to lead him upwards.

(2) One given to killing living beings has abstention from killing living beings to lead him upwards.

(3–43) One given to…to lead him upwards.

(44) One given to adhere to his own views, who holds on to them tenaciously and relinquishes them with difficulty, has non-adherence to his own views, not holding on to them tenaciously and relinquishing them easily, to lead him upwards.

The Way of Extinguishing

"Cunda, that one who is himself sinking in the mud should pull out another who is sinking in the mud is impossible; that one who is not himself sinking in the mud should pull out another who is sinking in the mud is possible. That one who is himself untamed, undisciplined, with defilements unextinguished, should tame another, discipline him, and help extinguish his defilements is impossible; that one who is himself tamed, disciplined, with defilements extinguished, should tame another, discipline him, and help extinguish his defilements is possible. So too:

(1) A person given to cruelty has non-cruelty by which to extinguish it.

(2) One given to killing living beings has abstention from killing living beings by which to extinguish it.

(3–43) One given to… …by which to extinguish it.

(44) One given to adhere to his own views, who holds on to them tenaciously and relinquishes them with difficulty, has non-adherence to his own views, not holding on to them tenaciously and relinquishing them easily, by which to extinguish it.

Conclusion

"So, Cunda, the way of effacement has been taught by me, the way of inclining the mind has been taught by me, the way of avoidance has been taught by me, the way leading upwards has been taught by me, and the way of extinguishing has been taught by me.

"What should be done for his disciples out of compassion by a teacher who seeks their welfare and has compassion for them, that I have done for you, Cunda. There are these roots of trees, these empty huts. Give up grasping conventions by observing your thoughts, Cunda, do not delay or else you will regret it later. This is our instruction to you."

That is what the Blessed One said. Mahā Cunda was satisfied and delighted in the Blessed One's words."

Chapter 11

Middle Discourses 9: Sammādiṭṭhisutta

Right View

This discourse records Arahant Sāriputta giving a detailed explanation of the right view, the first factor of the noble eightfold path. The right view of an ordinary person is understanding the ways of universal functioning and, universally applicable law of karma to a reasonable standard.

People are born at random places at random times. The universe functions in such a way that, when a person is born, birth brings death. Illnesses, losses, gains, falls and rises are part of life, the way of life. Once born, people can do many things and make certain choices that helps them to refine the quality of living, improve lives and their karma. What is commonly agreed by the society is not the agreement by universal functioning, rather each and every individual come to experience consequences of their own karma. Each being is responsible for one's own karma, and life experience is individually experienced by each, so as Nibbana is a personal experience for each. Life is an interaction between the universe and conventions. What is commonly agreed by the society is not the agreement by universal functioning, Nibbana, rather each and every individual come to experience consequences of their own karma. Each being is responsible for one's own karma, and life experience is individually experienced by each, so as Nibbana is a personal experience for each. Instead, Nibbana is a universal happening just like birth, and just like birth happens at random time without control or will of a person, Nibbana happens at a random time to a random person who has fulfilled the requisites for Nibbana, wisdom and merits.

Everything is a convention. There are only a few things that people can't do through conventions or collective agreements across societies. They cannot retain conventions with stability, decide on certain birth related aspects, where they will be born, etc. The universe functions in such a way that conventions can function only within the universe. The sun shines as the function of the universe, birth brings death, illnesses to all are functions of the universe.

When people don't apply reasoning, it is not possible to gain progress in Dhamma. When reasoning is not applied, conventional Dhamma can flourish instead of noble Dhamma. When wise people ask wise questions, they find that science provide answers and solutions in a reasonable manner.

Seeking truth requires investigation by questioning and findings reasons. Yet, if anyone tells you that the path to Nibbana and Arahantship meaning a living a lifestyle based on conventions, in line with Buddha's interpretation, one who aspire Nibbana should reject such claims with reasoning; this is developing the right view of Noble Path. Nibbana is a universal happening.

One of the confusions over Buddha's Dhamma is that who is a monk? Natural transformation takes place in a person's mental continuum across stages and that transformation which allow to abandon the mental fetters out of rituals, is a monk in Noble Path. At Anagami state, a person naturally transforms into someone who maintains chastity. Conscious transformation of a person can change because consciousness is subject to change. Ritualistic transformation can be temporary as life is temporary. It's not that one becomes a monk by taking the monastic rules, but one becomes a monk through natural transformation, transformation that makes a person abandoning the mental attachment to the fetters; self-view, rituals, shaped by the universal functioning. Across stages of Nibbana, a person naturally transforms into someone who eat meals before noon, not harming trees, chastity, not seeing movies, etc. underlying tendency for desire is abandoned. You might find Buddha's footprint in person from any conventional background. The path that Buddha wanted to open for people who are suffering has been kept open not just for one category of people (ritual, division, tradition, lifestyle), instead to all those who are seeking for it, practice is universally applicable to all.

Progress in the Dhamma path is determined by one's levels of understanding with wisdom, attainment across fourfold Nibbana and not determined by the number of years in practice, external factors (eg. age, gender, life style etc.) nor by memorized passages from textbooks.

Right view of a Sotapanna is possessing confirmed confidence in the Triple Gem and not grasping in to three fetters (self-view, rituals, precepts). Right view of a Sakadagami is confirmed confidence in the Triple Gem and abandoning the first three fetters. Right view of an Anagami is possessing confirmed confidence in the Triple Gem and abandoning sense desires, ill will and previous three fetters. Right view of an Arahant is giving up desire and not having desires to form (and other fetters), giving up middle and cessation. Thus, understanding of deep Dhamma differs based on one's level of attainment. Ideally, one should have completed four-fold Nibbana before explaining to another.

Lacking a full understanding of what Nibbana is, some practitioners mix up various other subjects and spend their time talking about things that are not directly relevant to gaining Nibbana. They may engage in doing things that are not part of a practice that leads to Nibbana. Due to their lack of training in the mind, they may possess a strong sense of self-view, and their minds will have a tendency to cling to various divisions, and their tendency of a mind of grasping to self-view can be expressed in their speech. They may divide the teachings based on division and geographical locations, because they are still ordinary and are yet to understand Dhamma practice, which is universally applicable to gaining Nibbana.

Not understanding Nibbana in full, ordinary views of Dhamma are many. Altered versions of teaching that are built upon in-correct views and that claim to be Buddha's teachings lead to confused Dhamma (non-Dhamma). The wrong understanding of Dhamma prevents Nibbana or liberation for those who aspire for it, and those who practice Dhamma in common ways. Right understanding of Dhamma will allow one to gain benefit of a practice.

Those who practice the teachings by understanding the teachings beyond ordinary understanding to reach the understanding of a Stream-enterer (Sotapanna) will be able to gain realization. Right view of an ordinary person (mundate view) is acceptance of karma. Thus, all those who practice Dhamma, if they will be humble and honest to take the responsibility to self-declare their attainment before sharing Dhamma with others, this will be helpful for themselves and others to clarify Dhamma as Taught by Buddha. For example, ordinary friends can introduce the basics of Dhamma, still discuss theoretical aspects of Dhamma by acknowledging that they are yet to gain a noble state and share Dhamma at the ordinary level. They can still gain benefits, such as materials that are needed for their survival, and, by continuing in their own practice, in that manner, Dhamma can be purified for the benefit of all.

The training path leading to Nibbana can be developed by developing one's understanding to gain an understanding of a Stream-enterer. To gain to a Stream-entry (Sotapanna), what you could do is engage in ten wholesome deeds while ensuring you are reducing the fetters and developing the confirmed confidence in the Triple Gem.

To get to cessation, the mind has to be trained in a correct manner, and knowing the right practice leading to Stream-entry (Sotapanna) is beneficial for practitioners, and practitioners should train thus:

"We take precepts and training rules to develop noble virtues (the purpose of maintaining virtue and training rules should be to develop noble virtues); we meditate to develop confirmed confidence in the Triple Gem (the purpose of developing concentration as meditation practice is to develop confirmed confidence in the Triple Gem)", *the purpose of any lifestyle should be to develop merits, engage in wholesome activities, the end purpose of training the mind is to gain freedom from precepts, a lifestyle, and mind; giving up getting attached to one's thoughts that create self- view, and others towards the end of noble training path"*.

By understanding what Dhamma and non-Dhamma are, understanding who Buddha and non-Buddha, understanding noble Sangha and non-noble Sangha, and understanding Triple Gem, one can abandon fetters, and, by abandoning fetters, one can under- stand Triple Gem. Triple Gem and fetters are linked, and Dhamma means Triple Gem and Triple Gem means Dhamma. By eradicating doubts and gaining a clear comprehension, those who wish to aspire to Nibbana may fulfil their wishes.

"Thus have I heard. On one occasion the Blessed One was living at Sāvatthī in Jeta's Grove, Anāthapiṇḍika's Park. There Arahant Sāriputta addressed the spiritual companions thus: "Friends, companions."—"Friend," they replied. Arahant Sāriputta said this:

"'One of right view, one of right view,' is said, friends. In what way is a noble disciple one of right view, whose view is straight, who has unwavering confidence in the Dhamma: four-fold nibbana, and has arrived at this true Dhamma; Sotapanna?"

"Indeed, friend, we would come from far away to learn from the Arahant Sāriputta the meaning of this statement. It would be good if Arahant Sāriputta would explain the meaning of this statement. Having heard it from him, the companions will remember it."

"Then, friends, listen and attend closely to what I shall say."

"Yes, friend," the bhikkhus replied. Arahant Sāriputta said this:

The Wholesome and the Unwholesome

"When, friends, a noble disciple understands the unwholesome and the root of the unwholesome, the wholesome and the root of the wholesome, in that way he is one of right view, whose view is straight, who has unwavering confidence in the Dhamma and has arrived at this true Dhamma (four-fold nibbana).

"And what, friends, is the unwholesome, what is the root of the unwholesome, what is the wholesome, what is the root of the wholesome? Killing living beings is unwholesome; taking what is not given is unwholesome; misconduct in sensual pleasures is unwholesome; false speech is unwholesome; malicious speech is unwholesome; harsh speech is unwholesome; gossip is unwholesome; covetousness is unwholesome; ill will is unwholesome; wrong view is unwholesome. This is called the unwholesome.

"And what is the root of the unwholesome? Greed is a root of the unwholesome; hate is a root of the unwholesome; delusion is a root of the unwholesome. This is called the root of the unwholesome.

"And what is the wholesome? Abstention from killing living beings is wholesome; abstention from taking what is not given is wholesome; abstention from misconduct in sensual pleasures is wholesome; abstention from false speech is wholesome; abstention from malicious speech is wholesome; abstention from harsh speech is wholesome; abstention from gossip is wholesome; uncovetousness is wholesome; non-ill will is wholesome; right view is wholesome.

This is called the wholesome.

"And what is the root of the wholesome? Non-greed is a root of the wholesome; non-hate is a root of the wholesome; non-delusion is a root of the wholesome. This is called the root of the wholesome.

"When a noble disciple has thus understood the unwholesome and the root of the unwholesome, the wholesome and the root of the wholesome, he entirely abandons the underlying tendency to lust, he abolishes the underlying tendency to aversion, one extirpates the underlying tendency to the view and conceit 'I am,' and by abandoning ignorance and arousing true knowledge he here and now makes an end of suffering.

In that way too a noble disciple is one of right view, whose view is straight, who has unwavering confidence in the Dhamma (four-fold nibbana) and has arrived at this true Dhamma (Sotapanna)."

Nutriment

Saying, "Good, friend," the companions delighted and rejoiced in the Arahant Sāriputta's words. Then they asked him a further question: "But, friend, might there be another way in which a noble disciple is one of right view…and has arrived at this true Dhamma (Sotapanna)?"— "There might be, friends.

"When, friends, a noble disciple understands nutriment, the origin of nutriment, the cessation of nutriment, and the way leading to the cessation of nutriment, in that way he is one of right view…and has arrived at this true Dhamma (Sotapanna).

"And what is nutriment, what is the origin of nutriment, what is the cessation of nutriment, what is the way leading to the cessation of nutriment? There are four kinds of nutriment for the maintenance of beings that already have come to be and for the support of those about to come to be.

What four? They are: physical food as nutriment, gross or subtle; contact as the second; mental volition as the third; and consciousness as the fourth. With the arising of craving there is the arising of nutriment. With the cessation of craving there is the cessation of nutriment. The way leading to the cessation of nutriment is just this Noble Eightfold Path; that is, right view, right intention, right speech, right action, right livelihood, right effort, right mindfulness, and right concentration.

"When a noble disciple has thus understood nutriment, the origin of nutriment, the cessation of nutriment, and the way leading to the cessation of nutriment, one entirely abandons the underlying tendency to greed, he abolishes the underlying tendency to aversion, he extirpates the underlying tendency to the view and conceit 'I am,' and by abandoning ignorance and arousing true knowledge he here and now makes an end of suffering. In that way too a noble disciple is one of right view, whose view is straight, who has unwavering confidence in the Dhamma (four-fold nibbana) and has arrived at this true Dhamma (four-fold nibbana)."

The Four Noble Truths

Saying, "Good, friend," the companions delighted and rejoiced in the Arahant Sāriputta's words. Then they asked him a further question: "But, friend, might there be another way in which a noble disciple is one of right view…and has arrived at this true Dhamma (four-fold nibbana)?"—"There might be, friends.

"When, friends, a noble disciple understands suffering, the origin of suffering, the cessation of suffering, and the way leading to the cessation of suffering, in that way one is one of right view…and has arrived at this true Dhamma (four-fold nibbana).

"And what is suffering, what is the origin of suffering, what is the cessation of suffering, what is the way leading to the cessation of suffering? Birth is suffering; ageing is suffering; sickness is suffering; death is suffering; sorrow, lamentation, pain, grief, and despair are suffering; not to obtain what one wants is suffering; in short, the five aggregates affected by clinging are suffering. This is called suffering.

"And what is the origin of suffering? It is craving, which brings renewal of being, is accompanied by delight and lust, and delights in this and that; that is, craving for sensual pleasures, craving for being, and craving for non-being. This is called the origin of suffering.

"And what is the cessation of suffering? It is the remainderless fading away and ceasing, the giving up, relinquishing, letting go, and rejecting of that same craving. This is called the cessation of suffering.

"And what is the way leading to the cessation of suffering? It is just this Noble Eightfold Path; that is, right view…right concentration. This is called the way leading to the cessation of suffering.

"When a noble disciple has thus understood suffering, the origin of suffering, the cessation of suffering, and the way leading to the cessation of suffering…he here and now makes an end of suffering. In that way too a noble disciple is one of right view…and has arrived at this true Dhamma (four-fold nibbana)."

Ageing and Death

Saying, "Good, friend," the companions delighted and rejoiced in Arahant Sāriputta's words. Then they asked him a further question: "But, friend, might there be another way in which a noble disciple is one of right view…and has arrived at this true Dhamma (four-fold nibbana)?"—"There might be, friends.

"When, friends, a noble disciple understands ageing and death, the origin of ageing and death, the cessation of ageing and death, and the way leading to the cessation of ageing and death, in that way he is one of right view…and has arrived at this true Dhamma (four-fold nibbana).

"And what is ageing and death, what is the origin of ageing and death, what is the cessation of ageing and death, what is the way leading to the cessation of ageing and death? The ageing of beings in the various orders of beings, their old age, brokenness of teeth, greyness of hair, wrinkling of skin, decline of life, weakness of faculties—this is called ageing. The passing of beings out of the various orders of beings, their passing away, dissolution, disappearance, dying, completion of time, dissolution of the aggregates, laying down of the body—this is called death. So this ageing and this death are what is called ageing and death. With the arising of birth there is the arising of ageing and death. With the cessation of birth there is the cessation of ageing and death. The way leading to the cessation of ageing and death is just this Noble Eightfold Path; that is, right view…right concentration.

"When a noble disciple has thus understood ageing and death, the origin of ageing and death, the cessation of ageing and death, and the way leading to the cessation of ageing and death…he here and now makes an end of suffering. In that way too a noble disciple is one of right view…and has arrived at this true Dhamma (four-fold nibbana)."

Birth

Saying, "Good, friend," the companions delighted and rejoiced in the Arahant Sāriputta's words. Then they asked him a further question: "But, friend, might there be another way in which a noble disciple is one of right view…and has arrived at this true Dhamma (four-fold nibbana)?" — "There might be, friends.

"When, friends, a noble disciple understands birth, the origin of birth, the cessation of birth, and the way leading to the cessation of birth, in that way he is one of right view…and has arrived at this true Dhamma (four-fold nibbana).

"And what is birth, what is the origin of birth, what is the cessation of birth, what is the way leading to the cessation of birth? The birth of beings in the various orders of beings, their coming to birth, precipitation in a womb, generation, manifestation of the aggregates, obtaining the bases for contact—this is called birth. With the arising of being there is the arising of birth. With the cessation of being there is the cessation of birth. The way leading to the cessation of birth is just this Noble Eightfold Path; that is, right view…right concentration.

"When a noble disciple has thus understood birth, the origin of birth, the cessation of birth, and the way leading to the cessation of birth…he here and now makes an end of suffering. In that way too a noble disciple is one of right view…and has arrived at this true Dhamma (four-fold nibbana)."

Being

Saying, "Good, friend," the bhikkhus delighted and rejoiced in the Arahant Sāriputta's words. Then they asked him a further question: "But, friend, might there be another way in which a noble disciple is one of right view…and has arrived at this true Dhamma (four-fold nibbana)?" — "There might be, friends.

"When, friends, a noble disciple understands being, the origin of being, the cessation of being, and the way leading to the cessation of being, in that way he is one of right view…and has arrived at this true Dhamma (four-fold nibbana).

"And what is being, what is the origin of being, what is the cessation of being, what is the way leading to the cessation of being? There are these three kinds of being: sense-sphere being, fine-material being, and immaterial being. With the arising of clinging there is the arising of being. With the cessation of clinging there is the cessation of being. The way leading to the cessation of being is just this Noble Eightfold Path; that is, right view…right concentration.

"When a noble disciple has thus understood being, the origin of being, the cessation of being, and the way leading to the cessation of being…one here and now makes an end of suffering. In that way too a noble disciple is one of right view…and has arrived at this true Dhamma (four-fold nibbana)."

Clinging

Saying, "Good, friend," the bhikkhus delighted and rejoiced in the Arahant Sāriputta's words. Then they asked him a further question: "But, friend, might there be another way in which a noble disciple is one of right view…and has arrived at this true Dhamma (four-fold nibbana)?"—"There might be, friends.

"When, friends, a noble disciple understands clinging, the origin of clinging, the cessation of clinging, and the way leading to the cessation of clinging, in that way one is one of right view… and has arrived at this true Dhamma (four-fold nibbana).

"And what is clinging, what is the origin of clinging, what is the cessation of clinging, what is the way leading to the cessation of clinging? There are these four kinds of clinging: clinging to sensual pleasures, clinging to views, clinging to rules and observances, and clinging to a doctrine of self. With the arising of craving there is the arising of clinging. With the cessation of craving there is the cessation of clinging. The way leading to the cessation of clinging is just this Noble Eightfold Path; that is, right view…right concentration.

"When a noble disciple has thus understood clinging, the origin of clinging, the cessation of clinging, and the way leading to the cessation of clinging…he here and now makes an end of suffering. In that way too a noble disciple is one of right view… and has arrived at this true Dhamma (four-fold nibbana)."

Craving

Saying, "Good, friend," the bhikkhus delighted and rejoiced in the Arahant Sāriputta's words. Then they asked him a further question: "But, friend, might there be another way in which a noble disciple is one of right view…and has arrived at this true Dhamma (four-fold nibbana)?"—"There might be, friends.

"When, friends, a noble disciple understands craving, the origin of craving, the cessation of craving, and the way leading to the cessation of craving, in that way one is one of right view… and has arrived at this true Dhamma (four-fold nibbana).

"And what is craving, what is the origin of craving, what is the cessation of craving, what is the way leading to the cessation of craving? There are these six classes of craving: craving for forms, craving for sounds, craving for odours, craving for flavours, craving for tangibles, craving for mind-objects. With the arising of feeling there is the arising of craving. With the cessation of feeling there is the cessation of craving. The way leading to the cessation of craving is just this Noble Eightfold Path; that is, right view…right concentration.

"When a noble disciple has thus understood craving, the origin of craving, the cessation of craving, and the way leading to the cessation of craving…he here and now makes an end of suffering. In that way too a noble disciple is one of right view… and has arrived at this true Dhamma (four-fold nibbana)."

Feeling

Saying, "Good, friend," the companions delighted and rejoiced in the Arahant Sāriputta's words. Then they asked him a further question: "But, friend, might there be another way in which a noble disciple is one of right view…and has arrived at this true Dhamma (four-fold nibbana)?"—"There might be, friends.

"When, friends, a noble disciple understands feeling, the origin of feeling, the cessation of feeling, and the way leading to the cessation of feeling, in that way one is one of right view…and has arrived at this true Dhamma (four-fold nibbana).

"And what is feeling, what is the origin of feeling, what is the cessation of feeling, what is the way leading to the cessation of feeling? There are these six classes of feeling: feeling born of eye-contact, feeling born of ear-contact, feeling born of nose-contact, feeling born of tongue-contact, feeling born of body-contact, feeling born of mind-contact. With the arising of contact there is the arising of feeling. With the cessation of contact there is the cessation of feeling. The way leading to the cessation of feeling is just this Noble Eightfold Path; that is, right view… right concentration.

"When a noble disciple has thus understood feeling, the origin of feeling, the cessation of feeling, and the way leading to the cessation of feeling…one here and now makes an end of suffering. In that way too a noble disciple is one of right view…and has arrived at this true Dhamma (four-fold nibbana)."

Contact

Saying, "Good, friend," the companions delighted and rejoiced in the Arahant Sāriputta's words. Then they asked him a further question: "But, friend, might there be another way in which a noble disciple is one of right view…and has arrived at this true Dhamma (four-fold nibbana)?"—"There might be, friends.

"When, friends, a noble disciple understands contact, the origin of contact, the cessation of contact, and the way leading to the cessation of contact, in that way one is one of right view…and has arrived at this true Dhamma (four-fold nibbana).

"And what is contact, what is the origin of contact, what is the cessation of contact, what is the way leading to the cessation of contact? There are these six classes of contact: eye-contact, ear-contact, nose-contact, tongue-contact, body-contact, mind-contact. With the arising of the sixfold base there is the arising of contact. With the cessation of the sixfold base there is the cessation of contact. The way leading to the cessation of contact is just this Noble Eightfold Path; that is, right view…right concentration.

"When a noble disciple has thus understood contact, the origin of contact, the cessation of contact, and the way leading to the cessation of contact…one here and now makes an end of suffering. In that way too a noble disciple is one of right view…and has arrived at this true Dhamma (four-fold nibbana)."

The Sixfold Base

Saying, "Good, friend," the companions delighted and rejoiced in the Arahant Sāriputta's words. Then they asked him a further question: "But, friend, might there be another way in which a noble disciple is one of right view…and has arrived at this true Dhamma (four-fold nibbana)?"—"There might be, friends.

"When, friends, a noble disciple understands the sixfold base, the origin of the sixfold base, the cessation of the sixfold base, and the way leading to the cessation of the sixfold base, in that way he is one of right view…and has arrived at this true Dhamma (four-fold nibbana).

"And what is the sixfold base, what is the origin of the sixfold base, what is the cessation of the sixfold base, what is the way leading to the cessation of the sixfold base? There are these six bases: the eye-base, the ear-base, the nose-base, the tongue-base, the body-base, the mind-base. With the arising of mentality-materiality there is the arising of the sixfold base. With the cessation of mentality-materiality there is the cessation of the sixfold base. The way leading to the cessation of the sixfold base is just this Noble Eightfold Path; that is, right view…right concentration.

"When a noble disciple has thus understood the sixfold base, the origin of the sixfold base, the cessation of the sixfold base, and the way leading to the cessation of the sixfold base…he here and now makes an end of suffering. In that way too a noble disciple is one of right view…and has arrived at this true Dhamma (four-fold nibbana)."

Mentality-Materiality

Saying, "Good, friend," the companions delighted and rejoiced in the Arahant Sāriputta's words. Then they asked him a further question: "But, friend, might there be another way in which a noble disciple is one of right view…and has arrived at this true Dhamma (four-fold nibbana)?"—"There might be, friends.

"When, friends, a noble disciple understands mentality-materiality, the origin of mentality-materiality, the cessation of mentality-materiality, and the way leading to the cessation of mentality-materiality, in that way one is one of right view…and has arrived at this true Dhamma (four-fold nibbana).

"And what is mentality-materiality, what is the origin of mentality-materiality, what is the cessation of mentality-materiality, what is the way leading to the cessation of mentality-materiality? Feeling, perception, volition, contact, and attention—these are called mentality. The four great elements and the material form derived from the four great elements—these are called materiality. So this mentality and this materiality are what is called mentality-materiality. With the arising of consciousness there is the arising of mentality-materiality. With the cessation of consciousness there is the cessation of mentality-materiality. The way leading to the cessation of mentality-materiality is just this Noble Eightfold Path; that is, right view…right concentration.

"When a noble disciple has thus understood mentality-materiality, the origin of mentality-materiality, the cessation of mentality-materiality, and the way leading to the cessation of mentality-materiality…one here and now makes an end of suffering. In that way too a noble disciple is one of right view…and has arrived at this true Dhamma (four-fold nibbana)."

Consciousness

Saying, "Good, friend," the bhikkhus delighted and rejoiced in the Arahant Sāriputta's words. Then they asked him a further question: "But, friend, might there be another way in which a noble disciple is one of right view…and has arrived at this true Dhamma (four-fold nibbana)?"—"There might be, friends.

"When, friends, a noble disciple understands consciousness, the origin of consciousness, the cessation of consciousness, and the way leading to the cessation of consciousness, in that way he is one of right view…and has arrived at this true Dhamma (four-fold nibbana).

"And what is consciousness, what is the origin of consciousness, what is the cessation of consciousness, what is the way leading to the cessation of consciousness? There are these six classes of consciousness: eye-consciousness, ear-consciousness, nose-consciousness, tongue-consciousness, body-consciousness, mind-consciousness. With the arising of formations there is the arising of consciousness. With the cessation of formations there is the cessation of consciousness. The way leading to the cessation of consciousness is just this Noble Eightfold Path; that is, right view…right concentration.

"When a noble disciple has thus understood consciousness, the origin of consciousness, the cessation of consciousness, and the way leading to the cessation of consciousness …he here and now makes an end of suffering. In that way too a noble disciple is one of right view…and has arrived at this true Dhamma (four-fold nibbana)."

Formations

Saying, "Good, friend," the companions delighted and rejoiced in the Arahant Sāriputta's words. Then they asked him a further question: "But, friend, might there be another way in which a noble disciple is one of right view…and has arrived at this true Dhamma (four-fold nibbana)?"—"There might be, friends.

"When, friends, a noble disciple understands formations, the origin of formations, the cessation of formations, and the way leading to the cessation of formations, in that way one is one of right view…and has arrived at this true Dhamma (four-fold nibbāna).

"And what are formations, what is the origin of formations, what is the cessation of formations, what is the way leading to the cessation of formations? There are these three kinds of formations: the bodily formation, the verbal formation, the mental formation.

With the arising of ignorance there is the arising of formations. With the cessation of ignorance there is the cessation of formations. The way leading to the cessation of formations is just this Noble Eightfold Path; that is, right view…right concentration.

"When a noble disciple has thus understood formations, the origin of formations, the cessation of formations, and the way leading to the cessation of formations…one here and now makes an end of suffering. In that way too a noble disciple is one of right view…and has arrived at this true Dhamma (four-fold nibbana)."

Ignorance

Saying, "Good, friend," the companions delighted and rejoiced in the Arahant Sāriputta's words. Then they asked him a further question: "But, friend, might there be another way in which a noble disciple is one of right view…and has arrived at this true Dhamma (four-fold nibbana)?"—"There might be, friends.

"When, friends, a noble disciple understands ignorance, the origin of ignorance, the cessation of ignorance, and the way leading to the cessation of ignorance, in that way one is one of right view…and has arrived at this true Dhamma (four-fold nibbāna).

"And what is ignorance, what is the origin of ignorance, what is the cessation of ignorance, what is the way leading to the cessation of ignorance? Not knowing about suffering, not knowing about the origin of suffering, not knowing about the cessation of suffering, not knowing about the way leading to the cessation of suffering—this is called ignorance.

With the arising of the taints there is the arising of ignorance. With the cessation of the taints there is the cessation of ignorance. The way leading to the cessation of ignorance is just this Noble Eightfold Path; that is, right view…right concentration.

"When a noble disciple has thus understood ignorance, the origin of ignorance, the cessation of ignorance, and the way leading to the cessation of ignorance…one here and now makes an end of suffering. In that way too a noble disciple is one of right view…and has arrived at this true Dhamma (four-fold nibbana)."

Taints

Saying, "Good, friend," the companions delighted and rejoiced in the Arahant Sāriputta's words. Then they asked him a further question: "But, friend, might there be another way in which a noble disciple is one of right view, whose view is straight, who has unwavering confidence in the Dhamma, and has arrived at this true Dhamma (four-fold nibbana)?"—"There might be, friends.

"When, friends, a noble disciple understands the taints, the origin of the taints, the cessation of the taints, and the way leading to the cessation of the taints, in that way one is one of right view, whose view is straight, who has unwavering confidence in the Dhamma, and has arrived at this true Dhamma (four-fold nibbana).

"And what are the taints, what is the origin of the taints, what is the cessation of the taints, what is the way leading to the cessation of the taints? There are these three taints: the taint of sensual desire, the taint of being, and the taint of ignorance.

With the arising of ignorance there is the arising of the taints. With the cessation of ignorance there is the cessation of the taints. The way leading to the cessation of the taints is just this Noble Eightfold Path; that is, right view, right intention, right speech, right action, right livelihood, right effort, right mindfulness, and right concentration.

"When a noble disciple has thus understood the taints, the origin of the taints, the cessation of the taints, and the way leading to the cessation of the taints, he entirely abandons the underlying tendency to lust, he abolishes the underlying tendency to aversion, he extirpates the underlying tendency to the view and conceit 'I am,' and by abandoning ignorance and arousing true knowledge he here and now makes an end of suffering. In that way too a noble disciple is one of right view, whose view is straight, who has unwavering confidence in the Dhamma, and has arrived at this true Dhamma (four-fold nibbana)."

That is what Arahant Sāriputta said. The companions were satisfied and delighted in the Arahant Sāriputta's words.

Chapter 12

Middle Discourses 10: Mahāsatipaṭṭhānasutta

Discourse on the Applications of Mindfulness

The limited explanation of Dhamma and partial explanations provided by ordinary people seem to have prevented many others from developing the right view of Dhamma. The way in which an ordinary person explains Nibbana can be illustrated in the story: the parable of the blind men and elephant, where men who have never seen an elephant before learn and imagine what the elephant is like and try to describe an elephant based on their limited experiences and their descriptions differ from one another, so as conventional dhamma. Partial explanations, limited vision and misinterpretations of Dhamma have prevented Nibbana for many. In this manner, ordinary people following an ordinary teacher of dhamma are likely to go in samsara. Yet, by linking ordinary dhamma understanding to the Noble Path, those who aspire to Nibbana and are wise will cross the shore that is rare to cross.

Sotapanna (or Sakagami) can practice Dhamma in a way that abandons sensual desires and ill will by reflecting and applying four kinds of mindfulness to become an Anagami. The same is not applicable to an ordinary person. Thus, an ordinary person would benefit from focusing on the practice of becoming a Sotapanna.

There are many meditation practices, to gain Sotapanna, the most appropriate meditation is reflecting the qualities of the Triple Gem. Alternatively, for those who are unable to do so, they may try engage in "chittanupassana" or understanding the causes, and analysing thoughts. One way to do that is understanding self; instead of allowing self to bring sufferings, by understanding yourself you can find a refuge in yourself that is rare to find. How can you understand yourself? You can begin to understand yourself by exploring the causes for your taught as they come and go. This is what is referred to as "chittanupassana".

Your automatic thoughts can be or cannot be accurate. Finding the causes for your thoughts as they occur, and reasons are an important route for understanding self. You can understand self by making an effort to understand reasons for your thoughts, self-view and changes happening in your self-view. For example, you can ask yourself why you think as the way you think when you experience distress in daily life. For example, when you feel sad, or distressed, explore the cause and reasons for your sadness, or distress. Ask yourself why you feel sad and upset or distressed? You will find your sadness arise due to attachment; thing that you desire, when you don't get what you like or expected, and when you get what you dislike or unexpected, you experience sadness, or distress. Then ask yourself, what made you think that you can get what you like and expected, is it realistic or not? If something is not realistic, why make it a cause to make distress? Instead, learn to accept the truth; that not all what you desire can be fulfilled, sometimes, they come to be fulfilled, sometimes not by constantly reminding yourself about the truth. If you think you are a beginner to this technique of analysing the cause of your thinking and you feel that it's too much for you that you are unable to go that far as reframing your thoughts, you could just start with smaller steps, you could begin by taking a few relaxed breaths and try and simply exploring the causes for your thoughts; for example, when you feel thirsty, ask yourself why do I feel thirsty? You may find the reason, that you feel thirsty because didn't drink enough water, and you continue to drink water and subsidies your thirst while knowing the cause. In this manner, if you continue to explore causes for your thinking, eventually you will learn to reduce grasping to your thoughts over time. Since a birth, you experienced many autonomic thoughts without exploring reasons but from now, you can learn to experience things while exploring the causes for your thinking, a technique through which you can progress into reduce grasping to self-view. By hearing these words, you may continue with your usual daily life. To practice Dhamma, there are no unusual things to do. At times, you may remember these words while going and doing usual things. Sometimes, these words can make you think again, and at such instances, you may consider, these words have come to meet you "within you".

A person who is seeking Nibbana and wishes to gain peace of mind should try to develop good qualities within. It is somewhat both; people who have completed paramis in previous birth and who have natural good qualities to some extent require further development, practice, refinement, and further development of wisdom and wholesome intentional actions/deeds until perfection, just as improving other skills, singing, drawing, etc. Those who genuinely appreciate Dhamma tend to constantly want to improve themselves. Those who do not appreciate Dhamma tend not to want to improve qualities within.

For an ordinary person wishing to progress into noble mindfulness can be developed by maintaining mindfulness towards one's own thoughts and choosing to do good and avoid bad within daily activities. For example, a mind can make up a past when the past is gone, and, at times, thoughts can pass on without a person noticing them. Whether a person recognizes such thoughts or not, they can produce or prolong sufferings. Instead, to develop the Noble Path, if a person can watch over the person's own mind and thoughts and choose to do good and avoid bad, this will be a way to develop noble mindfulness to reduce stress. For example, when thoughts making up a past bring up sufferings, a person can do wholesome things, such as picking up from thoughts anything that needs resolving and attempt to resolve things that need resolving and avoid unwholesome things that bring stress. In that sense, unwholesomeness is clinging to things that are gone, as they are gone, and it is meaningless to worry about such things excessively. Letting go of things that are gone will allow a person to gain peace of mind, middle-way practice, a step come closer to the realization of truth, and walk the noble path towards Sotapanna.

One technique that can be used to reduce self-view is trying to be happy with things as they are. When these habits develop within a person, ordinary ways can't seem to get enough of worldly experiences in one's mind and tend to feel and say in one's mind, "not enough". They tend to feel too upset when faced with difficulties in life (thinking that's not ok), instead letting go of things that are gone, doing what is needed to be done while resolve things, you can reduce clinging to self-view. These techniques that allow a person to deal better with life difficulties are particularly useful when circumstances are not favourable. Too much sadness can sometimes paralyse a person in mind to the extent that sometimes people may struggle to do things that they need to do. In this manner, applying wisdom, reducing clinging to self-view will allow a person to focus more on resolving things rather than worrying too much about such things in one's mind.

Similarly, the way of letting go of self-others and the world is also a practice in thoughts, a subjective process. In this manner, doing things that are beneficial without keeping too many expectations is a noble way of doing. For example, if a student puts all efforts to preparing an exam without keeping too many expectations either to pass or to fail, that will help the student to succeed and keep worries down at the same time.

Instead of positive and negative thinking, if a person is told that there are two sides in life that are possible and that uncertainty is a way of life and that ups and downs are what are usual, this will help the person to deal better with life experiences. Therefore, reducing expectations and just doing things that are beneficial will allow a person to extend happiness coming through worldly experiences. In that sense, middle way training is very practical. For instance, getting too upset, too worried about self, others and the world can produce depression, anxiety, addictions and similar things, and giving up on self physically or emotionally can harm a person. Quitting an ordinary world and conventions are not practical and feasible, as wherever one goes, whether in the forest or in the town, whatever role one plays, whether it's living as a monk based on conventions, a householder based on conventions, a friend based on conventions or a parent based on conventions, given that the ordinary world we live in is filled with conventions, one only gets to live with conventions. Either in the forest or in the town, both are still conventions. Instead, middle way shows how a person can find inner satisfaction while living with conventions in an ordinary world by giving up clinging to such conventions in the person's mind.

Thus, engaging in jhana practice through conscious efforts and conscious sila has limits and is not good enough. They need further development to make such things happen naturally without an effort ending with the universal ways.

First things first and training to Sotapanna comes first. The training path leading to Nibbana can be developed by developing one's understanding of a Sotapanna. To gain to the Stream-entry (Sotapanna), you could engage in ten wholesome deeds while ensuring you are reducing the fetters and developing the confirmed confidence in the Triple Gem. One thing you want to do is you want to give up all and renunciate in mind in the presence or absence of others, material things and the world.

"Thus have I heard:

At one time the Lord was staying among the Kuru people in the township of the Kurus called Kammāssadhamma. While he was there, the Lord addressed the companions, saying:

"Companions."

"Venerable sir," these companions answered the Lord in assent. The Lord spoke thus:

"There is this one way, companions, for the purification of beings, for the overcoming of sorrows and griefs, for the going down of sufferings and miseries, for winning the right path, for realising four-fold Nibbāna, that is to say, the four applications of mindfulness is helpful for a Sotapanna or Sakadagami.

What are the four?

Herein, companions, a noble person fares along contemplating the body in the body, ardent, clearly conscious (of it), mindful (of it) so as to control the covetousness and dejection in the world; he fares along contemplating the feelings in the feelings, ardent, clearly conscious (of them), mindful (of them) so as to control the covetousness and dejection in the world; one fares along contemplating the mind in the mind, ardent, clearly conscious (of it), mindful (of it) so as to control the covetousness and dejection in the world; one fares along contemplating the mental objects in the mental objects, ardent, dearly conscious (of them), mindful (of them) so as to control the covetousness and dejection in the world.

Contemplating the Body in the Body

And how, companions, does a noble person fare along contemplating the body in the body? Herein, companions, a person who is forest-gone or gone to the root of a tree or gone to an empty place, maintain a comfortable posture (sitting, lying, walking etc.), arousing mindfulness in front of one.

Mindful one breathes in, mindful one breathes out.

Whether one is breathing in a long (breath) one comprehends, 'I am breathing in a long (breath)'; or whether one is breathing out a long (breath) one comprehends, 'I am breathing out a long (breath)'; or whether one is breathing in a short (breath) one comprehends, 'I am breathing in a short (breath)'; or whether one is breathing out a short (breath) one comprehends, 'I am breathing out a short (breath).'

One trains oneself, thinking: 'I shall breathe in experiencing the whole body. One trains oneself, thinking: 'I shall breathe out experiencing the whole body.'

One trains oneself, thinking: 'I shall breathe in tranquillising the activity of the body.' One trains oneself, thinking: 'I shall breathe out tranquillising the activity of the body.'

Companions, it is like a clever turner or turner's apprentice who, making a long (turn), comprehends, 'I am making a long (turn)'; or when making a short (turn) comprehends, 'I am making a short (turn).' Even so, does a person who is breathing in a long (breath) comprehend, 'I am breathing in a long (breath)'; or when breathing out a long (breath) he comprehends, 'I am breathing out a long (breath)'; or when breathing in a short (breath) he comprehends, 'I am breathing in a short (breath)'; or when breathing out a short (breath) he comprehends, 'I am breathing out a short (breath).'

One trains oneself with the thought: 'I shall breathe in experiencing the whole body.'

One trains oneself with the thought: 'I shall breathe out experiencing the whole body.'

One trains oneself with the thought: 'I shall breathe in tranquillising the activity of the body.'

One trains oneself with the thought: 'I shall breathe out tranquillising the activity of the body.'

In this way, companions, one fares along contemplating the body in the body internally, or one fares along contemplating the body in the body externally, or one fares along contemplating the body in the body internally and externally; or one fares along contemplating origination-things in the body, or one fares along contemplating dissolution-things in the body, or one fares along contemplating origination-and-dissolution things in the body; or, thinking, 'There is the body,' one's mindfulness is established precisely to the extent necessary just for knowledge, just for remembrance, and one fares along independently of and not grasping anything in the world. It is thus too, that a person fares along contemplating the body in the body.

And again, companions, a noble person, when he is walking, comprehends, 'I am walking'; or when one is standing still, comprehends, 'I am standing still'; or when one is sitting down, comprehends, 'I am sitting down'; or when one is lying down, comprehends, 'I am lying down.' So that however his body is disposed he comprehends that it is like that.

Thus one fares along contemplating the body in the body internally, or one fares along contemplating the body in the body externally, or one fares along contemplating the body in the body internally and externally; or one fares along contemplating origination-things in the body, or one fares along contemplating dissolution-things in the body, or one fares along contemplating origination-and-dissolution things in the body; or, thinking,

'There is the body,' one's mindfulness is established precisely to the extent necessary just for knowledge, just for remembrance, and one fares along independently of and not grasping anything in the world.

It is thus too, that a person fares along contemplating the body in the body.

And again, companions, a noble person, when one is setting out or returning is one, acting in a clearly conscious way; when one is looking in front or looking around is one, acting in a clearly conscious way; when one has bent in or stretched out (his arm) is one, acting in a clearly conscious way; when one is carrying his outer cloak, bowl and robe is one, acting in a clearly conscious way; when one is eating, drinking, chewing, tasting is one, acting in a clearly conscious way; when one is obeying the calls of nature is one, acting in a clearly conscious way; when one is walking, standing, sitting, asleep, awake, talking, silent, one is one acting in a clearly conscious way.

Thus one fares along contemplating the body in the body internally, or one fares along contemplating the body in the body externally, or one fares along contemplating the body in the body internally and externally; or one fares along contemplating origination-things in the body, or one fares along contemplating dissolution-things in the body, or one fares along contemplating origination-and-dissolution things in the body; or, thinking,

'There is the body,' one's mindfulness is established precisely to the extent necessary just for knowledge, just for remembrance, and one fares along independently of and not grasping anything in the world. It is thus too, friends, that a person fares along contemplating the body in the body.

And again, companions, a noble person reflects on precisely this body itself, encased in skin and full of various impurities, from the soles of the feet up and from the crown of the head down, that: 'There is connected with this body hair of the head, hair of the body, nails, teeth, skin, flesh, sinews, bones, marrow, kidneys, heart, liver, membranes, spleen, lungs, intestines, mesentery, stomach, excrement, bile, phlegm, pus, blood, sweat, fat, tears, serum, saliva, mucus, synovic fluid, urine.'

Companions, it is like a double-mouthed provision bag that is full of various kinds of grain such as hill-paddy, paddy, kidney beans, peas, sesamum, rice; and a keen-eyed man, pouring them out, were to reflect: 'That's hill-paddy, that's paddy, that's kidney beans, that's peas, that's sesamum, that's rice.'

Even so, companions, does a noble person reflect on precisely this body itself, encased in skin and full of various impurities, from the soles of the feet up and from the crown of the head down, that: 'There is connected with this body hair of the head, hair of the body, nails, teeth, skin, flesh, sinews, bones, marrow, kidneys, heart, liver, membranes, spleen, lungs, intestines, mesentery, stomach, excrement, bile, phlegm, pus, blood, sweat, fat, tears, serum, saliva, mucus, synovic fluid, urine.'

Thus one fares along contemplating the body in the body internally, or one fares along contemplating the body in the body externally, or one fares along contemplating the body in the body internally and externally.; or he fares along contemplating origination-things in the body, or one fares along contemplating dissolution-things in the body, or one fares along contemplating origination-and-dissolution things in the body; or, thinking, '

There is the body,' one's mindfulness is established precisely to the extent necessary just for knowledge, just for remembrance, and one fares along independently of and not grasping anything in the world. It is thus too, friends, that a person fares along contemplating the body in the body.

And again, companions, a person reflects on this body according to how it is placed or disposed in respect of the elements, thinking: 'In this body there is the element of extension, the element of cohesion, the element of heat, the element of motion.'

Companions, even as a skilled cattle-butcher, or his apprentice, having slaughtered a cow, might sit displaying its carcass at the cross-roads, even so, does a person reflect on this body itself according to how it is placed or disposed in respect of the elements, thinking: 'In this body there is the element of extension, the element of cohesion, the element of heat, the element of motion.' Thus one fares along contemplating the body in the body internally, or one fares along contemplating the body in the body externally, or one fares along contemplating the body in the body internally and externally; or one fares along contemplating origination-things in the body, or one fares along contemplating dissolution-things in the body, or one fares along contemplating origination-and-dissolution things in the body; or, thinking,

'There is the body,' one's mindfulness is established precisely to the extent necessary just for knowledge, just for remembrance, and one fares along independently of and not grasping anything in the world. It is thus too, friends, that a person fares along contemplating the body in the body.

And again, companions, as a noble person might see a body thrown aside in a cemetery, dead for one day or for two days or for three days, swollen, discoloured, decomposing; one focuses on this body itself, thinking: 'This body, too, is of a similar nature a similar constitution, it has not got past that (state of things).'

Thus one fares along contemplating the body in the body internally, or one fares along contemplating the body in the body externally, or one fares along contemplating the body in the body internally and externally; or one fares along contemplating origination-things in the body, or one fares along contemplating dissolution-things in the body, or one fares along contemplating origination-and-dissolution things in the body; or, thinking, 'There is the body,' one's mindfulness is established precisely to the extent necessary just for knowledge, just for remembrance, and one fares along independently of and not grasping anything in the world. It is thus too, friends, that a person fares along contemplating the body in the body.

And again, companions, a noble person might see a body thrown aside in a cemetery, and being devoured by crows or ravens or vultures or wild dogs or jackals or by various small creatures; one focuses on this body itself, thinking: 'This body too is of a similar nature a similar constitution, it has not got past that (state of things).'

Thus one fares along contemplating the body in the body internally, or one fares along contemplating the body in the body externally, or one fares along contemplating the body in the body internally and externally; or one fares along contemplating origination-things in the body, or one fares along contemplating dissolution-things in the body, or one fares along contemplating origination-and-dissolution things in the body; or, thinking, 'There is the body,' his mindfulness is established precisely to the extent necessary just for knowledge, just for remembrance, and one fares along independently of and not grasping anything in the world. It is thus too, friends, that a person fares along contemplating the body in the body.

And again, companions, as a noble person might see a body thrown aside in a cemetery a skeleton with (some) flesh and blood, sinew-bound; one focuses on this body itself, thinking: 'This body too is of a similar nature a similar constitution, it has not got past that (state of things).'

Thus one fares along contemplating the body in the body internally, or one fares along contemplating the body in the body externally, or one fares along contemplating the body in the body internally and externally; or one fares along contemplating origination-things in the body, or one fares along contemplating dissolution-things in the body, or one fares along contemplating origination-and-dissolution things in the body; or, thinking,

'There is the body,' one's mindfulness is established precisely to the extent necessary just for knowledge, just for remembrance, and one fares along independently of and not grasping anything in the world. It is thus too, friends, that a person fares along contemplating the body in the body.

And again, companions, as a noble person might see a body thrown aside in a cemetery fleshless but blood-bespattered, sinew-bound; one focuses on this body itself, thinking: 'This body too is of a similar nature a similar constitution, it has not got past that (state of things).'

Thus one fares along contemplating the body in the body internally, or one fares along contemplating the body in the body externally, or one fares along contemplating the body in the body internally and externally; or one fares along contemplating origination-things in the body, or one fares along contemplating dissolution-things in the body, or one fares along contemplating origination-and-dissolution things in the body; or, thinking,

'There is the body,' one's mindfulness is established precisely to the extent necessary just for knowledge, just for remembrance, and one fares along independently of and not grasping anything in the world. It is thus too, friends, that a person fares along contemplating the body in the body.

And again, companions, as a noble person might see a body thrown aside in a cemetery without flesh and blood, sinew-bound; he focuses on this body itself, thinking:

'This body too is of a similar nature a similar constitution, it has not got past that (state of things).' Thus one fares along contemplating the body in the body internally, or one fares along contemplating the body in the body externally, or one fares along contemplating the body in the body internally and externally; or one fares along contemplating origination-things in the body, or he fares along contemplating dissolution-things in the body, or he fares along contemplating origination-and-dissolution things in the body.; or, thinking, 'There is the body,' one's mindfulness is established precisely to the extent necessary just for knowledge, just for remembrance, and one fares along independently of and not grasping anything in the world. It is thus too, friends, that a person fares along contemplating the body in the body.

And again, companions, as a noble person might see a body thrown aside in a cemetery the bones scattered here and there, no longer held together: here a bone of the hand, there a foot-bone, here a leg-bone, there a rib, here a hip-bone, there a back-bone, here the skull; he focuses on this body itself, thinking: 'This body too is of a similar nature a similar constitution, it has not got past that (state of things).' Thus one fares along contemplating the body in the body internally, or one fares along contemplating the body in the body externally, or one fares along contemplating the body in the body internally and externally; or one fares along contemplating origination-things in the body, or one fares along contemplating dissolution-things in the body, or one fares along contemplating origination-and-dissolution things in the body; or, thinking, 'There is the body,' one's mindfulness is established precisely to the extent necessary just for knowledge, just for remembrance, and one fares along independently of and not grasping anything in the world. It is thus too, friends, that a person fares along contemplating the body in the body.

And again, companions, a noble person might see a body thrown aside in a cemetery: the bones white and something like sea-shells a heap of dried up bones more than a year old, he focuses on this body itself, thinking: 'This body too is of a similar nature a similar constitution, it has not got past that (state of things).' Thus one fares along contemplating the body in the body internally, or one fares along contemplating the body in the body externally, or he fares along contemplating the body in the body internally and externally, or one fares along contemplating origination-things in the body, or one fares along contemplating dissolution-things in the body, or one fares along contemplating origination-and-dissolution things in the body.; or, thinking, 'There is the body,' one's mindfulness is established precisely to the extent necessary just for knowledge, just for remembrance, and one fares along independently of and not grasping anything in the world. It is thus too, friends, that a person fares along contemplating the body in the body.

And again, companions, a noble person might see a body thrown aside in a cemetery: the bones gone rotten and reduced to powder; one focuses on this body itself, thinking: 'This body, too, is of a similar nature a similar constitution, it has not got past that (state of things).' Thus one fares along contemplating the body in the body internally, or one fares along contemplating the body in the body externally, or one fares along contemplating the body in the body internally and externally; or one fares along contemplating origination-things in the body, or one fares along contemplating dissolution-things in the body, or one fares along contemplating origination-and-dissolution things in the body; or, thinking, 'There is the body,' one's mindfulness is established precisely to the extent necessary just for knowledge, just for remembrance, and one fares along independently of and not grasping anything in the world. It is thus too, friends, that a person fares along contemplating the body in the body.

Contemplating the Feelings in the Feelings

And how, companions, does a noble person fare along contemplating the feelings in the feelings? Herein, friends, while one is experiencing a pleasant feeling he comprehends: 'I am experiencing a pleasant feeling;' while he is experiencing a painful feeling he comprehends, 'I am experiencing a painful feeling'; while one is experiencing a feeling that is neither painful nor pleasant one comprehends: 'I am experiencing a feeling that is neither painful nor pleasant.'

While one is experiencing a pleasant feeling in regard to material things he comprehends, 'I am experiencing a pleasant feeling in regard to material things;

While one is experiencing a painful feeling in regard to material things one comprehends, 'I am experiencing a painful feeling in regard to material things; while one is experiencing a feeling that is neither painful nor pleasant in regard to material things one comprehends: 'I am experiencing a feeling that is neither painful nor pleasant in regard to material things; While one is experiencing a pleasant feeling in regard to non-material things one comprehends, 'I am experiencing a pleasant feeling in regard to non-material things; While one is experiencing a painful feeling in regard to non-material things one comprehends, 'I am experiencing a painful feeling in regard to non-material things; while one is experiencing a feeling that is neither painful nor pleasant in regard to non-material things one comprehends: 'I am experiencing a feeling that is neither painful nor pleasant in regard to non-material things; Thus one fares along contemplating the feelings in the feelings internally, or one fares along contemplating the feelings in the feelings externally, or one fares along contemplating the feelings in the feelings internally and externally; or one fares along contemplating origination-things in the feelings, or one fares along contemplating dissolution-things in the feelings, or one fares along contemplating origination-dissolution-things in the feelings; or, thinking, 'There is feeling,' one's mindfulness is established precisely to the extent necessary just for knowledge, just for remembrance, and one fares along independently of and not grasping anything in the world.

It is thus too, friends, that a person fares along contemplating feelings in the feelings.

Contemplating Mind in the Mind

And how, companions, does a person fare along contemplating mind in the mind? Herein, a person knows intuitively the mind with attachment as a mind with attachment;

one knows intuitively the mind without attachment, as a mind without attachment;

one knows intuitively the mind with hatred, as a mind with hatred;

one knows intuitively the mind without hatred, as a mind without hatred;

one knows intuitively the mind with confusion, as a mind with confusion;

one knows intuitively the mind without confusion, as a mind without confusion;

one knows intuitively the mind that is contracted, as a mind that is contracted;

one knows intuitively the mind that is distracted, as a mind that is distracted;

one knows intuitively the mind that has become great, as a mind that has become great;

one knows intuitively the mind that has not become great, as a mind that has not become great;

one knows intuitively the mind with (some other mental state) superior to it, as a mind with (some other mental state) superior to it;

one knows intuitively the mind with no (other mental state) superior to it, as a mind with no (other mental state) superior to it;

one knows intuitively the mind that is composed, as a mind that is composed;

one knows intuitively the mind that is not composed, as a mind that is not composed;

one knows intuitively the mind that is freed, as a mind that is freed;

one knows intuitively the mind that is not freed, as a mind that is not freed.

Thus one fares along contemplating the mind in the mind internally, or he fares along contemplating the mind in the mind externally, or one fares along contemplating the mind in the mind internally and externally, or one fares along contemplating origination-things in the mind, or one fares along contemplating dissolution-things in the mind, or one fares along contemplating origination-dissolution-things in the mind.; or, thinking, 'There is mind,' one's mindfulness is established precisely to the extent necessary just for knowledge, just for remembrance, and one fares along independently of and not grasping anything in the world. It is thus too, friends, that a person fares along contemplating mind in the mind.

Contemplating Mental Objects in Mental Objects

And how, companions, does a noble person fare along contemplating mental objects in mental objects? Herein, friends, a person fares along contemplating mental objects in mental objects from the point of view of the five hindrances.

And how, monks, does a person fare along contemplating mental objects in mental objects from the point of view of the five hindrances?

(1) Herein, friends, when a subjective desire for sense-pleasures is present a person comprehends that one has a subjective desire for sense-pleasures; or when a subjective desire for sense-pleasures is not present one comprehends that he has no subjective desire for sense-pleasures. And in so far as there comes to be an uprising of desire for sense-pleasures that had not arisen before, one comprehends that; and in so far as there comes to be a getting rid of desire for sense-pleasures that has arisen, one comprehends that. And in so far as there comes to be no future uprising of desire for the sense-pleasures that has been got rid of, he comprehends that.

(2) Or when ill-will is subjectively present a person comprehends that one has ill-will subjectively present; or when ill-will is subjectively not present one comprehends that he has no subjective ill-will.

And in so far as there comes to be an uprising of ill-will that had not arisen before, one comprehends that; and in so far as there comes to be a getting rid of ill-will that has arisen, one comprehends that.

And in so far as there comes to be no future uprising of ill-will that has been got rid of, one comprehends that.

(3) Or when sloth and torpor is subjectively present a person comprehends that one has sloth and torpor subjectively present; or when sloth and torpor is subjectively not present one comprehends that one has no subjective sloth and torpor. And in so far as there comes to be an uprising of sloth and torpor that had not arisen before, one comprehends that; and in so far as there comes to be a getting rid of sloth and torpor that has arisen, one comprehends that. And in so far as there comes to be no future uprising of sloth and torpor that has been got rid of, one comprehends that.

(4) Or when restlessness and worry is subjectively present a person comprehends that one has restlessness and worry subjectively present; or when restlessness and worry is subjectively not present one comprehends that one has no subjective restlessness and worry. And in so far as there comes to be an uprising of restlessness and worry that had not arisen before, one comprehends that; and in so far as there comes to be a getting rid of restlessness and worry that has arisen, one comprehends that. And in so far as there comes to be no future uprising of restlessness and worry that has been got rid of, one comprehends that.

Or when restlessness and worry is subjectively present a person comprehends that one has restlessness and worry subjectively present; or when restlessness and worry is subjectively not present one comprehends that one has no subjective restlessness and worry. And in so far as there comes to be an uprising of restlessness and worry that had not arisen before, one comprehends that; and in so far as there comes to be a getting rid of restlessness and worry that has arisen, one comprehends that. And in so far as there comes to be no future uprising of restlessness and worry that has been got rid of, he comprehends that. (5) Or when doubt is present subjectively he comprehends that one has subjective doubt; or when doubt is not present subjectively one comprehends that he has no subjective doubt. And in so far as there is an uprising of doubt that had not arisen before, he comprehends that; and in so far as there is a getting rid of doubt that has arisen, one comprehends that; and in so far as there is in the future no uprising of the doubt that has been got rid of, one comprehends that.

It is thus that he fares along contemplating mental objects in mental objects internally, or one fares along contemplating mental objects in mental objects externally, or one fares along contemplating mental objects in mental objects internally and externally; or one fares along contemplating origination-things in mental objects, or one fares along contemplating dissolution-things in mental objects, or one fares along contemplating origination-things and dissolution-things in mental objects; or, thinking, 'There are mental objects,' one's mindfulness is established precisely to the extent necessary just for knowledge, just for remembrance, and one fares along independently of and not grasping anything in the world. It is thus; that a person fares along contemplating mental objects in mental objects from the point of view of the five hindrances.

And again, companions, a noble person fares along contemplating mental objects in mental objects from the point of view of the five groups of grasping. And how does a person fare along contemplating mental objects in mental objects from the point of view of the five groups of grasping? (1) Herein, a person thinks, 'Such is material shape, such is the arising of material shape, such is the setting of material shape; (2) such is feeling, such the arising of feeling, such the setting of feeling; (3) such is perception, such the arising of perception such the setting of perception; (4) such are the tendencies, such the arising of the tendencies such the setting of the tendencies; (5) such is consciousness, such the arising of consciousness, such the setting of consciousness.' It is thus that he fares along contemplating mental objects in mental objects internally, or he fares along contemplating mental objects in mental objects externally, or he fares along contemplating mental objects in mental objects internally and externally; or he fares along contemplating origination-things in mental objects, or he fares along contemplating dissolution-things in mental objects, or he fares along contemplating origination-things and dissolution-things in mental objects; or, thinking, 'There are mental objects,' his mindfulness is established precisely to the extent necessary just for knowledge, just for remembrance, and he fares along independently of and not grasping anything in the world. It is thus; that a person fares along contemplating mental objects in mental objects from the point of view of the five groups of grasping.

And again, companions, a noble person fares along contemplating mental objects in mental objects from the point of view of the six internal-external sense-bases. And how, does a person fare along contemplating mental objects in mental objects from the point of view of the six internal-external sense-bases? (1) Herein, a person comprehends the eye and he comprehends material shapes, and he comprehends the fetter that arises dependent on both, and he comprehends the uprising of the fetter not arisen before, and he comprehends the getting rid of the fetter that has arisen, and he comprehends the non-uprising in the future of the fetter that has been got rid of. (2) And he comprehends the ear and he comprehends sounds, and he comprehends the fetter that arises dependent on both, and he comprehends the uprising of the fetter not arisen before, and he comprehends the getting rid of the fetter that has arisen, and he comprehends the non-uprising in the future of the fetter that has been got rid of. (3) And he comprehends the nose and he comprehends smells, and he comprehends the fetter that arises dependent on both, and he comprehends the uprising of the fetter not arisen before, and he comprehends the getting rid of the fetter that has arisen, and he comprehends the non-uprising in the future of the fetter that has been got rid of. (4) And he comprehends the tongue and he comprehends flavours, and he comprehends the fetter that arises dependent on both, and he comprehends the uprising of the fetter not arisen before, and he comprehends the getting rid of the fetter that has arisen, and he comprehends the non-uprising in the future of the fetter that has been got rid of. (5) And he comprehends the body and he comprehends tactile objects, and he comprehends the fetter that arises dependent on both, and he comprehends the uprising of the fetter not arisen before, and he comprehends the getting rid of the fetter that has arisen, and he comprehends the non-uprising in the future of the fetter that has been got rid of. (6) And he comprehends the mind and he comprehends mental objects, and he comprehends the fetter that arises dependent on both, and he comprehends the uprising of the fetter not arisen before, and he comprehends the getting rid of the fetter that has arisen, and he comprehends the non-uprising in the future of the fetter that has been got rid of.

It is thus that he fares along contemplating mental objects in mental objects internally, or he fares along contemplating mental objects in mental objects externally, or he fares along contemplating mental objects in mental objects internally and externally; or he fares along contemplating origination-things in mental objects, or he fares along contemplating dissolution-things in mental objects, or he fares along contemplating origination-things and dissolution-things in mental objects; or, thinking, 'There are mental objects,' his mindfulness is established precisely to the extent necessary just for knowledge, just for remembrance, and he fares along independently of and not grasping anything in the world. It is thus, that a person fares along contemplating mental objects in mental objects from the point of view of the six internal-external sense bases.

And again, companions, a noble person fares along contemplating mental objects in mental objects from the point of view of the seven links in awakening. And how, companions, does a noble person fare along contemplating mental objects in mental objects from the point of view of the seven links in awakening? (1) Herein, companions, when the link in awakening that is mindfulness is present internally he comprehends that he has internally the link in awakening that is mindfulness; when the link in awakening that is mindfulness is not internally present he comprehends that he has not internally the link in awakening that is mindfulness. And in so far as there is an uprising of the link in awakening that is mindfulness that had not uprisen before, he comprehends that; and in so far as there is completion by the mental development of the uprisen link in awakening that is mindfulness, he comprehends that. (2) When the link in awakening that is investigation of mental objects is present internally he comprehends that he has internally the link in awakening that is investigation of mental objects; when the link in awakening that is investigation of mental objects is not internally present he comprehends that he has not internally the link in awakening that is investigation of mental objects. And in so far as there is an uprising of the link in awakening that is investigation of mental objects that had not uprisen before, he comprehends that; and in so far as there is completion by the mental development of the uprisen link in awakening that is investigation of mental objects, he comprehends that. (3) When the link in awakening that is energy is present internally he comprehends that he has internally the link in awakening that is energy; when the link in awakening that is energy is not internally present he comprehends that he has not internally the link in awakening that is energy. And in so far as there is an uprising of the link in awakening that is energy that had not uprisen before, he comprehends that; and in so far as there is completion by the mental development of the uprisen link in awakening that is energy, he comprehends that. (4) When the link in awakening that is rapture is present internally he comprehends that he has internally the link in awakening that is rapture; when the link in awakening that is rapture is not internally present he comprehends that he has not internally the link in awakening that is rapture. And in so far as there is an uprising of the link in awakening that is rapture that had not uprisen before, he comprehends that; and in so far as there is completion by the mental development of the uprisen link in awakening that is rapture, he comprehends that. (5) When the link in awakening that is serenity is present internally he comprehends that he has internally the link in awakening that is serenity; when the link in awakening that is serenity is not internally present he comprehends that he has not internally the link in awakening that is serenity. And in so far as there is an uprising of the link in awakening that is serenity that had not uprisen before, he comprehends that; and in so far as there is completion by the mental development of the uprisen link in awakening that is serenity, he comprehends that. (6) When the link in awakening that is concentration is present internally he comprehends that he has internally the link in awakening that is concentration; when the link in awakening that is concentration is not internally present he comprehends that he has not internally the link in awakening that is concentration. And in so far as there is an uprising of the link in awakening that is concentration that had not uprisen before, he comprehends that; and in so far as there is completion by the mental development of the uprisen link in awakening that is concentration, he comprehends that. When the link in awakening that is concentration is present internally he comprehends that he has internally the link in awakening that is concentration; when the link in awakening that is concentration is not internally present he comprehends that he has not internally the link in awakening that is concentration. And in so far as there is an uprising of the link in awakening that is concentration that had not uprisen before, he comprehends that; and in so far as there is completion by the mental development of the uprisen link in awakening that is concentration, he comprehends that. (7) When the link in awakening that is equanimity is present internally one comprehends that he has the link in awakening that is equanimity; when the link in awakening that is equanimity is not present internally, one comprehends that one has not the link in awakening that is equanimity. And in so far as there is an uprising of the link in awakening that is equanimity that had not uprisen before, one comprehends that; and in so far as there is completion by mental development of the uprisen link in awakening that is equanimity, he comprehends that.

It is thus that he fares along contemplating mental objects in mental objects internally, or he fares along contemplating mental objects in mental objects externally, or he fares along contemplating mental objects in mental objects internally and externally; or he fares along contemplating origination-things in mental objects, or he fares along contemplating dissolution-things in mental objects, or he fares along contemplating origination-things and dissolution-things in mental objects; or, thinking, 'There are mental objects,' his mindfulness is established precisely to the extent necessary just for knowledge, just for remembrance, and he fares along independently of and not grasping anything in the world. It is thus, companions, that a person fares along contemplating mental objects in mental objects from the point of view of the seven links in awakening.

And again, companions, a noble person fares along contemplating mental objects in mental objects from the point of view of the four Ariyan truths. And how, companions, does a noble person fare along contemplating mental objects in mental objects from the point of view of the four Ariyan truths? Herein, companions, a noble person comprehends as it really is, 'This is anguish'; he comprehends as it really is, 'This is the arising of anguish'; he comprehends as it really is, 'This is the stopping of anguish'; he comprehends as it really is, 'This is the course leading to the stopping of anguish.'

It is thus that he fares along contemplating mental objects in mental objects internally, or he fares along contemplating mental objects in mental objects externally, or he fares along contemplating mental objects in mental objects internally and externally; or he fares along contemplating origination-things in mental objects, or he fares along contemplating dissolution-things in mental objects, or he fares along contemplating origination-things and dissolution-things in mental objects; or, thinking, 'There are mental objects,' his mindfulness is established precisely to the extent necessary just for knowledge, just for remembrance, and he fares along independently of and not grasping anything in the world. It is thus, friends, that a person fares along contemplating mental objects in mental objects from the point of view of the four Ariyan truths.

Whoever: Sotapanna and Sakadagami, companions, should thus develop these four applications of mindfulness for seven years, one of two fruits is to be expected for him: either profound knowledge here-now, or, if there is any residuum remaining, the state of non-returning. Companions, let be the seven years. Whoever, companions, should thus develop these four applications of mindfulness for six years, five years, four years, three years, two years, for one year, one of two fruits is to be expected for him: either profound knowledge here-now, or, if there is any residuum remaining, the state of non-returning. Companions, let be the one year. Whoever Sotapanna or Sakadagami, companions, should thus develop these four applications of mindfulness for seven months, one of two fruits is to be expected for him: either profound knowledge here now, or, if there is any residuum remaining, the state of non-returning. Companions, let be the seven months. Whoever, companions, should thus develop these four applications of mindfulness with efforts for six months, five months, four months, three months, two months, for one month, for half a month… Companions, let be the half month. Whoever Sotapanna or Sakadagami, companions, should thus develop these four applications of mindfulness for seven days, one of two fruits is to be expected for him: either profound knowledge here-now, or, if there is any residuum remaining, the state of non-returning.

What has been spoken in this way has been spoken in reference to this: 'There is this one way, companions, for the purification of beings, for the overcoming of sorrows and griefs, for the going down of sufferings and miseries, for winning the right path, for realising higher stages of Nibbāna, that is to say, the four applications of mindfulness."

Thus spoke the Lord. Delighted, these companions rejoiced in what the Lord had said.

Chapter 13

Middle Discourses 11: Cūḷasīhanādasutta

The Shorter Discourse on the Lion's Roar

A person who seeks Nibbana should only approach those who have gained Nibbana. Otherwise, it would make little or no sense to ask how to train to Nibbana from someone who hasn't experienced at least Sotapanna. A person cannot explain the path leading to Nibbana if they don't know what Nibbana is through personal experience. Applying reasoning and logic can aid you in distinguishing truth from what is not true.

Thus, those who seek Nibbana should approach four kinds of Buddha's direct disciples, and these four are none other than Sotapanna, Sakadagami, Anagami and Arahant. Those who gain Nibbana can publicly declare their attainment just as a lion's roar, especially if that benefits others, as otherwise, in the absence of the Noble Path, others may be lost in the Dhamma path following ignoble ways. Those who gain Nibbana can confirm that there are four stages of Nibbana when they have experienced these for themselves and that they have confidence in the supreme Buddha and supreme Dhamma. They know who the noble Sangha are and are confident in them and that they possess noble virtues. For those who gain Nibbana, it is easy to know who other noble ones are just by hearing how a person describes Dhamma. This is because just as 2+2 is 4, Dhamma should be described in the same way, irrespective of who describes it.

The purpose of following Buddha's Dhamma is to gain cessation. The purpose is not to live a spiritual lifestyle, meditate, engage in rituals or follow traditions. The purposes of Nibbana, medical science, and engineering differ. Although some illnesses can be shaped by karma, the purpose of medical science is to improve the quality of life and provide medication for physical illness. The purpose of engineering is to aid the construction of buildings. The purpose of Nibbana is to end samsara and improve the quality of this life and the afterlife based on universal functioning. This is not to say one thing is better than another, but to say the purpose of each differs. Knowing the difference, a person can avoid misunderstandings and can gain benefit from each.

If someone who follows a different spiritual path asks you how many goals you have in Buddha's spiritual path, you may respond by saying there is one goal.

The goal is cessation that abandons greed, hate, and delusion, and that is achieved through giving up grasping to conventions in the middle way across stages. The Noble Path is suitable for those who aspire to develop wisdom but not for those who prefer living with ignorance. Wisdom refers to wisdom to understand worldly experiences based on true life experience. Those who ignore awakening to true life experiences are more likely to experience mental pain. Those who aspire to abandon the mental pain, if they develop wisdom, they are more likely to make progress in the Noble Path. Thinking that they are practicing Dhamma, some spiritual practitioners tend to practice in the wrong way by grasping into views favoring continued existence. Not understanding how to end suffering, they grasp into various views that suggest there is continued existence. For them, there will be a continuing process of samsara, meaning the cycle of thoughts.

On the other hand, those who experience Nibbana understand four-fold Nibbana. Sometimes, when questioned, certain spiritual practitioners who pretend to know all about Nibbana answer others who are questioning regarding the practice leading to Nibbana without insight. There are a high number of spiritual practitioners, including those who claim to follow monastic rules, who happily break five precepts and fail to maintain at least the bare minimum. They pretend to know all about Nibbana when they have not gained an insight. Instead of developing honesty, some develop dishonesty even within monastic lives. Without knowing and experiencing Nibbana, some spiritual practitioners can act as if they know everything about Nibbana. They say that they know everything about Nibbana with confidence. However, they are unable to explain the noble path in full due to not knowing Nibbana through personal experience.

The limited explanation of Dhamma and partial explanations provided by ordinary people seem to have prevented many others from developing the right view of Dhamma. Some practitioners may say that you have to give up grasping to sensual pleasures through a sila-based path without describing that you have to give up grasping to self-view, rituals, and social practices before giving up grasping to sensual pleasures. Some practitioners may describe that you have to give up grasping sensual pleasures through a sila-based path, rituals, and social practices without describing that you have to give up grasping to self-view and concepts and theories related to self. Those who have not personally experienced universal ways of functioning; Nibbana, may not fully comprehend and appreciate the Triple Gem simply because they don't know how the Triple Gem and universal functioning are linked. Unless one experiences and knows it for oneself, one can have doubts, which is reasonable. Yet, those who have doubts and those who have not personally experienced Nibbana pretend to know all about Nibbana. If they grasp into their limited knowledge without seeking, keeping a space for new discoveries, they will likely not discover Nibbana. Not exploring, not discovering, both ordinary dhamma teachers and their followers are likely to continue in samsara. Not knowing the link between universal functioning and the Triple Gem, they tend to grasp into what they know; conventions. Thus, ordinary practitioners might not give importance to the Triple Gem, and this explains why some ordinary people talk about personal stories and various other subject matters during the time they allocate to dhamma talks. Some ordinary practitioners may give more importance to graduating, attending conferences, collecting and saving dana they received for personal use alone. They may appreciate honor and materials. That is not to say not to engage in graduating, attending conferences, etc. It is to say, maintain Dhamma in thoughts while doing these activities.

Maintaining Dhamma in thoughts/hearts meaning reduce greediness for self, others and the world; materials, pride, comparing one another, reducing pretense instead maintaining true self, without acting, without pretending to know Dhamma in full and without misinterpreting Dhamma as long as you have not gained Nibbana. Those who do not maintain Dhamma in their hearts but are grasping conventions are considered outsiders (not to discriminate or to say one category of people is more precious than another or to compare them but simply to clarify the Noble Path). In general, what can be said is that, to a greater extent, Dhamma and Vinaya are badly established among ordinary practitioners; Dhamma refers to Sotapanna to Arahant. Not knowing how the universe functions in full, an ordinary person may possess too much like and dislike for what they experience (i.e., feelings) through sensory information. What they experience through sensory information is interpreted based on conventions; the self is stable. I am supposed to experience only the good and bad with an underlying tendency to believe the self is stable. Given that the self does not remain stable and is subject to change, if someone thinks "self is a stable," it is an erroneous understanding. Instead, awakening to true life experience makes you come a step closer to Nibbana.

In this manner, when a person who is not enlightened attempts to describe the enlightenment, they cannot explain in full but explain in limited ways, and explain with errors or misinterpretations, they are unable to describe the practice leading to four-fold Nibbana in full. This confuses others, as one says one thing and another says another thing. In this manner, ordinary views and erroneous interpretations have prevented you from developing the right view, the Noble Path.

Yet, when Buddha appears, a state of wisdom, they clarify a path leading to Nibbana for you with reasoning. Then, if you follow the path, you will get to see the truth for yourself, and when you see the truth, you may reach unshakable confidence in Dhamma. Some say you have to practice jhanas, yet they don't know that jhanas happens after Sotapanna. Partial explanations are provided by those who have a limited vision of Dhamma, and they are still ordinary people. Lack of explanations leads to a lack of understanding among those who follow fellow ordinary teachers of Dhamma. In this manner, both dhamma teachers and the followers tend to become trapped in a cycle of misunderstanding of Dhamma despite years of practice. They are unable to develop the right view, Nibbana. Among those who have not gained four-fold Nibbana, you will find that they lack confidence in the Buddha, Dhamma, Savaka Sangha, and noble virtues. Their lack of confidence can be noticed through words; they ignore Buddha, speak different subject matter and personal stories, divide Dhamma, and misinterpret Dhamma or explain Dhamma in limited ways.

Among those who attempt to understand Buddha's Dhamma (four-fold Nibbana) through ordinary practitioners, sometimes you can see that some of the spiritual practitioners don't truly understand conventional and ultimate views; some may favor conventions, some may favor an ultimate view, meaning they may interpret these two views in different ways not knowing how to grasp to each but practicing a middle path based on life experience, just grasping to words, grasping to views; they are unable to escape mental suffering. They're greedy, hateful, delusional, craving, grasping, and ignorant. They favor and oppose, and they enjoy proliferation. They're not freed from rebirth, old age, and death, from sorrow.

"Thus have I heard:

At one time the Lord was staying near Sāvatthī in the Jeta Grove in Anāthapiṇḍika's monastery. While he was there, the Lord addressed the spiritual companions, saying:

"Companions."

"Revered sir," these companions answered the Lord in assent. The Lord spoke thus:

"Companions, thinking: 'Just here is a Sotapanna, here a second Sakadagami, here a third Anagami, here a fourth Arahant; void of recluses are other (systems teaching) alien views to that of Buddha's teachings; four-fold nibbana.' it is thus, companions, that you may rightly declare your attainment of four-fold nibbana in public; roar a lion's roar. But this situation occurs, companions, when wanderers belonging to other sects might herein speak thus:

'What confidence have the venerable ones, what authority, by reason of which the venerable ones speak thus:

"Just here is a recluse (Sotapanna), here a second recluse (Sakadagami), here a third recluse (Anagami), here a fourth recluse (Arahant); void of recluses are other (systems teaching) alien views?"'

Companions, if there are wanderers belonging to other sects who speak thus, they should be spoken to thus:

'It is because we see for ourselves four things, qualities a Sotapanna (and above) possesses, things that are made known to us by the Lord who knows, who sees, perfected one, fully self-awakened one, that we speak thus:

"Just here is a recluse (Sotapanna), here a second recluse (Sakadagami), here a third recluse (Anagami), here a fourth recluse (Arahant); void of recluses are other (systems teaching) alien views." "What are the four?"

Respected friends, we have experimented confidence in the supreme Buddha, we have confidence in *four-fold nibbana*, there is fulfilment of the noble virtues, and we have confidence in our fellow noble companions; Sotapanna to Arahant, they may come from any conventional background (householders, monks, men, women, old, young, any country, any age etc.). It is, your reverences, because of these four matters, made known to us by the Lord who knows, who sees, perfected one, fully self-awakened one, that we speak thus:

"Just here is a recluse (Sotapanna), here a second recluse (Sakadagami), here a third recluse (Anagami), here a fourth recluse (Arahant); void of recluses are other (systems teaching) alien views."

But this situation occurs, when wanderers belonging to other sects might speak thus:

'Your reverences, we too have confidence in that teacher of ours who is our teacher, and we have confidence in that *Dhamma* of ours which is our *Dhamma*, and we fulfil those which are our moral habits, and we have confidence in our fellow *Dhamma*-people coming from any conventional background (householders, monks, etc.) So, your reverences, what is the distinction, what the divergence, what the difference between you and us?'

Friends, if there are wanderers belonging to other sects who speak thus, they should be spoken to thus:

'But, your reverences, is the goal one or is the goal manifold?' Companions, if answering rightly wanderers belonging to other sects would answer thus:

'The goal is one, your reverences, the goal is not manifold.'

'But, your reverences, is this goal for one with attachment or for one without attachment?' Companions, if answering rightly wanderers belonging to other sects would answer: 'This goal is for one without attachment, this goal is not for one with attachment.'

'But, your reverences, is this goal for someone with aversion or for someone without aversion?' Monks, if answering rightly wanderers belonging to other sects would answer: 'This goal is for someone without aversion.'

'But, your reverences, is this goal for someone with confusion or for someone without confusion?' Companions, if answering rightly wanderers belonging to other sects would answer: 'This goal is for someone without confusion.'

'But, your reverences, is this goal for someone with craving or for someone without craving?' Companions, if answering rightly wanderers belonging to other sects would answer: 'This goal is for someone without craving.'

'But, your reverences, is this goal for someone with grasping or for someone without grasping?' Companions, if answering rightly wanderers belonging to other sects would answer: 'This goal is for someone without grasping.'

'But, your reverences, is this goal for someone who is intelligent or for someone who is unintelligent?' Companions, if answering rightly wanderers belonging to other sects would answer: 'This goal is for someone who is intelligent.'

'But, your reverences, is this goal for someone who is yielding and hindered or for someone who is unyielding and unhindered?' Companions, if answering rightly wanderers belonging to other sects would answer: 'This goal is for someone who is unyielding and unhindered.'

'But, your reverences, is this goal for someone with delight in impediments or for someone without delight in impediments?' Companions, if answering rightly wanderers belonging to other sects would answer thus:

'This goal is for someone who is without delight in impediments, not for someone with delight in impediments.'

Companions, there are these two views: view of becoming, and view of annihilation. Companions, whatever recluses and brahmans adhere to the view of becoming, have come under the view of becoming, cleave to the view of becoming, these are obstructed from the view of annihilation. Companions, whatever recluses and brahmans adhere to the view of annihilation, have come under the view of annihilation, cleave to the view of annihilation, these are obstructed from the view of becoming.

Companions, whatever recluses or brahmans do not comprehend as they really are the rise and fall of, and satisfaction in, and peril of these two views and the escape from them, these have attachment, these have aversion, these have confusion, these have craving, these have grasping, these are unintelligent, these are yielding and hindered, these delight in impediments, these are not utterly freed from birth, ageing, dying, grief, sorrow, suffering, lamentation, despair, these are not utterly freed from anguish, I say.

But whatever recluses or brahmans comprehend as they really are the rise and fall of, and the satisfaction in, and the peril of these two views and the escape from them, these are without attachment, these are without aversion, these are without confusion, these are without craving, these are without grasping, these are intelligent, these are unyielding and unhindered, these do not delight in impediments, these are utterly freed from birth, ageing dying, grief, sorrow, suffering, lamentation, despair, these are utterly freed from anguish, I say.

Companions, there are these four (kinds of) grasping. What are the four? The grasping of sense-pleasures, the grasping of view, the grasping of rule and custom, the grasping of the theory of self. There are some recluses and brahmans who, although pretending to a comprehension of all the graspings, do not lay down rightly a comprehension of all the graspings; they lay down a comprehension of the grasping of sense-pleasures, but do not lay down a comprehension of the grasping of view, of the grasping of rule and custom, of the grasping of the theory of self. What is the cause of this?

It is that these worthy recluses and brahmans do not understand three situations as they really are. Therefore these worthy recluses and brahmans, although pretending to a comprehension of all the graspings, do not lay down rightly a comprehension of all the graspings; they lay down a comprehension of the grasping of sense-pleasures, but do not lay down a comprehension of the grasping of view, do not lay down a comprehension of the grasping of rule and custom, do not lay down a comprehension of the grasping of the theory of self.

Companions, there are some recluses and brahmans who, although pretending to a comprehension of all the graspings, do not lay down rightly a comprehension of all the graspings; they lay down a comprehension of the grasping of sense-pleasures, they lay down a comprehension of the grasping of view, but they do not lay down a comprehension of the grasping of rule and custom, they do not lay down a comprehension of the grasping of the theory of self.

What is the cause of this? It is that these worthy recluses and brahmans do not comprehend two situations as they really are. Therefore these worthy recluses and brahmans, although pretending to a comprehension of all the graspings, do not rightly lay down a comprehension of all the graspings; they lay down a comprehension of the grasping of sense-pleasure, they lay down a comprehension of the grasping of view, they do not lay down the comprehension of the grasping of rule and custom, they do not lay down a comprehension of the grasping of the theory of self.

Companions, there are some recluses and brahmans who although pretending to a comprehension of all the graspings, do not lay down rightly a comprehension of all the graspings; they lay down a comprehension of the grasping of sense-pleasures, they lay down a comprehension of the grasping of view, they lay down a comprehension of the grasping of rule and custom, but they do not lay down a comprehension of the grasping of the theory of self. What is the cause of this? It is that these worthy recluses and brahmans do not understand one situation as it really is. Therefore these worthy recluses and brahmans, although pretending to a comprehension of all the graspings, do not rightly lay down a comprehension of all the graspings; they lay down a comprehension of the grasping of sense-pleasure, they lay down a comprehension of the grasping of view, they lay down a comprehension of the grasping of rule and custom, but they do not lay down a comprehension of the grasping of the theory of self.

In such a *Dhamma* and discipline as this, companions, that which is confidence in the Teacher is shown to be not perfect, that which is confidence in *Dhamma* is shown to be not perfect, that which is fulfilment of the moral habits is shown to be not perfect, that which is regard and affection for one's fellow *Dhamma*-men is shown to be not perfect.

What is the cause of this? It comes to be thus, companions, in a *Dhamma* and discipline that are wrongly shown, wrongly taught, not leading onwards, not conducive to allayment, taught by one who is not fully self-awakened.

But the Tathagata, companions, perfected one, fully self-awakened one, claiming a comprehension of all the graspings, rightly lays down a comprehension of all the graspings; he lays down a comprehension of the grasping of sense-pleasures, he lays down a comprehension of the grasping of view, he lays down a comprehension of the grasping of rule and custom, he lays down a comprehension of the grasping of the theory of self. In such a *Dhamma* and discipline meaning: Sotapanna to Arahant as this, monks, that which is confidence in the Buddha is shown to be perfect, that which is confidence in *four-fold nibbana* is shown to be perfect, that which is fulfilment of the noble virtues is shown to be perfect, that which is regard and affection for one's fellow *noble friends* is shown to be perfect.

What is the cause of this?

It comes to be thus, companions, in a *Dhamma* and discipline meaning Sotapanna to Arahant that are rightly shown, rightly taught, leading onwards, conducive to allayment, taught by one who is fully self-awakened.

Companions, what is the provenance, what the origin, what the birth, what the source of these four (kinds of) grasping? Craving, companions, is the provenance, craving is the origin, craving is the birth, craving is the source of these four (kinds of) grasping.

And what, companions, is the provenance, what the origin, what the birth, what the source of craving? Feeling, companions, is the provenance, feeling is the origin, feeling is the birth, feeling is the source of craving.

And what, companions, is the provenance, the origin, the birth, the source of feeling? Sensory impingement is the provenance, sensory impingement is the origin, sensory impingement is the birth, sensory impingement is the source of feeling.

And what, companions, is the provenance, the origin, the birth, the source of sensory impingement? The six bases of sensory impression, companions, is the provenance, the six bases of sensory impression is the origin, the six bases of sensory impression is the birth, the six bases of sensory impression is the source of sensory impingement.

And what, companions, is the provenance, the origin, the birth, the source of the six bases of sensory impression?

Name-and-form is the provenance, name-and-form is the origin, name-and-form is the birth, name-and-form is the source of the six bases of sensory impression.

And what, companions, is the provenance, the origin, the birth, the source of name-and-form?

Consciousness is the provenance, consciousness is the origin, consciousness is the birth, consciousness is the source of name-and-form.

And what, companions, is the provenance, the origin, the birth, the source of consciousness? The karma-formations, monks, are the provenance, the karma-formations are the origin, the karma-formations are the birth, the karma-formations are the source of consciousness.

And what, companions, is the provenance, the origin, the birth, the source of the karma-formations?

Ignorance, companions, is the provenance, ignorance is the origin, ignorance is the birth, ignorance is the source of the karma-formations.

When, companions, ignorance is got rid of by a person and knowledge has arisen, one, by the going down of ignorance, by the uprising of knowledge, neither grasps after the grasping of sense-pleasures, nor grasps after the grasping of view, nor grasp after the grasping of rule and custom, nor grasps after the theory of self.

Not grasping, one is not troubled; being untroubled he himself is individually attained to nibbana and he comprehends: 'Destroyed is birth, brought to a close is the Brahma-faring (completion of Arahant state), done is what was to be done, there is no more of being such or such.'"

Thus spoke the Lord. Delighted, these companions rejoiced in what the Lord had said."

Chapter 14

Middle Discourses 12: Mahāsīhanādasutta

The Longer Discourse on the Lion's Roar

There are only four kinds of Buddha's disciples. They become monks through universal ways of functioning, purifying grasping conventions in their thoughts and intentional actions.

One cannot receive monkhood from others. However, one can receive monkhood from self by letting go of grasping self-views and conventions, developing wisdom similar to that of Buddha (hence why take refuge in the universal Buddha, universal Dhamma, and universal Sangha) and blending with the universal ways. Those who are not universal monks are not the disciples of the Buddha. However, they are still practicing to become the disciples of the Buddha, outsiders. As they are outsiders, not having entered the Stream-entry, they don't completely understand what Nibbana is (Dhamma). They also don't understand Buddha and the practice leading to Nibbana in full. As they don't experience blissful Nibbana, their minds still cling to lower pleasures, blissful things in worldly life and living a lifestyle, meditations, materials, honors, cling to past self (they share personal stories, and cling to past events such as graduating ceremonies etc.).

Buddha possesses ten knowledges:
1. Knows what is possible and what is impossible.
2. Knows the result of intentional actions that have been undertaken– past, present, or future.
3. Knows the practices that lead to every state of being (desires; greed, hate, delusion).
4. Knows the world with its various and diverse features.
5. Knows the diverse characters of beings.
6. Knows the capacities and abilities (higher or lower state of the faculties) of other beings, other people.
7. Knows the impurity (mind state of grasping conventions), purity (Sotapanna to Arahant), the emergence from attainments, naturally occurring jhanas at the Anagami state leading to noble concentration; Arahantship.
8. Knows his numerous past lives – one life, two lives, three lives... a hundred lives... and their characteristics in detail.

9. With divine vision, which is pure and surpasses human vision, sees beings falling and appearing – inferior and superior, beautiful and ugly, in good places and bad places based on their karma (intentional actions).

10. Lives without mental attachment by personally experiencing four-fold Nibbana.

People think Buddha is someone who receives flowers and candles. However, a doormat, like a mind, can't see from the outside.

When Buddha knows and sees beyond the ordinary through wisdom, if someone says Buddha does not see such things, they are likely to collect demerits. The universal truth: four-fold Nibbana makes a person confident, and fearless with loving kindness for all. This is because in Noble Path, one does not hurt self or another. A person whose mind does not have greed, hate and delusion has heartfelt confidence based on the universal truth, four-fold Nibbana.

There are four kinds of truths about self-knowledge (and attainment) that Buddha possesses. He claims his place as leader, roars his lion's roar in assemblies, and sets the universal Dhamma wheel in motion. These four confidences include: Buddha is truly fully awakened and has given up the relevant fetters. The phenomena of what was declared by the Buddha as obstacles are truly obstacles. When Dhamma is taught to a wise ordinary person, it leads to abandon sufferings if a person gets to hear true Dhamma (four-fold Nibbana) beyond common ways and applies Dhamma ways within themselves.

Some say you can gain purity through jhanas. Some say you can gain purity through sila. Some say you can gain purity through lifestyle. Some say you can gain purity through dana, sila, or bavana. Then you might want to ask the question and find the answers to such as, among dana, what kind of dana generates the highest merits? Giving to Buddha and Arahants generates the highest merits. Among sila, what kind of sila generates the highest merits? The Ajivatthamaka Sila corresponds to the sila (morality) group of the Noble Eightfold Path and generates the highest merits. Among bavana, what can generate the highest wisdom and merits? Reflecting the qualities of the Triple Gem generates the highest merits and wisdom.

People seem to think following a tradition is a Dhamma. Yet Dhamma means Sotapanna to Arahant, the practice means reducing greed, hate and delusion by giving up grasping fetters (self view, doubts, ill will) across four stages, and the practice remains the same for all. A person who seeks Nibbana should only approach those who have gained Nibbana. Otherwise, it would make little or no sense to ask how to train to Nibbana from someone who hasn't experienced at least Sotapanna. A person cannot explain the path leading to Nibbana if they don't know what Nibbana is through personal experience. Applying reasoning and logic can aid you in distinguishing truth from what is not true.

Thus, those who seek Nibbana should approach four kinds of Buddha's direct disciples, and these four are none other than Sotapanna, Sakadagami, Anagami and Arahant. Those who gain Nibbana can publicly declare their attainment just as a lion's roar, especially if that benefits others, as otherwise, in the absence of the Noble Path, others may be lost in the Dhamma path following ignoble ways.

Those who gain Nibbana can confirm that there are four stages of Nibbana when they have experienced these for themselves and that they have confidence in the supreme Buddha and supreme Dhamma. They know who the noble Sangha are and are confident in them and that they possess noble virtues. For those who gain Nibbana, it is easy to know who other noble ones are just by hearing how a person describes Dhamma. This is because just as 2+2 is 4, Dhamma should be described in the same way, irrespective of who describes it.

The purpose of following Buddha's Dhamma is to gain Cessation. The goal is cessation that abandons greed, hate, and delusion, and that is achieved through giving up grasping to conventions in the middle way across stages.

Evidence based Nibbana involve testing life experience with evidence based on worldly experience through sensory information is at the core of Buddha's dhamma, four-fold Nibbana. Testing life experience involves figuring out life is an interaction between the universe and conventions. The purpose is to let go of mental pain, and if you continue to reduce desires, you may initially understand the idea that desires create mental pain, and if you reduce desires, your actual experience relevant to your life would indicate your suffering has reduced (the evidence). You can use evidence-based life experience to make progress in four-fold Nibbana. These components are useful;
1. What is the end goal of practicing Dhamma?

The goal is cessation that abandons greed, hate, and delusion, and that is achieved through giving up grasping to conventions in the middle way across stages.

2. What do you gain through four-fold Nibbana?
End of sufferings, end of cravings and fetters.

The purpose of Nibbana (Dhamma) is not to live a spiritual lifestyle, meditate, engage in rituals or follow traditions. The purposes of Nibbana, and science (medical science, and engineering, and so on) differ. Although some illnesses can be shaped by karma, the purpose of medical science is to improve the quality of life and provide medication for physical illness. The purpose of engineering is to aid the construction of buildings. The purpose of Nibbana is to end samsara and improve the quality of this life and the afterlife based on universal functioning. This is not to say one thing is better than another, but to say the purpose of each differs. Knowing the difference, a person can avoid misunderstandings and can gain benefit from each.

If someone who follows a different spiritual path asks you how many goals you have in Buddha's spiritual path, you may respond by saying there is one goal. The goal is cessation that abandons greed, hate, and delusion, and that is achieved through giving up grasping to conventions in the middle way across stages. The Noble Path is suitable for those who aspire to develop wisdom but not for those who prefer living with ignorance. Wisdom refers to wisdom to understand worldly experiences based on true life experience. Those who ignore awakening to true life experiences are more likely to experience mental pain. Those who aspire to abandon the mental pain, if they develop wisdom, they are more likely to make progress in the noble path. Thinking that they are practicing Dhamma, some spiritual practitioners tend to practice in the wrong way by grasping into views favoring continued existence. Not understanding how to end suffering, they grasp into various views that suggest there is continued existence. For them, there will be a continuing process of samsara, meaning the cycle of thoughts.

On the other hand, those who experience Nibbana understand four-fold Nibbana. Sometimes, when questioned, certain spiritual practitioners who pretend to know all about Nibbana answer others who are questioning regarding the practice leading to Nibbana without insight. There are a high number of spiritual practitioners, including those who claim to follow monastic rules, who happily break five precepts and fail to maintain at least the bare minimum. They pretend to know all about Nibbana when they have not gained an insight, and that's an example of they are breaking five precepts. Instead of developing honesty, some develop dishonesty even within monastic lives. Without knowing and experiencing Nibbana, some spiritual practitioners can act as if they know everything about Nibbana. They say that they know everything about Nibbana with confidence. However, they are unable to explain the Noble Path in full due to not knowing Nibbana through personal experience.

A person who gains four-fold Nibbana opens up their wisdom across stages. Wisdom is gained through meritorious activities and bending with universal ways.

"So I have heard. At one time the Buddha was staying outside the city of Vesālī in a woodland grove west of the town. Now at that time Sunakkhatta the Licchavi had recently left this teaching and training. He was telling a crowd in Vesālī:

"The ascetic Gotama has no superhuman distinction in knowledge and vision worthy of the noble ones. He teaches what he's worked out by logic, following a line of inquiry, expressing his own perspective. And his teaching leads those who practice it to the complete ending of suffering, the goal for which it's taught."

Then Arahant Sāriputta robed up in the morning and, taking his bowl and robe, entered Vesālī for alms. He heard what Sunakkhatta was saying. Then he wandered for alms in Vesālī. After the meal, on his return from almsround, he went to the Buddha, bowed, sat down to one side, and told him what had happened.

"Sāriputta, Sunakkhatta, that futile man, is angry. His words are spoken out of anger. Thinking he criticizes the Realized One, in fact he just praises him. For it is praise of the Realized One to say: 'His teaching leads those who practice it to the complete ending of suffering, the goal for which it's taught.' But there's no way Sunakkhatta will infer about me from the teaching: 'That Blessed One is perfected, a fully awakened Buddha, accomplished in knowledge and conduct, holy, knower of the world, supreme guide for those who wish to train, teacher of gods and humans, awakened, blessed.' And there's no way Sunakkhatta will infer about me from the teaching: 'That Blessed One wields the many kinds of psychic power: multiplying himself and becoming one again; appearing and disappearing; going unobstructed through a wall, a rampart, or a mountain as if through space; diving in and out of the earth as if it were water; walking on water as if it were earth; flying cross-legged through the sky like a bird; touching and stroking with the hand the sun and moon, so mighty and powerful; controlling the body as far as the realm of divinity.'

And there's no way Sunakkhatta will infer about me from the teaching: 'That Blessed One, with clairaudience that is purified and superhuman, hears both kinds of sounds, human and heavenly, whether near or far.'

And there's no way Sunakkhatta will infer about me from the teaching: 'That Blessed One understands the minds of other beings and individuals, having comprehended them with his own mind. He understands mind with greed as "mind with greed," and mind without greed as "mind without greed." He understands mind with hate … mind without hate … mind with delusion … mind without delusion … constricted mind … scattered mind … expansive mind … unexpansive mind … mind that is supreme … mind that is not supreme … mind immersed in samādhi … mind not immersed in samādhi … freed mind as "freed mind," and unfreed mind as "unfreed mind."'

There are these ten powers of a Realized One that the Realized One possesses. With these he claims the bull's place, roars his lion's roar in the assemblies, and turns the divine wheel. What ten?

Firstly, the Realized One truly understands the possible as possible, and the impossible as impossible. Since he truly understands this, this is a power of the Realized One. Relying on this he claims the bull's place, roars his lion's roar in the assemblies, and turns the divine wheel.

Furthermore, the Realized One truly understands the result of deeds undertaken in the past, future, and present in terms of grounds and causes. Since he truly understands this, this is a power of the Realized One. …

Furthermore, the Realized One truly understands where all paths of practice lead. Since he truly understands this, this is a power of the Realized One. …

Furthermore, the Realized One truly understands the world with its many and diverse elements. Since he truly understands this, this is a power of the Realized One. …

Furthermore, the Realized One truly understands the diverse convictions of sentient beings. Since he truly understands this, this is a power of the Realized One. …

Furthermore, the Realized One truly understands the faculties of other sentient beings and other individuals after comprehending them with his mind. Since he truly understands this, this is a power of the Realized One. …

Furthermore, the Realized One truly understands corruption, cleansing, and emergence regarding the absorptions, liberations, immersions, and attainments. Since he truly understands this, this is a power of the Realized One. …

Furthermore, the Realized One recollects many kinds of past lives. That is: one, two, three, four, five, ten, twenty, thirty, forty, fifty, a hundred, a thousand, a hundred thousand rebirths; many eons of the world contracting, many eons of the world expanding, many eons of the world contracting and expanding. He remembers: 'There, I was named this, my clan was that, I looked like this, and that was my food. This was how I felt pleasure and pain, and that was how my life ended. When I passed away from that place I was reborn somewhere else. There, too, I was named this, my clan was that, I looked like this, and that was my food. This was how I felt pleasure and pain, and that was how my life ended. When I passed away from that place I was reborn here.' And so he recollects his many kinds of past lives, with features and details. Since he truly understands this, this is a power of the Realized One. …

Furthermore, with clairvoyance that is purified and superhuman, the Realized One sees sentient beings passing away and being reborn—inferior and superior, beautiful and ugly, in a good place or a bad place. He understands how sentient beings are reborn according to their deeds. 'These dear beings did bad things by way of body, speech, and mind. They spoke ill of the noble ones; they had wrong view; and they chose to act out of that wrong view. When their body breaks up, after death, they're reborn in a place of loss, a bad place, the underworld, hell. These dear beings, however, did good things by way of body, speech, and mind. They never spoke ill of the noble ones; they had right view; and they chose to act out of that right view. When their body breaks up, after death, they're reborn in a good place, a heavenly realm.' And so, with clairvoyance that is purified and superhuman, he sees sentient beings passing away and being reborn—inferior and superior, beautiful and ugly, in a good place or a bad place. He understands how sentient beings are reborn according to their deeds. Since he truly understands this, this is a power of the Realized One. …

Furthermore, the Realized One has realized the undefiled freedom of heart and freedom by wisdom in this very life, and lives having realized it with his own insight due to the ending of defilements. Since he truly understands this, this is a power of the Realized One. Relying on this he claims the bull's place, roars his lion's roar in the assemblies, and turns the divine wheel.

A Realized One possesses these ten powers of a Realized One. With these he claims the bull's place, roars his lion's roar in the assemblies, and turns the divine wheel.

When I know and see in this way, suppose someone were to say this: 'The ascetic Gotama has no superhuman distinction in knowledge and vision worthy of the noble ones. He teaches what he's worked out by logic, following a line of inquiry, expressing his own perspective.' Unless they give up that speech and that thought, and let go of that view, they will be cast down to hell. Just as a person accomplished in noble ethics (Sotapanna), noble immersion (Anagami), and wisdom (Arahant) would reach enlightenment in this very life, such is the consequence, I say. Unless they give up that speech and that thought, and let go of that view, they will be cast down to hell.

Sāriputta, a Realized One has four kinds of self-assurance. With these he claims the bull's place, roars his lion's roar in the assemblies, and turns the divine wheel. What four?

I see no reason for anyone—whether ascetic, brahmin, god, Māra, or the Divinity, or anyone else in the world—to legitimately scold me, saying: 'You claim to be a fully awakened Buddha, but you don't understand these things.' Since I see no such reason, I live secure, fearless, and assured.

I see no reason for anyone—whether ascetic, brahmin, god, Māra, or the Divinity, or anyone else in the world—to legitimately scold me, saying: 'You claim to have ended all defilements, but you still have these defilements.' Since I see no such reason, I live secure, fearless, and assured.

I see no reason for anyone—whether ascetic, brahmin, god, Māra, or the Divinity, or anyone else in the world—to legitimately scold me, saying: 'The acts that you say are obstructions are not really obstructions for the one who performs them.' Since I see no such reason, I live secure, fearless, and assured.

I see no reason for anyone—whether ascetic, brahmin, god, Māra, or the Divinity, or anyone else in the world—to legitimately scold me, saying: 'The teaching doesn't lead those who practice it to the complete ending of suffering, the goal for which it is taught.' Since I see no such reason, I live secure, fearless, and assured.

A Realized One has these four kinds of self-assurance. With these he claims the bull's place, roars his lion's roar in the assemblies, and turns the divine wheel. When I know and see in this way, suppose someone were to say this: 'The ascetic Gotama has no superhuman distinction in knowledge and vision worthy of the noble ones …' Unless they give up that speech and that thought, and let go of that view, they will be cast down to hell.

Sāriputta, there are these eight assemblies. What eight? The assemblies of noble ones (Sotapanna to Anagami), brahmins (Arahant), conventional householders, and ascetics. An assembly of the gods of the four great kings. An assembly of the gods of the thirty-three. An assembly of Māras. An assembly of divinities. These are the eight assemblies. Possessing these four kinds of self-assurance, the Realized One approaches and enters right into these eight assemblies.

I recall having approached an assembly of hundreds of noble ones. There I used to sit with them, converse, and engage in discussion. But I don't see any reason to feel afraid or insecure. Since I see no such reason, I live secure, fearless, and assured.

I recall having approached an assembly of hundreds of brahmins (Arahants) … conventional householders … ascetics … the gods of the four great kings … the gods of the thirty-three … Māras … divinities. There too I used to sit with them, converse, and engage in discussion. But I don't see any reason to feel afraid or insecure. Since I see no such reason, I live secure, fearless, and assured.

When I know and see in this way, suppose someone were to say this: 'The ascetic Gotama has no superhuman distinction in knowledge and vision worthy of the noble ones …' Unless they give up that speech and that thought, and let go of that view, they will be cast down to hell.

Sāriputta, there are these four kinds of reproduction. What four? Reproduction for creatures born from an egg, from a womb, from moisture, or spontaneously.

And what is reproduction from an egg? There are beings who are born by breaking out of an eggshell. This is called reproduction from an egg. And what is reproduction from a womb? There are beings who are born by breaking out of the amniotic sac. This is called reproduction from a womb. And what is reproduction from moisture? There are beings who are born in a rotten fish, in a rotten carcass, in rotten dough, in a cesspool or a sump. This is called reproduction from moisture. And what is spontaneous reproduction? Gods, hell-beings, certain humans, and certain beings in the lower realms. This is called spontaneous reproduction. These are the four kinds of reproduction.

When I know and see in this way, suppose someone were to say this: 'The ascetic Gotama has no superhuman distinction in knowledge and vision worthy of the noble ones …' Unless they give up that speech and that thought, and let go of that view, they will be cast down to hell.

There are these five destinations. What five? Hell, the animal realm, the ghost realm, humanity, and the gods.

I understand hell, and the path and practice that leads to hell. And I understand how someone practicing that way, when their body breaks up, after death, is reborn in a place of loss, a bad place, the underworld, hell. I understand the animal realm … the ghost realm … humanity … gods, and the path and practice that leads to the world of the gods.

And I understand how someone practicing that way, when their body breaks up, after death, is reborn in a good place, a heavenly realm. And I understand extinguishment, and the path and practice that leads to extinguishment. And I understand how someone practicing that way realizes the undefiled freedom of heart and freedom by wisdom in this very life, and lives having realized it with their own insight due to the ending of defilements.

When I've comprehended the mind of a certain person, I understand: 'This person is practicing in such a way and has entered such a path that when their body breaks up, after death, they will be reborn in a place of loss, a bad place, the underworld, hell.'

Some time later I see that they have indeed been reborn in hell, where they experience exclusively painful feelings, sharp and severe. Suppose there was a pit of glowing coals deeper than a man's height, full of glowing coals that neither flamed nor smoked. Then along comes a person struggling in the oppressive heat, weary, thirsty, and parched. And they have set out on a path that meets with that same pit of coals. If a person with clear eyes saw them, they'd say: 'This person is proceeding in such a way and has entered such a path that they will arrive at that very pit of coals.' Some time later they see that they have indeed fallen into that pit of coals, where they experience exclusively painful feelings, sharp and severe. …

When I've comprehended the mind of a certain person, I understand: 'This person … will be reborn in the animal realm.' Some time later I see that they have indeed been reborn in the animal realm, where they suffer painful feelings, sharp and severe. Suppose there was a sewer deeper than a man's height, full to the brim with feces.

Then along comes a person struggling in the oppressive heat, weary, thirsty, and parched. And they have set out on a path that meets with that same sewer. If a person with clear eyes saw them, they'd say: 'This person is proceeding in such a way and has entered such a path that they will arrive at that very sewer.' Some time later they see that they have indeed fallen into that sewer, where they suffer painful feelings, sharp and severe. …

When I've comprehended the mind of a certain person, I understand: 'This person … will be reborn in the ghost realm.' Some time later I see that they have indeed been reborn in the ghost realm, where they experience mostly painful feelings. Suppose there was a tree growing on rugged ground, with thin foliage casting dappled shade.

Then along comes a person struggling in the oppressive heat, weary, thirsty, and parched. And they have set out on a path that meets with that same tree. If a person with clear eyes saw them, they'd say: 'This person is proceeding in such a way and has entered such a path that they will arrive at that very tree.' Some time later they see them sitting or lying under that tree, where they experience mostly painful feelings. …

When I've comprehended the mind of a certain person, I understand: 'This person … will be reborn among human beings.' Some time later I see that they have indeed been reborn among human beings, where they experience mostly pleasant feelings. Suppose there was a tree growing on smooth ground, with abundant foliage casting dense shade.

Then along comes a person struggling in the oppressive heat, weary, thirsty, and parched. And they have set out on a path that meets with that same tree. If a person with clear eyes saw them, they'd say: 'This person is proceeding in such a way and has entered such a path that they will arrive at that very tree.' Some time later they see them sitting or lying under that tree, where they experience mostly pleasant feelings. …

When I've comprehended the mind of a certain person, I understand: 'This person … will be reborn in a good place, a heavenly realm.' Some time later I see that they have indeed been reborn in a heavenly realm, where they experience exclusively pleasant feelings. Suppose there was a stilt longhouse with a peaked roof, plastered inside and out, draft-free, with door fastened and window shuttered. And it had a couch spread with woolen covers—shag-piled, pure white, or embroidered with flowers—and spread with a fine deer hide, with a canopy above and red pillows at both ends.

Then along comes a person struggling in the oppressive heat, weary, thirsty, and parched. And they have set out on a path that meets with that same stilt longhouse. If a person with clear eyes saw them, they'd say: 'This person is proceeding in such a way and has entered such a path that they will arrive at that very stilt longhouse.' Some time later they see them sitting or lying in that stilt longhouse, where they experience exclusively pleasant feelings. …

When I've comprehended the mind of a certain person, I understand: 'This person is practicing in such a way and has entered such a path that they will realize the undefiled freedom of heart and freedom by wisdom in this very life, and live having realized it with their own insight due to the ending of defilements.' Some time later I see that they have indeed realized the undefiled freedom of heart and freedom by wisdom in this very life, and live having realized it with their own insight due to the ending of defilements, experiencing exclusively pleasant feelings. Suppose there was a lotus pond with clear, sweet, cool water, clean, with smooth banks, delightful. Nearby was a dense forest grove.

Then along comes a person struggling in the oppressive heat, weary, thirsty, and parched. And they have set out on a path that meets with that same lotus pond. If a person with clear eyes saw them, they'd say: 'This person is proceeding in such a way and has entered such a path that they will arrive at that very lotus pond.'

Some time later they would see that person after they had plunged into that lotus pond, bathed and drunk. When all their stress, weariness, and heat exhaustion had faded away, they emerged and sat or lay down in that woodland thicket, where they experienced exclusively pleasant feelings.

In the same way, when I've comprehended the mind of a person, I understand: 'This person is practicing in such a way and has entered such a path that they will realize the undefiled freedom of heart and freedom by wisdom in this very life, and live having realized it with their own insight due to the ending of defilements.' Some time later I see that they have indeed realized the undefiled freedom of heart and freedom by wisdom in this very life, and live having realized it with their own insight due to the ending of defilements, experiencing exclusively pleasant feelings. These are the five destinations.

When I know and see in this way, suppose someone were to say this: 'The ascetic Gotama has no superhuman distinction in knowledge and vision worthy of the noble ones. He teaches what he's worked out by logic, following a line of inquiry, expressing his own perspective.' Unless they give up that speech and that thought, and let go of that view, they will be cast down to hell.

Just as a person accomplished in noble ethics, noble immersion, and noble wisdom would reach enlightenment in this very life, such is the consequence, I say. Unless they give up that speech and that thought, and let go of that view, they will be cast down to hell.

Sāriputta, I recall having practiced a spiritual path consisting of four factors. I used to be a fervent mortifier, the ultimate fervent mortifier. I used to live rough, the ultimate rough-liver. I used to live in disgust of sin, the ultimate one living in disgust of sin. I used to be secluded, in ultimate seclusion.

And this is what my fervent mortification was like. I went naked, ignoring conventions. I licked my hands, and didn't come or stop when asked. I didn't consent to food brought to me, or food prepared specially for me, or an invitation for a meal. I didn't receive anything from a pot or bowl; or from someone who keeps sheep, or who has a weapon or a shovel in their home; or where a couple is eating; or where there is a woman who is pregnant, breastfeeding, or who has a man in her home; or where food for distribution is advertised; or where there's a dog waiting or flies buzzing. I accepted no fish or meat or liquor or wine, and drank no beer. I went to just one house for alms, taking just one mouthful, or two houses and two mouthfuls, up to seven houses and seven mouthfuls. I fed on one saucer a day, two saucers a day, up to seven saucers a day. I ate once a day, once every second day, up to once a week, and so on, even up to once a fortnight. I lived committed to the practice of eating food at set intervals.

I ate herbs, millet, wild rice, poor rice, water lettuce, rice bran, scum from boiling rice, sesame flour, grass, or cow dung. I survived on forest roots and fruits, or eating fallen fruit. I wore robes of sunn hemp, mixed hemp, corpse-wrapping cloth, rags, lodh tree bark, antelope hide (whole or in strips), kusa grass, bark, wood-chips, human hair, horse-tail hair, or owls' wings. I tore out hair and beard, committed to this practice.

I constantly stood, refusing seats. I squatted, committed to the endeavor of squatting. I lay on a mat of thorns, making a mat of thorns my bed. I was devoted to ritual bathing three times a day, including the evening. And so I lived committed to practicing these various ways of mortifying and tormenting the body.

Such was my practice of fervent mortification. And this is what my rough living was like. The dust and dirt built up on my body over many years until it started flaking off.

It's like the trunk of a pale-moon ebony tree, which builds up bark over many years until it starts flaking off. But it didn't occur to me: 'Oh, this dust and dirt must be rubbed off by my hand or another's.' That didn't occur to me. Such was my rough living. And this is what my living in disgust of sin was like.

I'd step forward or back ever so mindfully, so I was full of pity regarding even a drop of water, thinking: 'May I not injure any little creatures on unclear ground.' Such was my living in disgust of sin.

And this is what my seclusion was like. I would plunge deep into a wilderness region and stay there. When I saw a cowherd or a shepherd, or someone gathering grass or sticks, or a lumberjack, I'd flee from forest to forest, from thicket to thicket, from valley to valley, from uplands to uplands. Why is that? So that I wouldn't see them, nor they me. I fled like a wild deer seeing a human being. Such was my practice of seclusion. I would go on all fours into the cow-pens after the cattle had left and eat the dung of the young suckling calves. As long as my own urine and excrement lasted, I would even eat that. Such was my eating of most unnatural things.

I would plunge deep into an awe-inspiring forest grove and stay there. It was so awe-inspiring that normally it would make your hair stand on end if you weren't free of greed. And on days such as the cold spell when the snow falls in the January winter, I stayed in the open by night and in the forest by day. But in the last month of summer I'd stay in the open by day and in the forest by night. And then these verses, which were neither supernaturally inspired, nor learned before in the past, occurred to me: 'Scorched and frozen, alone in the awe-inspiring forest. Naked, no fire to sit beside, the sage still pursues his quest.'

I would make my bed in a charnel ground, with the bones of the dead for a pillow. Then village louts would come up to me. They'd spit and piss on me, throw mud on me, even poke sticks in my ears. But I don't recall ever having a bad thought about them. Such was my abiding in equanimity.

There are some ascetics and brahmins who have this doctrine and view: 'Purity comes from food.' They say: 'Let's live on jujubes.' So they eat jujubes and jujube powder, and drink jujube juice. And they enjoy many jujube concoctions. I recall eating just a single jujube. You might think that at that time the jujubes must have been very big. But you should not see it like this.

The jujubes then were at most the same size as today. Eating so very little, my body became extremely emaciated. Due to eating so little, my major and minor limbs became like the joints of an eighty-year-old or a dying man, my bottom became like a camel's hoof, my vertebrae stuck out like beads on a string, and my ribs were as gaunt as the broken-down rafters on an old barn. Due to eating so little, the gleam of my eyes sank deep in their sockets, like the gleam of water sunk deep down a well. Due to eating so little, my scalp shriveled and withered like a green bitter-gourd in the wind and sun. Due to eating so little, the skin of my belly stuck to my backbone, so that when I tried to rub the skin of my belly I grabbed my backbone, and when I tried to rub my backbone I rubbed the skin of my belly.

Due to eating so little, when I tried to urinate or defecate I fell face down right there. Due to eating so little, when I tried to relieve my body by rubbing my limbs with my hands, the hair, rotted at its roots, fell out.

There are some ascetics and brahmins who have this doctrine and view: 'Purity comes from food.' They say: 'Let's live on mung beans.' … 'Let's live on sesame.' … 'Let's live on ordinary rice.' … Due to eating so little, when I tried to relieve my body by rubbing my limbs with my hands, the hair, rotted at its roots, fell out.

But Sāriputta, I did not achieve any superhuman distinction in knowledge and vision worthy of the noble ones by that conduct, that practice, that grueling work. Why is that? Because I didn't achieve that noble wisdom that's noble and emancipating, and which delivers one who practices it to the complete ending of suffering.

There are some ascetics and contemplatives who have this doctrine and view: 'Purity comes from transmigration.' But it's not easy to find a realm that I haven't previously transmigrated to in all this long time, except for the gods of the pure abodes. For if I had transmigrated to the gods of the pure abodes I would not have returned to this realm again.

There are some ascetics and contemplatives who have this doctrine and view: 'Purity comes from rebirth.' But it's not easy to find any rebirth that I haven't previously been reborn in …

There are some ascetics and contemplatives who have this doctrine and view: 'Purity comes from abode of rebirth.' But it's not easy to find an abode where I haven't previously abided …

There are some ascetics and contemplatives who have this doctrine and view: 'Purity comes from sacrifice.' But it's not easy to find a sacrifice that I haven't previously offered in all this long time, when I was an anointed aristocratic king or a well-to-do brahmin.

There are some ascetics and contemplatives who have this doctrine and view: 'Purity comes from serving the sacred flame.' But it's not easy to find a fire that I haven't previously served in all this long time, when I was an anointed aristocratic king or a well-to-do brahmin.

There are some ascetics and contemplatives who have this doctrine and view: 'So long as this gentleman is youthful, young, with pristine black hair, blessed with youth, in the prime of life he will be endowed with perfect lucidity of wisdom.

But when he's old, elderly, and senior, advanced in years, and has reached the final stage of life—eighty, ninety, or a hundred years old—he will lose his lucidity of wisdom.' But you should not see it like this. For now I am old, elderly, and senior, I'm advanced in years, and have reached the final stage of life. I am eighty years old. Suppose I had four disciples with a lifespan of a hundred years. And they each were perfect in memory, range, retention, and perfect lucidity of wisdom.

Imagine how easily a well-trained expert archer with a strong bow would shoot a light arrow across the shadow of a palm tree. That's how extraordinary they were in memory, range, retention, and perfect lucidity of wisdom.

They'd bring up questions about the reflecting four kinds of mindfulness again and again, and I would answer each question. They'd remember the answers and not ask the same question twice. And they'd pause only to eat and drink, go to the toilet, and sleep to dispel weariness.

But the Realized One would not run out of Dhamma teachings, words and phrases of the teachings, or spontaneous answers. And at the end of a hundred years my four disciples would pass away. Even if you have to carry me around on a stretcher, there will never be any deterioration in the Realized One's lucidity of wisdom.

And if there's anyone of whom it may be rightly said that a being not liable to delusion has arisen in the world for the welfare and happiness of the people, out of sympathy for the world, for the benefit, welfare, and happiness of gods and humans, it's of me that this should be said."

Now at that time Nāgasamāla was standing behind the Buddha fanning him. Then he said to the Buddha:

"It's incredible, sir, it's amazing! While I was listening to this exposition of the teaching my hair stood up! What is the name of this exposition of the teaching?"

"Well then, Nāgasamāla, you may remember this exposition of the teaching as 'The Hair-raising Discourse'." That is what the Buddha said. Satisfied, Venerable Nāgasamāla approved what the Buddha said.

Chapter 15

Middle Discourses 13: Mahādukkhakkhandhasutta

The Longer Discourse on the Mass of Suffering

It is not possible for those who have not experienced Nibbana to instruct another person to gain Nibbana. A person with integrity would not describe a path to Nibbana before at least becoming a Sotapanna. However, they may explain what's commonly known as keeping a space to discover for self and encouraging others to keep a space to discover Nibbana without grasping to existing knowledge, as keeping a space to grow in new knowledge allows a person to transform to higher knowledge across four-fold Nibbana. Buddha has tried many ways, such as extreme asceticism and jhanas through concentration with effort and comforts but didn't find Nibbana in such ways. Rejecting both, Buddha established the middle way.

The words of the Buddha that provide the path to Nibbana, Buddhahood gained through immeasurable scarifies, and completion of Paramis for the wellbeing of many, the route to escape samsara, and blocking the path by misinterpreting Dhamma can prevent Nibbana for such bhikkhus and many attendees.

Throughout history, you can find many occasions when bhikkhus misinterpret Dhamma. Not exploring but merely ignoring, people just go in circles again and again without gaining Nibbana. If anyone thinks they are worth listening to, they will block their chances of gaining Nibbana.

For those who seek universal Dhamma: Nibbana as taught by the Buddha, it's crucial for them to distinguish between what is Buddha's rare universal dhamma and what is made up as Dhamma by some ordinary Sanga and labeled as Buddha's Dhamma merely through conventions. In this world, without considering whether they are teachers, those who guide them to a spiritual path talk about the practice leading to Nibbana based on personal experience, whether they have gained Nibbana for themselves before speaking about the path. Some people can follow a spiritual path with ignorance. By applying reason, if you ask yourself; how anyone can be 100% sure of what one says unless one has gained Nibbana, it will become obvious that it is not possible to clarify a practice without having gained Nibbana. Then allow a bit space for yourself to discover new things without grasping to existing knowledge, allowing yourself to develop new knowledge and to seek truth that is universally applicable to all.

Among spiritual companions, there may be those who are happy to follow a made-up version of dhamma by ordinary Sangha. Respecting personal choice is dhamma, as respecting other 's choices is a matter related to dignity, and ethics. Dhamma (Sotapanna to Arahant) can only be understood subject to one's wisdom[14]. Every person is entitled to make their own choices. At the same time, speaking truth is dhamma. Speaking the truth because of made-up dhamma by ordinary Sangha over centuries, either with good intentions, bad intentions, or neither, among those spiritual practitioners, those who are genuinely seeking Buddha's Dhamma have been prevented from developing the right vision, understanding the path leading to universally applicable four-fold Nibbana.

Arahants can be like door mats. They can do things that an ordinary person may struggle to do due to grasp to self-view and conventions. Instead of becoming a king, asking for respect and materials, Buddha walked miles just to provide Nibbana, stable peace, to many.

Arahants provide higher merits, higher Dhamma, higher respect to others beyond socially accepted standards. One way to recognize an Arahant is by analyzing the words that the Arahant says. Arahants don't divide the universally applicable teachings. One way to recognize noble disciples is that they explain Nibbana as a universal teaching applicable for all with reason.

The ordinary state is characterized by an ongoing cycle of worldly experiences, such as sadness and happiness in cycles. The intentional action of a Sotapanna carries dhamma actions; reducing efforts to grasp conventions, fulfilling responsibilities to others, and not worrying excessively about bad things in self,

---

[14] See Dhp 11 & 12: "…The two Chief Disciples then related to the Buddha how they went to the Giragga festival, the meeting with arahant Assaji and their attainment of Sotapatti Fruition. They also told the Buddha about their former teacher Sanjaya, who refused to accompany them. Sanjaya had said, "Having been a teacher to so many pupils, for me to become his pupil would be like a jar turning into a drinking cup. Besides, only few people are wise and the majority are foolish; let the wise go to the wise Gotama, the foolish would still come to me. Go your way, my pupils."

others and the world. While you are an ordinary, you may develop a Dhamma doing similar to that of a Sotapanna within your lifestyle.

At Sotapanna and Sakadagami states, one doesn't become a monk created by the universal functioning and karma due to retaining sensual pleasures; instead, one remains a very happy householder, At the Anagami state, one comes to realize that one is free from the ill will and sensual pleasures. Thereafter, at the Arahant stage, one does not like or dislike things.

Food is simply for the survival of residuals. Dress and accommodations are simply to protect residuals. Without liking or disliking worldly experiences, whatever one does and every thought of an Arahant functions simply to provide Nibbana for those who seek it, a monk in universal making. Self-declaration is simply for sharing merits, and Nibbana is for those who seek it. Arahants don't grasp into tradition, rituals, divisions, lifestyles, or conventions, and they don't divide beings; they don't undermine others, ask for respect, material or honor but simply share what they have with others. When you are in the dark, and you've found a light that diminish darkness, you pass it on to others simply so that they can diminish their darkness to find light for themselves within.

Since birth, if you've experienced worldly life, you've developed likes and dislikes based on your experiences coming from sensory experiences, and, during the process, you've noticed that all that you like and dislike don't come as you wish, and you've experienced frustration and a lack of happiness that made you seek more ways to find happiness. You might have heard of a practice of Dhamma, and you've practiced in many ways and might have gained some sort of temporary relief through certain practices (meditation, jhanas etc.). Yet, if you still experience dissatisfaction and frustrations in worldly life, you may want to seek genuine Nibbana that gives you stable peace. By trying to discover yourself, come to know all about you, your good qualities, bad qualities without hiding such things from you. Try to purify self-meaning letting go of the mental attachment to self-view and conventions and develop the Noble Path. By associating with those who have given up fetters, integrating Triple Gem, listening to Dhamma from Arahants, and receiving guidance and merits from those who do not undermine your potential for gaining Nibbana but those who treat you with immense respect despite your conventional background, you can develop the Noble Path that will allow you to discover self, freedom from conventional life experience.

Sensual pleasures in the Noble Path refer to information coming from sensory experiences. Desiring sensual pleasures causes mental suffering. People tend to experience difficulties when engaged in livelihood because of sensual pleasures. People engage in fights for sensual pleasures. People tend to do bad deeds in mind, body and speech because of sensual pleasures. Worldly pleasures don't stay long, and worldly pleasures turn into displeasures. As pleasures turn to displeasure, people may experience distress and suffering on an ongoing basis. People who endured too many displeasures due to changing pleasures may seek a way to escape the changing nature of pleasures that come from worldly life experiences. By understanding, a person can escape suffering. Anagami comes to give up sensual pleasures. Four-fold Nibbana is not a sila-based path but a wisdom and merit-based path. Thus, Nibbana is a happening. For those who have not experienced Nibbana, it is not possible for them to instruct another person to gain Nibbana.

There is a strong link between the Triple Gem and Nibbana, and during the times there is an absence of genuine Triple Gem, looks like Triple Gem comes to appear and prevent Nibbana for many. When seeds of flowering trees are planted, flowers only blossoms during short period. Same way, when the wheel of Dhamma, Sasana is established, Arahant appear during certain time periods. Whoever cares, respect the Triple Gem, reduce grasping to conventions (rituals, divisions lifestyles etc.) by seeing the universal teachings, they come a step closer to gaining Nibbana.

Buddha is the knower of all worlds. There are five modes of birth: hell, human realm, animal realm and so on. People are born into random paces at random times. The universe functions in such a way that, when a person is born, birth brings death. Illnesses, losses, gains, falls and rises are part of life, the way of life. Once born, people can do many things and make certain choices that helps them to refine the quality of living, improve lives and their karma. You may engage in developing wholesome deeds to develop merits and wisdom;

1. Dana: There are many ways a person can give dana; giving material, giving non materials; skills, efforts, time, words of friendship and words of wisdom, etc.

Among all "Dana", giving Sotapanna to Arahant brings an end to your worldly suffering, it is the dana that Arahants gift to you. Among the laws, there are certain ways of universal functioning; one of the orders which operate in the universe is that rice is produced from rice-seed, sugary taste from sugar-cane, Sotapanna to Arahant is produced from those who gained Nibbana and bear the fruition of Nibbana.

Among the laws, certain ways of universal functioning, and one of the orders which operate in the universe is that intentional actions produce corresponding consequences; when you start a practice of reducing clinging to conventions, as a consequence, your mental pain will subside. Among the laws, certain ways of universal functioning, and one of the orders that operate in the universe is that intentional actions produce corresponding consequences; when you establish a friendship and offer "Dana" (your time, your skills, your friendship, materials, non-materials) to those who have given up mental attachment to Ten fetters, as a consequence, your mental attachment to fetters disappears, and your mental pain will subside.

2. Sila: There are many ways a person can take silas, taking noble precepts - Ajivatthamaka Sila (Eight Precepts with Right Livelihood as the Eighth) can contribute to enhance your merits and wisdom.

3. Meditation: There are many ways you can meditate, reflecting the qualities of Triple Gem and analysing the causes for your thoughts can contribute to enhance your merits and wisdom.

4. Respect Triple Gem: Triple Gem meaning those who have given up mental attachment to fetters.

For those who aspire to Nibbana, it is of benefit to them not to neglect or disrespect the Triple Gem (Buddha's footprint seen among Sotapanna to Arahant) or prevent others from progressing to the Noble path by dividing the universal teachings because in doing so, they will be taking a step away from Nibbana, and their potential for gaining Nibbana can be affected.

Likelihood of conventional bhikkhu/Sangha misinterpreting Dhamma is high, misinterpretations have prevented Nibbana. There are both look alike and genuine Triple Gem. Look alike Triple Gem can misinterpret Dhamma. Whoever cares, respect the Triple Gem, reduce grasping to conventions (rituals, divisions lifestyles etc.) by seeing the universal teachings, they come a step closer to gaining universal happening; four-fold Nibbana.

5. Pay homage to Buddha and Arahant's places, take care of such places, etc. (i.e., temples etc.)
6. Transfer of merits to others, contribute to other's well-being as the way you can, and fulfilling responsibilities towards others.

7. Rejoicing (accepting or participating) in other's merits, maintaining good thoughts about others, avoiding bad thoughts about others, being happy for their well-being, when they progress in what they do and what they want to achieve, and so on.
8. Hearing Dhamma from Arahants.
9. Teaching Dhamma to others once after gaining at least Sotapanna.
10. Correcting one's wrong views about Nibbana, giving up grasping to conventions and giving up mental attachment to fetters (Conventions; self-view, social practices, and rituals etc.)

"So I have heard. At one time the Buddha was staying near Sāvatthī in Jeta's Grove, Anāthapiṇḍika's monastery.

Then several spiritual companions dressed up in the morning and, taking their bowls and robes, entered Sāvatthī for alms. Then it occurred to them, "It's too early to wander for alms in Sāvatthī. Why don't we visit the monastery of the wanderers of other religions?"

Then they went to the monastery of the wanderers of other religions and exchanged greetings with the wanderers there. When the greetings and polite conversation were over, they sat down to one side. The wanderers said to them:

"Reverends, the ascetic Gotama advocates the complete understanding of sensual pleasures, and so do we. The ascetic Gotama advocates the complete understanding of forms, and so do we.

The ascetic Gotama advocates the complete understanding of feelings, and so do we. What, then, is the difference between the ascetic Gotama's teaching and instruction and ours?"

Those companions neither approved nor dismissed that statement of the wanderers of other religions. They got up from their seat, thinking, "We will learn the meaning of this statement from the Buddha himself."

Then, after the meal, when they returned from almsround, they went up to the Buddha, bowed, sat down to one side, and told him what had happened. The Buddha said:

"Companions, when wanderers of other religions say this, you should say to them: 'But reverends, what's the gratification, the drawback, and the escape when it comes to sensual pleasures? What's the gratification, the drawback, and the escape when it comes to forms? What's the gratification, the drawback, and the escape when it comes to feelings?' Questioned like this, the wanderers of other religions would be stumped, and, in addition, would get frustrated.

Why is that? Because they're out of their element. I don't see anyone in this world—with its gods, Māras, and Divinities, this population with its ascetics and brahmins, its gods and humans—who could provide a satisfying answer to these questions except for the Realized One or his disciple or someone who has heard it from them.

And what is the gratification of sensual pleasures? There are these five kinds of sensual stimulation. What five? Sights known by the eye, which are likable, desirable, agreeable, pleasant, sensual, and arousing. Sounds known by the ear … Smells known by the nose … Tastes known by the tongue … Touches known by the body, which are likable, desirable, agreeable, pleasant, sensual, and arousing.

These are the five kinds of sensual stimulation. The pleasure and happiness that arise from these five kinds of sensual stimulation: this is the gratification of sensual pleasures.

And what is the drawback of sensual pleasures? It's when a gentleman earns a living by means such as arithmetic, accounting, calculating, farming, trade, raising cattle, archery, government service, or one of the professions. But they must face cold and heat, being hurt by the touch of flies, mosquitoes, wind, sun, and reptiles, and risking death from hunger and thirst. This is a drawback of sensual pleasures apparent in the present life, a mass of suffering caused by sensual pleasures.

That gentleman might try hard, strive, and make an effort, but fail to earn any money. If this happens, they sorrow and wail and lament, beating their breast and falling into confusion, saying: 'Oh, my hard work is wasted. My efforts are fruitless!' This too is a drawback of sensual pleasures apparent in the present life, a mass of suffering caused by sensual pleasures.

That gentleman might try hard, strive, and make an effort, and succeed in earning money. But they experience pain and sadness when they try to protect it, thinking: 'How can I prevent my wealth from being taken by rulers or bandits, consumed by fire, swept away by flood, or taken by unloved heirs?' And even though they protect it and ward it, rulers or bandits take it, or fire consumes it, or flood sweeps it away, or unloved heirs take it.

They sorrow and wail and lament, beating their breast and falling into confusion: 'What once was mine is gone.' This too is a drawback of sensual pleasures apparent in the present life, a mass of suffering caused by sensual pleasures.

Furthermore, for the sake of sensual pleasures ordinary people fight with ordinary people; kings fight with kings, aristocrats fight with aristocrats, spiritual practitioners fight with spiritual practitioners, and householders fight with householders.

A mother fights with her child, child with mother, father with child, and child with father. Brother fights with brother, brother with sister, sister with brother, and friend fights with friend. Once they've started quarreling, arguing, and disputing, they attack each other with fists, stones, rods, and swords, resulting in death and deadly pain. This too is a drawback of sensual pleasures apparent in the present life, a mass of suffering caused by sensual pleasures.

Furthermore, for the sake of sensual pleasures they don their sword and shield, fasten their bow and arrows, and plunge into a battle massed on both sides, with arrows and spears flying and swords flashing. There they are struck with arrows and spears, and their heads are chopped off, resulting in death and deadly pain. This too is a drawback of sensual pleasures apparent in the present life, a mass of suffering caused by sensual pleasures.

Furthermore, for the sake of sensual pleasures they don their sword and shield, fasten their bow and arrows, and charge wetly plastered bastions, with arrows and spears flying and swords flashing. There they are struck with arrows and spears, splashed with dung, crushed by a superior force, and their heads are chopped off, resulting in death and deadly pain. This too is a drawback of sensual pleasures apparent in the present life, a mass of suffering caused by sensual pleasures.

Furthermore, for the sake of sensual pleasures they break into houses, plunder wealth, steal from isolated buildings, commit highway robbery, and commit adultery.

The rulers would arrest them and subject them to various punishments—whipping, caning, and clubbing; cutting off hands or feet, or both; cutting off ears or nose, or both; the 'porridge pot', the 'shell-shave', the 'Rāhu's mouth', the 'garland of fire', the 'burning hand', the 'bulrush twist', the 'bark dress', the 'antelope', the 'meat hook', the 'coins', the 'caustic pickle', the 'twisting bar', the 'straw mat'; being splashed with hot oil, being fed to the dogs, being impaled alive, and being beheaded.

These result in death and deadly pain. This too is a drawback of sensual pleasures apparent in the present life, a mass of suffering caused by sensual pleasures.

Furthermore, for the sake of sensual pleasures, they conduct themselves badly by way of body, speech, and mind. When their body breaks up, after death, they're reborn in a place of loss, a bad place, the underworld, hell. This is a drawback of sensual pleasures to do with lives to come, a mass of suffering caused by sensual pleasures.

And what is the escape from sensual pleasures? Removing and giving up desire and greed for sensual pleasures: this is the escape from sensual pleasures.

There are ascetics and brahmins who don't truly understand sensual pleasures' gratification, drawback, and escape in this way for what they are. It's impossible for them to completely understand sensual pleasures themselves, or to instruct another so that, practicing accordingly, they will completely understand sensual pleasures. There are ascetics and brahmins who do truly understand sensual pleasures' gratification, drawback, and escape in this way for what they are. It is possible for them to completely understand sensual pleasures themselves, or to instruct another so that, practicing accordingly, they will completely understand sensual pleasures.

And what is the gratification of forms? Suppose there was a girl from any cast (e.g. the brahmins, aristocrats etc.) in her fifteenth or sixteenth year, neither too tall nor too short, neither too thin nor too fat, neither too dark nor too fair. Is she not at the height of her beauty and prettiness?"

"Yes, sir."

"The pleasure and happiness that arise from this beauty and prettiness is the gratification of forms.

And what is the drawback of forms? Suppose that some time later you were to see that same sister—eighty, ninety, or a hundred years old—bent double, crooked, leaning on a staff, trembling as they walk, ailing, past their prime, with teeth broken, hair grey and scanty or bald, skin wrinkled, and limbs blotchy.

What do you think, companions? Has not that former beauty vanished, and the drawback become clear?"

"Yes, sir."

"This is the drawback of forms.

Furthermore, suppose that you were to see that same sister sick, suffering, gravely ill, collapsed in her own urine and feces, being picked up by some and put down by others.

What do you think, companions? Has not that former beauty vanished, and the drawback become clear?"

"Yes, sir."

"This too is the drawback of forms.

Furthermore, suppose that you were to see that same sister as a corpse discarded in a charnel ground. And it had been dead for one, two, or three days, bloated, livid, and festering.

What do you think, companions? Has not that former beauty vanished, and the drawback become clear?" "Yes, sir."

"This too is the drawback of forms.
Furthermore, suppose that you were to see that same sister as a corpse discarded in a charnel ground. And it was being devoured by crows, hawks, vultures, herons, dogs, tigers, leopards, jackals, and many kinds of little creatures …

Furthermore, suppose that you were to see that same sister as a corpse discarded in a charnel ground. And it had been reduced to a skeleton with flesh and blood, held together by sinews … a skeleton rid of flesh but smeared with blood, and held together by sinews … a skeleton rid of flesh and blood, held together by sinews … bones rid of sinews scattered in every direction. Here a hand-bone, there a foot-bone, here an ankle bone, there a shin-bone, here a thigh-bone, there a hip-bone, here a rib-bone, there a back-bone, here an arm-bone, there a neck-bone, here a jaw-bone, there a tooth, here the skull. …

Furthermore, suppose that you were to see that same sister as a corpse discarded in a charnel ground. And it had been reduced to white bones, the color of shells … decrepit bones, heaped in a pile … bones rotted and crumbled to powder.

What do you think, companions? Has not that former beauty vanished and the drawback become clear?"

"Yes, sir."

"This too is the drawback of forms.

And what is the escape from forms? Removing and giving up desire and greed for forms: this is the escape from forms.

There are ascetics and brahmins who don't truly understand forms' gratification, drawback, and escape in this way for what they are. It's impossible for them to completely understand forms themselves, or to instruct another so that, practicing accordingly, they will completely understand forms.

There are ascetics and brahmins who do truly understand forms' gratification, drawback, and escape in this way for what they are. It is possible for them to completely understand forms themselves, or to instruct another so that, practicing accordingly, they will completely understand forms.

And what is the gratification of feelings?

It's when a person, quite secluded from sensual pleasures, secluded from unskillful qualities, enters and remains in the first absorption, which has the rapture and bliss born of seclusion, while placing the mind and keeping it connected. At that time a mendicant doesn't intend to hurt themselves, hurt others, or hurt both; they feel only feelings that are not hurtful. Freedom from being hurt is the ultimate gratification of feelings, I say.

Furthermore, a person enters and remains in the second absorption … third absorption … fourth absorption. At that time a mendicant doesn't intend to hurt themselves, hurt others, or hurt both; they feel only feelings that are not hurtful. Freedom from being hurt is the ultimate gratification of feelings, I say.

And what is the drawback of feelings?

That feelings are impermanent, suffering, and perishable: this is their drawback.

And what is the escape from feelings?

Removing and giving up desire and greed for feelings: this is the escape from feelings.

There are ascetics and brahmins who don't truly understand feelings' gratification, drawback, and escape in this way for what they are.

It's impossible for them to completely understand feelings themselves, or to instruct another so that, practicing accordingly, they will completely understand feelings.

There are ascetics and brahmins who do truly understand feelings' gratification, drawback, and escape in this way for what they are. It is possible for them to completely understand feelings themselves, or to instruct another so that, practicing accordingly, they will completely understand feelings."

That is what the Buddha said. Satisfied, the companions approved what the Buddha said".

Chapter 16

Middle Discourses 14: Cūḷadukkhakkhandhasutta

The Shorter Discourse on the Mass of Suffering

Mhanama, a Sakyan, went to meet Buddha and have a discussion with the Buddha. During their conversation, he says to Buddha that although he understands that greed, hate and delusion are unwholesome things in the mind that lead to mental suffering, he finds such qualities reside within his mind despite knowing. In response, Buddha says to him before completing four-fold Nibbana, he understood that greed, hate and delusion bring mental attachment, and mental attachment causes pain, yet until he developed higher stages of Nibbana, he was unable to give up grasping sensual pleasures; instead he enjoys sensual pleasures coming from sensory information despite knowing.

Buddha says it's only after the Anagami stage that he declared he would not return to the lay life (i.e enjoying sensual pleasures is lay life, and sensual pleasures give up at Anagami state out of precepts and training rules). That is because when a person finds something better, they find it easier to give up other things. So when Buddha gained rapture (joy in the mind and body) and experienced something better than sensual pleasures, he left the lay life for the Anagami state.

Due to sensual pleasure, people experience various difficulties; maintaining a lifestyle is difficult, environmental pressures, hardships people have to endure because of sensual pleasures, quarrels, misunderstandings, and hurts between family, friends, employers and other parties all happen due to sensual pleasures. Besides, due to sensual pleasure, people commit various unwholesome activities through body, mind, and speech.

Buddha says that on one occasion, he met with Jains, spiritual practitioners of a different tradition, who believed that they could end their former lives' bad deeds by enduring difficulties in the present life. Yet, when Buddha asked Jains if they could see their former lives, they replied that they don't see their former lives, and not seeing, they still followed a spiritual path. Yet, Buddha describes the Noble Path by seeing former lives, and following Buddha's path, his noble disciples get to see former lives as well. This only happens after they abandon attachment to the mind and body, which allows vision to grow beyond mind and body. Attachment to mind and body makes vision limited. Non-attachment makes a vision broader than conventions. Nibbana is not something that a person gets to experience after death, but something that a person gets to experience while living their life.

Without having to wait until one dies, if a person can experience an outcome gained through a spiritual life while still living, it would be beneficial to follow a spiritual path that gives fruition immediately in this life. It would make sense for a wise person to continue such a spiritual path and to see for oneself. Knowing, and continuing the practice leading to four-fold Nibbana, a person can go on making progress in finding inner peace and happiness. Having experienced insight, Buddha and Arahants experience cessation and bliss.

"So I have heard. At one time the Buddha was staying in the land of the Sakyans, near Kapilavatthu in the Banyan Tree Monastery.

Then Mahānāma the Sakyan went up to the Buddha, bowed, sat down to one side, and said to him, "For a long time, sir, I have understood your teaching like this: 'Greed, hate, and delusion are corruptions of the mind.' Despite understanding this, sometimes my mind is occupied by thoughts of greed, hate, and delusion. I wonder what qualities remain in me that I have such thoughts?"

"Mahānāma, there is a quality that remains in you that makes you have such thoughts. For if you had given up that quality you would not still be living at home and enjoying sensual pleasures. But because you haven't given up that quality you are still living at home and enjoying sensual pleasures.

Sensual pleasures give little gratification and much suffering and distress, and they are all the more full of drawbacks. So, Mahānāma, even though a noble disciple has clearly seen this with right wisdom, as long as they do not achieve the rapture and bliss that are apart from sensual pleasures and unskillful qualities, or something even more peaceful than that, they can return to sensual pleasures. But when they do achieve that rapture and bliss, or something more peaceful than that, they do not return to sensual pleasures.

Before my awakening—when I was still unawakened but intent on awakening—I too clearly saw with right wisdom that: 'Sensual pleasures give little gratification and much suffering and distress, and they are all the more full of drawbacks.' But so long as I didn't achieve the rapture and bliss that are apart from sensual pleasures and unskillful qualities, or something even more peaceful than that, I didn't announce that I would not return to sensual pleasures. But when I did achieve that rapture and bliss, or something more peaceful than that, I announced that I would not return to sensual pleasures.

And what is the gratification of sensual pleasures? There are these five kinds of sensual stimulation. What five? Sights known by the eye, which are likable, desirable, agreeable, pleasant, sensual, and arousing. Sounds known by the ear … Smells known by the nose … Tastes known by the tongue … Touches known by the body, which are likable, desirable, agreeable, pleasant, sensual, and arousing. These are the five kinds of sensual stimulation. The pleasure and happiness that arise from these five kinds of sensual stimulation: this is the gratification of sensual pleasures.

And what is the drawback of sensual pleasures? It's when a person has desire (likes, dislikes), whatever the activities they do, livelihood (arithmetic, accounting, calculating, farming, trade, raising cattle, archery, government service, and so on one of the professions) and lifestyle (householder or bhikkhu life) bring sufferings. But they must face cold and heat, being hurt by the touch of flies, mosquitoes, wind, sun, and reptiles, and risking death from hunger and thirst. This is a drawback of sensual pleasures apparent in the present life, a mass of suffering caused by sensual pleasures.

A person might try hard, strive, and make an effort, but fail to fulfil their desires, gain the requisites for living. If this happens, they sorrow and wail and lament, beating their breast and falling into confusion, saying: 'Oh, my hard work is wasted. My efforts are fruitless!' This too is a drawback of sensual pleasures apparent in the present life, a mass of suffering caused by sensual pleasures.

A person might try hard, strive, and make an effort, and succeed in fulfilling their desires, gain the requisites for living. But they experience pain and sadness when they try to protect it, thinking: 'How can I prevent my wealth from being taken by rulers or bandits, consumed by fire, swept away by flood, or taken by unloved heirs?' And even though they protect it and ward it, rulers or bandits take it, or fire consumes it, or flood sweeps it away, or unloved heirs take it. They sorrow and wail and lament, beating their breast and falling into confusion: 'What once was mine is gone.' This too is a drawback of sensual pleasures apparent in the present life, a mass of suffering caused by sensual pleasures.

Furthermore, for the sake of sensual pleasures kings fight with kings, aristocrats fight with aristocrats, brahmins fight with brahmins, and ordinary people fight with ordinary people. A mother fights with her child, child with mother, father with child, and child with father.

Brother fights with brother, brother with sister, sister with brother, and friend fights with friend. Once they've started quarreling, arguing, and disputing, they attack each other with fists, stones, rods, and swords, resulting in death and deadly pain. This too is a drawback of sensual pleasures apparent in the present life, a mass of suffering caused by sensual pleasures and desires.

Furthermore, for the sake of sensual pleasures and desires they don their sword and shield, fasten their bow and arrows, and plunge into a battle massed on both sides, with arrows and spears flying and swords flashing.

There they are struck with arrows and spears, and their heads are chopped off, resulting in death and deadly pain. This too is a drawback of sensual pleasures apparent in the present life, a mass of suffering caused by sensual pleasures.

Furthermore, for the sake of sensual pleasures and desires they don their sword and shield, fasten their bow and arrows, and charge wetly plastered bastions, with arrows and spears flying and swords flashing. There they are struck with arrows and spears, splashed with dung, crushed by a superior force, and their heads are chopped off, resulting in death and deadly pain.

This too is a drawback of sensual pleasures apparent in the present life, a mass of suffering caused by sensual pleasures.

Furthermore, for the sake of sensual pleasures and desires they break into houses, plunder wealth, steal from isolated buildings, commit highway robbery, and commit adultery. The rulers would arrest them and subject them to various punishments—whipping, caning, and clubbing; cutting off hands or feet, or both; cutting off ears or nose, or both; the 'porridge pot', the 'shell-shave', the 'Rāhu's mouth', the 'garland of fire', the 'burning hand', the 'bulrush twist', the 'bark dress', the 'antelope', the 'meat hook', the 'coins', the 'caustic pickle', the 'twisting bar', the 'straw mat'; being splashed with hot oil, being fed to the dogs, being impaled alive, and being beheaded. These result in death and deadly pain. This too is a drawback of sensual pleasures apparent in the present life, a mass of suffering caused by sensual pleasures.

Furthermore, for the sake of sensual pleasures and desires, they conduct themselves badly by way of body, speech, and mind. When their body breaks up, after death, they're reborn in a place of loss, a bad place, the underworld, hell.

This is a drawback of sensual pleasures to do with lives to come, a mass of suffering caused by sensual pleasures.

Mahānāma, this one time I was staying near Rājagaha, on the Vulture's Peak Mountain. Now at that time several Jain ascetics on the slopes of Isigili at the Black Rock were constantly standing, refusing seats. And they felt painful, sharp, severe, acute feelings due to overexertion.

Then in the late afternoon, I came out of retreat and went to the Black Rock to visit those Jain ascetics. I said to them, 'Reverends, why are you constantly standing, refusing seats, so that you suffer painful, sharp, severe, acute feelings due to overexertion?'

When I said this, those Jain ascetics said to me, 'Reverend, the Jain ascetic of the Ñātika clan claims to be all-knowing and all-seeing, to know and see everything without exception, thus: "Knowledge and vision are constantly and continually present to me, while walking, standing, sleeping, and waking."

He says, "O Jain ascetics, you have done bad deeds in a past life. Wear them away with these severe and grueling austerities. And when in the present you are restrained in body, speech, and mind, you're not doing any bad deeds for the future.

So, due to eliminating past deeds by fervent mortification, and not doing any new deeds, there's nothing to come up in the future. With no future consequence, deeds end. With the ending of deeds, suffering ends. With the ending of suffering, feeling ends. And with the ending of feeling, all suffering will have been worn away." We endorse and accept this, and we are satisfied with it.'

When they said this, I said to them, 'But reverends, do you know for sure that you existed in the past, and it is not the case that you did not exist?'

'No we don't, reverend.'

'But reverends, do you know for sure that you did bad deeds in the past?'

'No we don't, reverend.'

'But reverends, do you know that you did such and such bad deeds?'

'No we don't, reverend.'

'But reverends, do you know that so much suffering has already been worn away? Or that so much suffering still remains to be worn away? Or that when so much suffering is worn away all suffering will have been worn away?'

'No we don't, reverend.'

'But reverends, do you know about giving up unskillful qualities in the present life and embracing skillful qualities?'

'No we don't, reverend.'

'So it seems that you don't know any of these things. That being so, when those in the world who are violent and bloody-handed and of cruel livelihood are reborn among humans they go forth as Jain ascetics.'

'Reverend Gotama, pleasure is not gained through pleasure; pleasure is gained through pain. For if pleasure were to be gained through pleasure, King Seniya Bimbisāra of Magadha would gain pleasure, since he lives in greater pleasure than Venerable Gotama.'

'Clearly the venerables have spoken rashly, without reflection. Rather, I'm the one who should be asked about who lives in greater pleasure, King Bimbisāra or Venerable Gotama?'

'Clearly we spoke rashly and without reflection. But let that be. Now we ask Venerable Gotama: "Who lives in greater pleasure, King Bimbisāra or Venerable Gotama?"'

'Well then, reverends, I'll ask you about this in return, and you can answer as you like. What do you think, reverends? Is King Bimbisāra capable of experiencing perfect happiness for seven days and nights without moving his body or speaking?'

'No he is not, reverend.'

'What do you think, reverends? Is King Bimbisāra capable of experiencing perfect happiness for six days … five days … four days … three days … two days … one day?'

'No he is not, reverend.'

'But I am capable of experiencing perfect happiness for one day and night without moving my body or speaking. I am capable of experiencing perfect happiness for two days … three days … four days … five days … six days … seven days. What do you think, reverends? This being so, who lives in greater pleasure, King Bimbisāra or I?'

'This being so, Venerable Gotama lives in greater pleasure than King Bimbisāra.'"

That is what the Buddha said. Satisfied, Mahānāma the Sakyan approved what the Buddha said.

Chapter 17

Middle Discourses 15: Anumānasutta

Measuring Up

A person who is seeking Nibbana and wishes to gain peace of mind should try to develop good qualities within. It is a two-part situation; those who genuinely appreciate Dhamma tend to constantly want to improve themselves. Those who do not appreciate Dhamma tend not to want to improve qualities within. It is somewhat both; people who have completed paramis in pervious birth and who have natural good qualities require practice, refinement, and further development until perfection, just as improving other skills, singing, etc.

Those who are Arahants, when they only approach people, speak about Nibbana and approach those who have the potential to understand Nibbana, those who are easy to speak with, and who possess an open mind, are able to apply logic and reasoning, are wise and possess humble, and good inner qualities. Arahants don't instruct those who have no potential for understanding Nibbana. The qualities that make a person not have the potential to gain Nibbana include:

- An ordinary person who possesses too many unwholesome intentions (i.e evil desires) due to a lack of wisdom to understand karma.
- An ordinary person who tends to be fond of comparing one to another, excessively boasts of self and degrades others.
- An ordinary person who gets angry for no apparent reason.
- An ordinary person who tends to be constantly engaged in finding faults in others but is not able to find faults within self.
- An ordinary person who tends to get too bitter for no apparent reason.
- An ordinary person who is inclined to use hurtful and harsh words with the intent to cause distress to another due to ill will.
- An ordinary person who rejects another person's valuable suggestions regarding the practice leading to four-fold Nibbana without any valid reason.
- An ordinary person who insults another person or person's well-intended suggestions regarding the practice leading to four-fold Nibbana without any valid reason.

- An ordinary person who tends to criticize the one who pointed out the areas for improvement to experience Nibbana (without a valid reason).
- An ordinary person who lacks interest in Dhamma (four-fold Nibbana); a person who ignores Dhamma-related matters but is fond of talking of issues that are not related to Dhamma and manifests unwholesome qualities (i.e. anger, ill will, and sulkiness).
- An ordinary person who pays no attention when higher Dhamma has been taught (Sotapanna to Arahant) and is unwilling to practice (or put effort into following the noble path).
- A person is unfair and wicked.
- A person is envious and resentful.
- A person is devious and deceitful.
- A person is too stubborn and proud.
- A person is not open-minded, and who does not keep space to discover new things, to discover Nibbana/self.

On the other hand, Arahants approach and instruct people who possess potential for gaining Nibbana and those who possess good qualities.

- An ordinary person who has fewer or no evil desires/ unwholesome intentions due to wisdom to understand beyond conventions/karma.
- An ordinary person who tends to not compare one to another excessively boasts of self and degrades others.
- An ordinary person who is not extremely angry.
- An ordinary person who is not excessively engaged in finding faults in others but is willing to focus on self; can identify weaknesses in self and is willing to work on improving the weaknesses.
- An ordinary person who is not extremely angry and who is not expressing excessive bitterness.
- An ordinary person who does not use harsh words with the intent to cause distress to another with anger.
- An ordinary person who is capable of understanding and accepting another person's valuable suggestions regarding the practice leading to Nibbana with reasoning.
- An ordinary person who can understand and appreciate another person's well-intended suggestions regarding the practice leading to Nibbana with reasoning.

- An ordinary person who does not criticize the person who provided valuable suggestions regarding the practice leading to Nibbana with reasoning.
- An ordinary person has a genuine interest in Dhamma and is not too much fond of gossiping/ talking excessively about issues that are not relevant to Dhamma (possessing low degree of unwholesome qualities; a low degree of anger, ill will, and sulkiness).
- An ordinary person who is willing to practice or put effort into following the Noble Path.
- An ordinary person who is fair and not wicked.
- An ordinary person who is not envious and resentful.
- An ordinary person who is not devious and deceitful.
- An ordinary person who is not stubborn and proud.
- An ordinary person who keeps space to discover new things, is open-minded, and does not grasp existing knowledge which makes it possible to grow knowledge to discover Nibbana/self.

Yet, when a person who aspires to Nibbana and who possesses good qualities is able to apply logic in thinking and is wise and humble and can think and discover self, and Nibbana, to them, Arahants come to instruct about Nibbana. Therefore, those who seek Nibbana would benefit if they develop good inner qualities within.

"So I have heard. At one time Arahant Mahāmoggallāna was staying in the land of the Bhaggas at Crocodile Hill, in the deer park at Bhesakaḷā's Wood. There Arahant Mahāmoggallāna addressed the companions: "Respected, companions!"

"Venerable sir," they replied. Arahant Mahāmoggallāna said this:

"Suppose a person invites another person to instruct them to Nibbana. But they're hard to instruct, having qualities that make them hard to instruct. They're impatient, and don't take instruction respectfully. So their spiritual companions don't think it's worth advising and instructing them, and that person doesn't gain their trust.

And what are the qualities that make them hard to instruct? Firstly, a person has corrupt wishes, having fallen under the sway of corrupt wishes. This is a quality that makes them difficult to admonish.

Furthermore, a person glorifies themselves and puts others down. ...

They're irritable, overcome by anger ...

They're irritable, and acrimonious due to anger …

They're irritable, and stubborn due to anger …

They're irritable, and blurt out words bordering on anger …

When accused, they object to the accuser …

When accused, they rebuke the accuser …

When accused, they retort to the accuser …

When accused, they dodge the issue, distract the discussion with irrelevant points, and display annoyance, hate, and bitterness …

When accused, they are unable to account for the evidence …

They are offensive and contemptuous …

They're jealous and stingy …

They're devious and deceitful …

They're obstinate and arrogant …

Furthermore, a person is attached to their own views, holding them tight, and refusing to let go. This too is a quality that makes them difficult to admonish.

These are the qualities that make them hard to admonish.

Suppose a person doesn't invite another person to instruct them to Nibbana. But they're easy to instruct, having qualities that make them easy to instruct. They're accepting, and take instruction respectfully. So their spiritual companions think it's worth advising and instructing them, and that person gains their trust.

And what are the qualities that make them easy to instruct? Firstly, a person doesn't have corrupt wishes …

Furthermore, a person isn't attached to their own views, not holding them tight, but letting them go easily.

These are the qualities that make them easy to admonish.

In such a case, a person should measure themselves like this. 'This person has corrupt wishes, having fallen under the sway of corrupt wishes. And I don't like or approve of this person. And if I were to fall under the sway of corrupt wishes, others wouldn't like or approve of me.' A person who knows this should give rise to the thought: 'I will not fall under the sway of corrupt wishes.' …

'This person is attached to their own views, holding them tight and refusing to let go. And I don't like or approve of this person. And if I were to be attached to my own views, holding them tight and refusing to let go, others wouldn't like or approve of me.'

A person who knows this should give rise to the thought: 'I will not be attached to my own views, holding them tight, but will let them go easily.'

In such a case, a person should check themselves like this: 'Do I have corrupt wishes? Have I fallen under the sway of corrupt wishes?' Suppose that, upon checking, a person knows that they have fallen under the sway of corrupt wishes. Then they should make an effort to give up those bad, unskillful qualities.

But suppose that, upon checking, a person knows that they haven't fallen under the sway of corrupt wishes. Then they should complete Sotapanna and experience rapture and joy reflecting the qualities of the triple gem, training day and night in skillful qualities. …

Suppose that, upon checking, a person knows that they are attached to their own views, holding them tight, and refusing to let go. Then they should make an effort to give up those bad, unskillful qualities. Suppose that, upon checking, a person knows that they're not attached to their own views, holding them tight, but let them go easily.

Then they should complete Sotapanna and experience rapture and joy reflecting the qualities of the triple gem, training day and night in skillful qualities.

Suppose that, upon checking, a person sees that they haven't given up all these bad, unskillful qualities. Then they should make an effort to give them all up. But suppose that, upon checking, a person sees that they have given up all these bad, unskillful qualities.

Then they should complete sotapanna and experience rapture and joy reflecting the qualities of the triple gem, training day and night in skillful qualities.

Suppose there was a woman or man who was young, youthful, and fond of adornments, and they check their own reflection in a clean bright mirror or a clear bowl of water. If they see any dirt or blemish there, they'd try to remove it. But if they don't see any dirt or blemish there, they're happy, thinking: 'How fortunate that I'm clean!'

In the same way, suppose that, upon checking, a person sees that they haven't given up all these bad, unskillful qualities. Then they should make an effort to give them all up. But suppose that, upon checking, a person sees that they have given up all these bad, unskillful qualities. Then they should complete Sotapanna and experience rapture and joy reflecting the qualities of the triple gem, training day and night in skillful qualities."

This is what Arhant Mahāmoggallāna said. Satisfied, the companions approved what Arahant Mahāmoggallāna said.

Chapter 18

Middle Discourses 16: Cetokhilasutta

Hard-heartedness

There are five kinds of mental unwholesomeness that a person has in mind and five barriers to making progress in the training path in mind and gaining Nibbana. A person can give up greed and hate that develop based on delusion (due to the lack of the right view) only in one's mind and not outside the mind.

What are the five kinds of mental unwholesomeness a person has in mind that, unless the person gives them up, will prevent the person from gaining Nibbana?

The first mental unwholesomeness is when a person has doubts about Buddha. Is Buddha the teacher of all? Is it real? Is it Gutama Buddha, who became the universal Buddha, an imaginary figure or a made-up second person? Doubts about Buddha can prevent Nibbana for those who seek Nibbana. This is because ordination in noble lineage is gained directly through Buddha. Noble ordination can only be gained in a person's mental continuum and not outside a person's mind. Natural transformation occurs in a person's mental continuum across stages, and that transformation, which allows abandoning mental fetters out of rituals, is a monk in Noble Path.

Triple Gem is universal. Buddha is the teacher of all noble Sangha, this does not change. Thus, irrespective of conventions, traditions, and rituals, a person from any background should refuge in the Universal Buddha if they aspire Nibbana to find a refuge for self towards the end of four-fold Nibbana. Refuge in Buddha can be achieved by refuge in universal Dhamma. Refuge in universal Dhamma can be achieved by refuge in universal (Savaka) Sangha. Refuge in universal Buddha, universal Dhamma, and Universal Sangha is simply finding a refuge in self by abandoning the ten fetters to gain four-fold Nibbana. For example, from a conventional perspective, an ordinary person who lives in a monastic setting and a non-monastic setting (householder setting) must pay respect and gain merits in the same way by attending to the universal Buddha to gain Nibbana through the noble Sangha route. An ordinary person who lives in a monastic setting and a householder setting must respect universal Dhamma (four-fold Nibbana) and gain merits in the same way by following noble Dhamma in mind to gain Nibbana through the noble

Sangha route. An ordinary person who lives in a monastic setting and a householder setting can gain merits that are required to gain universal Dhamma by respecting universal (Savaka) Sangha in the same way in mind and to develop inner qualities to that of universal (Savaka) Sangha within to gain Nibbana through the noble Sangha route.

The second mental unwholesomeness is: A person has doubts about the four-fold Nibbana (Dhamma); is Sotapanna to Arahant, is it for real? Is it possible to gain Nibbana these days?

The third mental unwholesomeness is: Among spiritual companions, some people can have doubts about enlightened beings or Savaka Sangha coming from any conventional background. They may raise doubts in their thoughts and words. Has the person who claims to have gained Nibbana gained Nibbana or not?

The fourth mental unwholesomeness is that a person has doubts about what to practice and what not to practice to gain Nibbana, they practice what is known only to noble ones.

Furthermore, the fifth, a person maintains ill will towards fellow practitioners of Dhamma, those who attempt to enter the path and are in the path.

By developing a reasonable understanding of Dhamma (four-fold Nibbana), by applying logic and reasoning based on true life experience and wisdom, an ordinary person may develop stronger confidence in its validity.

When someone feels that their heart calls them to practice Dhamma, doing good and avoiding doing bad in daily life, that's when they start a practice. As they practice, they may gain temporary satisfaction by doing so, and, when they find temporary satisfaction, and if they want to extend happiness, they may continue to practice Dhamma in a way that leads to four-fold Nibbana. Barriers to progressing in the Noble Path include possessing and developing too many likes, dislikes, and expectations towards worldly experiences. When a person is unable to reduce grasping conventions, eats too much or sleeps too much, and lacks motivation for practicing Dhamma, excessive desire for the physical body (which prevents gaining the Anagami state), and growing desires instead of reducing desires (i.e. practicing Dhamma to become a deva and so on), these factors can act as barriers to gaining Nibbana.

To give up five kinds of mental unwholesomeness and give up five barriers, you may develop an intent to overcome doubts by applying reasoning and logic to discover truth. The path to Nibbana can be found in those who have gained Nibbana and are able to provide higher merits and wisdom. Thereafter, you may strive to associate with noble ones to develop similar wisdom and inner qualities within. Therefore, what you can do is observe your mind to maintain noble qualities and wisdom day and night, investigate your mind to identify strengths and weaknesses in you that prevent purifying from grasping conventions, and maintain a determined effort to reduce mental pain, discover self, and discover Nibbana.

Triple Gem and Nibbana are linked, because higher merits and a higher training path leading to Nibbana can be shared only by Arahants. In the absence of Arahants, one may approach an Anagami. In the absence of Anagami, one may approach a Sakadagami. In the absence of Sakadagami, one may approach Sotapanna. In the absence of Sotapanna, one may approach an ordinary person who has confidence in the universal Buddha and universal Dhamma: four-fold Nibbana to a reasonable extent.

"So I have heard. At one time the Buddha was staying near Sāvatthī in Jeta's Grove, Anāthapiṇḍika's monastery. There the Buddha addressed the spiritual companions, "Companions!"

"Venerable sir," they replied. The Buddha said this:

"Companions, when a person has not given up five kinds of hard-heartedness and severed five shackles of the heart, it's not possible for them to achieve growth, improvement, or maturity in this teaching and training.

What are the five kinds of hard-heartedness they haven't given up?

Firstly, a person has doubts about the universal Buddha. They're uncertain, undecided, and lacking confidence. This being so, their mind doesn't incline toward keenness, commitment, persistence, and striving. This is the first kind of hard-heartedness they haven't given up.

Furthermore, a person has doubts about the universal Dhamma: four-fold nibbana … This is the second kind of hard-heartedness.

They have doubts about the universal Savaka Saṅgha … This is the third kind of hard-heartedness.

They have doubts about the noble training … This is the fourth kind of hard-heartedness.

Furthermore, a person is angry and upset with their spiritual companions, resentful and closed off. This being so, their mind doesn't incline toward keenness, commitment, persistence, and striving.

This is the fifth kind of hard-heartedness they haven't given up. These are the five kinds of hard-heartedness they haven't given up.

What are the five shackles of the heart they haven't severed? Firstly, a person isn't free of greed, desire, fondness, thirst, passion, and craving for sensual pleasures. This being so, their mind doesn't incline toward keenness, commitment, persistence, and striving. This is the first shackle of the heart they haven't severed.

Furthermore, a person isn't free of greed for the body … This is the second shackle of the heart.

Furthermore, a person isn't free of greed for form … This is the third shackle of the heart.

They eat as much as they like until their belly is full, then indulge in the pleasures of sleeping, lying down, and drowsing … This is the fourth heart shackle.

They lead the spiritual life hoping to be reborn in one of the orders of gods, thinking: 'By this precept or observance or fervent austerity or spiritual life, may I become one of the gods!' This being so, their mind doesn't incline toward keenness, commitment, persistence, and striving. This is the fifth shackle of the heart they haven't severed. These are the five shackles of the heart they haven't severed.

When a person has not given up these five kinds of hard-heartedness and severed these five shackles of the heart, it's not possible for them to achieve growth, improvement, or maturity in this teaching and training.

When a person has given up these five kinds of hard-heartedness and severed these five shackles of the heart, it is possible for them to achieve growth, improvement, and maturity in this teaching and training.

What are the five kinds of hard-heartedness they've given up? Firstly, a person has no doubts about the universal Buddha. They're not uncertain, undecided, or lacking confidence. This being so, their mind inclines toward keenness, commitment, persistence, and striving. This is the first kind of hard-heartedness they've given up.

Furthermore, a person has no doubts about the Dhamma; four-fold nibbana …

They have no doubts about the Savaka Saṅgha …

They have no doubts about the noble training …

They're not angry and upset with their spiritual companions, not resentful or closed off. This being so, their mind inclines toward keenness, commitment, persistence, and striving. This is the fifth kind of hard-heartedness they've given up. These are the five kinds of hard-heartedness they've given up.

What are the five shackles of the heart they've severed? Firstly, a person is rid of greed, desire, fondness, thirst, passion, and craving for sensual pleasures. This being so, their mind inclines toward keenness, commitment, persistence, and striving. This is the first shackle of the heart they've severed.

Furthermore, a person is rid of greed for the body …

They're rid of greed for form …

They don't eat as much as they like until their belly is full, then indulge in the pleasures of sleeping, lying down, and drowsing …

They don't lead the spiritual life hoping to be reborn in one of the orders of gods, thinking: 'By this precept or observance or fervent austerity or spiritual life, may I become one of the gods!'

This being so, their mind inclines toward keenness, commitment, persistence, and striving. This is the fifth shackle of the heart they've severed. These are the five shackles of the heart they've severed.

When a person has given up these five kinds of hard-heartedness and severed these five shackles of the heart, it is possible for them to achieve growth, improvement, or maturity in this teaching and training.

They develop the basis of psychic power that has immersion due to enthusiasm, and active effort … the basis of psychic power that has immersion due to energy, and active effort … the basis of psychic power that has immersion due to mental development, and active effort … the basis of psychic power that has immersion due to inquiry, and active effort. And the fifth is sheer vigor.

A person who possesses these fifteen factors, including vigor, is capable of breaking out, becoming awakened, and reaching the supreme sanctuary from the yoke. Suppose there was a chicken with eight or ten or twelve eggs. And she properly sat on them to keep them warm and incubated. Even if that chicken doesn't wish: 'If only my chicks could break out of the eggshell with their claws and beak and hatch safely!' Still they can break out and hatch safely.

In the same way, a person who possesses these fifteen factors, including vigor, is capable of breaking out, becoming awakened, and reaching the supreme sanctuary from the yoke (Arahantship)."

That is what the Buddha said. Satisfied, the companions approved what the Buddha said".

Chapter 19

Middle Discourses 17: Vanapatthasutta

Jungle Thickets

Irrespective of conventions, if a person who aspires to Nibbana does not get to experience Nibbana through what they practice, instead of grasping to what they know, they want to discover new ways of practicing to discover Nibbana. Those who aspire to Nibbana would benefit if they consider altering and making changes to their former practices by allowing new ways, trying new ways to discover self and discovering Nibbana.

If a person lives in a forest and a forest monk does not gain Nibbana, such a monk might consider reflecting and making changes to the practice. A person who lives in a village, city, temple, or house does not get to experience Nibbana. They might reconsider shaping their practice and try new ways based on Arahants' Dhamma. When a person is supported by another, they might consider reflecting and reshaping their practice to be in line with Arahants' Dhamma.

The end purpose of any spiritual practitioner should be to gain cessation and Nibbana. Whatever practice means, despite conventions that are different, practicing the universal path, the Noble Path that allows a person to gain Nibbana, is what benefits a person. The purpose of spiritual practice should be to at least gain Sotapanna. Anyone who is not a Sotapanna should consider whether or not their practices are fruitful, and make necessary changes, leave their practices to renew ways of practices that allow them to gain Sotapanna to Arahant.

Noble mindfulness differs from ordinary mindfulness. Noble mindfulness, jhanas happen to a Sakadagami paving the path to Anagami state at a random instance shaped by one's merits, karma, due to the completion of Paramis in previous births, one's training of the mind to reduce grasping to conventions.

When a person engages in developing a spiritual practice, whether it's in an isolated place or a crowded place, whether it's a monk based on rituals or not, wherever it is, unless they gain four-fold Nibbana, they all continue to go in samsara. If they realize the same practice (Crowded place or isolated place etc.) is not helping them gain Nibbana, they should be able to leave or to change such practices (or places), considering that their practice hasn't aided them in gaining Nibbana. Whichever practice does not allow them to gain Nibbana is not fruitful for them. Thus, those who seek end to end suffering; Nibbana should help themselves by developing and shaping their practice in a way that is possible to gain Nibbana.

"So I have heard. At one time the Buddha was staying near Sāvatthī in Jeta's Grove, Anāthapiṇḍika's monastery. There the Buddha addressed the companions, "Companions!"

"Venerable sir," they replied. The Buddha said this:

"Companions, I will teach you an exposition about jungle thickets. Listen and apply your mind well, I will speak."

"Yes, sir," they replied. The Buddha said this:

"Companions, take the case of a person who lives close by a jungle thicket. As they do so, their noble mindfulness does not become established, their mind does not become immersed in noble mindfulness (Anagami), they don't give up grasping ten fetters (their defilements do not come to an end), and they do not arrive at the Arahantship (supreme sanctuary from the yoke). And the necessities of life that a spiritual practitioner walking the Noble Path (renunciate in mind) requires—clothing, food, accommodation, and medicines and supplies for the sick—are hard to come by.

That person should reflect: 'While living close by this jungle thicket, my mindfulness does not become established, my mind does not become immersed in noble concentration (Sotapanna to Anagami etc.), my defilements (grasping ten fetters) do not come to an end, and I do not arrive at the Arahantship (supreme sanctuary from the yoke). And the necessities of life that a spiritual practitioner walking the Noble Path (renunciate in mind) requires—clothing, food, accommodation, and medicines —are hard to come by.' That person should leave that jungle thicket that very time of night or day; they should not stay there.

Take another case of a person who lives close by a jungle thicket. Their mindfulness does not become established … But the necessities of life are easy to come by.

That person should reflect: 'While living close by this jungle thicket, my mindfulness does not become established … But the necessities of life are easy to come by. But my intent on taking a noble practice is to give up mental attachment not merely for the sake of gaining clothing, food, accommodation, and medicines and supplies for the sick. Moreover, while living close by this jungle thicket, my mindfulness does not become established …' That person should, after appraisal, leave that jungle thicket; they should not stay there.

Take another case of a person who lives close by a jungle thicket. As they do so, their mindfulness becomes established, their mind becomes immersed in noble concentration (Anagami), they give up grasping ten fetters (their defilements come to an end) and arrive at the Arahantship. But the necessities of life are easy to come by. But my intent on taking the noble practice is to give up mental attachment not merely for the sake of gaining clothing, food, accommodation, and medicines and supplies for the sick.

That person should reflect: 'While living close by this jungle thicket, my mindfulness becomes established … But the necessities of life are hard to come by. But my intent on taking a noble practice is to give up mental attachment not merely for the sake of gaining donations (i.e. clothing, food, accommodation, and medicines etc.). Moreover, while living close by this jungle thicket, my mindfulness becomes established …' That person should, after appraisal, stay in that jungle thicket; they should not leave.

Take another case of a person who lives close by a jungle thicket. Their mindfulness becomes established … And the necessities of life are easy to come by. That person should reflect: 'While living close by this jungle thicket, my mindfulness becomes established … And the necessities of life are easy to come by.' That person should stay in that jungle thicket for the rest of their life; they should not leave.

Take the case of a person who lives supported by a village … town … city … country … an individual. As they do so, their mindfulness does not become established, their mind does not become immersed in noble concentration (Anagami), they do not give up grasping ten fetters (their defilements do not come to an end), and they do not arrive at the Arahantship.

And the necessities of life that a spiritual practitioner walking the Noble Path (renunciate in mind) requires—clothing, food, accommodation, and medicines —are hard to come by. That person should reflect: '… my mindfulness does not become established … And the necessities of life are hard to come by.' That person should leave that person at any time of the day or night, without taking leave; they should not follow them. …

Take another case of a person who lives supported by an individual. Their mindfulness does not become established … But the necessities of life are easy to come by. That person should reflect: '… my mindfulness does not become established … But the necessities of life are easy to come by.' … That person should, after appraisal, leave that person having taken leave; they should not follow them. …

Take another case of a person who lives supported by an individual. Their mindfulness becomes established … But the necessities of life are hard to come by. That person should reflect: '… my mindfulness becomes established … But the necessities of life are hard to come by.' … That person should, after appraisal, follow that person; they should not leave.

Take another case of a person who lives supported by an individual. As they do so, their mindfulness becomes established, their mind becomes immersed in noble concentration (Anagami), they give up grasping ten fetters (their defilements come to an end), and they arrive at the Arahantship.

And the necessities of life that a spiritual practitioner walking the Noble Path (renunciate in mind) requires—clothing, food, accommodation, and medicines —are hard to come by. That person should reflect—are easy to come by. That person should reflect: 'While living supported by this person, my mindfulness becomes established ... And the necessities of life are easy to come by.' That person should follow that person for the rest of their life; they should not leave them, even if sent away."

That is what the Buddha said. Satisfied, the person approved what the Buddha said".

Chapter 20

Middle Discourses 18: Madhupiṇḍikasutta

The Honey-Cake

This discourse discuss that Buddha explains to Daṇḍapāṇi that Buddha's Dhamma leading to Nibbana does not lead to hurt self and others. Worldly experiences don't bother a person who does not grasp into their thoughts, the end of craving across four-fold Nibbana.

The four-fold Nibbana brings an end to mental attachment[15]. When you grasp into your thoughts, your thoughts get the power to hurt you. Not all your thoughts are your friends. If all you're taught is that they were your friends, thoughts should not make you distressed. Yet, thoughts do bring mental pain. It is your thoughts that bring the most pain to you as you live with your thoughts. Thoughts are simply a stream of flaws that respond to sensory experiences for which you make a belonging. Thoughts function autonomously without your control. When you understand your thoughts are a flow of thoughts arising and ceasing while responding to sensory information, you can try to reduce getting attached to your own thoughts.

It's because you grasp into your thoughts that your thoughts tend to bother you. Instead, when you don't grasp into the things you think, feel, or perceive, your thoughts don't bother you. Attachment to what you think or what others think or say can bring mental pain. Arahants don't get attached to their thoughts, so the thoughts responding to sensory information do not bother them as they don't give too much value to such thoughts. Thus, they don't get distressed or upset if others disagree, or they don't experience happiness when others agree. This is what it meant by the statement below:

"If they don't find anything worth grasping to, by getting attached to the source from which these arise, just this is the end of the underlying tendencies to desire, repulsion, views, doubt, conceit, the desire to be reborn, and ignorance."

---

[15] The four-fold Nibbana brings an end to attachment, and that's what it means by the statement:*"Judgments driven by proliferating perceptions beset a person. If they don't find anything worth approving, welcoming, or getting attached to in the source from which these arise, this is just the end of the underlying tendencies to desire, repulsion, views, doubt, conceit, the desire to be reborn, and ignorance."*

When you receive sensory information, you may experience worldly things. You may experience and feel pleasure, displeasure or be neutral. You tend to interpret what you feel as you feel. Your feelings make you interpret your experience based on conventions. Based on your experiences, you may tend to think again and again. When you think again and again about certain things, you're taught to consume your happiness and make yourself weary and heavy in mind. So, in this manner, by grasping to your thoughts, you tend to get hurt by what you are thinking, and the way you think can hurt you. Learning how to think beneficially can help you avoid or reduce suffering.

When your eye meets a sight, information coming from the eye is processed with mind-based conventions. When you interpret such information based on conventions, you tend to experience a feeling as "I am experiencing a feeling", and if you grasp into such feelings with too much liking or disliking, you are likely to think more and more about it. What you think about excessively can bother you and disturb you, especially when you don't get what you want or what you want changes. This can make you distressed, and the same goes for past, present and future.

When you maintain and develop excessive liking or disliking or expectations towards what you see and what you feel after seeing and what you interpret based on conventions out of feelings, and what you tend to think based on your interpreting, and when you tend to think again and again with attachment to your worldly experiences, you tend to get hurt. Instead, when you don't have too many likes, dislikes, or expectations, meaning that you understand your likes, dislikes, and expectations don't always come to fulfilment, you will experience less pain. When you know, you won't always get what you like based on your true-life experience, you won't be surprised or shocked at life's circumstances. When you know without a doubt that your worldly experiences are impermanent and subject to change, your thoughts will not bother you.

When you experience feelings without grasping (as an Arahant), you will not grasp into giving value to what you feel. You will not make up various ideas or mental images about it and get attached to such images. When you don't give any importance to what you feel just as you would not care much about a leave falling off a random tree, taking what you feel as important or belonging to you, your feelings will not broadcast you. When you don't care about what you feel and don't get attached to your feelings, you are free from them. In this manner, your thoughts don't bother you anymore, and distress ends. To come into such a state, you should have completed Sotapanna to the Arahant state.

Residuals of Arahants are merely for offering higher wisdom and merits to others, so they can also develop their wisdom and merits/wholesome intentions to cease sufferings and experience Cessation, Nibbana.

Just as a hungry person would enjoy a tasty honey cake, a person with integrity and wisdom will gain joy and clarity by hearing the words of wisdom opening the Noble Path.

The Noble Path is universal. This is because every person can only experience their world through sensory information, which is universal to all. Sensuality in the Noble Path refers to greed: too much liking, or hate: too much disliking, or delusion: expectations (desire) towards the worldly experiences coming from sensory information. The route out of sensuality and worldly experiences remains the same for all, abandoning the mental attachment (desire) across four-fold Nibbana.

"So I have heard. At one time the Buddha was staying in the land of the Sakyans, near Kapilavatthu in the Banyan Tree Monastery.

Then the Buddha dressed up in the morning and, entered Kapilavatthu for alms. He wandered for alms in Kapilavatthu. After the meal, on his return from almsround, he went to the Great Wood for the day's stay, plunged deep into it, and sat at the root of a young wood apple tree to rest.

Daṇḍapāṇi the Sakyan, while going for a walk, plunged deep into the Great Wood. He approached the Buddha and exchanged greetings with him. When the greetings and polite conversation were over, he stood to one side leaning on his staff, and said to the Buddha, "What is the ascetic's doctrine? What does he assert?"

"Sir, my doctrine is such that one does not conflict with anyone in this world with its gods, Māras, and Divinities, this population with its ascetics and brahmins, its gods and humans. And it is such that perceptions do not underlie the brahmin who lives detached from sensual pleasures, without doubting, stripped of worry, and rid of craving for rebirth in this or that state. That is my doctrine, and that is what I assert."

When he had spoken, Daṇḍapāṇi shook his head, waggled his tongue, raised his eyebrows until his brow puckered in three furrows, and he departed leaning on his staff.

Then in the late afternoon, the Buddha came out of retreat and went to the Banyan Tree Monastery, sat down on the seat spread out, and told the spiritual companions what had happened.

When he had spoken, one of the companions said to him, "But venerable sir, asserting what doctrine does the Buddha not conflict with anyone in this world with its gods, Māras, and Divinities, this population with its ascetics and brahmins, its gods and humans? And how is it that perceptions do not underlie the Buddha, the brahmin who lives detached from sensual pleasures, without indecision, stripped of worry, and rid of craving for rebirth in this or that state?"

"Companion, judgments driven by proliferating perceptions beset a person. If they don't find anything worth approving, welcoming, or getting attached to in the source from which these arise, just this is the end of the underlying tendencies to desire, repulsion, views, doubt, conceit, the desire to be reborn, and ignorance.

This is the end of taking up the rod and the sword, the end of quarrels, arguments, and disputes, of accusations, divisive speech, and lies. This is where these bad, unskillful qualities cease without anything left over."

That is what the Buddha said. When he had spoken, the Holy One got up from his seat and entered his dwelling.

Soon after the Buddha left, those companions considered, "The Buddha gave this brief summary recital, then entered his dwelling without explaining the meaning in detail. Who can explain in detail the meaning of this brief summary recital given by the Buddha?"

Then those companions thought, "This Arahant Mahākaccāna is praised by the Buddha and esteemed by his sensible spiritual companions. He is capable of explaining in detail the meaning of this brief summary recital given by the Buddha. Let's go to him, and ask him about this matter."

Then those companions went to Arahant Mahākaccāna, and exchanged greetings with him. When the greetings and polite conversation were over, they sat down to one side. They told him what had happened and said: "May Arahant Mahākaccāna please explain this."

"Respected friends, suppose there was a person in need of heartwood. And while wandering in search of heartwood he'd come across a large tree standing with heartwood. But he'd pass over the roots and trunk, imagining that the heartwood should be sought in the branches and leaves. Such is the consequence for the companions.

Though you were face to face with the Buddha, you overlooked him, imagining that you should ask me about this matter. For he is the Buddha, the one who knows and sees. He is vision, he is knowledge, he is the manifestation of principle, he is the manifestation of divinity.

He is the teacher, the proclaimer, the elucidator of meaning, the bestower of freedom from death, the lord of truth, the Realized One. That was the time to approach the Buddha and ask about this matter. You should have remembered it in line with the Buddha's answer."

"Certainly, he is the Buddha, the one who knows and sees. He is vision, he is knowledge, he is the manifestation of principle, he is the manifestation of divinity. He is the teacher, the proclaimer, the elucidator of meaning, the bestower of freedom from death, the lord of truth, the Realized One. That was the time to approach the Buddha and ask about this matter.

We should have remembered it in line with the Buddha's answer. Still, Arahant Mahākaccāna is praised by the Buddha and esteemed by his sensible spiritual companions. You are capable of explaining in detail the meaning of this brief summary recital given by the Buddha. Please explain this, if it's no trouble."

"Well then, respected companions, listen and apply your mind well, I will speak."

"Yes, venerable sir," they replied. Arahant Mahākaccāna said this:

"Respected friends, the Buddha gave this brief summary recital, then entered his dwelling without explaining the meaning in detail: 'Judgments driven by proliferating perceptions beset a person. If they don't find anything worth approving, welcoming, or getting attached to in the source from which these arise, just this is the end of the underlying tendencies to desire, repulsion, views, doubt, conceit, the desire to be reborn, and ignorance.

This is the end of taking up the rod and the sword, the end of quarrels, arguments, and disputes, of accusations, divisive speech, and lies. This is where these bad, unskillful qualities cease without anything left over.' This is how I understand the detailed meaning of this summary recital.

Eye consciousness arises dependent on the eye and sights. The meeting of the three is contact. Contact is a condition for feeling. What you feel, you perceive. What you perceive, you think about. What you think about, you proliferate. What you proliferate is the source from which judgments driven by proliferating perceptions beset a person. This occurs with respect to sights known by the eye in the past, future, and present.

Ear consciousness arises dependent on the ear and sounds. ...

Nose consciousness arises dependent on the nose and smells. ...

Tongue consciousness arises dependent on the tongue and tastes. ...

Body consciousness arises dependent on the body and touches. …

Mind consciousness arises dependent on the mind and ideas. The meeting of the three is contact. Contact is a condition for feeling. What you feel, you perceive. What you perceive, you think about. What you think about, you proliferate. What you proliferate is the source from which judgments driven by proliferating perceptions beset a person.

This occurs with respect to ideas known by the mind in the past, future, and present.

Where there is the eye, sights, and eye consciousness, it will be possible to discover evidence of contact. Where there is evidence of contact, it will be possible to discover evidence of feeling. Where there is evidence of feeling, it will be possible to discover evidence of perception. Where there is evidence of perception, it will be possible to discover evidence of thought. Where there is evidence of thought, it will be possible to discover evidence of being beset by judgments driven by proliferating perceptions.

Where there is the ear … nose … tongue … body … mind, ideas, and mind consciousness, it will be possible to discover evidence of contact. … Where there is evidence of contact, it will be possible to discover evidence of feeling. Where there is evidence of feeling, it will be possible to discover evidence of perception. Where there is evidence of perception, it will be possible to discover evidence of thinking. Where there is evidence of thinking, it will be possible to discover evidence of being beset by judgments driven by proliferating perceptions.

Where there is no eye, no sights, and no eye consciousness, it will not be possible to discover evidence of contact. Where there is no evidence of contact, it will not be possible to discover evidence of feeling.

Where there is no evidence of feeling, it will not be possible to discover evidence of perception. Where there is no evidence of perception, it will not be possible to discover evidence of thinking. Where there is no evidence of thinking, it will not be possible to discover evidence of being beset by judgments driven by proliferating perceptions.

Where there is no ear … no nose … no tongue … no body … no mind, no ideas, and no mind consciousness, it will not be possible to discover evidence of contact. Where there is no evidence of contact, it will not be possible to discover evidence of feeling.

Where there is no evidence of feeling, it will not be possible to discover evidence of perception. Where there is no evidence of perception, it will not be possible to discover evidence of thinking.

Where there is no evidence of thinking, it will not be possible to discover evidence of being beset by judgments driven by proliferating perceptions.

This is how I understand the detailed meaning of that brief summary recital given by the Buddha. If you wish, you may go to the Buddha and ask him about this. You should remember it in line with the Buddha's answer."

Then those companions, approving and agreeing with what Arahant Mahākaccāna said, rose from their seats and went to the Buddha, bowed, sat down to one side, and told him what had happened, adding: "Arahant Mahākaccāna clearly explained the meaning to us in this manner, with these words and phrases."

"Arahant Mahākaccāna is astute, friends, he has great wisdom. If you came to me and asked this question, I would answer it in exactly the same way as Mahākaccāna. That is what it means, and that's how you should remember it."

When he said this, Ānanda said to the Buddha, "Sir, suppose a person who was weak with hunger was to obtain a honey-cake. Wherever they taste it, they would enjoy a sweet, delicious flavor.

In the same way, wherever a sincere, capable person might examine with wisdom the meaning of this exposition of the teaching they would only gain joy and clarity. Sir, what is the name of this exposition of the teaching?"

"Well then, Ānanda, you may remember this exposition of the teaching as 'The Honey-Cake Discourse'."

That is what the Buddha said. Satisfied, Ānanda approved what the Buddha said"

Chapter 21

Middle Discourses 19: Dvedhāvitakkasutta

Two Kinds of Thought

An ordinary person may observe one's thoughts by dividing them into two categories: wholesome thoughts and unwholesome thoughts, just as Buddha did before gaining Buddhahood. Wholesome thoughts refer to thoughts that don't hurt self or others. Unwholesome thoughts are thoughts that hurt self and others.

When you come to know that your thoughts are unwholesome thoughts, just as when you come to know them, your attachment to such thoughts can decline. Therefore, just becoming aware of what kind of thoughts you experience at a time, whether they are wholesome or unwholesome thoughts, can aid you in reducing attachment to such thoughts. When you want to develop awareness, it is when you experience distress within, taking discomfort as a wake-up call. Establish mindfulness to observe your thoughts to understand whether they are wholesome or unwholesome thoughts.

While an ordinary person may observe thoughts at times, observing thoughts at all times may not be practical as attention, mindfulness and concentration can be subject to change. However, striving to understand one's thoughts by observing them when possible can still help an ordinary person reduce too much distress. Unhelpful thoughts will make one suffer, and the way to see one's thoughts refers to Sotapanna to Arahant, a natural happening shaped by one's merits and karma.

Nibbana is not a sila based lifestyle but a wisdom and karma-based path and training. Things such as a person's good health and wisdom can be gained through both universal and conventional ways: previous merits, developing merits, putting efforts into developing self, working hard on tasks, etc.

The middle way means simply making use of universal ways and conventions without grasping but giving up grasping to reach cessation. Therefore, jhana practice among ordinary people and the practice of jhanas by an Anagami in the training path of four-fold Nibbana differs. The practice leading to Nibbana is the right view.

Right view for an ordinary person is understanding that life is an interaction between the universe and conventions, and the universal ways of functioning, karma to a reasonable level.

An ordinary person cannot see samsara due to attachment to limited vision. When your vision is stuck in conventions, you tend to forget universal ways of functioning. Yet, what your eyes cannot see, you can see with wisdom. In this way, wisdom can be developed by developing merits, shaping karma and putting efforts to practicing Dhamma in a way leading to four-fold Nibbana.

What makes people reborn in samsara? It is karma that makes people reborn in samsara. What is karma?

Intentional actions are karma. Actions without intentions free one from making new karma, which is the universal way of functioning.

You may live in any city, any country, or any place of accommodation. You may wear any dress and speak any language. If you want to practice universal Dhamma in a way leading to four-fold Nibbana, you have to practice in the same way: reduce greediness (too many likes), hatred (too many dislikes), and delusion (expectations) by giving up grasping to fetters across four-fold Nibbana. Greed, hate and delusion can burn you within. By understanding, you can let go of such burns.

When you have a limited vision, you don't see what lies beyond. When you look back on your past, you might notice that there were occasions when you did not see things and that your vision was limited. Attachment to mind and body makes someone stuck in mind and body, unable to see beyond mind and body. Non-attachment to mind and body across four-fold Nibbana makes it possible for a person to surpass mind and body to see beyond; previous births, birth and death of beings, understanding attainment of Nibbana through wisdom.

When faced with unpleasant events, an ordinary person is likely to suffer too much distress, particularly when the person's mind is in the habit of hiding certain aspects of life if they are not a part of life. Instead, stop hiding things that are a part of life to see with clarity by allowing the mind to understand and interpret real life experience to understand that ups and downs are natural for all of us. In doing so, let go of cognitive bias that results in clinging to mind-made things as if they are real. A wise person can develop an understanding to see beyond ordinary views. Having a limited and restricted understanding of life can produce too much stress. Instead, by reducing thinking erroneously with bias and becoming free from a limited understanding of life and the mind, a person can develop the right understanding of life and mind. The right view/correct understanding of life will allow a person to extend happiness gained through worldly experience (cutting off worldly experiences by cutting off sensory experiences is not practical, as worldly experiences are processed through sensory information in each person) while living with conventions.

Once born, a person comes to experience changes that are brought on by nature. Caught between nature in the universe and worldly experience coming from sensory information, a person may develop a self, others, and the world in the person's thoughts. While living on earth, a person may think certain things, and what a person is thinking may not happen in real life. When there is a discrepancy between what a person is thinking and what the person is experiencing on earth and in a person's life, a person can feel stress and inadequacy.

Not understanding the truth can produce mental pain. Understanding truth allows a person to experience worldly life without regret. Understanding that change is the nature for all of us, instead of just watching how things unfold, and without getting too worried over things that we cannot control or change, letting go of things that are gone, taking a reasonable course of action to do things that must be done, engaging to resolve things that can be resolved, and making the most of what is available, living life to the fullest is a wise thing to do. When a person understands with wisdom that certain things in the universe cannot be changed, that not everything can be gained, and that the person should therefore let go of things that cannot be changed but attend to doing the things that can be done without regret, this is a wise thing to do; it is a way of developing the middle mind training to abandoning self-view and to achieving the noble way of living. Instead of too much dependence on others and on society for approval or denial and expecting from others and society, a person chooses to do good and avoid doing bad and is true to one's heart, one can find inner peace within despite what other people think and say. In this manner, a person can remain satisfied and unaffected in the very presence of others and the world, not hurting oneself and not hurting others, and that is a way of developing the middle path.

Having attained four-fold Nibbana, Buddha showed the path to Nibbana to others so they too can experience Nibbana similar to Buddha while living by following the path.

"So I have heard. At one time the Buddha was staying near Sāvatthī in Jeta's Grove, Anāthapiṇḍika's monastery. There the Buddha addressed the companions, "Companions!"

"Venerable sir," they replied. The Buddha said this:

"Friends, before my awakening—when I was still unawakened but intent on awakening—I thought: 'Why don't I meditate by continually dividing my thoughts into two classes?' So I assigned sensual, malicious, and cruel thoughts to one class. And I assigned thoughts of renunciation, good will, and harmlessness to the second class.

Then, as I reflected on my thoughts—diligent, keen, and resolute—a sensual thought arose. I understood: 'This sensual thought has arisen in me. It leads to hurting myself, hurting others, and hurting both. It blocks wisdom, it's on the side of anguish, and it doesn't lead to extinguishment.' When I reflected that it leads to hurting myself, it went away. When I reflected that it leads to hurting others, it went away. When I reflected that it leads to hurting both, it went away. When I reflected that it blocks wisdom, it's on the side of anguish, and it doesn't lead to extinguishment, it went away. So I gave up, got rid of, and eliminated any sensual thoughts that arose.

Then, as I reflected on my thoughts—diligent, keen, and resolute—a malicious thought arose … a cruel thought arose. I understood: 'This cruel thought has arisen in me. It leads to hurting myself, hurting others, and hurting both. It blocks wisdom, it's on the side of anguish, and it doesn't lead to extinguishment.' When I reflected that it leads to hurting myself … hurting others … hurting both, it went away. When I reflected that it blocks wisdom, it's on the side of anguish, and it doesn't lead to extinguishment, it went away. So I gave up, got rid of, and eliminated any cruel thoughts that arose.

Whatever a person frequently thinks about and considers becomes their heart's inclination. If they often think about and consider sensual thoughts, they've given up the thought of renunciation to cultivate sensual thought. Their mind inclines to sensual thoughts. If they often think about and consider malicious thoughts … their mind inclines to malicious thoughts. If they often think about and consider cruel thoughts … their mind inclines to cruel thoughts.

Suppose it's the last month of the rainy season, in autumn, when the crops grow closely together, and a cowherd must take care of the cattle. He'd tap and poke them with his staff on this side and that to keep them in check. Why is that? For he sees that if they wander into the crops he could be executed, imprisoned, fined, or condemned.

In the same way, I saw that unskillful qualities have the drawbacks of sordidness and corruption, and that skillful qualities have the benefit and cleansing power of renunciation.

Then, as I reflected—diligent, keen, and resolute—a thought of renunciation arose. I understood: 'This thought of renunciation has arisen in me. It doesn't lead to hurting myself, hurting others, or hurting both. It nourishes wisdom, it's on the side of freedom from anguish, and it leads to extinguishment.' If I were to keep on thinking and considering this all night … all day … all night and day, I see no danger that would come from that. Still, thinking and considering for too long would tire my body. And when the body is tired, the mind is stressed.

And when the mind is stressed, it's far from immersion. So I stilled, settled, unified, and immersed my mind internally. Why is that? So that my mind would not be stressed.

Then, as I reflected—diligent, keen, and resolute—a thought of good will arose … a thought of harmlessness arose. I understood: 'This thought of harmlessness has arisen in me. It doesn't lead to hurting myself, hurting others, or hurting both. It nourishes wisdom, it's on the side of freedom from anguish, and it leads to extinguishment.' If I were to keep on thinking and considering this all night … all day … all night and day, I see no danger that would come from that. Still, thinking and considering for too long would tire my body.

And when the body is tired, the mind is stressed. And when the mind is stressed, it's far from immersion. So I stilled, settled, unified, and immersed my mind internally. Why is that? So that my mind would not be stressed.

Whatever a person frequently thinks about and considers becomes their heart's inclination. If they often think about and consider thoughts of renunciation, they've given up sensual thought to cultivate the thought of renunciation. Their mind inclines to thoughts of renunciation. If they often think about and consider thoughts of good will … their mind inclines to thoughts of good will. If they often think about and consider thoughts of harmlessness … their mind inclines to thoughts of harmlessness.

Suppose it's the last month of summer, when all the crops have been gathered within a village, and a cowherd must take care of the cattle. While at the root of a tree or in the open he need only be mindful that the cattle are there. In the same way I needed only to be mindful that those things were there.

My energy was roused up and unflagging, my mindfulness was established and lucid, my body was tranquil and undisturbed, and my mind was immersed in noble concentration (Anagami).

Upon gaining the Anagami state, having given up the relevant fetters (sensuality, ill will), I entered and remained in the first absorption, which has the rapture and bliss born of seclusion, while placing the mind and keeping it connected.

As the placing of the mind and keeping it connected were stilled, I entered and remained in the second absorption, which has the rapture and bliss born of immersion, with internal clarity and mind at one, without placing the mind and keeping it connected.

And with the fading away of rapture, I entered and remained in the third absorption, where I experienced equanimity, mindful and aware, personally experiencing the bliss of which the noble ones declare, 'Equanimous and mindful, one meditates in bliss.'

With the giving up of pleasure and pain, and the ending of former happiness and sadness, I entered and remained in the fourth absorption, without pleasure or pain, with pure equanimity and mindfulness.

When my mind had immersed in noble concentration like this—purified, bright, flawless, rid of corruptions, pliable, workable, steady, and imperturbable—I extended it toward recollection of past lives. I recollected many kinds of past lives, with features and details.

This was the first knowledge, which I achieved in the first watch of the night. Ignorance was destroyed and knowledge arose; darkness was destroyed and light arose, as happens for a person who is diligent, keen, and resolute.

When my mind had become immersed in noble concentration like this, I extended it toward knowledge of the death and rebirth of sentient beings.

With clairvoyance that is purified and superhuman, I saw sentient beings passing away and being reborn—inferior and superior, beautiful and ugly, in a good place or a bad place. I understood how sentient beings are reborn according to their deeds.

This was the second knowledge, which I achieved in the middle watch of the night.

Ignorance was destroyed and knowledge arose; darkness was destroyed and light arose, as happens for a person who is diligent, keen, and resolute.

When my mind had become immersed in noble concentration like this, I extended it toward knowledge of the ending of defilements; Arahantship and Buddhahood. I truly understood: 'This is suffering' … 'This is the origin of suffering' … 'This is the cessation of suffering' … 'This is the practice that leads to the cessation of suffering.'

I truly understood: 'These are defilements' … 'This is the origin of defilements' … 'This is the cessation of defilements' … 'This is the practice that leads to the cessation of defilements.' Knowing and seeing like this, my mind was freed from the defilements of sensuality, desire to be reborn, and ignorance.

I understood: 'Rebirth is ended; the spiritual journey has been completed; what had to be done has been done; there is nothing further for this place.'

This was the third knowledge, which I achieved in the last watch of the night. Ignorance was destroyed and knowledge arose; darkness was destroyed and light arose, as happens for a meditator who is diligent, keen, and resolute.

Suppose that in a forested wilderness there was an expanse of low-lying marshes, and a large herd of deer lived nearby. Then along comes a person who wants to harm, injure, and threaten them. They close off the safe, secure path that leads to happiness, and open the wrong path.

There they plant domesticated male and female deer as decoys so that, in due course, that herd of deer would fall to ruin and disaster. Then along comes a person who wants to help keep the herd of deer safe. They open up the safe, secure path that leads to happiness, and close off the wrong path. They get rid of the decoys so that, in due course, that herd of deer would grow, increase, and mature.

I've made up this simile to make a point. And this is what it means. 'An expanse of low-lying marshes' is a term for sensual pleasures. 'A large herd of deer' is a term for sentient beings.

'A person who wants to harm, injure, and threaten them' is a term for Māra the Wicked. 'The wrong path' is a term for the wrong eightfold path, that is, wrong view, wrong thought, wrong speech, wrong action, wrong livelihood, wrong effort, wrong mindfulness, and wrong immersion. 'A domesticated male deer' is a term for greed and relishing. 'A domesticated female deer' is a term for ignorance.

'A person who wants to help keep the herd of deer safe' is a term for the Realized One, the perfected one, the fully awakened Buddha. 'The safe, secure path that leads to happiness' is a term for the noble eightfold path, that is: right view, right thought, right speech, right action, right livelihood, right effort, right mindfulness, and right immersion.

So, companions, I have opened up the safe, secure path to happiness and closed off the wrong path. And I have got rid of the male and female decoys.

Out of sympathy, I've done what a teacher should do who wants what's best for their disciples. Here are these roots of trees, and here are these empty huts. Practice four-fold Nibbāna, companions! Don't be negligent! Don't regret it later! This is my instruction to you."

That is what the Buddha said. Satisfied, the companions approved what the Buddha said."

Chapter 22

Middle Discourses 20: Vitakkasaṇṭhānasutta

How to Stop Thinking

The one who purifies from unwholesome thoughts, thoughts that are grasping mind and body based on conventions (self-view, social practices, doubt to begin with) is the one who carries Dhamma within. The purified thoughts, and dhamma doing in intentional actions cannot be seen by the outside as a dress or appearance. Nibbana is a mental state; intentional actions that shape karma and not the external factors are relevant.

Dhamma can only be carried within a person's mind, as the world is created in the mind. Freedom from the world is experienced in mind. The conscious transformation of a person can change because consciousness is subject to change. Ritualistic transformation can be temporary, as life is temporary. One who carries Dhamma within (four-fold Nibbana) is one who represents Buddha. It should be understood that Dhamma does not mean a dress, a lifestyle or a celibate life based on rules but a mental state, intentional actions, actions free from grasping self, precepts and social practices, freedom from conventional ways of interpreting self, others and the world. Nibbana is a universal happening.

When you understand you have unwholesome thoughts flowing in your mind, you may adopt certain techniques to let go of unwholesome thoughts. You may distract your attention from such thoughts as distracting can change thoughts to a different topic or direction. You may ignore such thoughts, stop forming such thoughts through conscious efforts, use a strong will to stop such thoughts or be determined to stop these thoughts. Using these ways, you can reframe your thoughts until the natural process of four-fold Nibbana occurs in your thoughts. These techniques can help an ordinary person better manage their thoughts.

By understanding the consequences of wholesome and unwholesome thoughts, applying mindfulness to observe your thoughts to find Dhamma within your thoughts, not merely observing but observing to evaluate and discover self, to develop Dhamma within, a person can reframe thoughts and purify from grasping conventions. You may need to constantly adopt such a practice. At times, you may feel like you've lost track. Then, you start all over again and combine your practice of analyzing thoughts with engaging in ten wholesome deeds to blend with the universal ways. For example, when you feel sad, you might ask yourself, why do I feel sad? Then, you will analyze and try to evaluate the reason for your sadness or distress. You might notice that you feel sad or distressed because something you expected didn't come to fulfillment the way you had wished or because of your likes or dislikes for worldly experiences. Yet, the truth of life is that not all that you like, dislike or expect can be fulfilled. Instead of getting distressed, make the best of what is available, which is a wise thing to do. In this manner, by applying Dhamma and using wisdom, you can reduce mental pain from grasping unwholesome thoughts within you.

Mastering thoughts, a technique of developing the Noble Path or giving up getting attached to thoughts, can be done in stages. First, self-view and conventions are to be reduced in the middle way. Imagine you are riding a boat where you have to maintain some balance. In the same way, if you can try to maintain balance in your thoughts when thoughts occur, always remembering that nothing lasts forever, it will help you maintain the best of worldly experiences in a more balanced way. If you can see your thoughts, as it happens naturally for an Arahant, you may be able to stop giving up grasping to your thoughts. Yet, it is your desire (greed, hate, delusion) for thoughts that make you want to grasp into your thoughts. However, an ordinary person can learn to self-apply, not getting attached to self-view and conventions in mind. How can you do that?

You may constantly reflect and adopt certain techniques as below;

1. When unwholesome thoughts occur, try focus your attention on something else. The thoughts will go away.
2. When unwholesome/distressing thoughts appear in your mind, try and reflect that such thoughts occur because of desires (likes, dislikes, expectations), towards worldly experiences, and fetters, reflecting how difficult it is to endure pain, try and effectively give up grasping to distressing thoughts.
3. Continue to be mindful of how unwholesome thoughts bring you suffering. If likes, dislikes, hate, or delusions still come up, try and forget and ignore such thoughts.
4. As you try to forget and ignore bad and unwholesome thoughts that come to your mind because of desires (likes, dislikes, expectations) towards worldly experiences, try and give up forming such thoughts by questioning and answering and advising yourself; "Why I am fostering such thoughts that bother me?" and " Why don't I stop forming distressing thoughts?"

Strive to question and answer and analyze yourself. Eventually, you will be able to shape your thoughts and reframe your thoughts in the interest of your well-being, skilled in your thoughts to experience peace within.
5. As you mindfully stop forming your thoughts, if they continue to form bad thoughts connected with likes, dislikes, hate, and self-view as stable (greed, hate, delusion), then you should make an effort to cease and be free from such thoughts with strong determination (i.e clenched teeth, and pressed tongue) to gain your freedom from bothersome thoughts.

While engaging in observing, reflecting, analyzing, and reframing your thoughts, you may regularly engage in Dhamma activities, develop Dasa Kusal (*Ten Wholesome Deeds, intentional actions*). It will aid you in becoming a Sotapanna. Reducing mental attachment should be done in phases;
1. Reduce self-view.
   Reduce unwholesome thoughts that hurt self and others; too much sadness, anxiety, jealousy, pride, etc.
2. Reduce grasping conventions and social practices.
   Give up comparisons and grasping social practices by understanding social practices cannot retain stability within the universal ways of functioning; "I am better than them," "I am worse than them," "I am the same as them," etc.
3. Reduce grasping to sila ("I am better because I follow sila," etc.).
4. Develop the habit of sharing whatever you have with others and taking self-responsibility for your intentions/and actions.
5. Understand the universe functions in such a way that those who purify from grasping to conventions based on sensory information get to abandon mental suffering.
6. Nibbana is a matter dealing with the universe, as you are a part of the universe. Thus, pretending to gain Nibbana should be avoided at all costs.
7. Telling others how to gain Nibbana without you gaining Nibbana by misinterpreting Dhamma should be avoided by those who aspire to their own well-being and merit.

"So I have heard. At one time the Buddha was staying near Sāvatthī in Jeta's Grove, Anāthapiṇḍika's monastery. There the Buddha addressed the companions, "Companions!"

"Venerable sir," they replied. The Buddha said this:

"Companions, a companion committed to the higher mind should focus on five subjects from time to time. What five?

Take an ordinary person who is focusing on some subject that gives rise to bad, unskillful thoughts connected with desire, hate, and delusion. That person should focus on some other subject connected with the skillful.

As they do so, those bad thoughts are given up and come to an end. Their mind becomes stilled internally; it settles, calm down, and becomes immersed in concentration. It's like a deft carpenter or their apprentice who'd knock out or extract a large peg with a finer peg. In the same way, a person ... should focus on some other basis of reflecting connected with the skillful ...

Now, suppose that an ordinary person is focusing on some other subject connected with the skillful, but bad, unskillful thoughts connected with desire, hate, and delusion keep coming up. They should examine the drawbacks of those thoughts: 'So these thoughts are unskillful, they're blameworthy, and they result in suffering.'

As they do so, those bad thoughts are given up and come to an end. Their mind becomes stilled internally; it settles, unifies, and becomes immersed in concentrating.

Suppose there was a woman or man who was young, youthful, and fond of adornments. If the carcass of a snake or a dog or a human were hung around their neck, they'd be horrified, repelled, and disgusted. In the same way, a companion... should examine the drawbacks of those thoughts ...

Now, suppose that ordinary person is examining the drawbacks of those thoughts, but bad, unskillful thoughts connected with desire, hate, and delusion keep coming up. They should try to forget and ignore them. As they do so, those bad thoughts are given up and come to an end.

Their mind becomes stilled internally; it settles, calm down, and becomes immersed in concentration. Suppose there was a person with clear eyes, and some undesirable sights came into their range of vision. They'd just close their eyes or look away. In the same way, a companion ... those bad thoughts are given up and come to an end...

Now, suppose that ordinary person is ignoring and forgetting about those thoughts, but bad, unskillful thoughts connected with desire, hate, and delusion keep coming up.

They should focus on stopping the formation of thoughts. As they do so, those bad thoughts are given up and come to an end. Their mind becomes stilled internally; it settles, calm down, and becomes immersed in concentration. Suppose there was a person walking quickly. They'd think: 'Why am I walking so quickly? Why don't I slow down?' So they'd slow down. They'd think: 'Why am I walking slowly? Why don't I stand still?' So they'd stand still. They'd think: 'Why am I standing still? Why don't I sit down?' So they'd sit down. They'd think: 'Why am I sitting? Why don't I lie down?' So they'd lie down. And so that person would reject successively coarser postures and adopt more subtle ones.

In the same way, a person… those thoughts are given up and come to an end …

Now, suppose that person is focusing on stopping the formation of thoughts, but bad, unskillful thoughts connected with desire, hate, and delusion keep coming up. With teeth clenched and tongue pressed against the roof of the mouth, they should squeeze, squash, and crush mind with mind.

As they do so, those bad thoughts are given up and come to reduce or end. Their mind becomes stilled internally; it settles, unifies, and becomes immersed in concentration. It's like a strong man who grabs a weaker man by the head or throat or shoulder and squeezes, squashes, and crushes them. In the same way, a person… with teeth clenched and tongue pressed against the roof of the mouth, should squeeze, squash, and crush mind with mind. As they do so, those bad thoughts are given up and come to an end. Their mind becomes stilled internally; it settles, calm down, and becomes immersed in concentration.

Now, take the noble person, a trainee (Sotapanna or Sakadagami) who is focusing on some subject that gives rise to bad, unskillful thoughts connected with desire, hate, and delusion. They focus on some other subject connected with the skillful …

They examine the drawbacks of those thoughts … They try to forget and ignore about those thoughts …

They focus on stopping the formation of thoughts …

With teeth clenched and tongue pressed against the roof of the mouth, they squeeze, squash, and crush mind with mind.

When they succeed in each of these things, those bad thoughts are given up and come to an end. Their mind becomes stilled internally; it settles, calm down, and becomes immersed in noble concentration.

This is called a noble person who is a master of the ways of thought.

Arahant who gains four-fold Nibbana, naturally they will think what they want to think, and they won't think what they don't want to think. They've cut off craving, untied the fetters, and by rightly comprehending conceit have made an end of suffering."

That is what the Buddha said. Satisfied, the companions approved what the Buddha said."

Chapter 23

Middle Discourses 21: Kakacūpamasutta

The Simile of the Saw

This discourse discusses the mind state of an Anagami, and the advice given for those who aspire to develop the Noble Path is to try and refrain from developing ill will towards those who criticize you both reasonably and unreasonably. Practicing Dhamma to gain Nibbana requires training the mind to think beyond the ordinary within daily life. For example, when someone experiences criticism from others with a valid reason or without, it is useful to bring back mindfulness and make some effort to reflect on the teachings of the Buddha that remind us how criticism and praise from others with or without an edible reason, ups and downs are part of life, as that is the nature of life for all of us. Similarly, when one feels upset, it is useful to bring back mindfulness to reflect that context can be anything, so that feelings and thoughts, good times and bad times are normal things to expect in life, and everything is subject to change universally applicable to all beings. Applying such a Dhamma perspective into analyzing real-life experience is a helpful practice to maintain peace of mind.

Furthermore, for those who aspire to attain enlightenment, as a form of training, it will be beneficial to combine the practice of reflect on non-self-view in daily life and the qualities of Buddha, Dhamma, and noble Sangha to eliminate the first three fetters and to gain the non-self-view.

Below is a guided reflection that can be applied to giving up getting attached to one's thoughts related to self-view in daily life:

1. "Ups and downs, criticism and praise are a part of life, and such experiences can change",

2. "I am subject to decay, all beings are subject to decay, I have not gone beyond decay,"

3. "I am subject to illnesses, and all beings are subject to illnesses, and I have not gone beyond illnesses,"

4. "I am subject to death, and all beings are subject to death, and I have not gone beyond death,"

5. "I am the owner of my karma, all beings are subject to their karma, and I am not gone beyond my karma,"

6. "All that is mine, dear and delightful are subject to change," is always to be reflected upon.

7. "All that I wish, and I want, I will not get as the way I wish, and I like!" is always to be reflected upon.

It is by attaining to Anagmi you will not have intentional action to cause harm or ill will to others even when they cause difficulties for you. An ordinary person may try and develop such qualities, and may reflect on the true-life experience while going and doing within daily life. Although real life experience will show that both ups and downs are part of life for people, mind-made understanding of a person's world can be different from that of real-life experience. When there is a discrepancy between what is real and what is made up in one's mind, the difference between real life experience and a person's mind-made understanding of the person's world can create an ongoing tension and stress to the person when they mismatch, and harmony and peace can be lost in the person's mind. By bringing mind-made understanding of the person's world closer to real-life experience, the person will be able to gain harmony to restore satisfaction gained through worldly life.

Based on one's personal life experiences, if someone endures various kinds of worldly hardships and understands for themselves that life is not easy, that is the kind of an understanding that helps an ordinary practitioner want to practice middle mind training. At the next level, if an ordinary person understands that grasping worldly life can without a doubt produce mental pain, and it's not worth the pain, that kind of understanding helps an ordinary practitioner to continue training in the middle path. Otherwise, one may just hear and talk about the path and live a lifestyle without necessarily applying the middle path training.

Thus, practicing Dhamma for an ordinary practitioner means applying Dhamma to oneself, and, as the result of applying Dhamma practice, should reduce one's pride, greediness, and extreme sadness towards worldly experiences.

Life is an experience, an interaction between the universe and conventions, and that conventions can happen only within the universe, there are things beyond conventions that a person cannot control, such as the impermanent nature of beings. The teachings leading to Nibbana can be developed based on developing the right understanding of the deep teachings, right view, the first step towards the noble path. When Dhamma is understood, it produces benefit to those who aspire Nibbana.

The universe function in such a way that seasonal phenomena of winds, rain are a way of its functioning. Universe function in such a way that rice produced from rice-seed, sugary taste from sugar-cane or honey, and so on. Universe function in such a way that intentional actions lead to consequences. The universe functions in such a way that, when a person is born, birth brings death, illnesses, losses, gains, falls and rises are part of life, the way of life.

"So I have heard. At one time the Buddha was staying near Sāvatthī in Jeta's Grove, Anāthapiṇḍika's monastery.

Now at that time, ordinary monk Moliya Phagguna was spending too long mixing closely with some ordinary nuns. So much so that if any companions criticized those nuns in his presence, Phagguna got angry and upset, and even instigated disciplinary proceedings. And if any companion criticized Phagguna in their presence, those nuns got angry and upset, and even instigated disciplinary proceedings. That's how close Phagguna was with those nuns.

Then a spiritual companion went up to the Buddha, bowed, sat down to one side, and told him what was going on.

So the Buddha addressed one of the companions, "Please, friend, in my name tell the friend, Phagguna that the teacher calls him."

"Yes, sir," that companion replied. He went to Phagguna and said to him, "Friend Phagguna, the teacher calls you."

"As you say, friend," Phagguna replied.

He went to the Buddha, bowed, and sat down to one side. The Buddha said to him:

"Is it really true, Phagguna, that you've been spending too long mixing closely with some nuns? So much so that if any person criticizes those nuns in your presence, you get angry and upset, and even instigate disciplinary proceedings? And if any person criticizes you in those nuns' presence, they get angry and upset, and even instigate disciplinary proceedings? Is that how close you've become with those nuns?"

"Yes, sir."

"Phagguna, are you not a gentleman who has committed yourself to practicing the noble path by giving up mental attachment?"

"Yes, sir."

"As such, it's not appropriate for you to mix so closely and get mentally attached with those ordinary nuns. So if anyone criticizes those nuns in your presence, you should give up any desires or thoughts of the lay life. If that happens, you should train like this: 'My mind will not degenerate. I will blurt out no bad words. I will remain full of sympathy, with a heart of love and no secret hate.' That's how you should train.

So even if someone strikes those nuns with fists, stones, rods, and swords in your presence, you should give up any desires or thoughts of the lay life. If that happens, you should train like this: 'My mind will not live a lay life or degenerate. I will blurt out no bad words. I will remain full of sympathy, with a heart of love and no secret hate.' That's how you should train.

So if anyone criticizes you in your presence, you should give up any desires or thoughts of the lay life. If that happens, you should train like this: 'My mind will not degenerate. I will blurt out no bad words. I will remain full of sympathy, with a heart of love and no secret hate.' That's how you should train.

So Phagguna, even if someone strikes you with fists, stones, rods, and swords, you should give up any desires or thoughts of the ordinary life. If that happens, you should train like this: 'My mind will not degenerate. I will blurt out no bad words. I will remain full of sympathy, with a heart of love and no secret hate.' That's how you should train."

Then the Buddha said to the companions: "Companions, I used to be satisfied with the companions. Once, I addressed them: 'I eat my food in one sitting per day. Doing so, I find that I'm healthy and well, nimble, strong, and living comfortably. You too should eat your food in one sitting per day. Doing so, you'll find that you're healthy and well, nimble, strong, and living comfortably.' I didn't have to keep on instructing those companions; I just had to prompt their mindfulness.

Suppose a chariot stood harnessed to thoroughbreds at a level crossroads, with a goad ready. A deft horse trainer, a master charioteer, might mount the chariot, taking the reins in his right hand and goad in the left. He'd drive out and back wherever he wishes, whenever he wishes.

In the same way, I didn't have to keep on instructing those companions; I just had to prompt their mindfulness. So, companions, you too should give up what's unskillful and devote yourselves to skillful qualities. In this way you'll achieve growth, improvement, and maturity in this teaching (Sotapanna to Arahant) and training (The path).

Suppose that not far from a town or village there was a large grove of sal trees that was choked with castor-oil weeds. Then along comes a person who wants to help protect and nurture that grove.

They'd cut down the crooked sal saplings that were robbing the sap, and throw them out. They'd clean up the interior of the grove, and properly care for the straight, well-formed sal saplings. In this way, in due course, that sal grove would grow, increase, and mature.

In the same way, companions, you too should give up what's unskillful and devote yourselves to skillful qualities. In this way you'll achieve growth, improvement, and maturity in this teaching and training.

Once upon a time, companions, right here in Sāvatthī there was a housewife named Vedehikā. She had this good reputation: 'The housewife Vedehikā is sweet, even-tempered, and calm.' Now, Vedehikā had a bonded maid named Kāḷī who was deft, tireless, and well-organized in her work.

Then Kāḷī thought, 'My mistress has a good reputation as being sweet, even-tempered, and calm. But does she actually have anger in her and just not show it? Or does she have no anger? Or is it just because my work is well-organized that she doesn't show anger, even though she still has it inside? Why don't I test my mistress?'

So Kāḷī got up during the day. Vedehikā said to her, 'Oi wench, Kāḷī!'

'What is it, ma'am?'

'You're getting up in the day—what's up with you, wench?' 'Nothing, ma'am.'

'Oh, so nothing's up, you naughty maid, but you get up in the day!' Angry and upset, she scowled.

Then Kāḷī thought, 'My mistress actually has anger in her and just doesn't show it; it's not that she has no anger. It's just because my work is well-organized that she doesn't show anger, even though she still has it inside. Why don't I test my mistress further?'

So Kāḷī got up later in the day. Vedehikā said to her, 'Oi wench, Kāḷī!'

'What is it, ma'am?'

'You're getting up later in the day—what's up with you, wench?'

'Nothing, ma'am.'

'Oh, so nothing's up, you naughty maid, but you get up later in the day!' Angry and upset, she blurted out angry words.

Then Kāḷī thought, 'My mistress actually has anger in her and just doesn't show it; it's not that she has no anger. It's just because my work is well-organized that she doesn't show anger, even though she still has it inside. Why don't I test my mistress further?'

So Kāḷī got up even later in the day. Vedehikā said to her, 'Oi wench, Kāḷī!'

'What is it, ma'am?'

'You're getting up even later in the day—what's up with you, wench?' 'Nothing, ma'am.'

'Oh, so nothing's up, you naughty maid, but you get up even later in the day!' Angry and upset, she grabbed a door-pin and hit Kāḷī on the head, cracking it open.

Then Kāḷī, with blood pouring from her cracked skull, denounced her mistress to the neighbors, 'See, ladies, what the sweet one did! See what the even-tempered one did! See what the calm one did! How on earth can she grab a door-pin and hit her only maid on the head, cracking it open, just for getting up late?'

Then after some time the housewife Vedehikā got this bad reputation: 'The housewife Vedehikā is fierce, ill-tempered, and not calm at all.'

In the same way, a companion may be the sweetest of the sweet, the most even-tempered of the even-tempered, the calmest of the calm, so long as they don't encounter any disagreeable criticism.

But it's when they encounter disagreeable criticism that you'll know whether they're really sweet, even-tempered, and calm.

I don't say that a person is easy to admonish if they make themselves easy to admonish only for the sake of getting donations (i.e. clothing, food, accommodation, and medicines etc.).

Why is that? Because when they don't get donations (i.e. clothing, food, accommodation, and medicines etc.), they're no longer easy to admonish. But when a person is easy to admonish purely because they honor, respect, revere, worship, and venerate the teaching, then I say that they're easy to admonish.

So, companions, you should train yourselves: 'We will be easy to admonish purely because we honor, respect, revere, worship, and venerate the teaching.' That's how you should train.

Companions, there are these five ways in which others might criticize you. Their speech may be timely or untimely, true or false, gentle or harsh, beneficial or harmful, from a heart of love or from secret hate. When others criticize you, they may do so in any of these ways. If that happens, remembering the noble ones, you should train like this: 'Our minds will not degenerate. We will blurt out no bad words.

We will remain full of sympathy, with a heart of love and no secret hate. We will have a heart of love to that person. And with them as a basis, we will have a heart full of love to everyone in the world—abundant, expansive, limitless, free of enmity and ill will.' That's how you should train.

Suppose a person was to come along carrying a spade and basket and say, 'I shall make this great earth be without earth!' And they'd dig all over, scatter all over, spit all over, and urinate all over, saying, 'Be without earth! Be without earth!'

What do you think, companions? Could that person make this great earth be without earth?"

"No, sir. Why is that? Because this great earth is deep and limitless. It's not easy to make it be without earth. That person will eventually get weary and frustrated."

"In the same way, there are these five ways in which others might criticize you. Their speech may be timely or untimely, true or false, gentle or harsh, beneficial or harmful, from a heart of love or from secret hate. When others criticize you, they may do so in any of these ways.

If that happens, remembering the noble ones and their qualities, you should train like this: 'Our minds will not degenerate. We will blurt out no bad words. We will remain full of sympathy, with a heart of love and no secret hate. Anagami naturally possesses a heart of love, remembering that we will have a heart of love for that person.

And with them as a basis, we will possess a heart like the earth to everyone in the world—abundant, expansive, limitless, free of enmity and ill will.' That's how you should train. Suppose a person was to come along with dye such as red lac, turmeric, indigo, or rose madder, and say, 'I shall draw pictures in space, making pictures appear there.'

What do you think, companions? Could that person draw pictures in space?"

"No, sir. Why is that? Because space has no form or appearance. It's not easy to draw pictures there. That person will eventually get weary and frustrated."

"In the same way, if others criticize you in any of these five ways … you should train like this: '… We will have a heart of love to that person. And with them as a basis, we will have a heart like space to everyone in the world—abundant, expansive, limitless, free of enmity and ill will.' That's how you should train.

Suppose a person was to come along carrying a blazing grass torch, and say, 'I shall burn and scorch the river Ganges with this blazing grass torch.'

What do you think, companions? Could that person burn and scorch the river Ganges with a blazing grass torch?"

"No, sir. Why is that? Because the river Ganges is deep and limitless. It's not easy to burn and scorch it with a blazing grass torch. That person will eventually get weary and frustrated."

"In the same way, if others criticize you in any of these five ways … remembering the qualities of the noble ones, while you are still ordinary, you should train like this, the way of noble ones: '… We will have a heart of love to that person. And with them as a basis, we will have a heart like the Ganges to everyone in the world—abundant, expansive, limitless, free of enmity and ill will.' That's how you should train.

Suppose there was a catskin bag that was rubbed, well-rubbed, very well-rubbed, soft, silky, rid of rustling and crackling. Then a person comes along carrying a stick or a stone, and says, 'I shall make this soft catskin bag rustle and crackle with this stick or stone.'

What do you think, companions? Could that person make that soft catskin bag rustle and crackle with that stick or stone?"

"No, sir. Why is that? Because that catskin bag is rubbed, well-rubbed, very well-rubbed, soft, silky, rid of rustling and crackling. It's not easy to make it rustle or crackle with a stick or stone. That person will eventually get weary and frustrated."

"In the same way, there are these five ways in which others might criticize you. Their speech may be timely or untimely, true or false, gentle or harsh, beneficial or harmful, from a heart of love or from secret hate. When others criticize you, they may do so in any of these ways. If that happens, you should remember the noble ones and train like this, the way of noble ones: 'Our minds will not degenerate'.

We will blurt out no bad words. We will remain full of sympathy, with a heart of love and no secret hate. We will have a heart of love to that person. And with them as a basis, we will have a heart like a catskin bag to everyone in the world—abundant, expansive, limitless, free of enmity and ill will.' That's how you should train.

Even if low-down bandits were to sever your limb from limb with a two-handed saw, anyone who had a malevolent thought on that account would not be following my instructions. If that happens, you should train like this: 'Our minds will not degenerate.

We will blurt out no bad words. We will remain full of sympathy, with a heart of love and no secret hate. We will have a heart of love to that person. And with them as a basis, we will have a heart full of love to everyone in the world—abundant, expansive, limitless, free of enmity and ill will.' That's how you should train.

If you frequently reflect on this advice on the simile of the saw, do you see any criticism, large or small, that you could not endure?" "No, sir."

"So, companions, you should frequently reflect on this advice on the simile of the saw. This will be for your lasting welfare and happiness."

That is what the Buddha said. Satisfied, the companions approved what the Buddha said.

Chapter 24

Middle Discourses 22: Alagaddūpamasutta

The Simile of the Cobra

This discourse discusses the importance of understanding the Dhamma correctly– just as one must handle a viper in the proper way. A great number of ordinary monks have written books saying meditation is the way of letting go. This is an erroneous grasp of Dhamma.

The way of letting go is letting go of mental attachment, which means desires. This means letting go of greed, hate and delusion, which requires adopting a multifocal approach and not just focusing on meditation. This is because a person can meditate while having too much greediness, hatred and delusion and erroneous views; *"cosmos is me", "I am in the flower", "flower is me", "I exist after death", "I don't exist after death"* and like for years. Instead, the way to let go of desire is to understand life experience in daily life. Purity can be gained by engaging in ten wholesome deeds, especially by developing the right view.

Critical thinking enables one to expand one's understanding of various matters. Critical thinking, and reasoning if applied to Dhamma, one can expect to grow one's vision, right view leading to the Noble Path, and Nibbana. What is reasonable is that the Noble Path can be known only by those who have gained Nibbana. What is relevant for gaining Nibbana is the mind state, and thoughts. Often, thoughts are expressed in words. By analysing their words, those who compare one another and those who divide universal Dhamma are still grasping the fetters, and conventions have not yet gained Nibbana. It is important to discuss Dhamma matters openly and test the evidence of Dhamma-related matters for its validity.

Evidence by dress code, and appearance, some ordinary people follow a conventional Dhamma/ and conventional Sangha. Not exploring but merely ignoring, people just go in circles again and again without gaining Nibbana. If anyone thinks they are worth listening to, they will block their chances of gaining Nibbana. The words of the Buddha that provide the path to Nibbana, Buddhahood gained through immeasurable scarifies, and completion of Paramis for the wellbeing of many, the route to escape samsara, and blocking the training path by misinterpreting Dhamma can prevent Nibbana for such bhikkhus and many attendees.

Sometimes, bhikkhus misinterpret Dhamma, which leads to creating demerits. Therefore, it is the best for bhikkhus to become more vigilant and to look after themselves better, as demerits can prolong samsara. There is nothing wrong with saying "I became a bhikkhu because of my interest to gain Nibbana. According to these books and traditions, Nibbana is this. I teach based merely on books and traditions, but I have to yet gain Nibbana. I am not 100% sure what is the universal truth, Nibbana, as I have not yet experienced it myself. What I can explain is based on what I know. I may be right or wrong. I may know certain things, but I do not know all. Therefore, it's good to keep an open eye, a bit of space to discover truth for myself, and to keep seeking. In this manner, I can teach the basics without confirming, and encouraging others to seek truth without pretending to be Arahants." This will favor them and aid in gaining Nibbana.

Every person should be respected for who they are as an individual but exploring the subject matter (content) is needed for revealing the path leading the Nibbana simply for the benefit of many. It is important to discuss Dhamma matters openly and test the evidence of Dhamma-related matters for its validity. For a seeker of universal truth, it is important that they apply logic and reasoning to discover self and the universal truth: four-fold Nibbana. When critical appraisal is applied to subject matters, it allows hearers to use evidence to judge its trustworthiness and its value and relevance in the relevant context. Critical appraisal does not mean exploring a person. It simply means exploring the content, the subject matter written by a person. Despite who says irrespective of conventional background, four-fold Nibbana should be explained in the same manner no matter who explains.

A person's intentional actions (not actions alone as one can act with various intentions) are Dhamma. To a greater extent, an ordinary person cannot understand other person's intentional actions. Finding the Triple Gem through an appearance or an action alone can be a difficult task for another person, especially because an ordinary person cannot read another person's intentional actions. Instead, ordinary people may comprehend the Triple Gem through words of wisdom. The subject matter and the content related to four-fold Nibbana should be explained as universally applicable Dhamma that happens at a random occasion shaped by one's karma and merits by whoever explains.

Throughout history, you can find many occasions when bhikkhus misinterpreted Dhamma. Discussing this merely to discuss their interpretations related to Buddha's Dhamma so it allows others to grow understanding but not to discuss them as a person.

Below are some examples;

"Devadatta claimed that the rules proposed by him were much better than the existing rules of discipline, and some new bhikkhus agreed with him. One day, the Buddha asked Devadatta if it was true that he was trying to create a schism in the Order, and he admitted that it was so" -Dhp 163

"Now on that occasion a pernicious view had arisen in a bhikkhu named Sati, son of a fisherman, thus: "As I understand the Dhamma taught by the Blessed One, it is this same consciousness that runs and wanders through the round of rebirths, not another." Several bhikkhus, having heard about this, went to the bhikkhu Sati and asked him: "Friend Sati, is it true that such a pernicious view has arisen in you?"

…Then the Blessed One addressed the bhikkhus thus: "Bhikkhus, do you understand the Dhamma taught by me as this bhikkhu Sati does when he misrepresents us by his wrong grasp and injures himself and stores up much demerit?"

Then Bhikkhus replied: "No, venerable sir. For in many discourses the Blessed One has stated consciousness to be dependently arisen, since without a condition there is no origination of consciousness."

Buddha:" Good, bhikkhus. It is good that you understand the Dhamma taught by me thus. But this bhikkhu Sati misrepresents us by his wrong grasp and stores up much demerit; for this will lead to the harm and suffering of this misguided man for a long time. "

- Mahatanhasankhaya Sutta, MN 38

"Don't say that, Ariṭṭha! Don't misrepresent the Buddha, for misrepresentation of the Buddha is not good. And the Buddha would not say that."

- Alagaddūpamasutta, MN 22

Words and concepts are social constructs. They are things that are made as real by convention or collective agreement among people in society. Social constructs reflect shared ideas or perceptions that only exist because people in a group or society accept that they do. The word enlightenment, a social construct, is used by various people in various ways. For example, in the post-Buddha period (after *Buddhaparinirvana*), it is most common to hear about the word Dhamma and enlightenment as "one flash enlightenment that's different to four-fold Nibbana originally taught by the Buddha. Such different versions of dhamma and distorted versions of practices of dhamma created by ordinary Sangha have made a split in the universal Dhamma: four-fold Nibbana. The new version of enlightenment, "one flash enlightenment," such as being just here and now, just being Awareness, and remaining as the Awareness or Consciousness (Atman/Self), are all relatively easily done if you know how - including jhana practices. However, that is not what is meant by BODHI/AWAKENING, to experience cessation within genuine Buddha's Dhamma (four-fold Nibbana). This explains how look-alike dhamma has prevented the practice that leads to four-fold Nibbana for those who aspire to Nibbana through Buddha's Dhamma.

Throughout history, some ordinary monks who were unaware of practices leading to Nibbana have suggested (such as Buddhagosha, Mahasi Sayado and so on) that a person develops concentration to understand impermanence. "The Path of Purification (Visduddhimagga)" suggests that a person takes a meditation practice, a method called *kasina,* in which one stares at an external object until the image of the object is imprinted in one's mind. This image then gives rise to a countersign that is said to indicate the attainment of threshold concentration, a necessary prelude to jhana. When you develop the idea of impermanence through concentration, when you lose concentration, you will likely lose the idea of impermanence. Besides, impermanence is not merely an idea that you imprint through effort but a life experience.

"But when a man has had no such previous practice, he should make a kasióa, guarding against the four faults of a kasióa and not overlooking any of the directions for the meditation subject learnt from the teacher. Now, the four faults of the earth kasióa are due to the intrusion of blue, yellow, red or white.."

- The Path of Purification, Visuddhimagga, Buddhaghosa

When you understand impermanence through imprint, such an understanding can only be short-lived with an underlying tendency to grasp worldly experiences. Instead, when you understand impermanence through **life experience**, understanding can only be replaced by higher understanding, Sotapanna to Arahant.

"Once the mind has let go of external mind-objects, it means you will no longer feel disturbed by the sound of traffic or other noises. You won't feel irritated with anything outside. Whether it's forms, sounds or whatever, they won't be a source of disturbance, because the mind won't be paying attention to them - it will become centred upon the breath."

- From The Collected Teachings of Ajahn Chah

Yet, noble mindfulness to reduce mental attachment should be trained while keeping eyes open and engaging in daily activities in normal day-to-day life. This is because the world's pretty things and pleasures are not the fetters[16] but the desire (greed, hate, and delusion which means **likes, dislikes, and expectations**) to **experience or not experience** such things is what causes mental pain.

Noble mindfulness can be developed by maintaining mindfulness towards one's own thoughts and choosing to do good and avoid bad within daily activities. For example, a mind can make up a past when the past is gone, and, at times, thoughts can pass on without a person noticing them. Whether a person recognizes such thoughts or not, they can produce or prolong sufferings. Instead, to develop the Noble Path, if a person can watch over the person's own mind and thoughts and choose to do good and avoid bad, this will be a way to develop noble mindfulness to reduce stress. For example, when thoughts making up a past bring up sufferings, a person can do wholesome things, such as picking up from thoughts anything that needs resolving and attempt to resolve things that need resolving and avoid unwholesome things that bring stress. In that sense, unwholesomeness is clinging to things that are gone, as they are gone, and it is meaningless to worry about such things excessively. Letting go of things that are gone will allow a person to gain peace of mind, middle-way practice, a step come closer to the realization of truth, and walk the Noble Path towards Sotapanna.

What seems to be happening in the societies is that some of the common assumptions and practices based on such common assumptions have prevented Nibbana for those who understood and practiced in common ways. The path leading to four-fold Nibbana remains the same for all.

---

[16] "*The eye is not the fetter of sights, nor are sights the fetter of the eye. The fetter there is the desire and greed that arises from the pair of them. The ear ... nose ... tongue ... body ... mind is not the fetter of ideas, nor are ideas the fetter of the mind. The fetter there is the desire and greed that arises from the pair of them.*"
-SN 35.232, Koṭṭhikasutta

Middle Path (and Nibbana) is a universal remedy for mental pain experienced by people across the world and has nothing to do with any socially constructed religion, identities, divisions, or lifestyles. Dhamma (Sotapanna to Arahant) is universal.

"There are five detrimental things that lead to the decline and disappearance of the true teaching. What five? It's when the ordinary bhikkhus (male, female), ordinary householders (male, female) lack respect and reverence for the Buddha, the Buddha's Dhamma (Sotapanna to Arahant), the noble Saṅgha (Sotapanna to Arahant), the practice leading to four-fold Nibbana, and immersion. These five detrimental things lead to the decline and disappearance of the true teaching.

There are five things that lead to the continuation, persistence, and enduring of the true teaching. What five? It's when the ordinary bhikkhus (male, female), ordinary householders (male, female) lack respect and reverence for the Buddha, the Buddha's Dhamma (Sotapanna to Arahant), the noble Saṅgha (Sotapanna to Arahant), the practice leading to four-fold Nibbana, and immersion., and immersion. These five things lead to the continuation, persistence, and enduring of the true teaching."

-SN 16.13, Saddhammappatirūpakasutta

Ordinary practitioners seem to think and suggest that there are different ways to gain Nibbana for individuals from different backgrounds based on their assumptions. For example, one of the common assumptions is that individuals from different countries/traditions/lifestyles should follow different practices of Dhamma (e.g., Western and Eastern Buddhism). However, the middle-way practice including the path to Nibbana remains the same for all, abandoning the fetters and developing confirmed confidence in the Triple Gem.

A great many authors are narrating personal stories in their books of Dhamma. This is an indication of grasping self-view and a lack of noble virtues, as noble virtues include meaningless conversations. Talking about personal stories is not relevant for Dhamma. Someone who aspires to Nibbana would benefit if they avoided self-clinging to talk about self. Instead, they should focus on talking about dhamma-related matters directly.

What has been happening over centuries is that not knowing what to practice and what not to practice, not knowing whom to listen to for guidance and who are noble friends, and by grasping to conventional Dhamma and conventional Sangha who misinterpret and misrepresent Buddha, people will block their chances of gaining Nibbana.

A spiritual path with ignorance lead to outcomes with ignorance. In this world, without considering whether or not their teachers, those who guide them to a spiritual path talk about the practice leading to Nibbana based on personal experience, whether or not they have gained Nibbana for themselves before speaking about the path, some people can follow a spiritual path with ignorance. Not exploring but merely ignoring, people just go in circles again and again without gaining Nibbana. If anyone thinks they are worth listening to, they will block their chances of gaining Nibbana.

Commonly accepted as Buddha's Dhamma is not what is the universally accepted Dhamma; four-fold Nibbana. What is commonly seen, conventional Dhamma, are preliminary practices that require developing further to reach universal Dhamma; Nibbana. By applying reasons, if you ask yourself; how anyone can be 100% sure of what one say unless one gained Nibbana, the things will become obvious that it is not possible to clarify a practice without gaining Nibbana. Then allow a bit space for yourself to discover new things without grasping to existing knowledge, allowing to grow new knowledge, seek truth that is universally applicable to all.

A disciple of Buddha by conventions and a monk by rituals make a conventional Sangha. A disciple of Buddha by universal making and a monk out of rituals and out of mental attachment to conventional practices makes a noble Sangha.

Ordinary people misinterpret Dhamma. Misunderstanding can make someone unable to practice Dhamma in a way that leads to Nibbana. In fact, the reason people don't gain Nibbana is simply due to their misunderstanding of the Dhamma (Sotapanna to Arahant). This explains why, by abiding by the misunderstanding and developing confidence in the Triple Gem, one can become a Sotapanna. The quality of a Sotapanna is that they possess noble virtues and confirmed confidence in the Triple Gem.

When a person who gained four-fold Nibbana speaks of Dhamma, it is not important who the person is from a conventional perspective (personal stories, background, etc.,). However, it is their attainment and ability to share wisdom and merits that is relevant. By receiving wisdom and merits, try to grow wisdom and merits within you by giving up a self-view. Become an heir of Buddha's Dhamma and not the flesh. A practice to extinguish not grasping, practice giving up and not holding, thus use what is useful without overly grasping conventions.

Misinterpreting Dhamma and having the wrong gasp of Dhamma does not give fruition. Interpreting Dhamma correctly, with the right grasp of Dhamma, can lead to fruition and the end of suffering across four-fold Nibbana. By correctly understanding what Nibbana is and its practice, a person can develop four-fold Nibbana.

"So I have heard. At one time the Buddha was staying near Sāvatthī in Jeta's Grove, Anāthapiṇḍika's monastery.

Now at that time a companion called Ariṭṭha, who had previously been a vulture trapper, had the following harmful misconception: "As I understand the Buddha's teaching, the acts that he says are obstructions are not really obstructions for the one who performs them."

Several companions heard about this. They went up to Ariṭṭha and said to him, "Is it really true, friend, Ariṭṭha, that you have such a harmful misconception: 'As I understand the Buddha's teaching, the acts that he says are obstructions are not really obstructions for the one who performs them'?"

"Absolutely, friends. As I understand the Buddha's teaching, the acts that he says are obstructions are not really obstructions for the one who performs them."

Then, wishing to dissuade Ariṭṭha from his view, the companions pursued, pressed, and grilled him, "Don't say that, Ariṭṭha! Don't misrepresent the Buddha, for misrepresentation of the Buddha is not good. And the Buddha would not say that. In many ways the Buddha has said that obstructive acts are obstructive, and that they really do obstruct the one who performs them. The Buddha says that sensual pleasures give little gratification and much suffering and distress, and they are all the more full of drawbacks. With the similes of a skeleton ... a scrap of meat ... a grass torch ... a pit of glowing coals ... a dream ... borrowed goods ... fruit on a tree ... a butcher's knife and chopping board ... swords and spears ... a snake's head, the Buddha says that sensual pleasures give little gratification and much suffering and distress, and they are all the more full of drawbacks."

But even though the pursued, pressed, and grilled him in this way, Ariṭṭha obstinately stuck to his misconception and insisted on it.

When they weren't able to dissuade Ariṭṭha from his view, the companions went to the Buddha, bowed, sat down to one side, and told him what had happened.

So the Buddha addressed one of the practitioners, "Please, tell Ariṭṭha, formerly a vulture trapper, that the teacher calls him."

"Yes, sir," that monk replied. He went to Ariṭṭha and said to him, "Friend Ariṭṭha, the teacher calls you."

"Yes, friend," Ariṭṭha replied. He went to the Buddha, bowed, and sat down to one side. The Buddha said to him,

"Is it really true, Ariṭṭha, that you have such a harmful misconception: 'As I understand the Buddha's teaching, the acts that he says are obstructions are not really obstructions for the one who performs them'?"

"Absolutely, sir. As I understand the Buddha's teaching, the acts that he says are obstructions are not really obstructions for the one who performs them."

"Futile man, who on earth have you ever known me to teach in that way? Haven't I said in many ways that obstructive acts are obstructive, and that they really do obstruct the one who performs them? I've said that sensual pleasures give little gratification and much suffering and distress, and they are all the more full of drawbacks. With the similes of a skeleton … a scrap of meat … a grass torch … a pit of glowing coals … a dream … borrowed goods … fruit on a tree … a butcher's knife and chopping board … swords and spears … a snake's head, I've said that sensual pleasures give little gratification and much suffering and distress, and they are all the more full of drawbacks. But still you misrepresent me by your wrong grasp, harm yourself, and create much wickedness. This will be for your lasting harm and suffering."

Then the Buddha said to the companions, "What do you think, companions? Has this companion Ariṭṭha kindled even a spark of ardor in this teaching and training?"

"How could that be, sir? No, sir." When this was said, Ariṭṭha sat silent, dismayed, shoulders drooping, downcast, depressed, with nothing to say.

Knowing this, the Buddha said, "Futile man, you will be known by your own harmful misconception. I'll question the companions about this."

Then the Buddha said to the companions, "Companions, do you understand my teaching as Ariṭṭha does, when he misrepresents me by his wrong grasp, harms himself, and creates much wickedness?"

"No, sir. For in many ways the Buddha has told us that obstructive acts are obstructive, and that they really do obstruct the one who performs them. The Buddha has said that sensual pleasures give little gratification and much suffering and distress, and they are all the more full of drawbacks.

With the similes of a skeleton … a snake's head, the Buddha has said that sensual pleasures give little gratification and much suffering and distress, and they are all the more full of drawbacks."

"Good, good, companions! It's good that you understand my teaching like this. For in many ways I have said that obstructive acts are obstructive …

I've said that sensual pleasures give little gratification and much suffering and distress, and they are all the more full of drawbacks. But still this Ariṭṭha misrepresents me by his wrong grasp, harms himself, and creates much wickedness. This will be for his lasting harm and suffering. Truly, companions, it is quite impossible to perform sensual acts without sensual desires, sensual perceptions, and sensual thoughts.

Take a futile person who memorizes the teaching—statements, mixed prose & verse, discussions, verses, inspired exclamations, legends, stories of past lives, amazing stories, and elaborations. But they don't examine the meaning of those teachings with wisdom, and so don't come to an acceptance of them after deliberation.

They memorize the teaching for the sake of finding fault and winning debates. They don't realize the goal for which they memorized them. Because they're wrongly grasped, those teachings lead to their lasting harm and suffering. Why is that? Because of their wrong grasp of the teachings.

Suppose there was a person in need of a cobra. And while wandering in search of a cobra they'd see a big cobra, and grasp it by the coil or the tail. But that cobra would twist back and bite them on the hand or the arm or other major or minor limb, resulting in death or deadly pain. Why is that? Because of their wrong grasp of the cobra.

In the same way, a futile person memorizes the teaching … and those teachings lead to their lasting harm and suffering. Why is that? Because of their wrong grasp of the teachings.

Now, take a person who memorizes the teaching—statements, mixed prose & verse, discussions, verses, inspired exclamations, legends, stories of past lives, amazing stories, and elaborations. And once he's memorized them, one examines their meaning with wisdom, and comes to an acceptance of them after deliberation. One doesn't memorize the teaching for the sake of finding fault and winning debates. One gains four-fold Nibbana for which one memorized them. Because they're correctly grasped, those teachings lead to one's lasting welfare and happiness. Why is that? Because of his correct grasp of the teachings.

Suppose there was a person in need of a cobra. And while wandering in search of a cobra they'd see a big cobra and hold it down carefully with a cleft stick. Only then would they correctly grasp it by the neck. And even though that cobra might wrap its coils around that person's hand or arm or some other major or minor limb, that wouldn't result in death or deadly pain. Why is that? Because of their correct grasp of the cobra.

In the same way, a person memorizes the teaching … and those teachings lead to his lasting welfare and happiness. Why is that? Because of his correct grasp of the teachings.

So, companions, when you understand what I've said, you should remember it accordingly. But if I've said anything that you don't understand, you should ask me about it, or some competent companions.

Companions, I will teach you a simile of the teaching as a raft: for crossing over, not for holding on. Listen and apply your mind well, I will speak."

"Yes, sir," they replied. The Buddha said this:

"Suppose there was a person traveling along the road. They'd see a large deluge, whose near shore was dubious and perilous, while the far shore was a sanctuary free of peril. But there was no ferryboat or bridge for crossing over. They'd think, 'Why don't I gather grass, sticks, branches, and leaves and make a raft?

Riding on the raft, and paddling with my hands and feet, I can safely reach the far shore.' And so they'd do exactly that. And when they'd crossed over to the far shore, they'd think, 'This raft has been very helpful to me. Riding on the raft, and paddling with my hands and feet, I have safely crossed over to the far shore. Why don't I hoist it on my head or pick it up on my shoulder and go wherever I want?'

What do you think, companions? Would that person be doing what should be done with that raft?"

"No, sir."

"And what, companions, should that person do with the raft? When they'd crossed over they should think, 'This raft has been very helpful to me. … Why don't I beach it on dry land or set it adrift on the water and go wherever I want?' That's what that person should do with the raft.

In the same way, I have taught a simile of the teaching as a raft: for crossing over, not for holding on. By understanding the simile of the raft, you will even give up the teachings, let alone what is not the teachings.

Companions, there are these six grounds for views. What six? Take an unlearned ordinary person who has not seen the noble ones, and is neither skilled nor trained in the teaching of the noble ones. They've not seen noble disciples, and are neither skilled nor trained in the teaching of the noble ones. They regard form as: 'This is mine, I am this, this is my self.' They also regard feeling … perception … choices … whatever is seen, heard, thought, known, attained, sought, and explored by the mind as: 'This is mine, I am this, this is my self.' And as for this ground for views: 'The cosmos and the self are one and the same. After death I will be that, permanent, everlasting, eternal, imperishable, and will last forever and ever.' They regard this also as: 'This is mine, I am this, this is my self.'

But a learned noble disciple has seen the noble ones, and is skilled and trained in the teaching of the noble ones. They've seen true persons, and are skilled and trained in the teaching of the true persons. They regard form like this: 'This is not mine, I am not this, this is not my self.' They also regard feeling … perception … choices … whatever is seen, heard, thought, known, attained, sought, and explored by the mind like this: 'This is not mine, I am not this, this is not my self.' And the same for this ground for views: 'The cosmos and the self are one and the same. After death I will be that, permanent, everlasting, eternal, imperishable, and will last forever and ever.' They also regard like this: 'This is not mine, I am not this, this is not my self.'

Seeing in this way they're not anxious about what doesn't exist."

When he said this, one of the companions asked the Buddha, "Sir, can there be anxiety about what doesn't exist externally?"

"There can, companions," said the Buddha. "It's when someone thinks, 'Oh, it once was mine but is mine no more. Oh, it could be mine but I do not get it.' They sorrow and wail and lament, beating their breast and falling into confusion. That's how there is anxiety about what doesn't exist externally."

"But can there be no anxiety about what doesn't exist externally?"

"There can, companions," said the Buddha. "It's when someone doesn't think, 'Oh, it once was mine but is mine no more. Oh, it could be mine but I do not get it.' They don't sorrow and wail and lament, beating their breast and falling into confusion. That's how there is no anxiety about what doesn't exist externally."

"But can there be anxiety about what doesn't exist internally?"

"There can, companions," said the Buddha. "It's when someone has such a view: 'The cosmos and the self are one and the same. After death I will be that, permanent, everlasting, eternal, imperishable, and will last forever and ever.' They hear the Realized One or their disciple teaching Dhamma for the uprooting of all grounds, fixations, obsessions, insistences, and underlying tendencies regarding views; for the stilling of all activities, the letting go of all attachments, the ending of craving, fading away, cessation, extinguishment. They think, 'Whoa, I'm going to be annihilated and destroyed! I won't even exist any more!' They sorrow and wail and lament, beating their breast and falling into confusion. That's how there is anxiety about what doesn't exist internally."

"But can there be no anxiety about what doesn't exist internally?"

"There can," said the Buddha. "It's when someone doesn't have such a view: 'The cosmos and the self are one and the same. After death I will be that, permanent, everlasting, eternal, imperishable, and will last forever and ever.' They hear the Realized One or their disciple (Sotapanna to Arahant) teaching Dhamma for the uprooting of all grounds, fixations, obsessions, insistences, and underlying tendencies regarding views; for the stilling of all activities, the letting go of all attachments, the ending of craving, fading away, cessation, extinguishment. They don't think, 'Whoa, I'm going to be annihilated and destroyed! I won't even exist anymore!' They don't sorrow and wail and lament, beating their breast and falling into confusion. That's how there is no anxiety about what doesn't exist internally.

Companions, it would make sense to be possessive about something that's permanent, everlasting, eternal, imperishable, and will last forever and ever. But do you see any such possession?"

"No, sir."

"Good, companions! I also can't see any such possession.

It would make sense to grasp at a theory of self that didn't give rise to sorrow, lamentation, pain, sadness, and distress. But do you see any such theory of self?"

"No, sir."

"Good, companions! I also can't see any such theory of self.

It would make sense to rely on a view that didn't give rise to sorrow, lamentation, pain, sadness, and distress. But do you see any such view to rely on?"

"No, sir."

"Good, companions! I also can't see any such view to rely on.

Companions, were a self to exist, would there be the thought, 'Belonging to my self'?"

"Yes, sir."

"Were what belongs to a self to exist, would there be the thought, 'My self'?"

"Yes, sir."

"But since a self and what belongs to a self are not actually found, is not the following a totally foolish teaching: 'The cosmos and the self are one and the same. After death I will be that, permanent, everlasting, eternal, imperishable, and will last forever and ever'?"

"How could it not, sir? It's a totally foolish teaching."

"What do you think, companions? Is form permanent or impermanent?"

"Impermanent, sir."

"But if it's impermanent, is it suffering or happiness?"

"Suffering, sir."

"But if it's impermanent, suffering, and perishable, is it fit to be regarded thus: 'This is mine, I am this, this is my self'?"

"No, sir."

"What do you think, companions? Is feeling … perception … choices … consciousness permanent or impermanent?"

"Impermanent, sir."

"But if it's impermanent, is it suffering or happiness?"

"Suffering, sir."

"But if it's impermanent, suffering, and perishable, is it fit to be regarded thus: 'This is mine, I am this, this is my self'?"

"No, sir."

"So, companions, you should truly see any kind of form at all—past, future, or present; internal or external; solid or subtle; inferior or superior; far or near: all form—with right understanding: 'This is not mine, I am not this, this is not myself.' You should truly see any kind of feeling … perception … choices … consciousness at all—past, future, or present; internal or external; solid or subtle; inferior or superior; far or near: all consciousness—with right understanding: 'This is not mine, I am not this, this is not my self.'

Seeing this, a learned noble disciple grows disillusioned with form, feeling, perception, choices, and consciousness. Being disillusioned, desire fades away. When desire fades away they're freed. When they're freed, they know they're freed.

They understand: 'Rebirth is ended, the spiritual journey has been completed, what had to be done has been done, there is nothing further for this place.'

Such a companion is one who is called 'one who has lifted the cross-bar', 'one who has filled in the moat', 'one who has pulled up the pillar', 'one who is unimpeded', and also 'a noble one with banner lowered and burden dropped, detached'.

And how has a companion raised the cross-bar? It's when a companion has given up ignorance, cut it off at the root, made it like a palm stump, obliterated it, so it's unable to arise in the future. That's how a person has lifted the cross-bar.

And how has a companion filled in the moat? It's when a companion has given up transmigrating through births in future lives, cut it off at the root, made it like a palm stump, obliterated it, so it's unable to arise in the future. That's how a companion has filled in the moat.

And how has a companion pulled up the pillar? It's when a companions has given up craving, cut it off at the root, made it like a palm stump, obliterated it, so it's unable to arise in the future. That's how a companion has pulled up the pillar.

And how is a companion unimpeded? It's when a companion has given up the five lower fetters, cut them off at the root, made them like a palm stump, obliterated them, so they're unable to arise in the future. That's how a companion is unimpeded.

And how is a companion a noble one with banner lowered and burden dropped, detached? It's when a companion has given up the conceit 'I am', cut it off at the root, made it like a palm stump, obliterated it, so it's unable to arise in the future. That's how a companion is a noble one with banner lowered and burden dropped, detached.

When a companion's mind was freed like this, the gods together with Indra, the Divinity, and the Progenitor, search as they may, will not discover: 'This is the basis of that realized one's consciousness.' Why is that? Because even in the present life that realized one is not found, I say.

Though I state and assert this, certain ascetics and brahmins misrepresent me with the incorrect, hollow, false, untruthful claim: 'The ascetic Gotama is an exterminator. He advocates the annihilation, eradication, and obliteration of an existing being.' They misrepresent me as what I am not, and saying what I do not say. In the past, as today, what I describe is suffering and the cessation of suffering. This being so, if others abuse, attack, harass, and trouble the Realized One, he doesn't get resentful, bitter, and emotionally exasperated.

Or if others honor, respect, revere, or venerate him, he doesn't get thrilled, elated, and emotionally excited. If they praise him, he just thinks, 'They do such things for me regarding what in the past was completely understood.'

So, companions, if others abuse, attack, harass, and trouble you, don't make yourselves resentful, bitter, and emotionally exasperated.

Or if others honor, respect, revere, or venerate you, don't make yourselves thrilled, elated, and emotionally excited. If they praise you, just think, 'They do such things for us regarding what in the past was completely understood.'

So, companions, give up what isn't yours. Giving it up will be for your lasting welfare and happiness.

And what isn't yours? Form isn't yours: give it up. Giving it up will be for your lasting welfare and happiness.

Feeling … perception … choices … consciousness isn't yours: give it up. Giving it up will be for your lasting welfare and happiness.

What do you think, companions? Suppose a person was to carry off the grass, sticks, branches, and leaves in this Jeta's Grove, or burn them, or do what they want with them. Would you think, 'This person is carrying us off, burning us, or doing what they want with us'?"

"No, sir. Why is that? Because to us that's neither self nor belonging to self."

"In the same way, companions, give up what isn't yours. Giving it up will be for your lasting welfare and happiness. And what isn't yours? Form … feeling … perception … choices … consciousness isn't yours: give it up. Giving it up will be for your lasting welfare and happiness.

Thus the teaching has been well explained by me, made clear, opened, illuminated, and stripped of patchwork.

In this teaching there are companion who are perfected, who have ended the defilements, completed the spiritual journey, done what had to be done, laid down the burden, achieved their own goal, utterly ended the fetter of continued existence, and are rightly freed through enlightenment. For them, there is no cycle of rebirths to be found. …

In this teaching there are companions who have given up the five lower fetters.

All of them are reborn spontaneously. They are extinguished there, and are not liable to return from that world. …

In this teaching there are companions who, having given up three fetters, and weakened greed, hate, and delusion, are once-returners. All of them come back to this world once only, then make an end of suffering. …

In this teaching there are companions who have ended three fetters. All of them are stream-enterers, not liable to be reborn in the underworld, bound for awakening. …

In this teaching, there are companions who have the potential to become followers of teachings or followers by faith.

All of them are bound to awaken if they fulfill the requirements; four factors of stream-entry and abandoning the fetters.

Thus the teachings leading to four-fold Nibbana have been well explained by me, made clear, opened, illuminated, and stripped of patchwork. In this teaching, some have a degree of unshakable confidence grounded on evidence based on life experience and respect for me. Until they gain Arahantship, all of them are bound to awaken across stages and be reborn in good places (Those who have some faith and love are bound to be born in good places if they fulfil their merits and wisdom).

That is what the Buddha said. Satisfied, the companions approved what the Buddha said"

Chapter 25

Middle Discourses 23: Vammikasutta

The Termite Mound

This discourse attempts to discuss the entire process of four-fold Nibbana to gain Sotapanna by abandoning the fetters. As you abandon the fetters, you see the universal truth for yourself, that's when you come to possess unshakable confidence in the Buddha cross stages of four-fold Nibbana. Then, Sakadami reduces the relevant fetters. Anagami and Arahant reduce higher fetters. The first thing first: Sotapanna state should be completed to progress into higher stages of Nibbana. Nibbana is a karma-based path, Dasa Kusal (Ten wholesome intentional actions/deeds) is beneficial.

"So I have heard. At one time the Buddha was staying near Sāvatthī in Jeta's Grove, Anāthapiṇḍika's monastery. Now at that time Kassapa, the Prince was staying in the Dark Forest.

Then, late at night, a glorious deity, lighting up the entire Dark Forest, went up to Kassapa the Prince, stood to one side, and said:

"Monk, monk! This termite mound fumes by night and flames by day. The brahmin said, 'Dig, clever one, having picked up the sword!'

Picking up the sword and digging, the clever one saw a sticking point: 'A sticking point, sir!' The brahmin said, 'Throw out the sticking point! Dig, clever one, having picked up the sword!'

Picking up the sword and digging, the clever one saw a bullfrog: 'A bullfrog, sir!' The brahmin said, 'Throw out the bullfrog! Dig, clever one, having picked up the sword!'

Picking up the sword and digging, the clever one saw a forked path: 'A forked path, sir!' The brahmin said, 'Throw out the forked path! Dig, clever one, having picked up the sword!'

Picking up the sword and digging, the clever one saw a filter of ash: 'A filter of ash, sir!' The brahmin said, 'Throw out the filter of ash! Dig, clever one, having picked up the sword!'

Picking up the sword and digging, the clever one saw a tortoise: 'A tortoise, sir!' The brahmin said, 'Throw out the tortoise! Dig, clever one, having taken up the sword!'

Picking up the sword and digging, the clever one saw a butcher's knife and chopping board: 'A butcher's knife and chopping board, sir!' The brahmin said, 'Throw out the butcher's knife and chopping board! Dig, clever one, having picked up the sword!'

Picking up the sword and digging, the clever one saw a scrap of meat: 'A scrap of meat, sir!' The brahmin said, 'Throw out the scrap of meat! Dig, clever one, having picked up the sword!'

Picking up the sword and digging, the clever one saw a mighty serpent: 'A mighty serpent, sir!' The brahmin said, 'Leave the mighty serpent! Do not disturb the mighty serpent! Worship the mighty serpent!'

Companion, go to the Buddha and ask him about this riddle. You should remember it in line with his answer. I don't see anyone in this world—with its gods, Māras, and Divinities, this population with its ascetics and brahmins, its gods and humans—who could provide a satisfying answer to this riddle except for the Realized One or his disciple or someone who has heard it from them."

That is what that deity said before vanishing right there.

Then, when the night had passed, Kassapa the Prince went to the Buddha, bowed, sat down to one side, and told him what had happened. Then he asked:

"Sir, what is the termite mound? What is the fuming by night and flaming by day? Who is the brahmin, and who the clever one? What are the sword, the digging, the sticking point, the bullfrog, the forked path, the filter of ash, the tortoise, the butcher's knife and chopping board, and the scrap of meat? And what is the mighty serpent?"

"Companion, 'termite mound' is a term for this body made up of the four principal states, produced by mother and father, built up from rice and porridge, liable to impermanence, to wearing away and erosion, to breaking up and destruction.

Thinking and considering all night about what you did during the day—this is the fuming at night. The work you apply yourself to during the day by body, speech, and mind after thinking about it all night—this is the flaming by day.

'Brahmin' is a term for the Realized One, the perfected one, the fully awakened Buddha. 'Clever one' is a term for the trainee companion.

'Sword' is a term for noble wisdom. 'Digging' is a term for rousing energy.

'Sticking point' is a term for ignorance. 'Throw out the sticking point' means 'give up ignorance, dig, clever one, having picked up the sword.'

'Bullfrog' is a term for anger and distress. 'Throw out the bullfrog' means 'give up anger and distress' …

'A forked path' is a term for doubt. 'Throw out the forked path' means 'give up doubt' …

'A filter of ash' is a term for the five hindrances, that is: the hindrances of sensual desire, ill will, dullness and drowsiness, restlessness and remorse, and doubt. 'Throw out the filter of ash' means 'give up the five hindrances' …

'Tortoise' is a term for the five grasping aggregates, that is: form, feeling, perception, choices, and consciousness. 'Throw out the tortoise' means 'give up the five grasping aggregates' …

'Butcher's knife and chopping board' is a term for the five kinds of sensual stimulation. Sights known by the eye, which are likable, desirable, agreeable, pleasant, sensual, and arousing. Sounds known by the ear … Smells known by the nose … Tastes known by the tongue … Touches known by the body, which are likable, desirable, agreeable, pleasant, sensual, and arousing. 'Throw out the butcher's knife and chopping board' means 'give up the five kinds of sensual stimulation' …

'Scrap of meat' is a term for greed and relishing. 'Throw out the scrap of meat' means 'give up greed and relishing' …

'Mighty serpent' is a term for a person who has ended the defilements; ten fetters, an Arahant. This is the meaning of: 'Leave the mighty serpent! Do not disturb the mighty serpent! Worship the mighty serpent.'"

That is what the Buddha said. Satisfied, Kassapa the Prince approved what the Buddha said."

Chapter 26

Middle Discourses 24: Rathavinītasutta

Chariots at the Ready

Personally, having few wishes, one can speak to others and suggest that they may consider giving up too many expectations to avoid mental pain. Personally, not demanding; one should suggest to others that they may consider not to demand respect but to give respect. Personally, having given up grasping self-view, standard social practices and rituals, one should speak to others and suggest that they may consider giving up grasping self-view, standard social practices and rituals. Personally, having given up doubt, one should speak to others and suggest that they may consider giving up doubt. Personally, having given up desires (likes, dislikes, expectations), one should speak to others and suggest that they may consider giving up desires. Personally, having attained Nibbana, one should speak to others and suggest that they may consider gaining Nibbana if they wish to abandon mental pain and samsara. A person who has given up ten fetters shaped by universal ways, an Arahant; giving (friendship, time, skills, materials, non-materials, words of respect, etc.) to such a noble person (a monk in noble path irrespective of conventional background), allows an ordinary person to generate merits much needed for gaining Nibbana. Ordinary Sangha is not a substitute for noble Sangha. The purpose of noble Sangha cannot be replaced by ordinary Sangha, and if replaced, Nibbana cannot be gained as the noble order is linked to Nibbana.

The end purpose of Nibbana is the Cessation of attachment to thoughts; they cease to exist in the presence or absence of others and the world. The practice of reaching Cessation remains the same for all. You may build up a preliminary practice by taking refuge in the Triple Gem and precepts and building up on refuge and precepts. You may develop a concentration that allows you to engage in wholesome activities while purifying your mind from grasping conventions to let go of first three fetters; non-self-view, dependence on rites, ritual, ceremonies, social practices and doubt (Sotapanna). The purification of a non-self-view is merely to let go of doubts. Letting go of doubts is simply to understand the practice leading to Sotapanna. Understanding the practice is simply to gain Sakadagami and Anagami states. Gaining Sakadagami and Anagami states is simply to gain Arahantship. In the Arahant state, you come to extinguish in the mind. In the end, the purpose of engaging in precepts, wholesome activities, and Sotapanna to Anagami is simply to gain Arahantship.

"So I have heard. At one time the Buddha was staying near Rājagaha, in the Bamboo Grove, the squirrels' feeding ground.

Then several companions who had completed the rainy season residence in their native land went to the Buddha, bowed, and sat down to one side. The Buddha said to them:

"In your native land, companions, which of the native companions is esteemed in this way: 'Personally having few wishes, they speak to the companions on having few wishes. Personally having contentment, seclusion, aloofness, energy, noble ethics, immersion, noble wisdom, freedom, and the knowledge and vision of freedom, they speak to the companions on all these things. They're an adviser and counselor, one who educates, encourages, fires up, and inspires their spiritual companions.'"

"Arahant Puṇṇa, son of Mantāṇī, sir, is esteemed in this way in our native land."

Now at that time Arahant Sāriputta was sitting not far from the Buddha. Then he thought:

"Arahant Puṇṇa, son of Mantāṇī is fortunate, so very fortunate, in that his sensible spiritual companions praise him point by point in the presence of the Teacher, and that the Teacher seconds that appreciation. Hopefully, some time or other I'll get to meet Arahant Puṇṇa, and we can have a discussion."

When the Buddha had stayed in Rājagaha as long as he pleased, he set out for Sāvatthī. Traveling stage by stage, he arrived at Sāvatthī, where he stayed in Jeta's Grove, Anāthapiṇḍika's monastery. Puṇṇa heard that the Buddha had arrived at Sāvatthī.

Then he set his lodgings in order and, taking his bowl and robe, set out for Sāvatthī. Eventually he came to Sāvatthī and Jeta's Grove. He went up to the Buddha, bowed, and sat down to one side. The Buddha educated, encouraged, fired up, and inspired him with a Dhamma talk. Then, having approved and agreed with what the Buddha said, Puṇṇa got up from his seat, bowed, and respectfully circled the Buddha, keeping him on his right. Then he went to the Dark Forest for the day's stay.

Then a certain companion went up to Arahant Sāriputta, and said to him, "Arahant Sāriputta, the companion, Arahant Puṇṇa, of whom you have often spoken so highly, after being inspired by a talk of the Buddha's, left for the Dark Forest for the day's stay."

Arahant Sāriputta quickly grabbed his sitting cloth and followed behind Arahant Puṇṇa, keeping sight of his head. Arahant Puṇṇa plunged deep into the Dark Forest and sat at the root of a tree for the day'stay. And Arahant Sāriputta did likewise.

Then in the late afternoon, Arahant Sāriputta came out of retreat, went to Arahant Puṇṇa, and exchanged greetings with him. When the greetings and polite conversation were over, he sat down to one side and said to Arahant Puṇṇa:

"Respected friend, is our spiritual life lived under the Buddha?"

"Yes, respected friend."

"Is the spiritual life lived under the Buddha for the sake of purification of ethics?"

"Certainly not."

"Well, is the spiritual life lived under the Buddha for the sake of purification of mind?"

"Certainly not."

"Is the spiritual life lived under the Buddha for the sake of purification of view?"

"Certainly not."

"Well, is the spiritual life lived under the Buddha for the sake of purification by traversing doubt?"

"Certainly not."

"Is the spiritual life lived under the Buddha for the sake of purification of knowledge and vision of what is the path and what is not the path?"

"Certainly not."

"Well, is the spiritual life lived under the Buddha for the sake of purification of knowledge and vision of the practice?"

"Certainly not."

"Is the spiritual life lived under the Buddha for the sake of purification of knowledge and vision?"

"Certainly not."

"When asked each of these questions, you answered, 'Certainly not.' Then what exactly is the purpose of leading the spiritual life under the Buddha?"

"The purpose of leading the spiritual life under the Buddha is extinguishment by not grasping."

"Respected friend, is purification of ethics extinguishment by not grasping?"

"Certainly not, reverend."

"Is purification of mind …

purification of view …

purification by traversing doubt …

purification of knowledge and vision of what is the path and what is not the path …

purification of knowledge and vision of the practice …

Is purification of knowledge and vision extinguishment by not grasping?"

"Certainly not."

"Then is extinguishment by not grasping something apart from these things?"

"Certainly not."

"When asked each of these questions, you answered, 'Certainly not.' How then should we see the meaning of this statement?"

"If the Buddha had declared purification of ethics to be extinguishment by not grasping, he would have declared that which has fuel for grasping to be extinguishment by not grasping. If the Buddha had declared purification of mind … purification of view … purification by traversing doubt … purification of knowledge and vision of what is the path and what is not the path … purification of knowledge and vision of the practice … If the Buddha had declared purification of knowledge and vision to be extinguishment by not grasping, he would have declared that which has fuel for grasping to be extinguishment by not grasping. But if extinguishment by not grasping was something apart from these things, an ordinary person would become extinguished. For an ordinary person lacks these things.

Well then, reverend, I shall give you a simile. For by means of a simile some sensible people understand the meaning of what is said.

Suppose that, while staying in Sāvatthī, King Pasenadi of Kosala had some urgent business come up in Sāketa. Now, between Sāvatthī and Sāketa seven chariots were stationed at the ready for him. Then Pasenadi, having departed Sāvatthī, mounted the first chariot at the ready by the gate of the royal compound. The first chariot at the ready would bring him to the second, where he'd dismount and mount the second chariot. The second chariot at the ready would bring him to the third … The third chariot at the ready would bring him to the fourth … The fourth chariot at the ready would bring him to the fifth … The fifth chariot at the ready would bring him to the sixth … The sixth chariot at the ready would bring him to the seventh, where he'd dismount and mount the seventh chariot. The seventh chariot at the ready would bring him to the gate of the royal compound of Sāketa. And when he was at the gate, friends and colleagues, relatives and kin would ask him: 'Great king, did you come to Sāketa from Sāvatthī by this chariot at the ready?' If asked this, how should King Pasenadi rightly reply?"

"The king should reply: 'Well, while staying in Sāvatthī, I had some urgent business come up in Sāketa. Now, between Sāvatthī and Sāketa seven chariots were stationed at the ready for me. Then, having departed Sāvatthī, I mounted the first chariot at the ready by the gate of the royal compound. The first chariot at the ready brought me to the second, where I dismounted and mounted the second chariot. ... The second chariot brought me to the third ... the fourth ... the fifth ... the sixth ... The sixth chariot at the ready brought me to the seventh, where I dismounted and mounted the seventh chariot. The seventh chariot at the ready brought me to the gate of the royal compound of Sāketa.' That's how King Pasenadi should rightly reply."

"In the same way, respected sir, purification of ethics is only for the sake of purification of mind. Purification of mind is only for the sake of purification of view. Purification of view is only for the sake of purification by traversing doubt. Purification by traversing doubt is only for the sake of purification of knowledge and vision of what is the path and what is not the path. Purification of knowledge and vision of what is the path and what is not the path is only for the sake of purification of knowledge and vision of the practice. Purification of knowledge and vision of the practice is only for the sake of purification of knowledge and vision. Purification of knowledge and vision is only for the sake of extinguishment by not grasping. The spiritual life is lived under the Buddha for the sake of extinguishment by not grasping."

When he said this, Arahant Sāriputta said to Arahant Puṇṇa, "What is your name Arahant, respected friend? And how are you known among your spiritual companions?"

"Respected friend, my name is Arahant Puṇṇa. Formerly, I was known as 'son of Mantāṇī' among my spiritual companions."

"It's incredible, respected friend, it's amazing! Arahant Puṇṇa, formerly known as son of Mantāṇī has answered each deep question point by point, as a learned noble disciple who rightly understands the Buddha's instructions. It is fortunate for his spiritual companions, so very fortunate, that they get to see Arahant Puṇṇa and pay homage to him. Even if they only got to see him and pay respects to him by carrying him around on their heads on a roll of cloth, it would still be very fortunate for them! And it's fortunate for me, so very fortunate, that I get to see the Arahant and pay homage to him."

When he said this, Arahant Puṇṇa said to Arahant Sāriputta, "What is your name, respected Arahant? And how are you known among your spiritual companions?"

"Reverend, my ordinary birth name is Upatissa. And my noble birth name is Arahant Sāriputta, that's how I am known among my spiritual companions."

"Goodness! I had no idea I was consulting with Arahant Sāriputta, the disciple who is fit to be compared with the Buddha himself! If I'd known, I would not have said so much. It's incredible, reverend, it's amazing! Arahant Sāriputta has asked each deep question point by point, as a learned disciple who rightly understands the teacher's instructions. It is fortunate for his spiritual companions, so very fortunate, that they get to see Arahant Sāriputta and pay homage to him. Even if they only got to see him and pay respects to him by carrying him around on their heads on a roll of cloth, it would still be very fortunate for them! And it's fortunate for me, so very fortunate, that I get to see the venerable and pay homage to him."

And so these two Arahants agreed with each other's fine words"

Chapter 27

Middle Discourses 25: Nivāpasutta

Sowing

This discourse discusses an Anagami, who has abandoned sensual pleasures to reach full Nibbana; Arahanship and about the various kinds of practitioners. You may want to think again about your own practice and link your current practice to Noble Path if you were interested in discovering self, four-fold Nibbana.

Among the community of practitioners, there are various types of practitioners. Firstly, some of those who practice Dhamma among the ordinary community of practitioners (both conventional monks and conventional householders), engage in liking worldly experiences too much or disliking too much, and they ignore the middle way in which conventional life functions within universal ways of functioning. Due to ignorance, they are unable to develop wisdom to see beyond conventions. They go in to the Samsara. Secondly, some of those who practice Dhamma among the ordinary community of practitioners both conventional monks and conventional householders who live a strict life style. They manage to reduce too many likes and too many dislikes for some period of time only to fall back into their former habits of touching the worldly experiences in mind, grasping one's own thoughts. Thirdly, some of those who practice Dhamma among the ordinary community of practitioners (both conventional monks and conventional householders), there are those who follow a spiritual life with its requisites very closely. They may take precepts, monastic rules, but they have wrong views of grasping self and the world, such as "The cosmos is eternal" or "The cosmos is not eternal"; "The cosmos is finite" or "The cosmos is infinite"; "The soul and the body are the same thing" or "The soul and the body are different things"; or that, after death, "A realized one still exists" or "No longer exists" etc. They grasp into conventional words, fail to use conventions simply for understanding without grasping to such things in the middle way, and, consequently, they don't gain Nibbana but go into Samsara. Fourthly, among spiritual companions, those who follow a practice of Dhamma, having completed the first stages; Sotapanna and Skadagami, a person who has given up sensual desire will experience Jhanas at a random time. By entering the path of Arahantship at a random time, they may complete Nibbana.

"So I have heard. At one time the Buddha was staying near Sāvatthī in Jeta's Grove, Anāthapiṇḍika's monastery. There the Buddha addressed the companions, "Companions!"

"Venerable sir," they replied. The Buddha said this:

"Companions, a sower does not sow seed for deer thinking, 'May the deer, enjoying this seed, be healthy and in good condition. May they live long and prosper!' A sower sows seed for deer thinking, 'When these deer encroach on where I sow the seed, they'll recklessly enjoy eating it. They'll become indulgent, then they'll become negligent, and then I'll be able to do what I want with them on account of this seed.'

And indeed, the first herd of deer encroached on where the sower sowed the seed and recklessly enjoyed eating it. They became indulgent, then they became negligent, and then the sower was able to do what he wanted with them on account of that seed. And that's how the first herd of deer failed to get free from the sower's power.

So then a second herd of deer thought up a plan, 'The first herd of deer became indulgent … and failed to get free of the sower's power. Why don't we refrain from eating the seed altogether? Avoiding dangerous food, we can venture deep into a wilderness region and live there.' And that's just what they did. But when it came to the last month of summer, the grass and water ran out. Their bodies became much too thin, and they lost their strength and energy. So they returned to where the sower had sown the seed. Encroaching, they recklessly enjoyed eating it … And that's how the second herd of deer failed to get free from the sower's power.

So then a third herd of deer thought up a plan, 'The first … and second herds of deer … failed to get free of the sower's power. Why don't we set up our lair close by where the sower has sown the seed? Then we can encroach and enjoy eating without being reckless. We won't become indulgent, then we won't become negligent, and then the sower won't be able to do what he wants with us on account of that seed.' And that's just what they did.

So the sower and his helpers thought, 'Wow, this third herd of deer is so sneaky and devious, they must be some kind of strange spirits with magical abilities! For they eat the seed we've sown without us knowing how they come and go. Why don't we surround the seed on all sides by staking out high nets? Hopefully we might get to see the lair where they go to hide out.' And that's just what they did. And they saw the lair where the third herd of deer went to hide out. And that's how the third herd failed to get free from the sower's power.

So then a fourth herd of deer thought up a plan, 'The first … second … and third herds of deer … failed to get free of the sower's power. Why don't we set up our lair somewhere the sower and his helpers can't go? Then we can intrude on where the sower has sown the seed and enjoy eating it without being reckless. We won't become indulgent, then we won't become negligent, and then the sower won't be able to do with us what he wants on account of that seed.' And that's just what they did.

So the sower and his helpers thought, 'Wow, this fourth herd of deer is so sneaky and devious, they must be some kind of strange spirits with magical abilities! For they eat the seed we've sown without us knowing how they come and go. Why don't we surround the seed on all sides by staking out high nets? Hopefully we might get to see the lair where they go to hide out.' And that's just what they did. But they couldn't see the lair where the fourth herd of deer went to hide out. So the sower and his helpers thought, 'If we disturb this fourth herd of deer, they'll disturb others, who in turn will disturb even more. Then all of the deer will escape this seed we've sown. Why don't we just keep an eye on that fourth herd?' And that's just what they did. And that's how the fourth herd of deer escaped the sower's power.

I've made up this simile to make a point. And this is what it means.

'Seed' is a term for the five kinds of sensual stimulation.

'Sower' is a term for Māra the Wicked.

'Sower's helpers' is a term for Māra's assembly.

'Deer' is a term for ascetics and brahmins.

Now, the first group of ascetics and brahmins encroached on where the seed and the worldly pleasures of the flesh were sown by Māra and recklessly enjoyed eating it. They became indulgent, then they became negligent, and then Māra was able to do what he wanted with them on account of that seed and the worldly pleasures of the flesh. And that's how the first group of ascetics and brahmins failed to get free from Māra's power. This first group of ascetics and brahmins is just like the first herd of deer, I say.

So then a second group of ascetics and brahmins thought up a plan, 'The first group of ascetics and brahmins became indulgent … and failed to get free of Māra's power. Why don't we refrain from eating the seed and the worldly pleasures of the flesh altogether? Avoiding dangerous food, we can venture deep into a wilderness region and live there.' And that's just what they did. They ate herbs, millet, wild rice, poor rice, water lettuce, rice bran, scum from boiling rice, sesame flour, grass, or cow dung. They survived on forest roots and fruits, or eating fallen fruit.

But when it came to the last month of summer, the grass and water ran out. Their bodies became much too thin, and they lost their strength and energy. Because of this, they lost their heart's release, so they went back to where Māra had sown the seed and the worldly pleasures of the flesh. Intruding on that place, they recklessly enjoyed eating them … And that's how the second group of ascetics and brahmins failed to get free from Māra's power. This second group of ascetics and brahmins is just like the second herd of deer, I say.

So then a third group of ascetics and brahmins thought up a plan, 'The first ... and second groups of ascetics and brahmins ... failed to get free of Māra's power. Why don't we set up our lair close by where Māra has sown the seed and those worldly pleasures of the flesh? Then we can encroach on it and enjoy eating without being reckless. We won't become indulgent, then we won't become negligent, and then Māra won't be able to do what he wants with us on account of that seed and those worldly pleasures of the flesh.'

And that's just what they did. Still, they had such views as these: 'The cosmos is eternal' or 'The cosmos is not eternal'; 'The cosmos is finite' or 'The cosmos is infinite'; 'The soul and the body are the same thing' or 'The soul and the body are different things'; or that after death, a realized one still exists, or no longer exists, or both still exists and no longer exists, or neither still exists nor no longer exists. And that's how the third group of ascetics and brahmins failed to get free from Māra's power. This third group of ascetics and brahmins is just like the third herd of deer, I say.

So then a fourth group of ascetics and brahmins thought up a plan, 'The first ... second ... and third groups of ascetics and brahmins ... failed to get free of Māra's power. Why don't we set up our lair where Māra and his assembly can't go? Then we can encroach on where Māra has sown the seed and those worldly pleasures of the flesh, and enjoy eating without being reckless. We won't become indulgent, then we won't become negligent, and then Māra won't be able to do what he wants with us on account of that seed and those worldly pleasures of the flesh.'

And that's just what they did. And that's how the fourth group of ascetics and brahmins got free from Māra's power. This fourth group of ascetics and brahmins is just like the fourth herd of deer, I say.

And where is it that Māra and his assembly can't go? It's when a person (Sakadagami) entering the path to Anagami state, quite secluded from sensual pleasures, secluded from unskillful qualities, enters and remains in the first absorption, which has the rapture and bliss born of seclusion, while placing the mind and keeping it connected. This is called a person who has blinded Māra, put out his eyes without a trace, and gone where the Wicked One cannot see.

Furthermore, as the placing of the mind and keeping it connected are stilled, a person enters and remains in the second absorption, which has the rapture and bliss born of immersion, with internal clarity and mind at one, without placing the mind and keeping it connected. This is called a person who has blinded Māra ...

Furthermore, with the fading away of rapture, a person enters and remains in the third absorption, where they experience equanimity, mindful and aware in mind, personally experiencing the bliss of which the noble ones declare, 'Equanimous and mindful, one meditates in bliss.' This is called a person who has blinded Māra …

Furthermore, giving up pleasure and pain, and ending former happiness and sadness, a person enters and remains in the fourth absorption, without pleasure or pain, with pure equanimity and mindfulness. This is called a person who has blinded Māra …

Furthermore, having completed Anagami state, a person enters the path to Arahantship, going totally beyond perceptions of form, with the ending of perceptions of impingement, not focusing on perceptions of diversity, aware that 'space is infinite', enters and remains in the dimension of infinite space. This is called a person who has blinded Māra …

Furthermore, going totally beyond the dimension of infinite space, aware that 'consciousness is infinite', enters and remains in the dimension of infinite consciousness. This is called a person who has blinded Māra …

Furthermore, going totally beyond the dimension of infinite consciousness, aware that 'there is nothing at all', enters and remains in the dimension of nothingness. This is called a person who has blinded Māra …

Furthermore, going totally beyond the dimension of nothingness, enters and remains in the dimension of neither perception nor non-perception. This is called a person who has blinded Māra …

Furthermore, going totally beyond the dimension of neither perception nor non-perception, enters and remains in the cessation of perception and feeling. And, having seen with wisdom, their defilements come to an end. This is called an Arahant who has blinded Māra, put out his eyes without a trace, and gone where the Wicked One cannot see. And they've crossed over clinging to the world."

That is what the Buddha said. Satisfied, the companions approved what the Buddha said."

Chapter 28

Middle Discourses 26: Pāsarāsisutta

The Noble Quest

Noble friends are your whole spiritual life. This is because noble friends provide ordinary and trainee spiritual companions the opportunity to gain the higher merits and awakening to true life experience with wisdom, higher wisdom beyond ordinary wisdom blending with universal ways of functioning. In the Noble Path, all comparisons are given up. Whoever attains four-fold Nibbana from any conventional background is a noble person who carries a state of wisdom in mind and is a monk or an Arahant. Not all karma creates effects in the same manner, and sila can shape karma to a lesser degree. By attending to Buddha and Arahants, a person who aspires to Nibbana can gain the higher degree of merits. This is the basic thing about Buddha's Dhamma. If the basics are understood, one can make progress, and if not understood, one cannot make progress in the noble path leading to four-fold Nibbana. Also, it's not the flesh of a person that matters. However, the teachings, which means whoever the Arahant is as a person from a conventional perspective, are not relevant; the attainment of a person's four-fold Nibbana is relevant. Thus, bringing self into the picture and sharing personal stories is not relevant. However, sharing higher Dhamma (four-fold Nibbana), explaining the training path with reasoning and sharing merits are relevant.

Noble friends are the path to Nibbana. When someone who has not gained Nibbana seeks advice from someone who has not gained Nibbana about the training path leading to Nibbana, they are seeking ignoble ways, ways out of Nibbana. Instead, one who seeks peace may use whatever is necessary and available without getting too attached to such things in the mind. This is because a person creates an understanding of the external world in their mind: likes, dislikes, and expectations. The external world that is created in one's mind is merely a projection of the mind based on sensory experiences. When someone possesses a mental attachment to worldly experiences, an attachment can only reside within a person's mind, not outside. With friends and family, material and non-material things, they are likely to continue and grow in mental suffering due to such things given that worldly experiences are subject to change. Those who are liable to grow sick, old, and die possess greediness, hatred, and delusion and develop attachments towards others who are similar to them, and this is what everyone has done since their birth.

Instead, one who aspires to peace may choose to live anywhere feasible and practical and do things that need doing in a practical manner without developing too much of a mental attachment to the very same things. Attachment does not indicate that a person stops doing things, does not possess things physically, or does not maintain things that are liable to change, such as mind, body, friends, family, materials and non-materials. This is because giving up physically may indicate starting an extreme way of life that is not practical and feasible for many people; extreme ways are non-Dhamma. Instead, giving up in the middle way is subject to each individual and in one's mind. For a king, renunciation refers to reducing likes, dislikes and expectations within thoughts while continuing to live the lifestyle of a king (from a conventional sense) without getting attached to the view of self, others and the world experiences that are coming from sensory experiences. Buddha's Dhamma can be practiced by anyone anywhere within their lifestyle, and the practice remains the same for all times.

Giving up in the middle way is subjective to each individual; it is a practical thing to do in daily life. Letting go of attachment means doing things with wisdom, making use of materials and possessions with wisdom, and maintaining relationships with wisdom. Attachment means deluded understanding, understanding that self is stable (others are stable and the world is stable), and overly grasping conventions, thinking conventions can be retained for a long time by forgetting the universal functioning. A deluded understanding can make a person think that things a person likes can be retained forever, a person can gain everything they wish etc. When you reduce your attachment, which means reduce your deluded understanding, what you possess and what you do not possess, who you associate with and who you don't associate with, what others think or say and what others don't think or don't say, what your thoughts think, and feel, these things don't bother a person. To let go of attachment, which is the deluded understanding to the full, one must gain Arahantship. A Sotapanna lets go of attachment (gives up deluded understanding), and that self is stable, and conventions are great and stable.

This discourse discuss how Buddha sought ignoble ways and was developing attachment to worldly experiences before his enlightenment. Prince Siddhartha went to several teachers seeking Nibbana. The teachers who he approached, such as Āḷāra Kālāma and Uddaka Rāmaputta, taught jhana practices, but they did not gain Nibbana. Having studied under them, it became clear that their teachings didn't lead to Nibbana, and he found his own way. Nibbana, which is sublime, cannot be easily seen through conventions. It would be hard to explain such Dhamma to common people, and thinking that Buddha was hesitant to teach Dhamma. At that time, brahma appeared and invited him to teach Dhamma, saying that there would be few who would understand what is beyond conventions. It was simply of benefit to them if Dhamma is shared. When Buddha was surveying the world, thinking about who he should teach Dhamma, he understood that his former teachers, who had the potential to understand Nibbana, had passed away. Thus, Buddha decided to approach five friends who helped him before his full awakening. They did not believe Buddha had attained enlightenment and initially refused to accept it. Then, Buddha had to clarify Dhamma in depth. Eventually, they gained four-fold Nibbana and were willing to share Dhamma with others as the disciples of the Buddha.

There are spiritual practitioners who are attached to worldly experiences, and they continue in samsara. The practice of Nibbana requires learning to extinguishing not grasping, so when you start a preliminary practice whether it's a precept, or monastic training rules, or as a conventional monk or a conventional householder, if your mind tend to compare self and others, think you are better than others, this way you grasp into your self-view. In this manner when you become indulged in that what you think you are , and that what you do, you get more and more attachment to it. When you get attached, you become trapped in your worldly experiences, you become overly indulged in yourself, your become ignorant of the universal truth; impermanent of self applies to all beings that are born. Forgetting the truth, you become sad when truth comes to your life experience, interaction between conventions and the universe. This way your wrong grasp of Dhamma prevents you from Nibbana. In Noble Path, all comparisons given up. Given everyone is different, they are exposed various different contexts, whatever supports one to develop extinguishment, cessation is what is benefit one. Comparisons are needed for developing self-view (i.e. pride, and boasting etc.). Yet, Nibbana means giving up all, thus, if you wish to gain Nibbana, it will be of benefit to understand the practice leading to Nibbana blending with the universal ways, and ways in which you can grasp into conventional Dhamma; or Dhamma in wrong ways. If you give up comparisons that strengthening self-view, a wrong grasp of Dhamma, avoid grasping to conventional Dhamma, it will help you to grow and transform into new person with a noble vision, see noble Dhamma; Nibbana, universally applicable practice and the path. If you apply the words of wisdom to yourself, you will escape self-inflicted mental pain. Especially as you live with your mind day and night, purifying your mind will aid you to escape from the self that brings pain to self.

"So I have heard. At one time the Buddha was staying near Sāvatthī in Jeta's Grove, Anāthapiṇḍika's monastery.

Then the Buddha dressed in the morning and, taking his bowl and robe, entered Sāvatthī for alms. Then several spiritual companions went up to noble monk, Ānanda, a Sotapanna and said to him, "Respected friend, it's been a long time since we've heard a Dhamma talk from the Buddha. It would be good if we got to hear a Dhamma talk from the Buddha."

"Well then, respected friend, go to the brahmin Rammaka's hermitage. Hopefully you'll get to hear a Dhamma talk from the Buddha."

"Yes, reverend," they replied.

Then, after the meal, on his return from almsround, the Buddha addressed Ānanda, "Come, Ānanda, let's go to the stilt longhouse of Migāra's mother in the Eastern Monastery for the day's stay over."

"Yes, sir," Ānanda replied. So the Buddha went with Ānanda to the Eastern Monastery for spending the day. In the late afternoon the Buddha came out of retreat and addressed Ānanda, "Come, Ānanda, let's go to the eastern gate to bathe."

"Yes, sir," Ānanda replied.

So the Buddha went with Ānanda to the eastern gate to bathe. When he had bathed and emerged from the water he stood in one robe drying his limbs. Then Ānanda said to the Buddha, "Sir, the hermitage of the brahmin Rammaka is nearby. It's so delightful, so lovely. Please visit it out of sympathy." The Buddha consented with silence.

He went to the brahmin Rammaka's hermitage. Now at that time several people were sitting together in the hermitage talking about the teaching. The Buddha stood outside the door waiting for the talk to end. When he knew the talk had ended he cleared his throat and knocked on the door-panel. The spiritual practitioners opened the door for the Buddha, and he entered the hermitage, where he sat on the seat spread out and addressed the companions, "Companions, what were you sitting talking about just now? What conversation was left unfinished?"

"Sir, our unfinished discussion on the teaching was about the Buddha himself when the Buddha arrived."

"Good, companions! It's appropriate for gentlemen like you, who are interested in practicing the universal noble path to give up mental attachment, to sit together and talk about the universal teaching. When you're sitting together you should do one of two things: discuss the teachings or keep noble silence.

Companions, there are these two quests: the noble quest and the ignoble quest.

And what is the ignoble quest? It's when someone who is themselves liable to be reborn seeks what is also liable to be reborn. Themselves liable to grow old, fall sick, die, sorrow, and become corrupted, they seek what is also liable to these things.

And what should be described as liable to be changed, not permanent? Friends and associates (supporters, partners, parents, and children, male and female bondservants etc.), possessions (goats and sheep, chickens and pigs, elephants and cattle etc.), and materials (gold and currency, buildings, temples, homes etc.,) are liable to be change, impermanent. These attachments are not stable. Someone who is mentally tied, infatuated, and attached to such things, themselves liable to being changed, impermanent, seeks what is also liable to be changed, impermeant.

And what should be described as liable to grow old? Friends and associates (supporters, partners, parents, and children, male and female bondservants etc.), possessions (goats and sheep, chickens and pigs, elephants and cattle etc.) are liable to grow old. These people and possessions to which a person is attached are liable to grow old. Someone who is mentally tied, infatuated, and attached to such things, themselves liable to grow old, seeks what is also liable to grow old.

And what should be described as liable to fall sick? Friends and associates (supporters, partners, parents, and children, male and female bondservants etc.), possessions (goats and sheep, chickens and pigs, elephants and cattle etc.) are liable to fall sick. These people and animals to which a person is attached are liable to fall sick. Someone who is mentally tied, infatuated, and attached to such things, themselves liable to falling sick, seeks what is also liable to fall sick.

And what should be described as liable to die? Friends and associates (supporters, partners, parents, and children, male and female bondservants etc.), possessions (goats and sheep, chickens and pigs, elephants and cattle etc.) are liable to die. These people and animals to which a person is attached are liable to die. Someone who is mentally tied, infatuated, and attached to such things, themselves liable to die, seeks what is also liable to die.

And what should be described as liable to sorrow? Friends and associates (supporters, partners, parents, and children, male and female bondservants etc.), possessions (goats and sheep, chickens and pigs, elephants and cattle etc.) are liable to sorrow. These attachments are liable to sorrow. Someone who is mentally tied, infatuated, and attached to such things, themselves liable to sorrow, seeks what is also liable to sorrow.

And what should be described as liable to corruption? Friends and associates (supporters, partners, parents, and children, male and female bondservants etc.), possessions (goats and sheep, chickens and pigs, elephants and cattle etc.) are liable to corruption. These people and animals to which a person is attached are liable to corruption. Someone who is tied, infatuated, and attached to such things, themselves liable to corruption, seeks what is also liable to corruption. This is the ignoble quest.

And what is the noble quest? It's when someone who is themselves liable to be reborn, understanding the drawbacks in being liable to be reborn, seeks that which is free of rebirth, the supreme sanctuary from the yoke, four-fold nibbana. Themselves liable to grow old, fall sick, die, sorrow, and become corrupted, understanding the drawbacks in these things, they seek that which is free of old age, sickness, death, sorrow, and corruption, the supreme sanctuary from the yoke, four-fold nibbana. This is the noble quest.

Companions, before my awakening—when I was still unawakened but intent on awakening—I too, being liable to be reborn, sought what is also liable to be reborn. Myself liable to grow old, fall sick, die, sorrow, and become corrupted, I sought what is also liable to these things. Then it occurred to me: 'Why do I, being liable to be reborn, grow old, fall sick, sorrow, die, and become corrupted, seek things that have the same nature? Why don't I seek that which is free of rebirth, old age, sickness, death, sorrow, and corruption, the supreme sanctuary from the yoke, four-fold nibbana?'

Sometime later, while still with pristine black hair, blessed with youth, in the prime of life—though my mother and father wished otherwise, weeping with tearful faces—I went away from home seeking a spiritual life.

Once I had gone searching for a spiritual life, I set out to discover what is skillful, seeking the supreme state of sublime peace. I approached Āḷāra Kālāma and said to him, 'Reverend Kālāma, I wish to lead the spiritual life in this teaching and training.'

Āḷāra Kālāma replied, 'Stay, venerable. This teaching is such that a sensible person can soon realize their own tradition with their own insight and live having achieved it.'

I quickly memorized that teaching. As far as lip-recital and verbal repetition went, I spoke the doctrine of knowledge, the elder doctrine. I claimed to know and see, and so did others.

Then it occurred to me, 'It is not solely by mere faith that Āḷāra Kālāma declares: "I realize this teaching with my own insight, and live having achieved it." Surely he meditates knowing and seeing this teaching ("Jhanic" experience).'

So I approached Āḷāra Kālāma and said to him, 'Reverend Kālāma, to what extent do you say you've realized this teaching with your own insight?' When I said this, he declared the dimension of nothingness.

Then it occurred to me, 'It's not just Āḷāra Kālāma who has faith, energy, mindfulness, immersion, and wisdom; I too have these things. Why don't I make an effort to realize the same teaching that Āḷāra Kālāma says he has realized with his own insight ("Jhanic" experience).')?' I quickly realized that teaching with my own insight ("Jhanic" experience) and lived having achieved it.

So I approached Āḷāra Kālāma and said to him, 'Reverend Kālāma, is it up to this point that you realized this teaching with your own insight ("Jhanic" experience), and declare having achieved it?'

'I have, reverend.'

'I too, reverend, have realized this teaching with my own insight up to this point ("Jhanic" experience) and live having achieved it.'

'We are fortunate, reverend, so very fortunate to see a venerable such as yourself as one of our spiritual companions! So the teaching that I've realized with my own insight, and declare having achieved it, you've realized with your own insight, and dwell having achieved it. The teaching that you've realized with your own insight, and dwell having achieved it, I've realized with my own insight, and declare having achieved it. So the teaching that I know, you know, and the teaching that you know, I know. I am like you and you are like me. Come now, reverend! We should both lead this community together.'

And that is how my tutor Āḷāra Kālāma placed me, his pupil, on the same position as him, and honored me with lofty praise.

Then it occurred to me, 'This teaching doesn't lead to disillusionment, dispassion, cessation, peace, insight, awakening, and extinguishment. It only leads as far as rebirth in the dimension of nothingness.' Realizing that this teaching was inadequate, I left disappointed.

I set out to discover what is skillful, seeking the supreme state of sublime peace. I approached Uddaka son of Rāma and said to him, 'Reverend, I wish to lead the spiritual life in this teaching and training.'

Uddaka replied, 'Stay, venerable. This teaching is such that a sensible person can soon realize their own tradition with their own insight and live having achieved it.'

I quickly memorized that teaching. As far as lip-recital and verbal repetition went, I spoke the doctrine of knowledge, the elder doctrine. I claimed to know and see, and so did others.

Then it occurred to me, 'It is not solely by mere faith that Rāma declared: "I realize this teaching with my own insight, and live having achieved it." Surely he meditated knowing and seeing this teaching.'

So I approached Uddaka son of Rāma and said to him, 'Reverend, to what extent did Rāma say he'd realized this teaching with his own insight ("Jhanic" experience)?'

When I said this, Uddaka son of Rāma declared the dimension of neither perception nor non-perception.

Then it occurred to me, 'It's not just Rāma who had faith, energy, mindfulness, immersion, and wisdom; I too have these things. Why don't I make an effort to realize the same teaching that Rāma said he had realized with his own insight?' I quickly realized that teaching with my own insight ("Jhanic" experience) and lived having achieved it.

So I approached Uddaka son of Rāma and said to him, 'Reverend, had Rāma realized this teaching with his own insight up to this point, and declared having achieved it?'

'He had, reverend.'

'I too have realized this teaching with my own insight up to this point, and live having achieved it.'

'We are fortunate, reverend, so very fortunate to see a venerable such as yourself as one of our spiritual companions! So the teaching that Rāma had realized with his own insight, and declared having achieved it, you've realized with your own insight, and dwell having achieved it. The teaching that you've realized with your own insight, and dwell having achieved it, Rāma had realized with his own insight, and declared having achieved it. So the teaching that Rāma directly knew, you know, and the teaching you know, Rāma directly knew. Rāma was like you and you are like Rāma. Come now, reverend! You should lead this community.'

And that is how my spiritual companion Uddaka son of Rāma placed me in the position of a tutor and honored me with lofty praise.

Then it occurred to me, 'This teaching doesn't lead to disillusionment, dispassion, cessation, peace, insight, awakening, and extinguishment. It only leads as far as rebirth in the dimension of neither perception nor non-perception.' Realizing that this teaching was inadequate, I left disappointed.

I set out to discover what is skillful, seeking the supreme state of sublime peace. Traveling stage by stage in the Magadhan lands, I arrived at Senānigama in Uruvelā. There I saw a delightful park, a lovely grove with a flowing river that was clean and charming, with smooth banks. And nearby was a village for alms.

Then it occurred to me, 'This park is truly delightful, a lovely grove with a flowing river that's clean and charming, with smooth banks. And nearby there's a village to go for alms. This is good enough for striving for a gentleman wanting to strive.' So I sat down right there, thinking, 'This is good enough for striving.'

And so, being myself liable to be reborn, understanding the drawbacks in being liable to be reborn, I sought that which is free of rebirth, the supreme sanctuary from the yoke, extinguishment—and I found it. Being myself liable to grow old, fall sick, die, sorrow, and become corrupted, understanding the drawbacks in these things, I sought that which is free of old age, sickness, death, sorrow, and corruption, the supreme sanctuary from the yoke, extinguishment (Arahantship and four-fold Nibbāna)—and I found it.

Knowledge and vision arose in me: 'My freedom is unshakable; this is my last rebirth; now there'll be no more future lives.'

Then it occurred to me, 'This principle I have discovered is deep, hard to see, hard to understand, peaceful, sublime, beyond the scope of views, subtle, comprehensible to the astute. But people like clinging, they love it and enjoy it. It's hard for them to see this topic that goes beyond conventions; specific conditionality, dependent origination based on universal ways of functioning. It's also hard for them to understand; that is, the stilling of all activities, the letting go of all attachments, the ending of craving, fading away, cessation, extinguishment. And if I were to teach the universal Dhamma, others might not understand me, which would be wearying and troublesome for me.'

And then these verses, which were neither supernaturally inspired, nor learned before in the past, occurred to me:

'I've struggled hard to realize this, enough with trying to explain it! Those mired in greed and hate can't really understand this teaching.

It goes against the stream, subtle, deep, obscure, and very fine. Those besotted by greed cannot see, for they're shrouded in a mass of darkness.'

So, as I reflected like this, my mind inclined to remaining passive, not to teaching the Dhamma.

Then the divinity Sahampati, knowing my train of thought, thought, 'Alas! The world will be lost, the world will perish! For the mind of the Realized One, the perfected one, the fully awakened Buddha, inclines to remaining passive, not to teaching the Dhamma.'

Then, as easily as a strong person would extend or contract their arm, he vanished from the realm of divinity and reappeared in front of me. He arranged his robe over one shoulder, raised his joined palms toward me, and said, 'Sir, let the Blessed One teach the Dhamma! Let the Holy One teach the Dhamma! There are beings with little dust in their eyes. They're in decline because they haven't heard the teaching. There will be those who understand the teaching!'

That's what the divinity Sahampati said. Then he went on to say:

'Among the Magadhans there appeared in the past an impure teaching thought up by the stained. Fling open the door to freedom from death! Let them hear the teaching the immaculate one discovered.

Standing high on a rocky mountain, you can see the people all around. In just the same way, All-seer, so intelligent, having ascended the Temple of Truth, rid of sorrow, look upon the people swamped with sorrow, oppressed by rebirth and old age.

Rise, hero! Victor in battle, leader of the caravan, wander the world free of debt. Let the Blessed One teach the Dhamma! There will be those who understand!'

Then, understanding the Divinity's invitation, I surveyed the world with the eye of a Buddha, because of my compassion for sentient beings. And I saw sentient beings with little dust in their eyes, and some with much dust in their eyes; with keen faculties and with weak faculties, with good qualities and with bad qualities, easy to teach and hard to teach. And some of them lived seeing the danger in the fault to do with the next world, while others did not. It's like a pool with blue water lilies, or pink or white lotuses.

Some of them sprout and grow in the water without rising above it, thriving underwater. Some of them sprout and grow in the water reaching the water's surface. And some of them sprout and grow in the water but rise up above the water and stand with no water clinging to them. In the same way, I saw sentient beings with little dust in their eyes, and some with much dust in their eyes.

Then I replied in verse to the divinity Sahampati:

'Flung open are the doors to freedom from death! Let those with ears to hear commit to faith grounded by evidence to discover self, Nibbana. Thinking it would be troublesome, Divinity, I did not teach the sophisticated, sublime Dhamma among humans.'

Then the divinity Sahampati, knowing that his request for me to teach the Dhamma had been granted, bowed and respectfully circled me, keeping me on his right, before vanishing right there.

Then I thought, 'Who should I teach first of all? Who will quickly understand this teaching?'

Then it occurred to me, 'That Āḷāra Kālāma is astute, competent, clever, and has long had little dust in his eyes. Why don't I teach him first of all? He'll quickly understand the teaching.'

But a deity came to me and said, 'Sir, Āḷāra Kālāma passed away seven days ago.'

And knowledge and vision arose in me, 'Āḷāra Kālāma passed away seven days ago.'

I thought, 'This is a great loss for Āḷāra Kālāma. If he had heard the teaching, he would have understood it quickly.'

Then I thought, 'Who should I teach first of all? Who will quickly understand this teaching?'

Then it occurred to me, 'That Uddaka son of Rāma is astute, competent, clever, and has long had little dust in his eyes. Why don't I teach him first of all? He'll quickly understand the teaching.'

But a deity came to me and said, 'Sir, Uddaka son of Rāma passed away just last night.'

And knowledge and vision arose in me, 'Uddaka son of Rāma passed away just last night.'

I thought, 'This is a great loss for Uddaka. If he had heard the teaching, he would have understood it quickly.'

Then I thought, 'Who should I teach first of all? Who will quickly understand this teaching?'

Then it occurred to me, 'The group of five friends were very helpful to me. They looked after me during my time of resolute striving. Why don't I teach them first of all?'

Then I thought, 'Where are the group of five companions staying these days?' With clairvoyance that is purified and superhuman I saw that the group of five companions were staying near Varanasi, in the deer park at Isipatana. So, when I had stayed in Uruvelā as long as I pleased, I set out for Varanasi.

While I was traveling along the road between Gayā and Bodhgaya, the Ājīvaka ascetic Upaka saw me and said, 'Reverend, your faculties are so very clear, and your complexion is pure and bright. In whose name have you gone forth, reverend? Who is your Teacher? Whose teaching do you believe in?'

I replied to Upaka in verse:

'I am the champion, the knower of all, unsullied in the midst of all things. I've given up all, freed through the ending of craving. Since I know for myself, whose follower should I be?

I have no tutor. There is no-one like me. In the world with its gods, I have no rival.

For in this world, I am the Arahant, supremely enlightened Buddha; I am the supreme Teacher of men and gods. I alone am fully awakened, cooled, quenched.

I am going to the city of Kāsi to roll forth the Wheel of Dhamma. In this world that is so blind, I'll beat the drum of freedom from death!'

'According to what you claim, reverend, you ought to be the Infinite Victor.'

'The victors are those who, like me, have reached the ending of defilements. I have conquered bad qualities, Upaka—that's why I'm a victor.'

When I had spoken, Upaka said: 'If you say so, reverend.' Shaking his head, he took a wrong turn and left.

Traveling stage by stage, I arrived at Varanasi, and went to see the group of five spiritual practitioners in the deer park at Isipatana. The group of five practitioners saw me coming off in the distance and stopped each other, saying, 'Here comes the ascetic Gotama. He's so indulgent; he strayed from the struggle and returned to indulgence.

We shouldn't bow to him or rise for him or welcome him with extra respect. But we can set out a seat; he can sit if he likes.' Yet as I drew closer, the group of five spiritual practitioners were unable to stop themselves as they had agreed. Some came out to greet me and receive me with extra respect, some spread out a seat, while others set out water for washing my feet. But they still addressed me by name and as 'reverend'.

So I said to them, 'Friends, don't address me by name and as "reverend". The Realized One is perfected, a fully awakened Buddha. Listen up, companions: I have achieved freedom from death! I shall instruct you, I will teach you the Dhamma, four-fold nibbana. By practicing as instructed you will gain Arahantship in this very life. You will live having achieved with your own insight the goal for which a person follows a spiritual life.'

But they said to me, 'Reverend Gotama, even by that conduct, that practice, that grueling work you did not achieve any superhuman distinction in knowledge and vision worthy of the noble ones. How could you have achieved such a state now that you've become indulgent, strayed from the struggle and returned to indulgence?'

So I said to them, 'The Realized One has not become indulgent, strayed from the struggle and returned to indulgence. The Realized One is perfected, a fully awakened Buddha.

Listen up, companions: I have achieved freedom from death! I shall instruct you, I will teach you the Dhamma. By practicing as instructed you will soon realize the supreme end of the spiritual path in this very life.'

But for a second time they said to me, 'Reverend Gotama … you've returned to indulgence.'

So for a second time I said to them, 'The Realized One has not become indulgent …'

But for a third time they said to me, 'Reverend Gotama, even by that conduct, that practice, that grueling work you did not achieve any superhuman distinction in knowledge and vision worthy of the noble ones. How could you have achieved such a state now that you've become indulgent, strayed from the struggle and returned to indulgence?'

So I said to them, 'Companions, have you ever known me to speak like this before?'

'No sir, we have not.'

'The Realized One is perfected, a fully awakened Buddha. Listen up, friends: I have achieved freedom from death! I shall instruct you, I will teach you the Dhamma. By practicing as instructed you will soon realize the supreme end (Arahantship) of the spiritual path in this very life. You will live having achieved with your insight the goal for which a person follows a spiritual life.'

I was able to persuade the group of five spiritual friends. Then sometimes I advised two companions, while the other three went for alms. Then those three would feed all six of us with what they brought back. Sometimes I advised three companions, while the other two went for alms. Then those two would feed all six of us with what they brought back.

As the group of five spiritual friends were being advised and instructed by me like this, being themselves liable to be reborn, understanding the drawbacks in being liable to be reborn, they sought that which is free of rebirth, the supreme sanctuary from the yoke, extinguishment (Arahant state, four-fold Nibbana)—and they found it.

Being themselves liable to grow old, fall sick, die, sorrow, and become corrupted, understanding the drawbacks in these things, they sought that which is free of old age, sickness, death, sorrow, and corruption, the supreme sanctuary from the yoke, extinguishment (Arahant state, four-fold Nibbana)—and they found it. Knowledge and vision arose in them: 'Our freedom is unshakable; this is our last rebirth; now there'll be no more future lives.'

Companions, there are these five kinds of sensual stimulation. What five? Sights known by the eye, which are likable, desirable, agreeable, pleasant, sensual, and arousing. Sounds known by the ear … Smells known by the nose … Tastes known by the tongue

… Touches known by the body, which are likable, desirable, agreeable, pleasant, sensual, and arousing. These are the five kinds of sensual stimulation.

There are spiritual practitioners and trainees who enjoy these five kinds of sensual stimulation tied, infatuated, attached, blind to the drawbacks, and not understanding the escape.

You should understand that they have met with calamity and disaster, and the Wicked One can do with them what he wants.

Suppose a deer in the wilderness was lying caught on a pile of snares. You'd know that it has met with calamity and disaster, and the hunter can do with them what he wants. And when the hunter comes, it cannot flee where it wants.

In the same way, spiritual practitioners and trainees who enjoy these five kinds of sensual stimulation tied, infatuated, attached, blind to the drawbacks, and not understanding the escape.

You should understand that they have met with calamity and disaster, and the Wicked One can do with them what he wants.

There are spiritual practitioners and trainees who enjoy these five kinds of sensual stimulation without being tied, infatuated, or attached, seeing the drawbacks, and understanding the escape.

You should understand that they haven't met with calamity and disaster, and the Wicked One cannot do what he wants with them.

Suppose a deer in the wilderness was lying on a pile of snares without being caught. You'd know that it hasn't met with calamity and disaster, and the hunter cannot do what he wants with them. And when the hunter comes, it can flee where it wants.

In the same way, there are spiritual practitioners and trainees who enjoy these five kinds of sensual stimulation without being tied, infatuated, or attached, seeing the drawbacks, and understanding the escape.

You should understand that they haven't met with calamity and disaster, and the Wicked One cannot do what he wants with them.

Suppose there was a wild deer wandering in the forest that walked, stood, sat, and laid down in confidence. Why is that? Because it's out of the hunter's range.

In the same way, a companion who has completed first two stages of four-fold nibbana, quite secluded from sensual pleasures (upon gaining Anagami state), secluded from unskillful qualities, experiences the first absorption (path to Arahantship), which has the rapture and bliss born of seclusion, while placing the mind and keeping it connected. This is called a person who has blinded Māra, put out his eyes without a trace, and gone where the Wicked One cannot see.

Furthermore, as the placing of the mind and keeping it connected are stilled, a person experiences the second absorption, which has the rapture and bliss born of immersion, with internal clarity and mind at one, without placing the mind and keeping it connected. This is called a person who has blinded Māra …

Furthermore, with the fading away of rapture, a companion experiences the third absorption, where they experience equanimity, mindful and aware, personally experiencing the bliss of which the noble ones declare, 'Equanimous and mindful, one meditates in bliss.' This is called a person who has blinded Māra …

Furthermore, giving up pleasure and pain, and ending former happiness and sadness, a person experiences the fourth absorption, without pleasure or pain, with pure equanimity and mindfulness. This is called person who has blinded Māra …

Furthermore, a person, going totally beyond perceptions of form, with the ending of perceptions of impingement, not focusing on perceptions of diversity, aware that 'space is infinite', enters and remains in the dimension of infinite space. This is called a person who has blinded Māra …

Furthermore, a person, going totally beyond the dimension of infinite space, aware that 'consciousness is infinite', enters and remains in the dimension of infinite consciousness. This is called a person who has blinded Māra …

Furthermore, a person, going totally beyond the dimension of infinite consciousness, aware that 'there is nothing at all', enters and remains in the dimension of nothingness. This is called a person who has blinded Māra …

Furthermore, a person, going totally beyond the dimension of nothingness, enters and remains in the dimension of neither perception nor non-perception. This is called a person who has blinded Māra …

Furthermore, a person, going totally beyond the dimension of neither perception nor non-perception, enters and remains in the cessation of perception and feeling (complete Arahantship). And, having seen with wisdom, their defilements come to an end. This is called a person who has blinded Māra, put out his eyes without a trace, and gone where the Wicked One cannot see. They've crossed over clinging to the world. And they walk, stand, sit, and lie down in confidence. Why is that? Because they're out of the Wicked One's range."

That is what the Buddha said. Satisfied, the companions approved what the Buddha said."

Chapter 29

Middle Discourses 27: Cūḷahatthipadopamasutta

The Shorter Simile of the Elephant's Footprint

This discourse discusses the practice leading to four-fold Nibbana. One may practice precepts and move to noble virtues (Sotapanna) and noble concentration of an Anagami and Arahant. To understand the full meaning of this discourse it is important to understand who a monk on the Noble Path is. One of the confusions over Buddha's Dhamma is who is a monk. Natural transformation takes place in a person's mental continuum across stages, and that transformation, which allows abandoning mental fetters out of rituals, is a monk in Noble Path. At the Anagami state, a person naturally transforms into someone who maintains chastity. At least until one is established in the four factors of Stream-entry, one is not a disciple of the Buddha or Savaka Sangha representing the Triple Gem.

When asked, they claim to be venerable and act like Arahants, but they are not true Arahants. At least until one is established in the four factors of Stream-entry, one is not a disciple of the Buddha or Savaka Sangha representing the Triple Gem.

One cannot become a universal disciple (Savaka Sangha) of Buddha through ritualistic transformation. This is because ritualistic transformation can be temporary, as life is temporary.

One cannot become a universal disciple (Savaka Sangha) of Buddha through conscious transformation and concentration ("Jhanic" experience through conscious effort). This is because the conscious transformation of a person can change because consciousness is subject to change, and concentration can change. Instead, one must learn to blend with the universal rhythm to become a Savaka disciple of the Buddha and the practice remains the same for all. This explains why a Sotapanna abandons grasping conventions. Birth in noble linage a random happening. It's not that one becomes a monk by taking the monastic rules which are preliminary practices before Sotapanna; instead, one becomes a monk through natural transformation, transformation that makes a person abandon the mental attachment to the fetters; self-view, rituals, shaped by the universal functioning. Across stages of Nibbana, a person naturally transforms into someone who eats meals before noon, does not harm trees, is chaste, does not see movies, etc., because the underlying tendency for desire is abandoned. Thus, declaring Arahantship when one truly attains Arahantship is accepted and welcomed by the Buddha. Yet, Buddha rejects pretending to be Arahants, receiving special treatments from others, and misinterpreting Dhamma by preventing Nibbana for many.

True Arahants don't divide beings or act like they are special; instead, they unite the universal teachings and treat all beings as precious irrespective of conventions. No one of noble linage will make comparisons, or they will attempt to make one person superior, the same or inferior. Thus, anyone who wants to make progress in the Noble Path needs to give up thinking that they are special, similar, or inferior if they want to develop the Noble Path. Therefore, when those who are in monastic settings call themselves venerable, it appears as if they want to pretend like they are Arahants and that they want to be treated as special. Some monastics tell others that monastic rules are better than householder rules and that monastic life is superior to other lifestyles. When they compare one another, wanting and asking to be treated as if they are special, they are strengthening the self-view, grasping rituals and conventions. Instead, they need to give-up thinking that they are special, if they want to develop the Noble Path. The same can be said regarding practitioners of all settings. For example, when those who are in a householder setting compare one another and think that they can enjoy better than monastics, they are inferior to monastics, and they are strengthening the self-view and rituals. Self knows the best of self. Self is the best to give advice to self. When self attempts to purify self from grasping to self-view, the universe comes to know about it as self, a mere convention that functions within the universe. Purification of an Arahant is simply for sharing purification with those who are looking to purify themselves and to abandon the mental pain that comes from worldly experiences. Social practices and conventions are boxes within which people think and lenses through which people see the world.

One way in which people who seek Nibbana can go wrong is by trying to find the universally created truth in socially created ways. In this manner, if you grasp socially accepted ways and those who represent socially accepted monks as monks in Buddha's path, you can grasp into conventional Dhamma and conventional Sangha. By doing so, you can go into the wrong path where you can be barred from Nibbana, because monks who grasp conventions have no capacity to provide you the path to become free from conventions. They may teach you the basics of Dhamma, which you must develop further. Thus, conventional monks can be seen as pre-school teachers. Sotapanna is like primary school teachers. Sakadagami is like secondary school teachers. Anagamis are like higher education teachers. Arahants are like PhD supervisors, and, in this manner, one who wishes to make progress in Nibbana requires replacing existing knowledge with higher knowledge over stages in the noble path. If you grasp socially accepted Dhamma as Buddha's Dhamma, Nibbana can be kept from you due to blocking your right view. Social creations, such as the "jhana" practices proposed by some conventional monks of certain traditions, are subject to change.

Dhamma refers to Nibbana (Sotapanna to Arahant). If Dhamma were to depend solely on Arahants, the continuation of Dhamma would become impossible as Arahants are rare. Thus, conventional Sangha aids the continuation of Dhamma by caring about the preliminary Dhamma, and these preliminary stages of Dhamma require linking to the Noble Path by filling the gaps for the right understanding of Dhamma.

The reason that people grasp conventions is because they think conventions are great. Conventions don't stand alone but stand within the universe. The universe is bigger than conventions, and you can get support from the universe. That support from the universe can help you in conventional life and after. Thus, by understanding what benefits you, you can develop the Noble Path to let go of grasping conventions in the middle way.

Conventional Sangha who have not gained Nibbana can have various doubts about Nibbana, which is reasonable as unless you gain Nibbana, you wouldn't know, yet doubts lead to creating doubt in another and doubts among conventional Sangha make them entangled in circles of doubts, unable to find the practice leading to Nibbana, with the right vision leading to Nibbana. Instead, by not developing an ignoble vision but developing a wise vision by applying reasoning, a wise, ordinary person can develop a practice.

Before Sotapanna, one may believe in karma, and the Triple Gem. Belief indicates the likelihood of certainty but not certainty, and belief can be true or false. After gaining Sotapanna, one may be surprised to know that Dhamma is true, a turning point of understanding. Yet, Sotapanna does not know of the Sakadagami, Anagami, and Arahant stages and has no clue what it means to experience such things. It is only after the Arahant stage that one concludes that Buddha is the knower of all the world. They don't say that merely based on books but say it because they know it for themselves. Therefore, one way to recognize an Arahant is to say that they know Buddha is the knower of all.

Developing the right vision means understanding that life is an experience between the universe and conventions and giving up mental attachment to the fetters, self-view, social practices, and conventions.

Society encourages one to look Dhamma in appearance or certain places. Among practitioners, some people can feel delighted or scared (or ignored) when they see the appearance of a conventional Sangha and someone dressed up as a monk. Society teaches you to understand Dhamma through an appearance or a dress. Yet, universal Dhamma can be found beyond socially accepted ways in unexpected people. Nibbana is not a conscious effect, a natural happening while sitting or lying down at a random time. People who don't have a reasonable acceptance of karma can still meditate for years without the right vision. The right view means understanding the universal ways of Dhamma and the practices of Dhamma because without a right vision it makes their practice fruitless.

Those who give importance to conventions, they grasp into conventions. Those who has seen universal functioning through personal experience, having given up importance and not importance, simply for showing the training path to others, they talk about Dhamma (four-fold Nibbana). Those who make Dhamma alive within, they come to live with Nibbana.

Those who make Dhamma alive outside but do not make Dhamma alive within are running far short of Nibbana. Speaking the truth, practicing Dhamma refers to reducing desires and mental attachment to worldly experiences coming through sensory information. Reducing mental attachment refers to reducing too much liking, disliking, or having expectations for worldly experiences. Giving up liking, disliking, and expectations is higher Dhamma (this happens at Arahant state). Buddha is the knower of all worlds (without a doubt) and is the understanding of the noble ones, it is an understanding based on evidence gained from life experience. Dhamma is a universal happening is the understanding of the noble ones, it is an understanding based on evidence gained from their life experience. If you apply Dhamma within and make progress, you will get to experience universal Dhamma across four-fold Nibbana. When you understand non-dhamma as Dhamma, you can't make Dhamma grow within. Instead, when you understand Dhamma as Dhamma and make Dhamma grow within, your defilements and sufferings will cease within. You have two options. You can grow defilement and suffer mentally, or you can grow Dhamma within and give up suffering mentally.

Having seen Buddha through experiencing four-fold Nibbana, those who attain Arahantship do not misinterpret Buddha. Arahants are respectful of Buddha for it is because of Buddha that they could escape their sufferings, end of samsara. Those who have not seen Buddha (meaning Nibbana within) misinterpret Buddha. Although wisdom can be shared, an individual's ability to absorb wisdom remains subjective. Thus, refuge in the Triple Gem - not the lookalike Triple Gem, but the genuine - is the path to Nibbana.

"So I have heard. At one time the Buddha was staying near Sāvatthī in Jeta's Grove, Anāthapiṇḍika's monastery.

Now at that time the brahmin Jānussoṇi drove out from Sāvatthī in the middle of the day in an all-white chariot drawn by mares. He saw the wanderer Pilotika coming off in the distance, and said to him, "So, Mister Vacchāyana, where are you coming from in the middle of the day?"

"Just now, good sir, I've come from the presence of the ascetic Gotama."

"What do you think of the ascetic Gotama's lucidity of wisdom? Do you think he's astute?"

"My good man, who am I to judge the ascetic Gotama's lucidity of wisdom? You'd really have to be on the same level to judge his lucidity of wisdom."

"Mister Vacchāyana praises the ascetic Gotama with lofty praise indeed."

"Who am I to praise the ascetic Gotama? He is praised by the praised as the first among gods and humans."

"But for what reason are you so devoted to the ascetic Gotama?"

"Suppose that a skilled bull elephant tracker were to enter a bull elephant wood. There he'd see a large elephant's footprint, long and broad. He would come to the conclusion, 'This must be a big bull elephant.'

In the same way, because I saw four footprints (four-fold Nibbana) of the ascetic Gotama I came to the conclusion, 'The Blessed One is a fully awakened Buddha. The teaching is well explained. The Savaka Saṅgha is practicing well.'

What four? Firstly, I see some wise people from a high social rank who are subtle, accomplished in the doctrines of others, hair-splitters. You'd think they live to demolish convictions with their intellect. They hear, 'So, gentlemen, that ascetic Gotama will come down to such and such village or town.' They formulate a question, thinking, 'We'll approach the ascetic Gotama and ask him this question. If he answers like this, we'll refute him like that; and if he answers like that, we'll refute him like this.'

When they hear that he has come down they approach him. The ascetic Gotama educates, encourages, fires up, and inspires them with a Dhamma talk. They don't even get around to asking their question to the ascetic Gotama, so how could they refute his answer? Invariably, they become his disciples (Sotapanna to Arahant). When I saw this first footprint (Sotapanna) of the ascetic Gotama, I came to the conclusion, 'The Blessed One is a fully awakened Buddha. The teaching is well explained. The Savaka Saṅgha is practicing well.'

Furthermore, I see some wise religious leaders… some wise householders … they become his disciples (Sotapanna to Arahant).

Furthermore, I see some clever ascetics who are subtle, accomplished in the doctrines of others, hair-splitters. … They don't even get around to asking their question to the ascetic Gotama, so how could they refute his answer? Invariably, they ask the ascetic Gotama for the chance to gain four-fold Nibbana. And he gives them the chance to gain four-fold Nibbana. Soon after taking the refuge in the Triple Gem (Sotapanna), living withdrawn, diligent, keen, and resolute, they realize the supreme end of the spiritual path (Arahant) in this very life.

They live having achieved with their insight the goal for which a person follows a spiritual life by taking refuge in the triple gem.

They say, 'We were almost lost! We almost perished! For we used to claim that we were ascetics, brahmins, and perfected ones, but we were none of these things. But now we really are ascetics, brahmins, and perfected ones!' When I saw this fourth footprint of the ascetic Gotama, I came to the conclusion, 'The Blessed One is a fully awakened universal Buddha. The universal teaching-four-fold Nibbana is well explained. The universal (Savaka) Saṅgha is practicing well.'

It's because I saw these four footprints of the ascetic Gotama that I came to the conclusion, 'The Blessed One is a fully awakened universal Buddha. The universal teaching-four-fold Nibbana is well explained. The universal (Savaka) Saṅgha is practicing well.'

When he had spoken, Jānussoṇi got down from his chariot, arranged his robe over one shoulder, raised his joined palms toward the Buddha, and expressed this heartfelt sentiment three times:

"Homage to that Blessed One, the perfected one, the fully awakened universal Buddha!

Homage to that Blessed One, the perfected one, the fully awakened universal Buddha!

Homage to that Blessed One, the perfected one, the fully awakened universal Buddha!

Hopefully, some time or other I'll get to meet Mister Gotama, and we can have a discussion."

Then the brahmin Jānussoṇi went up to the Buddha, and exchanged greetings with him. When the greetings and polite conversation were over, he sat down to one side, and informed the Buddha of all he had discussed with the wanderer Pilotika.

When he had spoken, the Buddha said to him, "Brahmin, the simile of the elephant's footprint is not yet completed in detail. As to how it is completed in detail, listen and apply your mind well, I will speak."

"Yes sir," Jānussoṇi replied. The Buddha said this:

"Suppose a bull elephant tracker were to enter a bull elephant wood. There they'd see a large elephant's footprint, long and broad. A skilled bull elephant tracker does not yet come to the conclusion, 'This must be a big bull elephant.' Why not? Because in an elephant wood there are dwarf cow elephants with big footprints, and this footprint might be one of theirs.

They keep following the track until they see a big footprint, long and broad, and traces high up. A skilled bull elephant tracker does not yet come to the conclusion, 'This must be a big bull elephant.' Why not? Because in an elephant wood there are tall lofty cow elephants with big footprints, and this footprint might be one of theirs.

They keep following the track until they see a big footprint, long and broad, and traces and tusk-marks high up. A skilled bull elephant tracker does not yet come to the conclusion, 'This must be a big bull elephant.' Why not? Because in an elephant wood there are tall matriarch cow elephants with big footprints, and this footprint might be one of theirs.

They keep following the track until they see a big footprint, long and broad, and traces, tusk-marks, and broken branches high up. And they see that bull elephant walking, standing, sitting, or lying down at the root of a tree or in the open. Then they'd come to the conclusion, 'This is that big bull elephant.'

In the same way, brahmin, a Realized One arises in the world, perfected, a fully awakened Buddha, accomplished in knowledge and conduct, holy, knower of the world, supreme guide for those who wish to train, teacher of gods and humans, awakened, blessed. He realizes with his own insight this world—with its gods, Māras, and divinities, this population with its ascetics and brahmins, gods and humans—and he makes it known to others. He proclaims a teaching that is good in the beginning, good in the middle, and good in the end, meaningful and well-phrased. And he reveals a spiritual practice that's entirely complete and pure.

An ordinary person hears that teaching, or an ordinary person's child, or someone reborn in a good family. They gain faith in the Realized One, and reflect, 'Life with mental attachment as an ordinary person is cramped and dirty, life with detachment, noble path is wide open. It's not easy for me to living at home to lead the spiritual life by practicing mental detachment utterly full and pure, like a polished shell. Why don't I join a monastery, and live a life that can help me reduce mental attachment?' After some time, they give up a large or small fortune, and give up living with a large or small family circle. They dress up as ascetics and start living their lives in monasteries.

Once they begin their spiritual life, they attempt to practice the noble path universally applicable to all by taking the preliminary precepts. Ideally, an ordinary person should give up killing living creatures and renounce the rod and the sword. They should be scrupulous and kind, living full of sympathy for all living beings (Upon gaining Sotapanna, a person naturally has these qualities without having to take precepts due to the right view and giving up the relevant fetters).

Ideally, an ordinary person should give up stealing. They should take only what's given and expect only what's given. They should keep themselves clean by not thieving (Upon gaining Sotapanna, a person naturally has these qualities ...)

Ideally, an ordinary person should give up unchastity. They should be celibate, set apart, avoiding the vulgar act of sex. (Upon gaining Anagami, a person naturally has these qualities without having to take precepts due to the right view and giving up the relevant fetters).

Ideally, an ordinary person should give up lying. They should speak the truth and stick to the truth. They should become honest and dependable, and don't trick the world with their words. (Upon gaining Sotapanna, a person naturally has these qualities without having to take precepts due to the right view and giving up the relevant fetters).

Ideally, an ordinary person should give up divisive speech. They should not repeat in one place what they heard in another so as to divide people against each other. Instead, they reconcile those who are divided, supporting unity, delighting in harmony, loving harmony, speaking words that promote harmony (Upon gaining Anagami, a person naturally has these qualities without having to take precepts...)

Ideally, an ordinary person should give up harsh speech with an underlying tendency to possessing ill will. They should speak in a way that's mellow, pleasing to the ear, lovely, going to the heart, polite, likable, and agreeable to the people.

Ideally, an ordinary person should give up talking nonsense. Their words are timely, true, and meaningful, in line with the teaching and training. They say things at the right time that are valuable, reasonable, succinct, and beneficial.

Upon gaining Anagami state, a person naturally has these qualities; they refrain from injuring plants and seeds. They eat in one part of the day, abstaining from eating at night and at the wrong time. They do not have the desire forseeing shows of dancing, singing, and music. They do not have the desire for beautifying and adorn themselves with garlands, fragrances, and makeup. They do not have the desire to use high and luxurious beds with mental attachment to such things. They reduce their desire to receive gold and currency, raw grains, raw meat, women and girls, male and female bondservants, goats and sheep, chickens and pigs, elephants, cows, horses, mares, and fields and land. They do not have the desire for running errands and messages; buying and selling; falsifying weights, metals, or measures; bribery, fraud, cheating, and duplicity; mutilation, murder, abduction, banditry, plunder, and violence (Ideally, an ordinary person should refrain ….).

Upon gaining Arahant state, they are content with whatever robes they have and intend to use such things simply to look after the body and food to look after the belly. Wherever they go, they go without mental attachment to worldly experiences. They're like a free bird: wherever it flies, wings are its only burden. In the same way, an ordinary person should try becoming content with whatever robes they have (simply to look after the body) and whatever food to look after the belly. Wherever they go, they should try reducing mental attachment.

Upon gaining Arahant state, when they have this entire spectrum of noble ethics, they experience blameless happiness inside themselves. (Ideally, an ordinary person should try becoming content with whatever the robes they have and intend to use such things simply to look after the body and food to look after the belly. Wherever they go, they should try reducing attachment).

Arahant is like a bird: wherever it flies, wings are its only burden. In the same way, a person is content with whatever the robes they have to look after the body and food to look after the belly. Wherever they go, they go without mental attachment. When they have this entire spectrum of noble ethics, they experience a blameless happiness inside themselves (Ideally, an ordinary person should try becoming content with whatever the robes they have ….).

Upon gaining Arahant state, when they see a sight with their eyes, they don't get caught up in the features and details. If the faculty of sight were left unrestrained, bad unskillful qualities of covetousness and displeasure would become overwhelming. For this reason, they practice restraint, protecting the faculty of sight, and achieving its restraint. When they hear a sound with their ears … When they smell an odor with their nose … When they taste a flavor with their tongue … When they feel a touch with their body … When they know an idea with their mind, they don't get caught up in the features and details. If the faculty of mind were left unrestrained, bad unskillful qualities of covetousness and displeasure would become overwhelming. For this reason, they possess naturally occurring restraint due to wisdom, protecting the faculty of mind, and achieving its restraint.

When they have this noble sense restraint, they experience an unsullied bliss inside themselves (Ideally, an ordinary person should try reducing desire when they see a sight with their eyes....).

Upon gaining Arahant state, they naturally possess situational awareness when going out and coming back; when looking ahead and aside; when bending and extending the limbs; when doing daily activities such as dressing (i.e bearing the outer robe, robes), eating, drinking, chewing, and tasting; when urinating and defecating; when walking, standing, sitting, sleeping, waking, speaking, and keeping silent (Ideally, an ordinary person should try maintaining situational awareness...).

When they have this entire spectrum of noble ethics, this noble contentment, this noble sense of restraint, and this noble mindfulness and situational awareness, wherever they live (house, village, city, country, nature such as in a forest, etc.), they live unattached from others, and they are not fond of interacting with others but simply for sharing Dhamma— (Ideally, an ordinary person should try developing noble ethics, noble contentment...).

After the meal, they return to their places, they possess noble mindfulness naturally at all times. Giving up covetousness for the world, their heart is free of covetousness, their mind is free of covetousness. Giving up ill will and malevolence, their mind rid of ill will, full of sympathy for all living beings, cleansing the mind of ill will. Giving up dullness and drowsiness, their mind rid of dullness and drowsiness, perceiving light, mindful and aware, cleansing the mind of dullness and drowsiness.

Giving up restlessness and remorse, they mind becomes free of restlessness, their mind peaceful inside, cleansing the mind of restlessness and remorse. Giving up doubt, their mind gone beyond doubt, not undecided about skillful qualities, cleansing the mind of doubt (Ideally, an ordinary person should try maintaining mindfulness...).

They give up these five hindrances, corruptions of the heart that weaken wisdom (Ideally, an ordinary person should develop across four-fold Nibbana to give up hindrances...).

Walking the path to higher stages of four-fold nibbana, quite secluded from sensual pleasures, secluded from unskillful qualities, they enter and remain in the first absorption, which has the rapture and bliss born of seclusion, while placing the mind and keeping it connected.

This, brahmin, is that which is called 'a footprint of the Realized One' and also 'a trace of the Realized One' and also 'a mark of the Realized One'. But a noble disciple does not yet come to the conclusion, 'The Blessed One is a fully awakened universal Buddha. The universal Dhamma is well explained. The universal (Savakaa) Saṅgha is practicing well.'

Furthermore, as the placing of the mind and keeping it connected are stilled, a person enters and remains in the second absorption, which has the rapture and bliss born of immersion, with internal clarity and mind at one, without placing the mind and keeping it connected. This too is what is called 'a footprint of the Realized One' …

Furthermore, with the fading away of rapture, a person enters and remains in the third absorption, where they experience equanimity, mindful and awareness, personally experiencing the bliss of which the noble ones declare, 'Equanimous and mindful, one experiences bliss.' This too is what is called 'a footprint of the Realized One' …

Furthermore, giving up pleasure and pain, and ending former happiness and sadness, a person enters and remains in the fourth absorption, without pleasure or pain, with pure equanimity and mindfulness. This too is what is called 'a footprint of the Realized One' …

When their mind has become immersed in noble concentration like this—purified, bright, flawless, rid of corruptions, pliable, workable, steady, and imperturbable—they extend it toward recollection of past lives. They recollect many kinds of past lives, that is, one, two, three, four, five, ten, twenty, thirty, forty, fifty, a hundred, a thousand, a hundred thousand rebirths; many eons of the world contracting, many eons of the world expanding, many eons of the world contracting and expanding. …

They recollect their many kinds of past lives, with features and details. This too is what is called 'a footprint of the Realized One' …

When their mind has become immersed in noble concentration like this—purified, bright, flawless, rid of corruptions, pliable, workable, steady, and imperturbable—they extend it toward knowledge of the death and rebirth of sentient beings. With clairvoyance that is purified and surpasses the human, they understand how sentient beings are reborn according to their deeds. This too is what is called 'a footprint of the Realized One' …

When their mind has become immersed in noble concentration like this—purified, bright, flawless, rid of corruptions, pliable, workable, steady, and imperturbable—they extend it toward knowledge of the ending of defilements. They truly understand: 'This is suffering' … 'This is the origin of suffering' … 'This is the cessation of suffering' … 'This is the practice that leads to the cessation of suffering.' They truly understand: 'These are defilements' … 'This is the origin of defilements' … 'This is the cessation of defilements' … 'This is the practice that leads to the cessation of defilements.'

This, brahmin, is what is called 'a footprint of the Realized One' and also 'a trace of the Realized One' and also 'a mark of the Realized One'. At this point a noble disciple has not yet come to a conclusion, but they are coming to the conclusion, 'The Blessed One is a fully awakened universal Buddha. The universal Dhamma is well explained. The universal (Savakaa) Saṅgha is practicing well.'

Knowing and seeing like this, their mind is freed from the defilements of sensuality, desire to be reborn, and ignorance. When they're freed, they know they're freed.

They understand: 'Rebirth is ended, the spiritual journey has been completed, what had to be done has been done, there is nothing further for this place.' This, brahmin, is what is called 'a footprint of the Realized One' and also 'a trace of the Realized One' and also 'a mark of the Realized One'.

At this point a noble disciple has come to the conclusion, 'The Blessed One is a fully awakened universal Buddha. The universal Dhamma is well explained. The universal (Savaka) Saṅgha is practicing well.'

And it is at this point that the simile of the elephant's footprint has been completed in detail."

When he had spoken, the brahmin Jānussoṇi said to the Buddha, "Excellent, Mister Gotama! Excellent! As if he were righting the overturned, or revealing the hidden, or pointing out the path to the lost, or lighting a lamp in the dark so people with clear eyes can see what's there, Mister Gotama has made the teaching clear in many ways. I go for refuge to Mister Gotama, to the teaching, and to the universal (Savaka) Saṅgha.

From this day forth, may Mister Gotama remember me as an ordinary follower who has gone for refuge for life."

Chapter 30

Middle Discourses 28: Mahāhatthipadopama Suttaṁ

The Longer Simile of the Elephant's Footprint

This discourse discusses the importance of understanding the impermanent nature of worldly experience and the Triple Gem to gain Sotapanna. "At this point, much has been done by that person" means becoming a Sotapanna, establishing confirmed confidence in the Triple Gem.

Grasping at changing experiences is a common way of thinking since birth. Common ways of thinking are founded in social practices. Social practices based on standard ways of thinking teach people to think and behave in certain ways. Based on social learning and conditioning, people learn to associate happiness with winning and sadness with loosing, happiness at birth, and sadness at death. In this manner, since birth, people learn to connect certain things such as winning, gains, birth and the feelings of happiness that cause you to become happy. Similarly, people learn to connect certain things such as loosing, death and the feeling of sadness that cause you to become unhappy based on social learning and conditioning to interpret worldly experiences based on standard ways. Eventually, an association between events and responses is learned. You'll find that many, if not most, of your ways of thinking and actions can be traced back to standard ways of thinking and doing things. By understanding that life is impermanent and that ups and downs are part of life for all of us and are universally applicable to all beings, one can train the mind not to become disheartened when faced with bad events and, similarly, not to become overjoyed when experiencing good events, as they do not last long, and, in doing so, train the mind in the middle way in daily life (middle mind training is given up at the Arahant state to lead to Cessation; until then, middle mind training is useful).

Everything that a person thinks belongs to self can only fall short in worldly experiences. Based on sensory information and conventions, you tend to interpret self and the world in a limited way, which may not necessarily represent your true-life experience. For example, interpreting yourself as always gaining things or as not always gaining things as the way you would like to gain things are extreme ways of understanding life experience. Instead of making assumptions regarding what is possible to gain and what is not possible to gain and getting distressed when what is constructed in mind is not what is happening in life, a balanced mind can be maintained by understanding that there is no reason to be so worried over things that you lose, as loosing things is a part of life, both losses and gains are parts of life, both experiences subject to change. You can learn to develop a deeper understanding of life to maintain a balanced mind with wisdom to face events within daily life. The root cause of mental pain is how you interpret yourself and the situation based on too much greed you have for your thoughts, hatred you have in thoughts and your lack of (deluded) understanding the truth in your thoughts. Instead, by understanding how your thoughts work, you can take a step to free yourself from your mind when it brings too much mental pain to you. By applying wisdom, you can learn to make the most of your experiences. You can develop your wisdom both in universal (collecting merits etc.) and conventional ways (putting efforts etc.).

There is a strong link between the Triple Gem and Nibbana. For those who seek Nibbana, it would be of benefit to understand the Triple Gem. The shortest and quickest route to Nibbana is meeting with the Triple Gem, meaning understanding the Triple Gem. Confirmed confidence in the Triple Gem can be developed by reflecting on the qualities of the Triple Gem day and night; recollect the Tathagata; 'Supreme Gautama Buddha, the Blessed One is worthy and rightly self-awakened, possess perfect and highest knowledge & noble conduct, well-gone, an expert with regard to the world, excellent trainer for those people fit to be instructed, the Teacher of divine & human beings, fully enlightened, understood the path by himself and explained the path to us, and blessed'; recollect Dhamma; 'The Dhamma is well-explained by the Blessed One, those who practice correctly will get to experience Dhamma immediately, applicable for all times and thus, timeless, others can be invited to practice and see for themselves, inviting verification, pertinent, can be realized by those who are wise enough to see beyond ordinary ways', and recollect noble Sangha; 'The noble Sangha of the Blessed One's are the good in their practice, they have practiced Dhamma in a correct manner, they are systematic in their practice, they have practiced correctly, and skilfully and gained realization across four stages; noble Sangha of the blessed ones are the in- comparable field of merit for the world.' while walking, standing, sitting, and going about doing other things, and attending to the Triple Gem by giving priority to the Triple Gem in one's mind.

The truth is that there is no substitute for universal Buddha, as Buddha is the teacher of gods and men. So as universal Dhamma and universal Savaka Sangha. Thus, the Triple Gem is rare but precious as it allows another person wishing to escape pain to reach cessation. While it is up to each individual to make choices, those who genuinely aspire to Nibbana should prioritize Buddha in mind by avoiding putting anyone above the perfect Buddha if they want to walk the Noble Path. This is how a person can take refuge across stages by first taking refuge in the Buddha. One should give priority and avoid putting anything above universal Dhamma if they want to walk the Noble Path. This is how a person can find refuge across stages by taking refuge on the universal Dhamma at second. What you give priority is what you grow within. When you grow wisdom and qualities similar to Buddha by applying the universal Dhamma within, you become an heir to the teachings not the heir of flesh. Those who give priority to universal Buddha and universal Dhamma are the ones who become a Buddha through Arahantship or universal (Savaka) Sangha route. When you give priority to Noble Sangha in your mind, you can develop universal Buddha, Dhamma and Sangha within.

"So I have heard. At one time the Buddha was staying near Sāvatthī in Jeta's Grove, Anāthapiṇḍika's monastery. There Arahant Sāriputta addressed the companions, "Respected, friends!"

"Venerable sir," they replied. Arahant Sāriputta said this:

"The footprints of all creatures that walk can fit inside an elephant's footprint, so an elephant's footprint is said to be the biggest of them all. In the same way, all skillful qualities are included in the four noble truths. What four? The noble truths of suffering, the origin of suffering, the cessation of suffering, and the practice that leads to the cessation of suffering.

And what is the noble truth of suffering? Rebirth is suffering; old age is suffering; death is suffering; sorrow, lamentation, pain, sadness, and distress are suffering; not getting what you wish for is suffering. In brief, the five grasping aggregates are suffering. And what are the five grasping aggregates? They are as follows: the grasping aggregates of form, feeling, perception, choices, and consciousness.

And what is the grasping aggregate of form? The four principal states, and form derived from the four principal states.

And what are the four principal states? The elements of earth, water, fire, and air.

And what is the earth element? The earth element may be interior or exterior. And what is the interior earth element? Anything internal, pertaining to an individual, that's hard, solid, and appropriated. This includes: head hair, body hair, nails, teeth, skin, flesh, sinews, bones, bone marrow, kidneys, heart, liver, diaphragm, spleen, lungs, intestines, mesentery, undigested food, feces; or anything else internal, pertaining to an individual, that's hard, solid, and appropriated. This is called the interior earth element. The interior earth element and the exterior earth element are just the earth element. This should be truly seen with right understanding like this: 'This is not mine, I am not this, this is not my self.' When you truly see with right understanding, you grow disillusioned with the earth element, detaching the mind from the earth element.

There comes a time when the exterior water element flares up. At that time the exterior earth element vanishes. So for all its great age, the earth element will be revealed as impermanent, liable to end, vanish, and perish. What then of this ephemeral body appropriated by craving? Rather than 'I' or 'mine' or 'I am', they consider it to be none of these things.

If others abuse, attack, harass, and trouble that mendicant, they understand: 'This painful feeling born of ear contact has arisen in me. That's dependent, not independent. Dependent on what? Dependent on contact.' They see that contact, feeling, perception, choices, and consciousness are impermanent. Based on that element alone, their mind leaps forth, gains confidence, settles down, and becomes decided.

Others might treat that person with disliking, loathing, and detestation, striking them with fists, stones, sticks, and swords. They understand: 'This body is such that fists, stones, sticks, and swords strike it. But the Buddha has said in the Advice on the Simile of the Saw:

"Even if low-down bandits were to sever you limb from limb with a two-handed saw, anyone who had a malevolent thought on that account would not be following my instructions." My energy shall be roused up and unflagging, my mindfulness established and lucid, my body tranquil and undisturbed, and my mind immersed in noble concentration. Gladly now, let fists, stones, sticks, and swords strike this body! For this is how the instructions of the Buddhas are followed.'

While recollecting the universal Buddha, the universal Dhamma; and the universal Saṅgha in this way, equanimity based on the skillful may not become stabilized in them. In that case they stir up a sense of urgency: 'It's my loss, my misfortune, that while recollecting the universal Buddha, the universal Dhamma; and the universal Saṅgha in this way, equanimity based on the skillful does not become stabilized in me.' They're like a daughter-in-law who stirs up a sense of urgency when they see their father-in-law. But if, while recollecting the universal Buddha, the universal Dhamma; and the universal Saṅgha in this way in this way, equanimity based on the skillful does become stabilized in them, they're happy with that. At this point, much has been done by that companion.

And what is the water element? The water element may be interior or exterior. And what is the interior water element? Anything internal, pertaining to an individual, that's water, watery, and appropriated. This includes: bile, phlegm, pus, blood, sweat, fat, tears, grease, saliva, snot, synovial fluid, urine; or anything else internal, pertaining to an individual, that's water, watery, and appropriated.

This is called the interior water element. The interior water element and the exterior water element are just the water element. This should be truly seen with right understanding like this: 'This is not mine, I am not this, this is not my self.' When you truly see with right understanding, you grow disillusioned with the water element, detaching the mind from the water element.

There comes a time when the exterior water element flares up. It sweeps away villages, towns, cities, countries, and regions. There comes a time when the water in the ocean sinks down a hundred leagues, or two, three, four, five, six, up to seven hundred leagues. There comes a time when the water in the ocean stands just seven palm trees deep, or six, five, four, three, two, or even just one palm tree deep.

There comes a time when the water in the ocean stands just seven fathoms deep, or six, five, four, three, two, or even just one fathom deep. There comes a time when the water in the ocean stands just half a fathom deep, or waist deep, or knee deep, or even just ankle deep. There comes a time when there's not even enough water left in the great ocean to wet the tip of the toe. So for all its great age, the water element will be revealed as impermanent, liable to end, vanish, and perish. What then of this ephemeral body appropriated by craving? Rather than 'I' or 'mine' or 'I am', they consider it to be none of these things. ... If, while recollecting the universal Buddha, universal Dhamma; and the universal Saṅgha in this way in this way, equanimity based on the skillful does become stabilized in them, they're happy with that. At this point, much has been done by that companion.

And what is the fire element? The fire element may be interior or exterior. And what is the interior fire element? Anything internal, pertaining to an individual that's fire, fiery, and appropriated. This includes: that which warms, that which ages, that which heats you up when feverish, that which properly digests food and drink; or anything else internal, pertaining to an individual, that's fire, fiery, and appropriated. This is called the interior fire element.

The interior fire element and the exterior fire element are just the fire element. This should be truly seen with right understanding like this: 'This is not mine, I am not this, this is not my self.' When you truly see with right understanding, you grow disillusioned with the fire element, detaching the mind from the fire element.

There comes a time when the exterior fire element flares up. It burns up villages, towns, cities, countries, and regions until it reaches a green field, a roadside, a cliff's edge, a body of water, or cleared parkland, where it's extinguished due to not being fed. There comes a time when they go looking for a fire, taking just a chicken feather or a scrap of sinew as kindling. So for all its great age, the fire element will be revealed as impermanent, liable to end, vanish, and perish. What then of this ephemeral body appropriated by craving? Rather than 'I' or 'mine' or 'I am', they consider it to be none of these things. ...

If, while recollecting the universal Buddha, the universal Dhamma; and the universal Saṅgha in this way, equanimity based on the skillful does become stabilized in them, they're happy with that. At this point, much has been done by that companion.

And what is the air element? The air element may be interior or exterior. And what is the interior air element? Anything internal, pertaining to an individual, that's air, airy, and appropriated. This includes: winds that go up or down, winds in the belly or the bowels, winds that flow through the limbs, in-breaths and out-breaths; or anything else internal, pertaining to an individual, that's air, airy, and appropriated. This is called the interior air element. The interior air element and the exterior air element are just the air element. This should be truly seen with right understanding like this: 'This is not mine, I am not this, this is not my self.' When you truly see with right understanding, you grow disillusioned with the air element, detaching the mind from the air element.

There comes a time when the exterior air element flares up. It sweeps away villages, towns, cities, countries, and regions. There comes a time, in the last month of summer, when they look for wind by using a palm-leaf or fan, and even the grasses in the drip-fringe of a thatch roof don't stir. So for all its great age, the air element will be revealed as impermanent, liable to end, vanish, and perish. What then of this ephemeral body appropriated by craving?

Rather than 'I' or 'mine' or 'I am', they consider it to be none of these things.

If others abuse, attack, harass, and trouble that person, they understand: 'This painful feeling born of ear contact has arisen in me. That's dependent, not independent. Dependent on what? Dependent on contact.' They see that contact, feeling, perception, choices, and consciousness are impermanent. Based on that element alone, their mind leaps forth, gains confidence, settles down, and becomes decided.

Others might treat that person with disliking, loathing, and detestation, striking them with fists, stones, sticks, and swords. They understand: 'This body is such that fists, stones, sticks, and swords strike it.

But the Buddha has said in the Advice on the Simile of the Saw: "Even if low-down bandits were to sever you limb from limb with a two-handed saw, anyone who had a thought of hate on that account would not be following my instructions." My energy shall be roused up and unflagging, my mindfulness established and lucid, my body tranquil and undisturbed, and my mind immersed in noble mindfulness. Gladly now, let fists, stones, sticks, and swords strike this body! For this is how the instructions of the Buddhas are followed by the noble ones.'

While recollecting the universal Buddha, the universal Dhamma; and the universal Saṅgha in this way, equanimity based on the skillful may not become stabilized in them. In that case they stir up a sense of urgency: 'It's my loss, my misfortune, that while recollecting the universal Buddha, the teaching (four-fold nibbana), and the Savaka Saṅgha in this way, equanimity based on the skillful does not become stabilized in me.' They're like a daughter-in-law who stirs up a sense of urgency when they see their father-in-law. But if, while recollecting the while recollecting the universal Buddha, the universal Dhamma; and the universal Saṅgha in this way, equanimity based on the skillful does become stabilized in them, they're happy with that. At this point, much has been done by that person.

When a space is enclosed by sticks, creepers, grass, and mud it becomes known as a 'building'. In the same way, when a space is enclosed by bones, sinews, flesh, and skin it becomes known as a 'form'.

Reverends, though the eye is intact internally, so long as exterior sights don't come into range and there's no corresponding engagement, there's no manifestation of the corresponding type of consciousness. Though the eye is intact internally and exterior sights come into range, so long as there's no corresponding engagement, there's no manifestation of the corresponding type of consciousness. But when the eye is intact internally and exterior sights come into range and there is corresponding engagement, there is the manifestation of the corresponding type of consciousness.

The form produced in this way is included in the grasping aggregate of form. The feeling, perception, choices, and consciousness produced in this way are each included in the corresponding grasping aggregate.

They understand: 'So this is how there comes to be inclusion, gathering together, and joining together into these five grasping aggregates. But the Buddha has said: "One who sees dependent origination sees the teaching. One who sees the teaching sees dependent origination." And these five grasping aggregates are indeed dependently originated.

The desire, clinging, attraction, and attachment for these five grasping aggregates is the origin of suffering. Giving up and getting rid of desire and greed for these five grasping aggregates is the cessation of suffering.' At this point, much has been done by that person.

Though the ear … nose … tongue … body … mind is intact internally, so long as exterior ideas don't come into range and there's no corresponding engagement, there's no manifestation of the corresponding type of consciousness.

Though the mind is intact internally and exterior ideas come into range, so long as there's no corresponding engagement, there's no manifestation of the corresponding type of consciousness. But when the mind is intact internally and exterior ideas come into range and there is corresponding engagement, there is the manifestation of the corresponding type of consciousness.

The form produced in this way is included in the grasping aggregate of form. The feeling, perception, choices, and consciousness produced in this way are each included in the corresponding grasping aggregate. They understand: 'So this is how there comes to be inclusion, gathering together, and joining together into these five grasping aggregates.

But the Buddha has also said: "One who sees dependent origination sees the teaching. One who sees the teaching sees dependent origination." And these five grasping aggregates are indeed dependently originated. The desire, clinging, attraction, and attachment for these five grasping aggregates is the origin of suffering. Giving up and getting rid of desire and greed for these five grasping aggregates is the cessation of suffering.' At this point, much has been done by that person."

That's what Arahant Sāriputta said. Satisfied, the companions approved what Arahant Sāriputta said".

Chapter 31

Middle Discourses 29: Mahāsāropamasutta

The Longer Simile of the Heartwood

While they are ordinary, those who live in monastic settings would benefit if they avoided thinking they are the disciples of Buddha at least until gaining Sotapanna, instead they are practicing to become a disciple of Buddha. Those live in monastic settings would benefit if they avoided misinterpret and spread wrong interpretations of Buddha's Dhamma (i.e Sotapanna to Arahant), such as saying that monastic life is more supportive of gaining Nibbana than a householder's life. Similarly, householders would benefit if they avoided thinking they are the disciples of Buddha at least until gaining Sotapanna, instead they are practicing to become a disciple of Buddha. Those live in household settings would benefit if they avoided misinterpret and spread wrong interpretations of Buddha's Dhamma (i.e Sotapanna to Arahant), such as saying that a householder life is less supportive of gaining Nibbana than a monastic life. A male or female bhikkhu would benefit if they avoided thinking they are the disciples of Buddha (instead practicing becoming a disciple of Buddha) at least until gaining Sotapanna. They say they are better than householders because they take more precepts, misinterpreting and spreading wrong interpretations such as saying that monastic life is more supportive of gaining Nibbana than a householder life. A male or female householder would benefit if they avoided thinking they are the disciples of Buddha (instead practicing becoming a disciple of Buddha) at least until gaining Sotapanna. They can enjoy it better than monastics and avoid misinterpreting Dhamma, saying that a householder life is less supportive of gaining Nibbana than a monastic life. This is because Nibbana is not a lifestyle[17] but a birth in noble lineage, a random happening in the mental continuum shaped by one's merit and wisdom.

The path leading to Nibbana can only be developed by not boasting, praising self with pride and not putting others down. This is an important aspect of training in the Noble Path. It is often misunderstood that the Noble Path means dressing up and following monastic rules with an underlying tendency to grasp into conventions. This explains why Nibbana is rare. Instead, one who aspires to

---

[17] The expression of social positioning based on standard social practices.

Nibbana would benefit if they vigilantly observed their mind and corrected themselves when they fail to reach noble standards. Every time the mind is inclined to boast self with pride and put others down, try and correct yourself.

"So I have heard. At one time the Buddha was staying near Rājagaha, on the Vulture's Peak Mountain, not long after Devadatta had left. There the Buddha spoke to the companions about Devadatta:

"Companions, take the case of a person who practices dhamma to give up mental attachment by following the noble path universal to all, thinking, 'I'm swamped by rebirth, old age, and death; by sorrow, lamentation, pain, sadness, and distress. I'm swamped by suffering, mired in suffering. Hopefully I can find an end to this entire mass of suffering.' When they've gone forth they generate possessions, honor, and popularity. They're happy with that, and they've got all they wished for. And they glorify themselves and put others down because of that: 'I'm the one with possessions, honor, and popularity. These other companions are obscure and insignificant.' And so they become indulgent and fall into negligence on account of those possessions, honor, and popularity. And being negligent they live in suffering.

Suppose there was a person in need of heartwood. And while wandering in search of heartwood he'd come across a large tree standing with heartwood. But, passing over the heartwood, softwood, bark, and shoots, he'd cut off the branches and leaves and depart imagining they were heartwood. If a person with clear eyes saw him they'd say, 'This gentleman doesn't know what heartwood, softwood, bark, shoots, or branches and leaves are. That's why he passed them over, cut off the branches and leaves, and departed imagining they were heartwood. Whatever he needs to make from heartwood, he won't succeed.' …

This is called a person who has grabbed the branches and leaves of the spiritual life and stopped short with that.

Next, take an ordinary person who practices a spiritual path… When they're practicing a spiritual path, a lifestyle they generate possessions, honor, and popularity. They're not happy with that, and haven't got all they wished for. They don't glorify themselves and put others down on account of that. Nor do they become indulgent and fall into negligence on account of those possessions, honor, and popularity.

Being diligent, they achieve accomplishment in ethics. They're happy with that, and they've got all they wished for. And they glorify themselves and put others down on account of that: 'I'm the one who is ethical, of good character. These other companions are unethical, of bad character.' And so they become indulgent and fall into negligence regarding their accomplishment in ethics. And being negligent they live in suffering.

Suppose there was a person in need of heartwood. And while wandering in search of heartwood he'd come across a large tree standing with heartwood. But, passing over the heartwood, softwood, and bark, he'd cut off the shoots and depart imagining they were heartwood. If a person with clear eyes saw him they'd say, 'This gentleman doesn't know what heartwood, softwood, bark, shoots, or branches and leaves are. That's why he passed them over, cut off the shoots, and departed imagining they were heartwood. Whatever he needs to make from heartwood, he won't succeed.' …

This is called a person who has grabbed the shoots of the spiritual life and stopped short with that.

Next, take an ordinary person who practices a spiritual path… When they're practicing a spiritual path, a life style they generate possessions, honor, and popularity. … Being diligent, they achieve accomplishment in immersion. They're happy with that, and they've got all they wished for. And they glorify themselves and put others down on account of that: 'I'm the one with immersion and unified mind. These other companions lack immersion, they have straying minds.' And so they become indulgent and fall into negligence regarding that accomplishment in immersion. And being negligent they live in suffering.

Suppose there was a person in need of heartwood. And while wandering in search of heartwood he'd come across a large tree standing with heartwood. But, passing over the heartwood and softwood, he'd cut off the bark and depart imagining it was heartwood. If a person with clear eyes saw him they'd say: 'This gentleman doesn't know what heartwood, softwood, bark, shoots, or branches and leaves are. That's why he passed them over, cut off the bark, and departed imagining it was heartwood. Whatever he needs to make from heartwood, he won't succeed.' …

This is called a person who has grabbed the bark of the spiritual life and stopped short with that.

Next, take an ordinary person who practices a spiritual path… When they're practicing a spiritual path, a life style they generate possessions, honor, and popularity. … Being diligent, they achieve knowledge and vision. They're happy with that, and they've got all they wished for. And they glorify themselves and put others down on account of that, 'I'm the one who meditates knowing and seeing. These other people meditate without knowing and seeing.' And so they become indulgent and fall into negligence regarding that knowledge and vision. And being negligent they live in suffering.

Suppose there was a person in need of heartwood. And while wandering in search of heartwood he'd come across a large tree standing with heartwood. But, passing over the heartwood, he'd cut out the softwood and depart imagining it was heartwood. If a person with clear eyes saw him they'd say, 'This gentleman doesn't know what heartwood, softwood, bark, shoots, or branches and leaves are. That's why he passed them over, cut out the softwood, and departed imagining it was heartwood. Whatever he needs to make from heartwood, he won't succeed.' …

This is called a person who has grabbed the softwood of the spiritual life and stopped short with that.

Next, take an person who practices a spiritual path… When they're practicing a spiritual path, a life style, thinking, 'I'm swamped by rebirth, old age, and death; by sorrow, lamentation, pain, sadness, and distress. I'm swamped by suffering, mired in suffering. Hopefully I can find an end to this entire mass of suffering.' When they've gone forth they generate possessions, honor, and popularity. They're not happy with that, and haven't got all they wished for. They don't glorify themselves and put others down on account of that. Nor do they become indulgent and fall into negligence on account of those possessions, honor, and popularity.

Being diligent, they achieve accomplishment in noble ethics (Sotapanna). They're happy with that, but they haven't got all they wished for. They don't glorify themselves and put others down on account of that. Nor do they become indulgent and fall into negligence regarding that accomplishment in ethics. Being diligent, they achieve accomplishment in immersion. They're happy with that, but they haven't got all they wished for. They don't glorify themselves and put others down on account of that. Nor do they become indulgent and fall into negligence regarding that accomplishment in immersion. Being diligent, they achieve knowledge and vision. They're happy with that, but they haven't got all they wished for. They don't glorify themselves and put others down on account of that. Nor do they become indulgent and fall into negligence regarding that knowledge and vision. Being diligent, they achieve irreversible freedom (Arahantship). And it's impossible for that companion to fall away from that irreversible freedom.

Suppose there was a person in need of heartwood. And while wandering in search of heartwood he'd come across a large tree standing with heartwood. He'd cut out just the heartwood and depart knowing it was heartwood. If a person with clear eyes saw him they'd say, 'This gentleman knows what heartwood, softwood, bark, shoots, and branches and leaves are. That's why he cut out just the heartwood and departed knowing it was heartwood. Whatever he needs to make from heartwood, he will succeed.' …

It's impossible for that person to fall away from that irreversible freedom.

And so, friends, this spiritual life is not lived for the sake of possessions, honor, and popularity, or for accomplishment in ethics, or for accomplishment in immersion, or for knowledge and vision. Rather, the goal, heartwood, and final end of the spiritual life is the unshakable freedom of heart across four-fold Nibbana."

That is what the Buddha said. Satisfied, the companions approved what the Buddha said."

Chapter 32

Middle Discourses 30: Cūḷasāropamasutta

The Shorter Simile of the Heartwood

This discourse discusses that the end goal of Nibbana does not have gain, honor, and similar things for its benefit but freedom from all, a mind that is free from the events that are happening in the world, a mind that remains unaffected by the existence of the physical world. To get to cessation, the mind of an ordinary person has to be trained to reduce desires, give up grasping conventions, liking or disliking gains, honors, etc.

One way in which people who seek Nibbana can go wrong is by trying to find the universally created truth in socially created ways. In this manner, if you grasp socially accepted ways and those who represent socially accepted monks as monks in Buddha's path, you can grasp into conventional Dhamma and conventional Sangha. By doing so, you can go into the wrong path where you can be barred from Nibbana, because monks who grasp conventions have no capacity to provide you the path to become free from conventions. They may teach you the basics of Dhamma, which you must develop further[18].

One of the confusions over Buddha's Dhamma is who is a monk. Natural transformation takes place in a person's mental continuum across stages, and that transformation, which allows abandoning mental fetters out of rituals, is a monk in noble path. At the Anagami state, a person naturally transforms into someone who eats meals before noon, does not harm trees, is chaste, does not see movies, etc., because the underlying tendency for desire (i.e sensual desire, ill will) is abandoned. At Sotapama and Sakadagami stages, these things are not applicable or relevant due to retaining sensual desires.

Nibbana is not a ritualistic lifestyle where one comes to recognize by the society. Nibbana is a universal happening where universe come to recognize a

---

[18] One who wishes to make progress in Nibbana requires replacing existing knowledge with higher knowledge over stages in the noble path. If you grasp socially accepted Dhamma as Buddha's Dhamma, Nibbana can be kept from you due to blocking your right view. Instead, developing the right view leads to Nibbana.

purity of a random person, Gods and Devas know, and there are other people who have gained various stages of Nibbana and they know who Arahants are, wise people in the society comes to know later. How can an ordinary person recognize noble Sangha? You can understand an Arahant by analysing words, thoughts, and actions.

How can a person recognize another person's reduction in attachment to the fetters? Often, thoughts are expressed in words. By analysing their words, those who compare one another and those who divide universal Dhamma are still grasping the fetters. Progress in the Dhamma path is not measured by somebody's appearance or years of a meditation practice but by the extent to which mental attachment to fetters is reduced.

Among ordinary people, those who are wise when they hear wise words, get to see the state of wisdom, Buddhahood. Being born with certain wisdom is the result of good karma, being able to grow your wisdom is shaped by several factors including your efforts, good karma, hearing Dhamma from Arahants, applying Dhamma to oneself, and so on. Thus, engaging in Dasa Kusal (wholesome intentional actions/deeds) is a helpful way one can grow merits and wisdom through which path to Nibbana open up to those who aspire Nibbana.

The conscious transformation through practicing jhanas as suggest by some conventional monks/Sangha can change, because consciousness is subject to change. Ritualistic transformation can be temporary, as life is temporary. Nibbana brings end to the conscious transformation, and ritualistic transformation.

When you want to practice the Noble Path, you want to make sure you don't train yourself to a practice of grasping conventional Dhamma, such as rituals and divisions, as they are preliminary practices. Just as streams of water turn to rivers, and rivers meet and unite with the sea, all those who follow conventional Dhamma unite and become the same as they extinguish through cessation, and when they meet Nibbana; Sotapanna to Arahant.

True Arahants don't divide beings or act like they are special; instead, they unite the universal teachings and treat all beings as precious irrespective of conventions. No one of noble linage will make comparisons, or they will attempt to make one person superior, the same or inferior. Thus, anyone who wants to make progress in the Noble Path needs to give up thinking that they are special, similar, or inferior if they want to develop the noble path. Therefore, when those who are in monastic settings, some of them call themselves venerable, it appears as if they want to pretend like they are Arahants and that they want to be treated as special. Some monastics tell others that monastic rules are better than householder rules and that monastic life is superior to other lifestyles. When they compare one another, wanting and asking to be treated as if they are special, they are strengthening the self-view, grasping rituals and conventions. The same can be said regarding practitioners of all settings. For example, when those who are in a householder setting compare one another and think that they can enjoy better than monastics, they are inferior (same, superior) to monastics, and they are strengthening the self-view and rituals.

The path that Supreme Buddha wanted to open for people who are suffering has been kept open not just for one category of people based on conventions (ritual, division, tradition, lifestyle, country, age, etc.) but the Universal Dhamma; Nibbāna and the path is open for all those who want to escape sufferings.

Knowing the right practice leading to Stream Entry is beneficial for practitioners, and practitioners should train thus:

"We take precepts and training rules to develop noble virtues (the purpose of maintaining virtue and training rules should be to develop noble virtues); we meditate to develop confirmed confidence in the Triple Gem (the purpose of developing concentration as meditation practice is to develop confirmed confidence in the Triple Gem)", the purpose of any lifestyle should be to develop merits, engage in wholesome activities, the end purpose of training the mind is to gain freedom from precepts, a lifestyle, and mind; giving up getting attached to one's thoughts that create self- view, and others towards the end of noble training path".

"So I have heard. At one time the Buddha was staying near Sāvatthī in Jeta's Grove, Anāthapiṇḍika's monastery.

Then the brahmin Piṅgalakoccha went up to the Buddha, and exchanged greetings with him. When the greetings and polite conversation were over, he sat down to one side and said to the Buddha:

"Mister Gotama, there are those ascetics and brahmins who lead an order and a community, and teach a community. They're well-known and famous religious founders, deemed holy by many people.

Namely: Pūraṇa Kassapa, the bamboo-staffed ascetic Gosāla, Ajita of the hair blanket, Pakudha Kaccāyana, Sañjaya Belaṭṭhiputta, and the Jain ascetic of the Ñātika clan. According to their own claims, did all of them have direct knowledge, or none of them, or only some?"

"Enough, brahmin, let this be: 'According to their own claims, did all of them have direct knowledge, or none of them, or only some?' I will teach you the Dhamma. Listen and apply your mind well, I will speak."

"Yes sir," Piṅgalakoccha replied. The Buddha said this:

"Suppose there was a person in need of heartwood. And while wandering in search of heartwood he'd come across a large tree standing with heartwood. But, passing over the heartwood, softwood, bark, and shoots, he'd cut off the branches and leaves and depart imagining they were heartwood.

If a person with clear eyes saw him they'd say: 'This gentleman doesn't know what heartwood, softwood, bark, shoots, or branches and leaves are. That's why he passed them over, cut off the branches and leaves, and departed imagining they were heartwood. Whatever he needs to make from heartwood, he won't succeed.'

Suppose there was another person in need of heartwood … he'd cut off the shoots and depart imagining they were heartwood …

Suppose there was another person in need of heartwood … he'd cut off the bark and depart imagining it was heartwood …

Suppose there was another person in need of heartwood … he'd cut out the softwood and depart imagining it was heartwood …

Suppose there was another person in need of heartwood. And while wandering in search of heartwood he'd come across a large tree standing with heartwood. He'd cut out just the heartwood and depart knowing it was heartwood.

If a person with clear eyes saw him they'd say: 'This gentleman knows what heartwood, softwood, bark, shoots, or branches and leaves are. That's why he cut out just the heartwood and departed knowing it was heartwood. Whatever he needs to make from heartwood, he will succeed.'

In the same way, take a certain person who practices a spiritual path, thinking: 'I'm swamped by rebirth, old age, and death; by sorrow, lamentation, pain, sadness, and distress. I'm swamped by suffering, mired in suffering. Hopefully I can find an end to this entire mass of suffering.' When they've gone forth they generate possessions, honor, and popularity. They're happy with that, and they've got all they wished for. And they glorify themselves and put others down on account of that: 'I'm the one with possessions, honor, and popularity.

These other companions are obscure and insignificant.' They become lazy and slack on account of their possessions, honor, and popularity, not generating enthusiasm or trying to realize those things that are better and finer. … They're like the person who mistakes branches and leaves for heartwood, I say.

Next, take a person who practices a spiritual path… When a person who practices a spiritual path, they generate possessions, honor, and popularity. They're not happy with that and haven't got all they wished for. They don't glorify themselves and put others down on account of that. They don't become lazy and slack regarding their possessions, honor, and popularity, but generate enthusiasm and try to realize those things that are better and finer.

They achieve accomplishment in ethics. They're happy with that, and they've got all they wished for. And they glorify themselves and put others down on account of that: 'I'm the one who is ethical, of good character. These other companions are unethical, of bad character.' They become lazy and slack regarding their accomplishment in ethics, not generating enthusiasm or trying to realize those things that are better and finer.
… They're like the person who mistakes shoots for heartwood, I say.

Next, take a person who practices a spiritual path… They achieve accomplishment in ethics … and immersion. … They become lazy and slack regarding their accomplishment in immersion, not generating enthusiasm or trying to realize those things that are better and finer. … They're like the person who mistakes bark for heartwood, I say.

Next, take a person who practices a spiritual path… As an ordinary person, they achieve accomplishment in some ethics … some immersion … and some knowledge and some vision. They become lazy and slack regarding their knowledge and vision, not generating enthusiasm or trying to realize those things that are better and finer. … They're like the person who mistakes softwood for heartwood, I say.

Next, take a person who practices a spiritual path, thinking: 'I'm swamped by rebirth, old age, and death; by sorrow, lamentation, pain, sadness, and distress. I'm swamped by suffering, mired in suffering. Hopefully I can find an end to this entire mass of suffering.' When they've gone forth they generate possessions, honor, and popularity. They're not happy with that, and haven't got all they wished for.

They don't glorify themselves and put others down on account of that. They don't become lazy and slack on account of their possessions, honor, and popularity, but generate enthusiasm and try to realize those things that are better and finer. They become accomplished in ethics (Sotapanna). They're happy with that, but they haven't got all they wished for. They don't glorify themselves and put others down on account of that. They don't become lazy and slack regarding their accomplishment in ethics but generate enthusiasm and try to realize those things that are better and finer.

They become accomplished in immersion (Anagami). They're happy with that, but they haven't got all they wished for. They don't glorify themselves and put others down on account of that. They don't become lazy and slack regarding their accomplishment in immersion but generate enthusiasm and try to realize those things that are better and finer. They achieve knowledge and vision. They're happy with that, but they haven't got all they wished for. They don't glorify themselves and put others down on account of that. They don't become lazy and slack regarding their knowledge and vision but generate enthusiasm and try to realize those things that are better and finer.

And what are those things that are better and finer than knowledge and vision of a Sotapanna and a Sakadagami?

Take a person who is on the path to gaining Anagami state, quite secluded from sensual pleasures, secluded from unskillful qualities, enters and remains in the first absorption, which has the rapture and bliss born of seclusion, while placing the mind and keeping it connected. This is something better and finer than knowledge and vision.

Furthermore, as the placing of the mind and keeping it connected are stilled, a person enters and remains in the second absorption, which has the rapture and bliss born of immersion, with internal clarity and mind at one, without placing the mind and keeping it connected. This too is something better and finer than knowledge and vision.

Furthermore, with the fading away of rapture, a companion enters and remains in the third absorption, where they experience equanimity, mindfulness and awareness, personally experiencing the bliss of which the noble ones declare, 'Equanimous and mindful, one experiences bliss.' This too is something better and finer than knowledge and vision.

Furthermore, giving up pleasure and pain, and ending former happiness and sadness, a person enters and remains in the fourth absorption, without pleasure or pain, with pure equanimity and mindfulness. This too is something better and finer than knowledge and vision.

Take a person who is on the path to gaining Arahant state; furthermore, a person, going totally beyond perceptions of form, with the ending of perceptions of impingement, not focusing on perceptions of diversity, aware that 'space is infinite', enters and remains in the dimension of infinite space. This too is something better and finer than knowledge and vision.

Furthermore, a person, going totally beyond the dimension of infinite space, aware that 'consciousness is infinite', enters and remains in the dimension of infinite consciousness. This too is something better and finer than knowledge and vision.

Furthermore, a person, going totally beyond the dimension of infinite consciousness, aware that 'there is nothing at all', enters and remains in the dimension of nothingness. This too is something better and finer than knowledge and vision.

Furthermore, take a person who, going totally beyond the dimension of nothingness, enters and remains in the dimension of neither perception nor non-perception. This too is something better and finer than knowledge and vision.

Furthermore, take a person who, going totally beyond the dimension of neither perception nor non-perception, enters and remains in the cessation of perception and feeling. And, having seen with wisdom, their defilements come to an end. This too is something better and finer than knowledge and vision. These are the things that are better and finer than knowledge and vision.

Suppose there was a person in need of heartwood. And while wandering in search of heartwood he'd come across a large tree standing with heartwood. He'd cut out just the heartwood and depart knowing it was heartwood. Whatever he needs to make from heartwood, he will succeed. That's what this person is like, I say.

And so, brahmin, this spiritual life is not lived for the sake of possessions, honor, and popularity, or for accomplishment in ethics, or for accomplishment in immersion, or for knowledge and vision. Rather, the goal, heartwood, and final end of the spiritual life is the unshakable freedom of heart (i.e.four-fold Nibbana)."

When he had spoken, the brahmin Piṅgalakoccha said to the Buddha, "Excellent, Mister Gotama! Excellent! … From this day forth, may Mister Gotama remember me as an ordinary person who has gone for refuge for life."

Chapter 33

Middle Discourses 31: Cūḷagosiṅgasutta

The Shorter Discourse at Gosiṅga

Nibbana is not an appearance, most of the ordinary people could not understand Nibbana even when they were in the presence of the Buddha[19]. People who have not yet gained Nibbana will struggle to understand Nibbana, as Nibbana cannot be compared to anything we would know in this world or what is commonly heard about.

Buddha visited a group of spiritual practitioners, and asked if they live all right, whether they get alms food, live happily in each other's company, and to which they respond saying that they live as one mind. Supposed, Buddha asked them if they gained spiritual attainment of Nibbana, they explain they have gained Anagami state and Arahant states. When one talks about Dhamma, an enlightened person can easily understand whether or not the person who speaks of Dhamma have attained Nibbana, as a person's attainment of Nibbana is visible through words as they explain Dhamma. As in mathematics, 3+2 is 5 despite who says irrespective of conventional background, Nibbana should be explained in the same manner no matter who explains. Anyone who deviates from the standards, they have not gained Nibbana.

"So I have heard. At one time the Buddha was staying at Ñātika in the brick house.

Now at that time the respected Arahants; Arahant Anuruddha, Arahant Nandiya, and Arahant Kimbila were staying in the sal forest park at Gosiṅga.

Then in the late afternoon, the Buddha came out of retreat and went to that park. The park keeper saw the Buddha coming off in the distance and said to him, "Don't come into this park. There are three gentlemen staying here whose nature is to desire only the peace. Do not disturb them."

Arahant Anuruddha heard the park keeper conversing with the Buddha, and said to him, "Don't keep the Buddha out, good park keeper! Our Teacher, the Blessed One, has arrived." Then Arahant Anuruddha went to Arahant Nandiya and Arahant Kimbila, and

---

[19] *As illustrated in Sarakāni case (SN 55.2, Paṭhamasaraṇānisakkasutta) most of the ordinary people could not understand Nibbana even when they were in the presence of the Buddha. Most of the ordinary people could not recognize Buddha through an appearance (see MN 31).*

said to them, "Come forth, respected friends, come forth! Our Teacher, the Blessed One, has arrived!"

Then Arahant Anuruddha, Arahant Nandiya, and Arahant Kimbila came out to greet the Buddha. One greeted and welcomed Buddha, one spread out a seat, and one set out water for washing his feet. The Buddha sat on the seat spread out, and washed his feet. Those Arahants bowed and sat down to one side.

The Buddha said to Arahant Anuruddha, "I hope you're keeping well, Anuruddha and friends; I hope you're all right. And I hope you're having no trouble getting almsfood."

"We're keeping well, Blessed One, we're getting by. And we have no trouble getting almsfood."

"I hope you're living in harmony, appreciating each other, without quarreling, blending like milk and water, and regarding each other with kindly eyes?"

"Indeed, sir, we live in harmony like this."

"But how do you live this way?"

"In this case, venerable sir, I think, 'I'm fortunate, so very fortunate, to live together with spiritual companions such as these.' I consistently treat these Arahants with kindness by way of body, speech, and mind, both in public and in private. I think, 'Why don't I set aside my own ideas and just go along with these venerables' ideas?' And that's what I do. Though we're different in body, sir, we're one in mind, it seems to me."

And Arahant Nandiya and Arahant Kimbila spoke likewise, and they added: "That's how we live in harmony, appreciating each other, without quarreling, blending like milk and water, and regarding each other with kindly eyes."

"Good, good, Anuruddha and friends! But I hope you're living diligently, keen, and resolute?"

"Indeed, sir, we live diligently."

"But how do you live this way?"

"In this case, venerable sir, whoever returns first from almsround prepares the seats, and puts out the drinking water and the rubbish bin. If there's anything left over, whoever returns last eats it if they like. Otherwise they throw it out where there is little that grows, or drop it into water that has no living creatures. Then they put away the seats, drinking water, and rubbish bin, and sweep the refectory. If someone sees that the pot of water for washing, drinking, or the toilet is empty they set it up. If he can't do it, he summons another with a wave of the hand, and they set it up by lending each other a hand to lift. But we don't break into speech for that reason. And every five days we sit together for the whole night and discuss the teachings. That's how we live diligently, keen, and resolute."

"Good, good, Anuruddha and friends! But as you live diligently like this, have you achieved any superhuman distinction in knowledge and vision worthy of the noble ones, a comfortable mental state?"

"How could we not, venerable sir? Since we gained Anagami state, whenever we want, quite secluded from sensual pleasures, secluded from unskillful qualities, we enter and remain in the first absorption, which has the rapture and bliss born of seclusion, while placing the mind and keeping it connected. This is a superhuman distinction in knowledge and vision worthy of the noble ones, a comfortable mind state, that we have achieved while living diligent, keen, and resolute."

"Good, good! But have you achieved any other superhuman distinction for going beyond and stilling that absorption state?"

"How could we not, venerable sir? Whenever we want, as the placing of the mind and keeping it connected are stilled, we enter and remain in the second absorption, which has the rapture and bliss born of immersion, with internal clarity and mind at one, without placing the mind and keeping it connected. This is another superhuman distinction that we have achieved for going beyond and stilling that absorption."

"Good, good! But have you achieved any other superhuman distinction for going beyond and stilling that absorption?"

"How could we not, venerable sir? Whenever we want, with the fading away of rapture, we enter and remain in the third absorption, where we experience equanimity, mindfulness and awareness, personally experiencing the bliss of which the noble ones declare, 'Equanimous and mindful, one experiences bliss.' This is another superhuman distinction that we have achieved for going beyond and stilling that absorption."

"Good, good! But have you achieved any other superhuman distinction for going beyond and stilling that absorption?"

"How could we not, venerable sir? Whenever we want, with the giving up of pleasure and pain, and the ending of former happiness and sadness, we enter and remain in the fourth absorption, without pleasure or pain, with pure equanimity and mindfulness. This is another superhuman distinction that we have achieved for going beyond and stilling that absorption."

"Good, good! But have you achieved any other superhuman distinction for going beyond and stilling that absorption?"

"How could we not, venerable sir? Whenever we want, going totally beyond perceptions of form, with the ending of perceptions of impingement, not focusing on perceptions of diversity, aware that 'space is infinite', we enter and remain in the dimension of infinite space.

This is another superhuman distinction that we have achieved for going beyond and stilling that absorption."

"Good, good! But have you achieved any other superhuman distinction for going beyond and stilling that absorption?"

"How could we not, venerable sir? Whenever we want, going totally beyond the dimension of infinite space, aware that 'consciousness is infinite', we enter and remain in the dimension of infinite consciousness. … going totally beyond the dimension of infinite consciousness, aware that 'there is nothing at all', we enter and remain in the dimension of nothingness. … going totally beyond the dimension of nothingness, we enter and remain in the dimension of neither perception nor non-perception. This is another superhuman distinction that we have achieved for going beyond and stilling that absorption."

"Good, good! But have you achieved any other superhuman distinction for going beyond and stilling that absorption?"

"How could we not, venerable sir? Whenever we want, going totally beyond the dimension of neither perception nor non-perception, we enter and remain in the cessation of perception and feeling.

And, having seen with wisdom, our defilements (ten fetters) have come to an end. This is another superhuman distinction in knowledge and vision worthy of the noble ones, a comfortable mind state, that we have achieved for going beyond and stilling that absorption. And we don't see any better or finer way of absorption comfortably than this."

"Good, good! There is no better or finer way of experiencing the natural meditative states comfortably than this."

Then the Buddha educated, encouraged, fired up, and inspired the Arahants; Anuruddha, Nandiya, and Kimbila with a Dhamma talk, after which he got up from his seat and left.

Arahants then accompanied the Buddha for a little way before turning back. Arahant Nandiya and Arahant Kimbila said to Arahant Anuruddha, "Did we ever tell you that we had gained such and such absorptions and attainments, up to Arahant state, the ending of defilements, as you revealed to the Buddha?"

"You, great Arahants did not tell me that they had gained such absorption and attainment of Arahantship. But I discovered it by comprehending the words of Dhamma that you say, and your minds, and deities also told me. I answered when the Buddha directly asked about it."

Then the native spirit Dīgha Parajana went up to the Buddha, bowed, stood to one side, and said to him, "The Vajjis are lucky! The Vajjian people are so very lucky that the Realized One, the perfected one, the fully awakened Buddha stays there, as well as these three gentlemen, the Arahant Anuruddha, Arahant Nandiya, and Arahant Kimbila."

Hearing the cry of Dīgha Parajana, the earth gods raised the cry …

Hearing the cry of the earth gods, the gods of the four great kings … the gods of the thirty-three … the gods of Yama … the joyful gods … the gods who love to imagine … the gods who control what is imagined by others … the gods of the Divinity's host raised the cry, "The Vajjis are lucky!

The Vajjian people are so very lucky that the Realized One, the perfected one, the fully awakened Buddha stays there, as well as these three gentlemen, the Arahant Anuruddha, Arahant Nandiya, and Arahant Kimbila."

And so at that moment, that second, that hour, those Arahants were known as far as the realm of divinity.

"That's so true, Dīgha! That's so true! If the family from which those three gentlemen went into following and completing a spiritual path were to recollect those Arahants with confident heart, that would be for that family's lasting welfare and happiness. If the family circle … village … town … city … country … all the aristocrats … all the brahmins … all the peasants … all the workers were to recollect those Arahants with confident heart, that would be for all those menials' lasting welfare and happiness.

If the whole world—with its gods, Māras, and divinities, this population with its ascetics and brahmins, gods and humans—were to recollect those Arahants with confident heart, that would be for the whole world's lasting welfare and happiness.

See, Dīgha, how those three gentlemen are practicing for the welfare and happiness of the people, out of sympathy for the world, for the benefit, welfare, and happiness of gods and humans!"

That is what the Buddha said. Satisfied, the native spirit Dīgha Parajana approved what the Buddha said."

Chapter 34

Middle Discourses 32: Mahāgosiṅgasutta

The Longer Discourse at Gosiṅga

Several spiritual saints, reveling in the beauty of the night, discuss what kind of practitioner would adorn the park. Sariputta Arahant asks from Ananda, a Sotapanna, what kind of a person can beautify the park at night?

A Sotapanna, Ananda says; Those who have experienced four-fold Nibbana and know Sotapanna, Sakadagami, Anagami, and Arahant stages through personal experience, those who know the in-depth meaning of discourses and are able to explain Dhamma leading to Nibbana, they remember, rehearse them, mentally investigate, understand fully through personal experience. They teach Dhamma to community members (ordinary four assemblies, male and female bhikkhu, and householders) so that they can give up the underlying tendency of grasping conventions. They are the kind who can adorn a park. When asked the same question to Arahant Revata: those who experience peaceful Nibbana complete the Anaagami state. They are empty of desires; they are the ones who adorn the park.

When asked the same question to Arahant Anuruddha, a person who can surpass the human eye to see beyond what eyes cannot see through wisdom, Nibbana, they have the divine eye. They are able to see the universe with its various realms clearly, just as a man with good eyesight can see the royal house. That's the kind of person who adorns the park.

When asked the same question to Arahant Kssapa; A person who lives isolated from others in the very presence or absence of them in mind is happy with whatever food they get and content with whatever robes they have and has no desire to keep too much but what is needed. These are good things. They have few wishes, are content with what they have, live in isolation and have freedom in mind in the presence or absence of others. They're not fond of company but are living alone in mind in the presence or absence of others. They have noble virtues, they carry Dhamma within, wise, free from grasping conventions, and have attained Nibbana across four-fold Nibbana; that's the kind of a person who adorns the park.

When asked the same question to Arahant Moggallāna; it's when people talk about four-fold Nibbana they discuss with proper interpretation and the strength of Dhamma retains within conversations (meaningful conversations that make another gain Nibbana), that's the kind of people who adorn the park.

When asked the same question to Arahant Sariputta; when someone masters one's own mind, and there is no self-clinging with all fetters given up across stages, having attained four-fold Nibbana, they are free. They may do "whatever" they must do, go "wherever" they have to go, eat and dress "whatever" they have, and so on, they are free of mental attachment. Their minds are not affected by their worldly experiences and doing; just as a king's minister can wear different clothes in the day and night, they may do whatever they must, but they remain non-clinging as Arahants. That's the kind of people who adorn the park.

Having spoken in many ways, they mentioned what they spoke with each other to Buddha. Then Buddha says, you all have spoken well. Those who are Arahants are beautifying the park, and we can also include trainees in the category of those who beautify a park. While they are trainees (Ordinary wise practitioner to Anagami), a person who puts in constant effort to give up grasping to conventions while maintaining mindfulness to engage in Dhamma/wholesome intentional actions and not to engage in non-dhamma, and one who constantly strive to gain freedom Nibbana practicing in the right way, such a person adorns a park.

"So I have heard. At one time the Buddha was staying in the sal forest park at Gosiṅga, together with several well-known senior disciples, such as Arahant Sāriputta, Arahant Mahāmoggallāna, Arahant Mahākassapa, Arahant Anuruddha, Arahant Revata, A Sotapanna, Ānanda, and others.

Then in the late afternoon, Arahant Mahāmoggallāna came out of retreat, went to Arahant Mahākassapa, and said, "Come, Arahant Kassapa, let's go to Arahant Sāriputta to hear the teachings; four-fold Nibbana."

"Yes, respected friends," Arahant Mahākassapa replied. Then, together with Arahant Anuruddha, they went to Arahant Sāriputta to hear the teaching.

Seeing them, Arahant Ānanda went to Arahant Revata, told him what was happening, and invited him also.

Arahant Sāriputta saw them coming off in the distance and said to Ānanda, "Come, respected friend, Ānanda. Welcome to Ānanda, the Buddha's attendant, who is so close to the Buddha. Ānanda, the sal forest park at Gosiṅga is lovely, the night is bright, the sal trees are in full blossom, and heavenly scents seem to float on the air. What kind of person would beautify this park?"

"Arahant Sāriputta, it's a person who is very learned, remembering and keeping what they've learned. These teachings are good in the beginning (Sotapanna), good in the middle (Anagami), and good in the end (Arahant), meaningful and well-phrased, describing a spiritual practice that's entirely full and pure. They are very learned in such teachings, remembering them, rehearsing them, mentally scrutinizing them, and comprehending them through experience. And they teach the four assemblies in order to uproot the underlying tendencies with well-rounded and coherent words and phrases. That's the kind of person who would beautify this park."

When he had spoken, Arahant Sāriputta said to Arahant Revata, "Arahant Revata, Ānanda has answered by speaking from his heart. And now we ask you the same question."

"Arahant Sāriputta, it's a person who enjoys dhamma and loves dhamma. They're committed to inner path, noble path of the heart, they don't neglect absorption, they're endowed with discernment, and they frequent empty huts. That's the kind of person who would beautify this park."

When he had spoken, Arahant Sāriputta said to Arahant Anuruddha, "Arahant Anuruddha, Arahant has answered by speaking from his heart. And now we ask you the same question."

"Arahant Sāriputta, it's a person who surveys a thousandfold galaxy with clairvoyance that is purified and surpasses the human, just as a person with clear eyes could survey a thousand orbits from the upper floor of a royal longhouse. That's the kind of person who would beautify this park."

When he had spoken, Arahant Sāriputta said to Arahant Mahākassapa, "Arahant Kassapa, Arahant Anuruddha has answered by speaking from his heart. And now we ask you the same question."

"Arahant Sāriputta, it's a person who lives in the isolation in mind, eats whatever they get with ease, wears whatever they have with ease, and do not possess desire (likes, dislikes, expectations) for possessions; and they praise these things. They are of few wishes, content, secluded, aloof, and energetic; and they praise these things. They are accomplished in ethics (Sotapanna), immersion (Anagami), wisdom (Arahant), freedom, and the knowledge and vision of freedom; and they praise these things. That's the kind of person who would beautify this park."

When he had spoken, Arahant Sāriputta said to Arahant Mahāmoggallāna, "Arahant Moggallāna, Arahant Mahākassapa has answered by speaking from his heart. And now we ask you the same question."

"Arahant Sāriputta, it's when two people engage in discussion about the teaching. They question each other and answer each other's questions without faltering, and their discussion on the teaching flows on. That's the kind of person who would beautify this park."

Then Arahant Mahāmoggallāna said to Arahant Sāriputta, "Each of us has spoken from our heart. And now we ask you: Arahant Sāriputta, the sal forest park at Gosiṅga is lovely, the night is bright, the sal trees are in full blossom, and heavenly scents seem to float on the air. What kind of companion would beautify this park?"

"Arahant Moggallāna, it's when a person masters their mind and is not mastered by it. In the morning, they abide in whatever mental state they want. At midday, and in the evening, they abide in whatever mental state they want. Suppose that a ruler or their chief minister had a chest full of garments of different colors. In the morning, they'd don whatever pair of garments they wanted. At midday, and in the evening, they'd don whatever pair of garments they wanted.

In the same way, a companion masters their mind and is not mastered by it. In the morning, they abide in whatever mental state they want. At midday, and in the evening, they abide in whatever mental state they want. That's the kind of person who would beautify this park."

Then Arahant Sāriputta said to other Arahant, "Each of us has spoken from the heart. Come, reverends, let's go to the Buddha, and inform him about this. As he answers, so we'll remember it."

"Yes, venerable sir," they replied. Then those Arahants went to the Buddha, bowed, and sat down to one side. Arahant Sāriputta told the Buddha of how the companions had come to see him, and how he had asked Ānanda: "Ānanda, the sal forest park at Gosiṅga is lovely, the night is bright, the sal trees are in full blossom, and heavenly scents seem to float on the air.

What kind of companion would beautify this park?' When I had spoken, Ānanda, a Sotapanna said to me: 'Arahant Sāriputta, it's a person who is very learned … That's the kind of person who would beautify this park.'"

"Good, good, Sāriputta! Ānanda answered in the right way for him. For Ānanda is very learned …"

"Next I asked Arahant Revata the same question. He said: 'It's a person who enjoys retreat … That's the kind of person who would beautify this park.'"

"Good, good, Sāriputta! Revata answered in the right way for him. For Revata enjoys retreat …"

"Next I asked Arahant Anuruddha the same question. He said: 'It's a person who surveys the thousandfold galaxy with clairvoyance that is purified and surpasses the human … That's the kind of person who would beautify this park.'"

"Good, good, Sāriputta! Anuruddha answered in the right way for him. For Anuruddha surveys the thousandfold galaxy with clairvoyance that is purified and surpasses the human."

"Next I asked Arahant Mahākassapa the same question. He said: 'It's a person who lives in the wilderness … and is accomplished in the knowledge and vision of freedom; and they praise these things. That's the kind of person who would beautify this park.'"

"Good, good, Sāriputta! Kassapa answered in the right way for him. For Kassapa lives in the wilderness … and is accomplished in the knowledge and vision of freedom; and he praises these things."

"Next I asked Arahant Mahāmoggallāna the same question. He said: 'It's when two people engage in discussion about the teaching … That's the kind of person who would beautify this park.'"

"Good, good, Sāriputta! Moggallāna answered in the right way for him. For Moggallāna is a Dhamma speaker."

When he had spoken, Arahant Moggallāna said to the Buddha, "Next, I asked Arahant Sāriputta: 'Each of us has spoken from our heart. And now we ask you: Arahant Sāriputta, the sal forest park at Gosiṅga is lovely, the night is bright, the sal trees are in full blossom, and heavenly scents seem to float on the air.

What kind of person would beautify this park?' When I had spoken, Arahant Sāriputta said to me: 'Arahant Moggallāna, it's when a person masters their mind and is not mastered by it … That's the kind of person who would beautify this park.'"

"Good, good, Moggallāna! Sāriputta answered in the right way for him. For Sāriputta masters his mind and is not mastered by it …"

When he had spoken, Arahant Sāriputta asked the Buddha, "Venerable sir, who has spoken well?"

"You've all spoken well in your way. However, listen to me also as to what kind of a person would beautify this sal forest park at Gosiṅga.. It's a person who constantly strives to purify grasping conventions in any posture while sitting, walking, and lying down, and establishes mindfulness in their presence, thinking: 'I will not give up the spiritual practice until my mind is freed from the defilements by not grasping!' That's the kind of person who would beautify this park."

That is what the Buddha said. Satisfied, those Arahants and spiritual friends approved what the Buddha said."

Chapter 35

Middle Discourses 33: Mahāgopālakasutta

The Longer Discourse on the Cowherd

A person who is unable to develop certain qualities, as shown below, is unlikely to be able to make progress in the Dhamma practice, leading to Nibbana despite long years of practice:

- A person is unable to gain a deeper understanding of the impermanence; instead, they keep grasping things that are liable to change, and conventions[20].
- A person's intentional action remains excessively impure (Impurity refers to too much greediness, hatred, and delusions).
- A person makes no attempt to purify from unwholesome thoughts. Instead, they maintain them and keep developing unwholesome thoughts such as a high degree of sensual, malicious, and ill-will more and more.
- When a person receives sensory information, they tend to either excessively like or dislike such experiences. In doing so, they tend to develop unwholesome qualities: envies, jealousy, pride, sorrow, due to excessive (endless) desires.
- A person doesn't interpret Dhamma in the correct manner as intended by the Buddha.
- A person has doubts about Dhamma, and they do not get such doubts clarified by Arahants. Doubts can act as a barrier to making progress in the Noble Path. Thus, a wise practitioner should be allowed to clarify doubts.
- A person does not get inspired by the wise words leading to Nibbana and does not find satisfaction in Dhamma.
- A person does not understand how to practice Dhamma across the stages of Nibbana.

---

[20] For example, instead of understanding impermanence in self, a person continues to grasp into self-view and conventions.

- A person does not develop higher stages of Nibbana through noble mindfulness/jhanas happening naturally after the Sotapanna state.
- A person tends to not accept gifts in moderation, instead, accepts gifts without a limit due to excessive desires.
- A person doesn't respect Arahants, including universal (Savaka) Sangha.

Therefore, a person who aspires to Nibbana would benefit if they avoid forming thoughts as above, instead putting effort into developing wholesome thoughts.

"So I have heard. At one time the Buddha was staying near Sāvatthī in Jeta's Grove, Anāthapiṇḍika's monastery. There the Buddha addressed the companions, "Companions!"

"Venerable sir," they replied. The Buddha said this:

"Companions, a cowherd with eleven factors can't maintain and expand a herd of cattle. What eleven? It's when a cowherd doesn't know form, is unskilled in characteristics, doesn't pick out flies' eggs, doesn't dress wounds, doesn't spread smoke, doesn't know the ford, doesn't know satisfaction, doesn't know the trail, is not skilled in pastures, milks dry, and doesn't show extra respect to the bulls who are fathers and leaders of the herd. A cowherd with these eleven factors can't maintain and expand a herd of cattle.

In the same way, a person with eleven qualities can't achieve growth, improvement, or maturity in this teaching and training. What eleven? It's when a person doesn't know form, is unskilled in characteristics, doesn't pick out flies' eggs, doesn't dress wounds, doesn't spread smoke, doesn't know the ford, doesn't know satisfaction, doesn't know the trail, is not skilled in pastures, milks dry, and doesn't show extra respect to arahants of long standing, long gone forth, fathers and leaders of the Saṅgha.

And how does a companion not know form? It's when a person doesn't truly understand that all form is the four principal states, or form derived from the four principal states. That's how a person doesn't know form.

And how is a person not skilled in characteristics? It's when a person doesn't understand that a fool is characterized by their deeds (i.e intentional actions), and an astute person is characterized by their deeds. That's how a person isn't skilled in characteristics.

And how does a person not pick out flies' eggs? It's when a person tolerates a sensual, malicious, or cruel thought that has arisen. They tolerate any bad, unskillful qualities that have arisen. They don't give them up, get rid of them, eliminate them, and obliterate them. That's how a person doesn't pick out flies' eggs.

And how does a person not dress wounds? When a person sees a sight with their eyes, they get caught up in the features and details. Since the faculty of sight is left unrestrained, bad unskillful qualities of covetousness and displeasure become overwhelming. They don't practice restraint, they don't protect the faculty of sight, and they don't achieve its restraint. When they hear a sound with their ears … smell an odor with their nose … taste a flavor with their tongue … feel a touch with their body … know an idea with their mind, they get caught up in the features and details.

Since the faculty of the mind is left unrestrained, bad unskillful qualities of covetousness and displeasure become overwhelming. They don't practice restraint, they don't protect the faculty of the mind, and they don't achieve its restraint. That's how a person doesn't dress wounds.

And how does a person not spread smoke? It's when a person doesn't teach others the Dhamma in detail with correct interpretation as intended by the Buddha. That's how a person doesn't spread smoke.

And how does a person not know the ford? It's when a person doesn't from time to time go up to those disciples of the Buddha (Sotapanna to Arahant)—inheritors of the heritage, who experience four-fold Nibbana, the noble virtues, and the outlines—and ask them questions: 'Why, sir, does it say this? What does that mean?'

Those companions don't get to understand what is clarified, what is unclear, reveal what is obscure, and dispel doubt regarding the many doubtful matters. That's how a companion doesn't know the ford.

And how does a companion not know satisfaction? It's when a person, when the teaching and training proclaimed by the Realized One are being taught, finds no inspiration in the meaning and the teaching, and finds no joy connected with the teaching. That's how a person doesn't know satisfaction.

And how does a companion not know the trail? It's when a person doesn't truly understand the noble eightfold path. That's how a person doesn't know the trail.

And how is a companion not skilled in pastures? It's when a person doesn't truly understand the four kinds of mindfulness practices (i.e path to Anagami). That's how a person is not skilled in pastures.

And how does a companion milk dry? It's when a person is invited by an ordinary person to accept cloths, food, accommodation, and medicines and supplies for the sick, and that person doesn't know moderation in accepting. That's how a person milks dry.

And how does a companion not show extra respect to Arahants of long standing, long gone forth, fathers and leaders of the Saṅgha? It's when a person doesn't consistently treat senior disciples of the Buddha, long gained fruition, fathers and leaders of the Saṅgha with kindness by way of body, speech, and mind, both in public and in private.

That's how a person doesn't show extra respect to Arahants of long standing, long gained fruition, fathers and leaders of the Saṅgha.

A person with these eleven qualities can't achieve growth, improvement, or maturity in this teaching and training.

A cowherd with eleven factors can maintain and expand a herd of cattle. What eleven? It's when a cowherd knows form, is skilled in characteristics, picks out flies' eggs, dresses wounds, spreads smoke, knows the ford, knows satisfaction, knows the trail, is skilled in pastures, doesn't milk dry, and shows extra respect to the bulls who are fathers and leaders of the herd. A cowherd with these eleven factors can maintain and expand a herd of cattle.

In the same way, a person with eleven qualities can achieve growth, improvement, and maturity in this teaching and training. What eleven?

It's when a person knows form, is skilled in characteristics, picks out flies' eggs, dresses wounds, spreads smoke, knows the ford, knows satisfaction, knows the trail, is skilled in pastures, doesn't milk dry, and shows extra respect to senior disciples of the Buddha (Arahants), long gained fruition, fathers and leaders of the Saṅgha.

And how does a person know form? It's when a person truly understands that all form is the four principal states, or form derived from the four principal states. That's how a person knows form.

And how is a person skilled in characteristics? It's when a person understands that a fool is characterized by their deeds, and an astute person is characterized by their deeds (intentional actions). That's how a person is skilled in characteristics.

And how does a person pick out flies' eggs? It's when a person doesn't tolerate a sensual, malicious, or cruel thought that has arisen. They don't tolerate any bad, unskillful qualities that have arisen, but give them up, get rid of them, eliminate them, and obliterate them. That's how a person picks out flies' eggs.

And how does a person dress wounds? When a person sees a sight with their eyes, they don't get caught up in the features and details. If the faculty of sight were left unrestrained, bad unskillful qualities of covetousness and displeasure would become overwhelming.

For this reason, they practice restraint, protecting the faculty of sight, and achieving its restraint. When they hear a sound with their ears … smell an odor with their nose … taste a flavor with their tongue … feel a touch with their body … know an idea with their mind, they don't get caught up in the features and details. If the faculty of mind were left unrestrained, bad unskillful qualities of covetousness and displeasure would become overwhelming. For this reason, they practice restraint, protecting the faculty of mind, and achieving its restraint. That's how a person dresses wounds.

And how does a person spread smoke? It's when a person teaches others the Dhamma in detail as they experienced and understood it. That's how a person spreads smoke.

And how does a person know the ford? It's when from time to time a person goes up to those Arahants who know all about four-fold Nibbana, —inheritors of the heritage, who have understood the teachings, the noble virtues, and the outlines—and asks them questions: 'Why, sir, does it say this? What does that mean?'

They understand that those Arahants clarify what is unclear, reveal what is obscure, and dispel doubt regarding the many doubtful matters. That's how a person knows the ford.

And how does a person know satisfaction? It's when a companion, when the teaching and training proclaimed by the Realized One are being taught, finds inspiration in the meaning and the teaching, and finds joy connected with the teaching. That's how a person knows satisfaction.

And how does a person know the trail? It's when a companion truly understands the noble eightfold path. That's how a person knows the trail.

And how is a person skilled in pastures? It's when a person truly understands the four kinds of mindfulness meditation upon gaining Anagami state. That's how a person is skilled in pastures.

And how does a person not milk dry? It's when a person is invited by an ordinary person or trainee to accept clothing, food, lodgings, and medicines and supplies for the sick, and that person knows moderation in accepting. That's how a person doesn't milk dry.

And how does a person show extra respect to Arahants, long gained fruition, parenting like leaders of the Saṅgha? It's when a person consistently treats Arahants of long standing, long gone forth, parenting like leaders of the Saṅgha with kindness by way of body, speech, and mind, both in public and in private. That's how a person shows extra respect to Arahants of long standing, long gone forth, fathers and leaders of the Saṅgha.

A person with these eleven qualities can achieve growth, improvement, and maturity in this teaching and training."

That is what the Buddha said. Satisfied, the companions approved what the Buddha said.

Chapter 36

Middle Discourses 34: Cūḷagopālakasutta

The Shorter Discourse on the Cowherd

This discourse records the Buddha presenting four kinds of disciples who gain four-fold Nibbana.

In this world, without considering whether they are teachers, those who guide them to a spiritual path talk about the practice leading to Nibbana based on personal experience, whether they have gained Nibbana for themselves before speaking about the path. Some people can follow a spiritual path with ignorance.

Throughout history, you can find many occasions when bhikkhus misinterpret Dhamma. Not exploring but merely ignoring, people just go in circles again and again without gaining Nibbana. If anyone thinks they are worth listening to, they will block their chances of gaining Nibbana.

Those who have not personally experienced universal ways of functioning; Nibbana, may not fully comprehend and appreciate the Triple Gem. On the other hand, those who experience Nibbana understand four-fold Nibbana. It is only after experience four-fold Nibbana through personal experience, one can explain to another with accuracy. Thus, the Three Jewels and Three Roots are supports in which a person takes refuge at the beginning of a practice to escape mental pain across four-fold Nibbana. Tree Jewels are universal Buddha, Universal Dhamma (four-fold Nibbana), and universal Sangha (Sotapanna to Arahant). The Triple Gem offers spiritual protection and refuge to trainees (Ordinary to Anagami), helping them find refuge in themselves as they progress across four-fold Nibbana.

"So I have heard. At one time the Buddha was staying in the land of the Vajjis near Ukkacelā on the bank of the Ganges river. There the Buddha addressed the spiritual practitioners, "Friends!"

"Venerable sir," they replied. The Buddha said this:

"Once upon a time, companions, there was an unintelligent Magadhan cowherd. In the last month of the rainy season, in autumn, without inspecting the near shore or the far shore, he drove his cattle across a place with no ford on the Ganges river to the northern shore among the Suvidehans.

But the cattle bunched up in mid-stream and came to ruin right there. Why is that? Because the unintelligent cowherd failed to inspect the shores before driving the cattle across at a place with no ford. In the same way, there are ordinary monks and spiritual practitioners who are unskilled in this world and the other world, unskilled in Māra's domain and its opposite, and unskilled in Death's domain and its opposite. If anyone thinks they are worth listening to and trusting, it will be for their lasting harm and suffering.

Once upon a time, companions, there was an intelligent Magadhan cowherd. In the last month of the rainy season, in autumn, after inspecting the near shore and the far shore, he drove his cattle across a ford on the Ganges river to the northern shore among the Suvidehans.

First he drove across the bulls, the fathers and leaders of the herd. They breasted the stream of the Ganges and safely reached the far shore. Then he drove across the strong and tractable cattle. They too breasted the stream of the Ganges and safely reached the far shore. Then he drove across the bullocks and heifers. They too breasted the stream of the Ganges and safely reached the far shore.

Then he drove across the calves and weak cattle. They too breasted the stream of the Ganges and safely reached the far shore. Once it happened that a baby calf had just been born. Urged on by its mother's lowing, even it managed to breast the stream of the Ganges and safely reach the far shore. Why is that? Because the intelligent cowherd inspected both shores before driving the cattle across at a ford.

In the same way, there are noble ones (Perfected ones) and noble trainees (Sotapanna to Anagami) who are skilled in this world and the other world, skilled in Māra's domain and its opposite, and skilled in Death's domain and its opposite. If anyone thinks they are worth listening to and trusting, it will be for their lasting welfare and happiness.

Just like the bulls, fathers and leaders of the herd, who crossed the Ganges to safety are the mendicants who are perfected, who have ended the defilements, completed the spiritual journey, done what had to be done, laid down the burden, achieved their own goal, utterly ended the fetter of continued existence, and are rightly freed through enlightenment. Having breasted Māra's stream, they have safely crossed over to the far shore.

Just like the strong and tractable cattle who crossed the Ganges to safety are the companions who, with the ending of the five lower fetters, are reborn spontaneously. They're extinguished there, and are not liable to return from that world. They too, having breasted Māra's stream, will safely cross over to the far shore.

Just like the bullocks and heifers who crossed the Ganges to safety are the companions who, with the ending of three fetters, and the weakening of greed, hate, and delusion, are once-returners.

They come back to this world once only, then make an end of suffering. They too, having breasted Māra's stream, will safely cross over to the far shore.

Just like the calves and weak cattle who crossed the Ganges to safety are the companions who, with the ending of three fetters are stream-enterers, not liable to be reborn in the underworld, bound for awakening. They too, having breasted Māra's stream, will safely cross over to the far shore.

Just like the baby calf who had just been born, but, urged on by its mother's lowing, still managed to cross the Ganges to safety are the companions who have the potential to become followers of Dhamma (four-fold Nibbana), followers of Buddha by faith grounded on evidence based on life experience. They too, having breasted Māra's stream, will safely cross over to the far shore.

Companions, I am skilled in this world and the other world, skilled in Māra's domain and its opposite, and skilled in Death's domain and its opposite. If anyone thinks I am worth listening to and trusting, it will be for their lasting welfare and happiness."

That is what the Buddha said. Then the Holy One, the Teacher, went on to say:

"This world and the other world have been clearly explained by one who knows; as well as Māra's reach, and what's out of Death's reach.

Directly knowing the whole world, the Buddha who understands has opened the door to freedom from death, for finding the sanctuary, extinguishment.

The Wicked One's stream has been cut, it's blown away and mown down. Be full of joy, companions, set your heart on sanctuary!"

Chapter 37

Middle Discourses 35: Cūḷasaccakasutta

The Shorter Discourse with Saccaka

This discourse records an argumentative philosopher named Saccaka comes to the Buddha. He attempts to defeat the Buddha in debate – an attempt that fails spectacularly. Subsequently, the Buddha gives a detailed explanation of the impersonal nature of all phenomena that Saccaka finds quite convincing. Buddha's explanation can be mentioned as below:

Body cells change every minute, and the body can change due to various factors: lack of nutrition, lack of eating, overeating, illness, aging, weather conditions, etc. Although one can look after one's body to some extent, one cannot have full control of one's body just as one wishes. This is because the body is subject to change. By understanding that you can let go of overly getting attached to your body, simply use your body to engage in wholesome activities/end samsara if that's what you aspire to. Do things that need doing without making suffering out of it, not grasping and not ignoring in the middle way.

Feelings such as hunger, body aches, pleasure, and pain, neither pleasure nor pain can be subject to change. Feelings can rapidly change when responding to worldly experiences coming from sensory information. While you may shape certain feelings through conscious efforts, one does not have total control to retain or shape one's feelings that are responding to sensory information just as one wishes to, as feelings are subject to change in line with a universal rhythm and ways. By understanding that you can let go of getting overly attached to your feelings (meaning when feelings change due to pleasures, displeasures, neutral) and so on, by understanding the universal truth but simply using the feelings to engage in wholesome activities/intentional actions, do things that need doing without making sufferings out of feelings, not grasping and not ignoring the middle way.

Perception (how things seem based on conventions and interpretations based on conventions) can change at any time, and perception can change in response to sensory information. One does not have total control to retain or shape one's perceptions that are responding to sensory information just as one wishes to, as perceptions are subject to change in line with a universal rhythm and ways. By understanding that you can let go of getting overly attached to your perception (meaning when perceptions change based on conventions) etc, by understanding the universal truth but simply understanding how the perceptions are formed, without getting overly attached to such things to engage in wholesome activities/intentional actions, do things that need doing without making sufferings out of feelings, not grasping and not ignoring the middle way.

Fabrication (intentions and actions, intentional actions) can change at any time, and intentional actions change in response to sensory information. One does not have total control to retain one's fabrications that are responding to sensory information just as one wishes to, as fabrications are subject to change in line with a universal rhythm and ways. By understanding that you avoid getting overly attached to your fabrications. As an ordinary person, you may reduce your mental attachment to fabrications by understanding that fabrications change responding to worldly experiences, the universal truth applicable to all. Instead, you may engage in wholesome activities/intentional actions, do things that need doing without making sufferings out of fabrications, not grasping and not ignoring in the middle way.

Consciousness can change when oxygen is reduced in the body or due to illness. You may not have control over your consciousness, or you may not be able to overpower your consciousness that functions in line with universal ways. Instead, by understanding that you can let go of getting attached to your consciousness, simply use your consciousness to understand what you need to understand to reduce mental pain coming from worldly experience, not grasping and not ignoring it in the middle way.

Thus, form, feeling, how you perceive things, your intentional actions, and consciousness (as "I am self" etc.) can change. You may not have total control to retain or shape such things, and they are inconstant. By understanding with wisdom to see beyond conventions, you can reduce mental attachment for such things. The way to gain understanding can be developed by developing merits.

You may live in any city, any country, or any place of accommodation. You may wear any dress and speak any language. If you want to practice Dhamma in a way leading to Nibbana, you have to practice in the same way: reduce greediness (too many likes), hatred (too many dislikes), and delusion (expectations) by giving up grasping to fetters across four-fold Nibbana. Greed, hate and delusion can burn you within. By understanding, you can let go of such burns. Arahants are like fertile fields, for those who attend to fertile fields get fruition.

"So I have heard. At one time the Buddha was staying near Vesālī, at the Great Wood, in the hall with the peaked roof.

Now at that time Saccaka, the son of Jain parents, was staying in Vesālī. He was a debater and clever speaker deemed holy by many people. He was telling a crowd in Vesālī, "I don't see any ascetic or brahmin who would not shake and rock and tremble, sweating from the armpits, were I to take them on in debate—not a leader of an order or a community, or the tutor of a community, and not even one who claims to be a perfected one, a fully awakened Buddha. Even an insentient post would shake and rock and tremble were I to take it on in debate. How much more then a human being!"

Then Arahant Assaji got dressed in the morning and, went into gathering almsfood, and entered Vesālī for alms. As Saccaka was going for a walk he saw arahant Assaji coming off in the distance. He approached him and exchanged greetings with him.

When the greetings and polite conversation were over, Saccaka stood to one side and said to Assaji, "Mister Assaji, how does the ascetic Gotama guide his disciples? And on what topics does instruction to his disciples generally proceed?"

"Aggivessana, this is how the ascetic Gotama guides his disciples, and his instructions to disciples generally proceed on these topics: 'Form, feeling, perception, choices, and consciousness are impermanent. Form, feeling, perception, choices, and consciousness are not-self. All conditions are impermanent. All things are not-self.' This is how the ascetic Gotama guides his disciples, and how instruction to his disciples generally proceeds."

"It's sad to hear, Mister Assaji, that the ascetic Gotama has such a doctrine. Hopefully, some time or other I'll get to meet Mister Gotama, and we can have a discussion. And hopefully I can dissuade him from this harmful misconception."

Now at that time around five hundred Licchavis were sitting together at the town hall on some business. Then Saccaka went up to them and said, "Come forth, good Licchavīs, come forth! Today I am going to have a discussion with the ascetic Gotama. If he stands by the position stated to me by one of his well-known disciples—a mendicant named Assaji—I'll take him on in debate and drag him to and fro and roundabout, like a strong man would grab a fleecy sheep and drag it to and fro and round about! Taking him on in debate, I'll drag him to and fro and roundabout, like a strong brewer's worker would toss a large brewer's sieve into a deep lake, grab it by the corners, and drag it to and fro and round about! Taking him on in debate, I'll shake him down and about, and give him a beating, like a strong brewer's mixer would grab a strainer by the corners and shake it down and about and give it a beating! I'll play a game of ear-washing with the ascetic Gotama, like a sixty-year-old elephant would plunge into a deep lotus pond and play a game of ear-washing! Come forth, good Licchavīs, come forth! Today I am going to have a discussion with the ascetic Gotama."

At that, some of the Licchavis said, "How can the ascetic Gotama refute Saccaka's doctrine, when it is Saccaka who will refute Gotama's doctrine?"

But some of the Licchavis said, "Who is Saccaka to refute the Buddha's doctrine, when it is the Buddha who will refute Saccaka's doctrine?"

Then Saccaka, escorted by the five hundred Licchavis, went to the hall with the peaked roof in the Great Wood.

At that time several people were walking mindfully in the open air. Then Saccaka went up to them and said, "Good sirs, where is Mister Gotama at present? For we want to see him."

"Aggivessana, the Buddha has plunged deep into the Great Wood and is sitting at the root of a tree for simply resting during the day."

Then Saccaka, together with a large group of Licchavis, went to see the Buddha in the Great Wood, and exchanged greetings with him. When the greetings and polite conversation were over, he sat down to one side. Before sitting down to one side, some of the Licchavīs bowed, some exchanged greetings and polite conversation, some held up their joined palms toward the Buddha, some announced their name and clan, while some kept silent.

Then Saccaka said to the Buddha, "I'd like to ask Mister Gotama about a certain point, if you'd take the time to answer."

"Ask what you wish, Aggivessana."

"How does Mister Gotama guide his disciples? And on what topics does instruction to his disciples generally proceed?"

"This is how I guide my disciples, and my instructions to disciples generally proceed on these topics: 'Form, feeling, perception, choices, and consciousness are impermanent. Form, feeling, perception, choices, and consciousness are not-self. All conditions are impermanent. All things are not-self.' This is how I guide my disciples, and how instruction to my disciples generally proceeds."

"A simile strikes me, Mister Gotama."

"Then speak as you feel inspired," said the Buddha.

"All the plants and seeds that achieve growth, increase, and maturity do so depending on the earth and grounded on the earth. All the hard work that gets done depends on the earth and is grounded on the earth.

In the same way, an individual's self is form. Grounded on form they create merit and wickedness. An individual's self is feeling … perception … choices … consciousness. Grounded on consciousness they create merit and wickedness."

"Aggivessana, are you not saying this: 'Form is myself, feeling is myself, perception is myself, choices are myself, consciousness is myself'?"

"Indeed, Mister Gotama, that is what I am saying. And this big crowd agrees with me!"

"What has this big crowd to do with you? Please just unpack your own statement."

"Then, Mister Gotama, what I am saying is this: 'Form is myself, feeling is myself, perception is myself, choices are myself, consciousness is myself'."

"Well then, Aggivessana, I'll ask you about this in return, and you can answer as you like. What do you think, Aggivessana? Consider an anointed aristocratic king such as Pasenadi of Kosala or Ajātasattu of Magadha, son of the princess of Videha. Would they have the power in their own realm to execute those who have incurred execution, fine those who have incurred fines, or banish those who have incurred banishment?"

"An anointed king would have such power, Mister Gotama. Even federations such as the Vajjis and Mallas have such power in their own realm. So of course, an anointed king such as Pasenadi or Ajātasattu would wield such power, as is their right."

"What do you think, Aggivessana? When you say, 'Form is myself,' do you have power over that form to say: 'May my form be like this! May it not be like that'?" When he said this, Saccaka kept silent. The Buddha asked the question a second time, but Saccaka still kept silent. So the Buddha said to Saccaka, "Answer now, Aggivessana. Now is not the time for silence. If someone fails to answer a legitimate question when asked three times by the Buddha, their head explodes into seven pieces there and then."

Now at that time the spirit Vajirapāṇī, taking up a burning iron thunderbolt, blazing and glowing, stood in the air above Saccaka, thinking, "If this Saccaka doesn't answer when asked a third time, I'll blow his head into seven pieces there and then!" And both the Buddha and Saccaka could see Vajirapāṇī.

Saccaka was terrified, shocked, and awestruck. Looking to the Buddha for shelter, protection, and refuge, he said, "Ask me, Mister Gotama. I will answer."

"What do you think, Aggivessana? When you say, 'Form is myself,' do you have power over that form to say: 'May my form be like this! May it not be like that'?"

"No, Mister Gotama."

"Think about it, Aggivessana! You should think before answering. What you said before and what you said after don't match up. What do you think, Aggivessana? When you say, 'Feeling is myself,' do you have power over that feeling to say: 'May my feeling be like this! May it not be like that'?"

"No, Mister Gotama."

"Think about it, Aggivessana! You should think before answering. What you said before and what you said after don't match up. What do you think, Aggivessana? When you say, 'Perception is myself,' do you have power over that perception to say: 'May my perception be like this! May it not be like that'?"

"No, Mister Gotama."

"Think about it, Aggivessana! You should think before answering. What you said before and what you said after don't match up. What do you think, Aggivessana? When you say, 'Choices are myself,' do you have power over those choices to say: 'May my choices be like this! May they not be like that'?"

"No, Mister Gotama."

"Think about it, Aggivessana! You should think before answering. What you said before and what you said after don't match up. What do you think, Aggivessana? When you say, 'Consciousness is myself,' do you have power over that consciousness to say: 'May my consciousness be like this! May it not be like that'?"

"No, Mister Gotama."

"Think about it, Aggivessana! You should think before answering. What you said before and what you said after don't match up. What do you think, Aggivessana? Is form permanent or impermanent?"

"Impermanent."

"But if it's impermanent, is it suffering or happiness?"

"Suffering."

"But if it's impermanent, suffering, and perishable, is it fit to be regarded thus: 'This is mine, I am this, this is my self'?"

"No, Mister Gotama."

"What do you think, Aggivessana? Is feeling ... perception ... choices ... consciousness permanent or impermanent?"

"Impermanent."

"But if it's impermanent, is it suffering or happiness?"

"Suffering."

"But if it's impermanent, suffering, and perishable, is it fit to be regarded thus: 'This is mine, I am this, this is my self'?"

"No, Mister Gotama."

"What do you think, Aggivessana? Consider someone who resorts, draws near, and clings to suffering, regarding it thus: 'This is mine, I am this, this is my self.' Would such a person be able to completely understand suffering themselves, or live having wiped out suffering?"

"How could they? No, Mister Gotama."

"What do you think, Aggivessana? This being so, aren't you someone who resorts, draws near, and clings to suffering, regarding it thus: 'This is mine, I am this, this is my self'?"

"How could I not? Yes, Mister Gotama."

"Suppose, Aggivessana, there was a person in need of heartwood. Wandering in search of heartwood, they'd take a sharp axe and enter a forest. There they'd see a big banana tree, straight and young and grown free of defects. They'd cut it down at the base, cut off the top, and unroll the coiled sheaths. But they wouldn't even find sapwood, much less heartwood.

In the same way, when pursued, pressed, and grilled by me on your own doctrine, you turn out to be vacuous, hollow, and mistaken. But it was you who stated before the assembly of Vesālī: 'I don't see any ascetic or brahmin who would not shake and rock and tremble, sweating from the armpits, were I to take them on in debate—not a leader of an order or a community, or the tutor of a community, and not even one who claims to be an enlightened being in various spiritual paths.

Even an insentient post would shake, and rock and tremble were I to take it on in debate. How much more then a human being!' But sweat is pouring from your forehead; it's soaked through your robe and drips on the ground. While I now have no sweat on my body." So the Buddha revealed his golden body to the assembly. When this was said, Saccaka sat silent, dismayed, shoulders drooping, downcast, depressed, with nothing to say.

Knowing this, the Licchavi Dummukha said to the Buddha, "A simile strikes me, Blessed One."

"Then speak as you feel inspired," said the Buddha.

"Sir, suppose there was a lotus pond not far from a town or village, and a crab lived there. Then several boys or girls would leave the town or village and go to the pond, where they'd pull out the crab and put it on dry land. Whenever that crab extended a claw, those boys or girls would snap, crack, and break it off with a stick or a stone.

And when that crab's claws had all been snapped, cracked, and broken off it wouldn't be able to return down into that lotus pond. In the same way, sir, the Buddha has snapped, cracked, and broken off all Saccaka's twists, ducks, and dodges. Now he can't get near the Buddha again looking for a debate."

But Saccaka said to him, "Hold on, Dummukha, hold on! I wasn't talking with you; I was talking with Mister Gotama.

Mister Gotama, leave aside that statement I made—as did various other ascetics and brahmins—it was, like, just a bit of nonsense. How do you define a disciple of Mister Gotama who follows instructions and responds to advice; who has gone beyond doubt, got rid of indecision, gained assurance, and is independent of others in the Teacher's instructions?"

"It's when one of my disciples truly sees any kind of form at all—past, future, or present; internal or external; solid or subtle; inferior or superior; far or near: *all* form—with right understanding: 'This is not mine, I am not this, this is not myself.'

They truly see any kind of feeling ... perception ... choices ... consciousness at all—past, future, or present; internal or external; solid or subtle; inferior or superior; far or near: *all* consciousness—with right understanding: 'This is not mine, I am not this, this is not myself.' That's how to define one of my disciples who follows instructions and responds to advice, who has gone beyond doubt, got rid of indecision, gained assurance, and is independent of others in the Teacher's instructions."

"But how do you define a person who is a perfected one, Arahant with defilements ended, who has completed the spiritual journey, done what had to be done, laid down the burden, achieved their own true goal, utterly ended the fetter of continued existence, and is rightly freed through enlightenment?"

"It's when a person truly sees any kind of form at all—past, future, or present; internal or external; coarse or fine; inferior or superior; far or near: *all* form—with right understanding: 'This is not mine, I am not this, this is not myself.' And having seen this with right understanding they're freed by not grasping. They truly see any kind of feeling ... perception ... choices ... consciousness at all—past, future, or present; internal or external; solid or subtle; inferior or superior; far or near: *all* consciousness—with right understanding: 'This is not mine, I am not this, this is not myself.'

And having seen this with right understanding they're freed by not grasping. That's how to define a person who is a perfected one, with defilements ended, who has completed the spiritual journey, done what had to be done, laid down the burden, achieved their own true goal, utterly ended the fetter of continued existence, and is rightly freed through four-fold nibbana.

A person whose mind is freed like this has three unsurpassable qualities: unsurpassable seeing, practice, and freedom. They honor, respect, esteem, and venerate only the Realized One: 'The Blessed One is awakened, tamed, serene, crossed over, and quenched. And he teaches Dhamma for awakening, self-control, serenity, crossing over, and extinguishment.'"

When he had spoken, Saccaka said to him, "Mister Gotama, it was rude and impudent of me to imagine I could attack you in debate. For a person might find safety after attacking a rutting elephant, but not after attacking Mister Gotama. A person might find safety after attacking a blazing mass of fire, but not after attacking Mister Gotama.

They might find safety after attacking a poisonous viper, but not after attacking Mister Gotama. It was rude and impudent of me to imagine I could attack you in debate. Would Mister Gotama together with the community of Saṅgha please accept tomorrow's meal from me?" The Buddha consented with silence.

Then, knowing that the Buddha had consented, Saccaka addressed those Licchavis, "Listen, gentlemen. I have invited the ascetic Gotama together with the Saṅgha for tomorrow's meal. You may all bring me what you think is suitable."

Then, when the night had passed, those Licchavis presented Saccaka with an offering of five hundred servings of food. And Saccaka had delicious fresh and cooked foods prepared in his own park. Then he had the Buddha informed of the time, saying, "It's time, Mister Gotama, the meal is ready."

Then the Buddha robed up in the morning and, taking his bowl and robe, went to Saccaka's park, where he sat on the seat spread out, together with the Saṅgha. Then Saccaka served and satisfied the Saṅgha headed by the Buddha with his own hands with delicious fresh and cooked foods. When the Buddha had eaten and washed his hand and bowl, Saccaka took a low seat and sat to one side.

Then Saccaka said to the Buddha, "Mister Gotama, may the merit and the growth of merit in this gift be for the happiness of the donors."

"Aggivessana, whatever comes from giving to a recipient of a religious donation such as yourself—who is not free of greed, hate, and delusion—will accrue to the donors. Whatever comes from giving to a recipient of a religious donation such as myself—who is free of greed, hate, and delusion—will accrue to you."

Chapter 38

Middle Discourses 36: Mahāsaccakasutta

The Longer Discourse with Saccaka

This discourse records a discussion between Buddha and Saccaka. Saccaka follows a spiritual path different from that of Buddha's path. He said there are some practitioners who love a spiritual life and are committed to enduring physical pain without developing their minds. They suffer mentally when something physical goes wrong. Someone he knows they were paralyzed in tights; blood was coming out of their mouth, they went insane and lost their mind. Their body was subject to their mind. The mind had power over the body, and that is because they didn't develop their mind.

Saccaka says; it must be that Mister Gotama's path and disciples live committed to developing the mind without developing physical endurance.

Buddha asks from Aggivessana, what do you mean by enduring physical pain?

Aggivessana says; some people take extreme practices. Some go and walk on hard surfaces without shoes. Some without dresses, a person takes cold water baths and live in cold places without a dress, eating very little. Some practitioners might live a life that causes pain to the body and physical suffering.

In response, Buddha asks again, do they go on by always eating very little? To which Aggivessana replies, saying, that sometimes, they want a lot.

Then Buddha says that such physical endurance is not noble endurance and explains how to describe a person who is not developed in physique and mind; Take an ordinary person who experiences feelings. They grasp into feelings, both physically and mentally, meaning that for what they experience physically through sensory information, they either start liking or disliking such an experience too much. Such desires make one experience lust or suffer. When they experience lust or suffering, they continue to think more and more about it and develop an attachment with an underlying tendency to think such things should/should not happen. They experience both pleasant and painful feelings physically and in their mind.

On the other hand, in the case of an Arahant, they don't grasp pleasant or painful feelings when they experience physical pain, and they don't suffer in mind.

As they have developed physical endurance by not giving too much value/importance to such thoughts related to physical endurance by understanding impermanence without a doubt, pleasant feelings are not given a value/importance to such thoughts related to feelings by understanding impermanence without a doubt. When someone's mind is not affected too much by pleasant or painful feelings, they are free from the mental pain arising from such things, and they have developed physically and mentally.

Thereafter, Buddha explained to him that before gaining Buddhahood, he had tried all the hardships and techniques that were commonly adopted by spiritual practitioners of those times. Realizing that such practices don't lead to Nibbana, he found his own way. For example, jhana practice through conscious concentration was practiced by Prince Siddharta's (before gaining Buddhahood) teachers; Āḷāra Kālāma and Uddaka son of Rāma. Prince Siddhartha practiced hard ways, suppressing his mind, greed, hate delusion through his mind's conscious efforts, mindfulness in breathing, cutting off breath, taking no food, and several other ways of enduring suffering and realized such practices are not leading to cessation; Nibbana. Buddha says that eventually, having tried all the common ways, such practices will make a person tired and weary with no fruition whatsoever. Having tried all the common ways, he finally recalled how he concentrated as a child under a tree. He established his focus on the path that he's known since he was a child. On that occasion, his mind went through jhanas that naturally occur before Arahantship, Buddhahood was gained. As he was paying attention to childhood practice, naturally at that occasion, Prince Siddhartha experienced transformation in a mental continuum; Arahantship and ability to recollect past lives, death and birth of sentient beings, and understanding that cessation Nibbana gained, and came to understand rebirth is ended, Buddhahood is achieved, done all that needs doing.

Furthermore, Buddha says; I speak about the path to others but don't grasp into what I say. My mind remains free. Aggivessana asks; do you sleep during the day? To which Buddha responded, saying yes, and Aggivessana says that sleeping during the day is deluded abiding. Buddha explains to him that deluded abiding is not what he describes. It is one who thinks self is permanent in a deluded abiding and grasping fetters.

Often, it is easier to misunderstand Dhamma, yet people mix up and misinterpret four-fold Nibbana, and the basics should always be remembered by a spiritual practitioner who aspires to Nibbana: Nibbana is a universal happening, and the path leading to four-fold Nibbana is wisdom and merit-based.

"So I have heard. At one time the Buddha was staying near Vesālī, at the Great Wood, in the hall with the peaked roof.

Now at that time in the morning the Buddha, being properly dressed, took his bowl and robe, wishing to enter Vesālī for alms.

Then as Saccaka, the son of Jain parents, was going for a walk he approached the hall with the peaked roof in the Great Wood. A Sotapanna, Ānanda saw him coming off in the distance, and said to the Buddha, "Venerable sir, Saccaka, the son of Jain parents, is coming. He's a debater and clever speaker deemed holy by many people. He wants to discredit the Buddha, the teaching, and the Saṅgha. Please, sir, sit for an hour out of sympathy." The Buddha sat on the seat spread out.

Then Saccaka went up to the Buddha and exchanged greetings with him. When the greetings and polite conversation were over, he sat down to one side and said to the Buddha,

"Mister Gotama, there are some ascetics and brahmins who live committed to the practice of developing physical endurance, without developing the mind. They suffer painful physical feelings. This happened to someone once. Their thighs became paralyzed, their heart burst, hot blood gushed from their mouth, and they went mad and lost their mind. Their mind was subject to the body, and the body had power over it.

Why is that? Because their mind was not developed. There are some ascetics and brahmins who live committed to the practice of developing the mind, without developing physical endurance. They suffer painful mental feelings. This happened to someone once. Their thighs became paralyzed, their heart burst, hot blood gushed from their mouth, and they went mad and lost their mind. Their body was subject to the mind, and the mind had power over it. Why is that? Because their physical endurance was not developed. It occurs to me that Mister Gotama's disciples must live committed to the practice of developing the mind, without developing physical endurance."

"But Aggivessana, what have you heard about the development of physical endurance?"

"Take, for example, Nanda Vaccha, Kisa Saṅkicca, and the bamboo-staffed ascetic Gosāla. They go naked, ignoring conventions. They lick their hands, and don't come or wait when called. They don't consent to food brought to them, or food prepared on their behalf, or an invitation for a meal. They don't receive anything from a pot or bowl; or from someone who keeps sheep, or who has a weapon or a shovel in their home; or where a couple is eating; or where there is a woman who is pregnant, breastfeeding, or who has a man in her home; or where there's a dog waiting or flies buzzing.

They accept no fish or meat or liquor or wine and drink no beer. They go to just one house for alms, taking just one mouthful, or two houses and two mouthfuls, up to seven houses and seven mouthfuls. They feed on one saucer a day, two saucers a day, up to seven saucers a day. They eat once a day, once every second day, up to once a week, and so on, even up to once a fortnight. They live committed to the practice of eating food at set intervals."

"But Aggivessana, do they get by on so little?"

"No, Mister Gotama. Sometimes they eat luxury fresh and cooked foods and drink a variety of luxury beverages. They gather their body's strength, build it up, and get fat."

"What they earlier gave up, they later got back. That is how there is the increase and decrease of this body. But Aggivessana, what have you heard about development of the mind?" When Saccaka was questioned by the Buddha about development of the mind, he was stumped.

So the Buddha said to Saccaka, "The development of physical endurance that you have described is not the legitimate development of physical endurance in the noble one's training. And since you don't even understand the development of physical endurance, how can you possibly understand the development of the mind? Still, as to how someone is undeveloped in physical endurance and mind, and how someone is developed in physical endurance and mind, listen and apply your mind well, I will speak."

"Yes, sir," replied Saccaka. The Buddha said this:

"And how is someone undeveloped in physical endurance and mind? Take an unlearned ordinary person who has a pleasant feeling. When they experience a pleasant feeling, they become full of lust for it. Then that pleasant feeling ceases. And when it ceases, a painful feeling arises.

When they suffer painful feeling, they sorrow and wail and lament, beating their breast and falling into confusion. Because their physical endurance is undeveloped, pleasant feelings occupy the mind. And because their mind is undeveloped, painful feelings occupy the mind. Anyone whose mind is occupied by both pleasant and painful feelings like this is undeveloped both in physical endurance and in mind.

And how is someone developed in physical endurance and mind? Take a learned noble disciple who has a pleasant feeling. When they experience a pleasant feeling, they don't become full of lust for it. Then that pleasant feeling ceases. And when it ceases, painful feeling arises. When they suffer painful feelings, they don't sorrow or wail or lament, beating their breast and falling into confusion. Because their physical endurance is developed, pleasant feelings don't occupy the mind. And because their mind is developed, painful feelings don't occupy the mind. Anyone whose mind is not occupied by both pleasant and painful feelings like this is developed both in physical endurance and in mind."

"I am quite confident that Mister Gotama is developed in physical endurance and in mind."

"Your words are clearly invasive and intrusive, Aggivessana. Nevertheless, I will answer you. Ever since I shaved off my hair and beard, dressed in ocher robes, and went forth from the lay life to homelessness, it has not been possible for any pleasant or painful feeling to occupy my mind."

"Mister Gotama mustn't have experienced the kind of pleasant or painful feelings that would occupy the mind."

"How could I not, Aggivessana? Before my awakening—when I was still unawakened but intent on awakening—I thought: 'Life at home is cramped and dirty, life gone forth is wide open. It's not easy for someone living at home to practice a spiritual life utterly full and pure, like a polished shell. Why don't I leave home, and seek spiritual paths?'

Some time later, while still with pristine black hair, blessed with youth, in the prime of life—though my mother and father wished otherwise, weeping with tearful faces—I went away from home in search of a spiritual life, a spiritual practice while promising to return after finding the path.

I was seeking a spiritual practice, to discover what is skillful, seeking the supreme state of sublime peace. I approached Āḷāra Kālāma and said to him, 'Reverend Kālāma, I wish to lead the spiritual life in this teaching and training.'

Āḷāra Kālāma replied, 'Stay, respected sir. This teaching is such that a sensible person can soon realize their own tradition with their own insight and live having achieved it.'

I quickly memorized that teaching. As far as lip-recital and verbal repetition went, I spoke the doctrine of knowledge, the elder doctrine. I claimed to know and see, and so did others.

Then it occurred to me, 'It is not solely by mere faith that Āḷāra Kālāma declares: "I realize this teaching with my own insight, and live having achieved it." Surely he meditates knowing and seeing this teaching.'

So I approached Āḷāra Kālāma and said to him, 'Reverend Kālāma, to what extent do you say you've realized this teaching with your own insight?' When I said this, he declared the dimension of nothingness.

Then it occurred to me, 'It's not just Āḷāra Kālāma who has faith, energy, mindfulness, immersion, and wisdom; I too have these things. Why don't I make an effort to realize the same teaching that Āḷāra Kālāma says he has realized with his own insight?' I quickly realized that teaching with my own insight and lived having achieved it.

So I approached Āḷāra Kālāma and said to him, 'Reverend Kālāma, is it up to this point that you realized this teaching with your own insight, and declare having achieved it?'

'I have, reverend.'

'I too have realized this teaching with my own insight up to this point, and live having achieved it.'

'We are fortunate, reverend, so very fortunate to see a venerable such as yourself as one of our spiritual companions! So the teaching that I've realized with my own insight, and declare having achieved it, you've realized with your own insight, and dwell having achieved it. The teaching that you've realized with your own insight, and dwell having achieved it, I've realized with my own insight, and declare having achieved it. So the teaching that I know, you know, and the teaching you know, I know. I am like you and you are like me.

Come now, reverend! We should both lead this community together.' And that is how my tutor Āḷāra Kālāma placed me, his pupil, on the same position as him, and honored me with lofty praise.

Then it occurred to me, 'This teaching doesn't lead to disillusionment, dispassion, cessation, peace, insight, awakening, and extinguishment. It only leads as far as rebirth in the dimension of nothingness.' Realizing that this teaching was inadequate, I left disappointed.

I set out to discover what is skillful, seeking the supreme state of sublime peace. I approached Uddaka son of Rāma and said to him, 'Reverend, I wish to lead the spiritual life in this teaching and training.'

Uddaka replied, 'Stay, respected sir. This teaching is such that a sensible person can soon realize their own tradition with their own insight and live having achieved it.'

I quickly memorized that teaching. As far as lip-recital and verbal repetition went, I spoke the doctrine of knowledge, the elder doctrine. I claimed to know and see, and so did others.

Then it occurred to me, 'It is not solely by mere faith that Rāma declared: "I realize this teaching with my own insight, and live having achieved it." Surely he meditated knowing and seeing this teaching.'

So I approached Uddaka son of Rāma and said to him, 'Reverend, to what extent did Rāma say he'd realized this teaching with his own insight?' When I said this, Uddaka son of Rāma declared the dimension of neither perception nor non-perception.

Then it occurred to me, 'It's not just Rāma who had faith, energy, mindfulness, immersion, and wisdom; I too have these things. Why don't I make an effort to realize the same teaching that Rāma said he had realized with his own insight?' I quickly realized that teaching with my own insight, and lived having achieved it.

So I approached Uddaka son of Rāma and said to him, 'Reverend, had Rāma realized this teaching with his own insight up to this point, and declared having achieved it?'

'He had, reverend.'

'I too have realized this teaching with my own insight up to this point, and live having achieved it.'

'We are fortunate, reverend, so very fortunate to see a venerable such as yourself as one of our spiritual companions! The teaching that Rāma had realized with his own insight, and declared having achieved it, you have realized with your own insight, and dwell having achieved it. The teaching that you've realized with your own insight, and dwell having achieved it, Rāma had realized with his own insight, and declared having achieved it.

So the teaching that Rāma directly knew, you know, and the teaching you know, Rāma directly knew. Rāma was like you and you are like Rāma. Come now, reverend! You should lead this community.' And that is how my spiritual companion Uddaka son of Rāma placed me in the position of a tutor and honored me with lofty praise.

Then it occurred to me, 'This teaching doesn't lead to disillusionment, dispassion, cessation, peace, insight, awakening, and extinguishment. It only leads as far as rebirth in the dimension of neither perception nor non-perception.' Realizing that this teaching was inadequate, I left disappointed.

I set out to discover what is skillful, seeking the supreme state of sublime peace. Traveling stage by stage in the Magadhan lands, I arrived at Senānigama in Uruvelā. There I saw a delightful park, a lovely grove with a flowing river that was clean and charming, with smooth banks. And nearby was a village to go for alms.

Then it occurred to me, 'This park is truly delightful, a lovely grove with a flowing river that's clean and charming, with smooth banks. And nearby there's a village to go for alms. This is good enough for striving for a gentleman wanting to strive.' So I sat down right there, thinking: 'This is good enough for striving.'

And then these three similes, which were neither supernaturally inspired, nor learned before in the past, occurred to me. Suppose there was a green, sappy log, and it was lying in water. Then a person comes along with a drill-stick, thinking to light a fire and produce heat. What do you think, Aggivessana? By drilling the stick against that green, sappy log lying in the water, could they light a fire and produce heat?"

"No, Mister Gotama. Why not? Because it's a green, sappy log, and it's lying in the water. That person will eventually get weary and frustrated."

"In the same way, there are ascetics and brahmins who don't live withdrawn in body and mind from sensual pleasures. They haven't internally given up or stilled desire, affection, infatuation, thirst, and passion for sensual pleasures.

Regardless of whether or not they feel painful, sharp, severe, acute feelings due to overexertion, they are incapable of knowledge and vision, of supreme awakening. This was the first example that occurred to me.

Then a second example occurred to me. Suppose there was a green, sappy log, and it was lying on dry land far from the water. Then a person comes along with a drill-stick, thinking to light a fire and produce heat. What do you think, Aggivessana? By drilling the stick against that green, sappy log on dry land far from water, could they light a fire and produce heat?"

"No, Mister Gotama. Why not? Because it's still a green, sappy log, despite the fact that it's lying on dry land far from water. That person will eventually get weary and frustrated."

"In the same way, there are ascetics and brahmins who live withdrawn in body and mind from sensual pleasures. But they haven't internally given up or stilled desire, affection, infatuation, thirst, and passion for sensual pleasures. Regardless of whether or not they suffer painful, sharp, severe, acute feelings due to overexertion, they are incapable of knowledge and vision, of supreme awakening. This was the second example that occurred to me.

Then a third example occurred to me. Suppose there was a dried up, withered log, and it was lying on dry land far from the water. Then a person comes along with a drill-stick, thinking to light a fire and produce heat. What do you think, Aggivessana? By drilling the stick against that dried up, withered log on dry land far from water, could they light a fire and produce heat?"

"Yes, Mister Gotama. Why is that? Because it's a dried up, withered log, and it's lying on dry land far from water."

"In the same way, there are ascetics and brahmins who live withdrawn in body and mind from sensual pleasures. And they have internally given up and stilled desire, affection, infatuation, thirst, and passion for sensual pleasures. Regardless of whether or not they suffer painful, sharp, severe, acute feelings due to overexertion, they are capable of knowledge and vision, of supreme awakening. This was the third example that occurred to me. These are the three similes, which were neither supernaturally inspired, nor learned before in the past, that occurred to me.

Then it occurred to me, 'Why don't I, with teeth clenched and tongue pressed against the roof of my mouth, squeeze, squash, and scorch mind with mind?' So that's what I did, until sweat ran from my armpits. It was like when a strong man grabs a weaker man by the head or throat or shoulder and squeezes, squashes, and crushes them.

In the same way, with teeth clenched and tongue pressed against the roof of my mouth, I squeezed, squashed, and crushed mind with mind until sweat ran from my armpits. My energy was roused up and unflagging, and my mindfulness was established and lucid, but my body was disturbed, not tranquil, because I'd pushed too hard with that painful striving. But even such painful feeling did not occupy my mind.

Then it occurred to me, 'Why don't I practice the breathless absorption?' So I cut off my breathing through my mouth and nose. But then winds came out my ears making a loud noise, like the puffing of a blacksmith's bellows. My energy was roused up and unflagging, and my mindfulness was established and lucid, but my body was disturbed, not tranquil, because I'd pushed too hard with that painful striving. But even such painful feeling did not occupy my mind.

Then it occurred to me, 'Why don't I keep practicing the breathless absorption?' So I cut off my breathing through my mouth and nose and ears. But then strong winds ground my head, like a strong man was drilling into my head with a sharp point. My energy was roused up and unflagging, and my mindfulness was established and lucid, but my body was disturbed, not tranquil, because I'd pushed too hard with that painful striving. But even such painful feeling did not occupy my mind.

Then it occurred to me, 'Why don't I keep practicing the breathless absorption?' So I cut off my breathing through my mouth and nose and ears. But then I got a severe headache, like a strong man was tightening a tough leather strap around my head. My energy was roused up and unflagging, and my mindfulness was established and lucid, but my body was disturbed, not tranquil, because I'd pushed too hard with that painful striving. But even such painful feeling did not occupy my mind.

Then it occurred to me, 'Why don't I keep practicing the breathless absorption?' So I cut off my breathing through my mouth and nose and ears. But then strong winds carved up my belly, like a deft butcher or their apprentice was slicing my belly open with a sharp meat cleaver. My energy was roused up and unflagging, and my mindfulness was established and lucid, but my body was disturbed, not tranquil, because I'd pushed too hard with that painful striving. But even such painful feeling did not occupy my mind.

Then it occurred to me, 'Why don't I keep practicing the breathless absorption?' So I cut off my breathing through my mouth and nose and ears. But then there was an intense burning in my body, like two strong men grabbing a weaker man by the arms to burn and scorch him on a pit of glowing coals. My energy was roused up and unflagging, and my mindfulness was established and lucid, but my body was disturbed, not tranquil, because

I'd pushed too hard with that painful striving. But even such painful feeling did not occupy my mind.

Then some deities saw me and said, 'The ascetic Gotama is dead.' Others said, 'He's not dead, but he's dying.' Others said, 'He's not dead or dying. The ascetic Gotama is a perfected one, for that is how the perfected ones live.'

Then it occurred to me, 'Why don't I practice completely cutting off food?' But deities came to me and said, 'Good sir, don't practice totally cutting off food. If you do, we'll infuse heavenly nectar into your pores and you will live on that.' Then I thought, 'If I claim to be completely fasting while these deities are infusing heavenly nectar in my pores, that would be a lie on my part.' So I dismissed those deities, saying, 'There's no need.'

Then it occurred to me, 'Why don't I just take a little bit of food each time, a cup of broth made from mung beans, horse gram, chickpeas, or green gram?' So that's what I did, until my body became extremely emaciated. Due to eating so little, my major and minor limbs became like the joints of an eighty-year-old or a dying man, my bottom became like a camel's hoof, my vertebrae stuck out like beads on a string, and my ribs were as gaunt as the broken-down rafters on an old barn. Due to eating so little, the gleam of my eyes sank deep in their sockets, like the gleam of water sunk deep down a well. Due to eating so little, my scalp shriveled and withered like a green bitter-gourd in the wind and sun.

Due to eating so little, the skin of my belly stuck to my backbone, so that when I tried to rub the skin of my belly I grabbed my backbone, and when I tried to rub my backbone I rubbed the skin of my belly. Due to eating so little, when I tried to urinate or defecate I fell face down right there. Due to eating so little, when I tried to relieve my body by rubbing my limbs with my hands, the hair, rotted at its roots, fell out.

Then some people saw me and said: 'The ascetic Gotama is black.' Some said: 'He's not black, he's brown.' Some said: 'He's neither black nor brown. The ascetic Gotama has tawny skin.' That's how far the pure, bright complexion of my skin had been ruined by taking so little food.

Then I thought, 'Whatever ascetics and brahmins have experienced painful, sharp, severe, acute feelings due to overexertion—whether in the past, future, or present—this is as far as it goes, no-one has done more than this. But I have not achieved any superhuman distinction in knowledge and vision worthy of the noble ones by this severe, grueling work. Could there be another path to awakening?'

Then it occurred to me, 'I recall sitting in the cool shade of a black plum tree while my father the Sakyan was off working. Quite secluded from sensual pleasures, secluded from unskillful qualities, I entered and remained in the first absorption, which has the rapture and bliss born of seclusion, while placing the mind and keeping it connected. Could that be the path to awakening?'

Stemming from that memory came the realization: '*That* is the path to awakening!'

Then it occurred to me, 'Why am I afraid of that pleasure, for it has nothing to do with sensual pleasures or unskillful qualities?' Then I thought, 'I'm not afraid of that pleasure, for it has nothing to do with sensual pleasures or unskillful qualities.'

Then I thought, 'I can't achieve that pleasure with a body so excessively emaciated. Why don't I eat some solid food, some rice and porridge?' So I ate some solid food.

Now at that time the five friends were attending on me, thinking, 'The ascetic Gotama will tell us of any truth that he realizes.' But when I ate some solid food, they left disappointed in me, saying, 'The ascetic Gotama has become indulgent; he has strayed from the struggle and returned to indulgence.'

After eating solid food and gathering my strength, quite secluded from sensual pleasures, secluded from unskillful qualities, I entered and remained in the first absorption (gained anagami state and experienced absorption), which has the rapture and bliss born of seclusion, while placing the mind and keeping it connected. But even such pleasant feeling did not occupy my mind.

As the placing of the mind and keeping it connected were stilled, I entered and remained in the second absorption, which has the rapture and bliss born of immersion, with internal clarity and mind at one, without placing the mind and keeping it connected. But even such pleasant feeling did not occupy my mind.

And with the fading away of rapture, I entered and remained in the third absorption, where I experience equanimity, mindfulness and awareness, personally experiencing the bliss of which the noble ones declare, 'Equanimous and mindful, one experience bliss.' But even such pleasant feeling did not occupy my mind. With the giving up of pleasure and pain, and the ending of former happiness and sadness, I entered and remained in the fourth absorption, without pleasure or pain, with pure equanimity and mindfulness. But even such pleasant feeling did not occupy my mind.

When my mind had immersed in noble concentration like this—purified, bright, flawless, rid of corruptions, pliable, workable, steady, and imperturbable—I extended it toward recollection of past lives. I recollected my many kinds of past lives, with features and details.

This was the first knowledge, which I achieved in the first watch of the night. Ignorance was destroyed and knowledge arose; darkness was destroyed and light arose, as happens for a person who is diligent, keen, and resolute. But even such pleasant feeling did not occupy my mind.

When my mind had immersed in noble concentration like this—purified, bright, flawless, rid of corruptions, pliable, workable, steady, and imperturbable—I extended it toward knowledge of the death and rebirth of sentient beings. With clairvoyance that is purified and superhuman, I saw sentient beings passing away and being reborn—inferior and superior, beautiful and ugly, in a good place or a bad place. I understood how sentient beings are reborn according to their deeds.

This was the second knowledge, which I achieved in the middle watch of the night. Ignorance was destroyed and knowledge arose; darkness was destroyed and light arose, as happens for a person who is diligent, keen, and resolute. But even such pleasant feeling did not occupy my mind.

When my mind had immersed in noble concentration like this—purified, bright, flawless, rid of corruptions, pliable, workable, steady, and imperturbable—I extended it toward knowledge of the ending of defilements. I truly understood: 'This is suffering' … 'This is the origin of suffering' … 'This is the cessation of suffering' … 'This is the practice that leads to the cessation of suffering.' I truly understood: 'These are defilements' … 'This is the origin of defilements' … 'This is the cessation of defilements' … 'This is the practice that leads to the cessation of defilements.'

Knowing and seeing like this, my mind was freed from the defilements of sensuality, desire to be reborn, and ignorance. When it was freed, I knew it was freed.

I understood: 'Rebirth is ended; the spiritual journey has been completed; what had to be done has been done; there is nothing further for this place.'

This was the third knowledge, which I achieved in the last watch of the night. Ignorance was destroyed and knowledge arose; darkness was destroyed and light arose, as happens for a person who is diligent, keen, and resolute. But even such pleasant feeling did not occupy my mind.

Aggivessana, I recall teaching the Dhamma to an assembly of many hundreds, and each person thought that I was teaching the Dhamma especially for them. But it should not be seen like this. The Realized One teaches others only so that they can understand.

When that talk was finished, I stilled, settled, unified, and immersed my mind in samādhi internally, experiencing blissful nibbana and various mind states (jhanas in noble path including seeing past, birth of beings etc.)."

"I'd believe that of Mister Gotama, just like a perfected one, a fully awakened Buddha. But do you ever recall sleeping during the day?"

"I do recall that in the last month of the summer, I have spread out my outer robe folded in four and lain down in the lion's posture—on the right side, placing one foot on top of the other—mindful and aware."

"Some ascetics and brahmins call that a deluded abiding."

"That's not how to define whether someone is deluded or not. But as to how to define whether someone is deluded or not, listen and apply your mind well, I will speak."

"Yes, sir," replied Saccaka.

The Buddha said this: "Anyone who has not given up the defilements that are corrupting, leading to future lives, hurtful, resulting in suffering and future rebirth, old age, and death is deluded, I say. For it's not giving up the defilements that makes you deluded. Anyone who has given up the defilements that are corrupting, leading to future lives, hurtful, resulting in suffering and future rebirth, old age, and death—is not deluded, I say. For it's giving up the defilements that makes you not deluded.

The Realized One has given up the defilements that are corrupting, leading to future lives, hurtful, resulting in suffering and future rebirth, old age, and death. He has cut them off at the root, made them like a palm stump, obliterated them so they are unable to arise in the future. Just as a palm tree with its crown cut off is incapable of further growth, in the same way, the Realized One has given up the defilements so they are unable to arise in the future."

When he had spoken, Saccaka said to him, "It's incredible, Mister Gotama, it's amazing! How when Mister Gotama is repeatedly attacked with inappropriate and intrusive criticism, the complexion of his skin brightens and the color of his face becomes clear, just like a perfected one, a fully awakened Buddha! I recall taking on Pūraṇa Kassapa in debate. He dodged the issue, distracting the discussion with irrelevant points, and displaying annoyance, hate, and bitterness. But when Mister Gotama is repeatedly attacked with inappropriate and intrusive criticism, the complexion of his skin brightens and the color of his face becomes clear, just like a perfected one, a fully awakened Buddha.

I recall taking on the bamboo-staffed ascetic Gosāla, Ajita of the hair blanket, Pakudha Kaccāyana, Sañjaya Belaṭṭhiputta, and the Jain ascetic of the Ñātika clan in debate. They all dodged the issue, distracting the discussion with irrelevant points, and displaying annoyance, hate, and bitterness. But when Mister Gotama is repeatedly attacked with inappropriate and intrusive criticism, the complexion of his skin brightens and the color of his face becomes clear, just like a perfected one, a fully awakened Buddha.

Well, now, Mister Gotama, I must go. I have many duties, and much to do."

"Please, Aggivessana, go at your convenience."

Then Saccaka, the son of Jain parents, having approved and agreed with what the Buddha said, got up from his seat and left."

Chapter 39

Middle Discourses 37: Cūḷataṇhāsaṅkhayasutta

The Shorter Discourse on the Ending of Craving

How to understand the state of mind of an Arahant? One who is not bothered by worldly experiences, an Arahant. This discourse explains the mind state of an Arahant, someone who grasps to nothing in the world and worldly experiences in mind, simply functional without desires.

Ordinary people may not fully comprehend the state of mind of an Arahant. This is because a person can only comprehend another person's mind within one's mind. Yet, it is possible to explain, and there may be wise people who may comprehend the mind state of an Arahant at least to some extent.

Arahants don't like or dislike or expect things from sensory experiences based on worldly life. Cease in mind is different from cease in body, meaning the end or death of desires (likes, dislikes, expectations in mind) as opposed to bodily death. Death in desires brings an end to craving, mental sufferings, and one's binding to Earth in mind, to earthy experiences with a distorted understanding that they are permanent, stable pleasures that can be retained forever, and so on. When grasping is completely ended, one experiences Arahantship.

"So I have heard. At one time the Buddha was staying near Sāvatthī in the stilt longhouse of Migāra's mother in the Eastern Monastery.

And then Sakka, lord of gods, went up to the Buddha, bowed, stood to one side, and said to him:

"Sir, how do you briefly define a person who is freed through the ending of craving, an Arahant, who has reached the ultimate end, the ultimate sanctuary from the yoke, the ultimate spiritual life, the ultimate goal, and is best among gods and humans?"

"Lord of gods, take a person who has heard: 'Nothing is worth insisting on.' When a person has heard that nothing is worth insisting on, they directly know all things. Directly knowing all things, they completely understand all things. Completely understanding all things, when they experience any kind of feeling—pleasant, unpleasant, or neutral—they reflect observing impermanence, dispassion, cessation, and letting go in those feelings. Reflecting in this way, they don't grasp at anything in the world. Not grasping, they're not anxious. Not being anxious, they personally become extinguished. They understand: 'Rebirth is ended, the spiritual journey has been completed, what had to be done has been done, there is nothing further for this place.' That's how I briefly define a mendicant who is freed through the ending of craving, who has reached the ultimate end, the ultimate sanctuary from the yoke, the ultimate spiritual life, the ultimate goal, and is best among gods and humans."

Then Sakka, lord of gods, having approved and agreed with what the Buddha said, bowed and respectfully circled the Buddha, keeping him on his right, before vanishing right there.

Now at that time Arahant Mahāmoggallāna was sitting not far from the Buddha. He thought, "Did that spirit comprehend what the Buddha said when he agreed with him, or not? Why don't I find out?"

And then Arahant Mahāmoggallāna, as easily as a strong person would extend or contract their arm, vanished from the Eastern Monastery and reappeared among the gods of the thirty-three. Now at that time Sakka was amusing himself in the Single Lotus Park, supplied and provided with a heavenly orchestra.

Seeing Arahant Mahāmoggallāna coming off in the distance, he dismissed the orchestra, approached Mahāmoggallāna, and said, "Come, my good friend Arahant Moggallāna! Welcome, good sir! It's been a long time since you took the opportunity to come here. Sit, my dear friend Arahant Moggallāna, this seat is for you." Arahant Mahāmoggallāna sat down on the seat spread out, while Sakka took a low seat and sat to one side.

Arahant Mahāmoggallāna said to him, "Kosiya, how did the Buddha briefly explain freedom through the ending of craving? Please share this talk with me so that I can also get to hear it."

"My good friend Arahant Moggallāna, I have many duties, and much to do, not only for myself, but also for the gods of the thirty-three. Still, what is properly heard, learned, attended, and memorized does not vanish all of a sudden. Once upon a time, a battle was fought between the gods and the titans. In that battle the gods won and the titans lost. When I returned from that battle as a conqueror, I created the Palace of Victory. The Palace of Victory has a hundred towers. Each tower has seven hundred chambers. Each chamber has seven nymphs. Each nymph has seven maids. Would you like to see the lovely Palace of Victory?" Arahant Mahāmoggallāna consented with silence.

Then, putting Arahant Mahāmoggallāna in front, Sakka, lord of gods, and Vessavaṇa, the Great King, went to the Palace of Victory. When they saw Arahant Moggallāna coming off in the distance, Sakka's maids, being discreet and prudent, each went to her own bedroom. They were just like a daughter-in-law who is discreet and prudent when they see their father-in-law.

Then Sakka and Vessavaṇa encouraged Arahant Moggallāna to wander and explore the palace, saying, "See, in the palace, my dear friend, Arahant Moggallāna, this lovely thing! And that lovely thing!"

"That looks beautiful for the respected friend Kosiya, as befits one who has made merit in the past. Humans, when they see something lovely, also say: 'It looks beautiful enough for the gods of the thirty-three!' That looks beautiful for the venerable Kosiya, as befits one who has made merit in the past."

Then Arahant Moggallāna thought, "This spirit lives much too negligently. Why don't I stir up a sense of urgency in him?"

Then Arahant Moggallāna used his psychic power to make the Palace of Victory shake and rock and tremble with his big toe. Then Sakka, Vessavaṇa, and the gods of the thirty-three, their minds full of wonder and amazement, thought, "Oh, how incredible, how amazing! The ascetic has such power and might that he makes the god's home shake and rock and tremble with his big toe!"

Knowing that Sakka was shocked and awestruck, Arahant Moggallāna said to him, "Kosiya, how did the Buddha briefly explain freedom through the ending of craving? Please share this talk with me so that I can also get to hear it."

"My dear Arahant Moggallāna, I approached the Buddha, bowed, stood to one side, and said to him, 'Sir, how do you briefly define a person who is freed with the ending of craving, who has reached the ultimate end, the ultimate sanctuary from the yoke (Arahant), the ultimate spiritual life, the ultimate goal, and is best among gods and humans?'

When I had spoken the Buddha said to me: 'lord of gods, it's when a person has heard: "Nothing is worth insisting on" When a companion has heard that nothing is worth insisting on, they directly know all things. Directly knowing all things, they completely understand all things. Having completely understood all things, when they experience any kind of feeling—pleasant, unpleasant, or neutral—they reflect impermanence, dispassion, cessation, and letting go in those feelings.

Reflecting in this way, they don't grasp at anything in the world. Not grasping, they're not anxious. Not being anxious, they personally become extinguished.

They understand: "Rebirth is ended, the spiritual journey has been completed, what had to be done has been done, there is nothing further for this place." That's how I briefly define a companion who is freed through the ending of craving, who has reached the ultimate end, the ultimate sanctuary from the yoke (Arahantship), the ultimate spiritual life, the ultimate goal, and is best among gods and humans.' That's how the Buddha briefly explained freedom through the ending of craving to me."

Arahant Moggallāna approved and agreed with what Sakka said. As easily as a strong person would extend or contract their arm, he vanished from among the gods of the thirty-three and reappeared in the Eastern Monastery.

Soon after Arahant Moggallāna left, Sakka's maids said to him, "Good sir, was that the Blessed One, your Teacher?"

"No, it was not. That was my spiritual companion Arahant Mahāmoggallāna."

"You're fortunate, good sir, so very fortunate, to have a spiritual companion of such power and might! We can't believe that's not the Blessed One, your Teacher!"

Then Arahant Mahāmoggallāna went up to the Buddha, bowed, sat down to one side, and said to him, "Sir, do you recall briefly explaining freedom through the ending of craving to a certain well-known and illustrious spirit?"

"I do, Moggallāna." And the Buddha retold all that happened when Sakka came to visit him, adding:

"That's how I recall briefly explaining freedom through the ending of craving to Sakka, lord of gods."

That is what the Buddha said. Satisfied, Arahant Mahāmoggallāna approved what the Buddha said."

Chapter 40

Middle Discourses 38: Mahātaṇhāsaṅkhaya Sutta

The Greater Discourse on the Complete Elimination of Craving

This discourse discusses four-fold Nibbana and how it transforms a person across four stages. You may initially practice precepts. By engaging in ten wholesome deeds, especially by developing the right view, you may reach a Sotapanna.

A harmful grasp of Dhamma, misunderstanding the Dhamma taught by the Buddha in the mind of a conventional monk named Sati leads to creating demerits. It can prevent Nibbana for him, and for his followers.

Sometimes, conventional bhikkhus/Sangha misinterpret Dhamma, which leads to creating demerits. It can prevent Nibbana for them. Therefore, it is the best for bhikkhus to become more vigilant and to look after themselves better, as demerits can prevent Nibbana, and can extend Samsara. There is nothing wrong with saying "I became a bhikkhu because of my interest to gain Nibbana. According to these books and traditions, Nibbana is this. I teach based merely on books and traditions, but I have to yet gain Nibbana. I am not 100% sure what is the universal truth, Nibbana, as I have not yet experienced it myself. What I can explain is based on what I know. I may be right or wrong. I may know certain things, but I do not know all. Therefore, it's good to keep an open eye, a bit of space to discover truth for myself, and to keep seeking. In this manner, I can teach the basics without confirming, and encouraging myself and others to seek truth without pretending to know all, and without pretending to be Arahants." This will favor them and aid in gaining Nibbana.

Throughout history, you can find many occasions when bhikkhus misinterpret Dhamma. Not exploring but merely ignoring, people just go in circles again and again without gaining Nibbana. If anyone thinks they are worth listening to, they will block their chances of gaining Nibbana. In this world, without considering whether they are teachers, those who guide them to a spiritual path talk about the practice leading to Nibbana based on personal experience, whether they have gained Nibbana for themselves before speaking about the path. Some people can follow a spiritual path with ignorance.

The conscious transformation of a person can change, because consciousness is subject to change. Ritualistic transformation can be temporary, as life is temporary. It's not that one becomes a monk by taking the monastic rules; one becomes a monk through natural transformation, transformation that makes a person abandon the mental attachment to the fetters; self-view, rituals, shaped by the universal functioning. Across stages of Nibbana, a person naturally transforms into someone who eats meals before noon, does not harm trees, is chaste, does not see movies, and so on, because the underlying tendency for desire is abandoned.

The ordinary state is characterized by an ongoing cycle of worldly experiences, such as sadness and happiness in cycles. The intentional action of a Sotapanna carries Dhamma actions; reducing efforts to grasp conventions, fulfilling responsibilities to others, and not worrying excessively about bad things in self, others and the world. While you are an ordinary, you may develop a Dhamma doing similar to that of a Sotapanna within your lifestyle.

One of the confusions over Buddha's Dhamma is who is a monk. Natural transformation takes place in a person's mental continuum across stages, and that transformation, which allows abandoning mental fetters out of rituals, is a monk in Noble Path. At the Anagami state, a person naturally transforms into someone who maintains chastity.

Common and ordinary ways of thinking that everyone follows since a birth include getting attached to worldly experiences. Touching worldly experiences too much in mind is a common way, as is the inability to be satisfied with whatever way one presently has and instead seeking more and more worldly experiences. Thinking that it is possible to retain stability in self and worldly experiences, a person may develop a habit of touching worldly experiences too much in mind since birth. Thinking that the things on earth belong to a person, a person may grasp at changing worldly experiences. In this manner, what you think may not align with your true-life experiences.

Identity views and social divisions are socially created constructs. What is socially constructed is subject to change. The underlying tendency you have for interpreting yourself as someone who should not face problems in life is deluded understanding. Understanding and accepting yourself as someone who should not experience problems can make you feel too upset when upsetting things happen in real life. In this manner, the screening of information coming through sense organs is processed based on how you understand and interpret things, which is how you make sense of you, others and the world and experience worldly life.

Understanding self as someone who can retain wordily experiences with stability can make you feel too upset when self and the experiences change following illnesses and changes in friendships and relationships and situations. Interpreting someone as your friend and another person as not a friend can bring stress to you when a friend acts in a way that is opposed to what you interpreted. In this manner, how you understand and interpret self, others, situations, and worldly experiences will lead to your thoughts related to feelings and what you say and how you behave in situations. By understanding how your thoughts work, you can take a step to free yourself from your mind when it brings too much mental pain to you. By applying wisdom, you can learn to make the most of your experiences. Thoughts can behave like an ongoing stream just below your understanding, and, by understanding your thoughts, you can make gradual changes that will help you to think better and, in turn, pave your way to gaining peace and freedom from an ongoing stream of thoughts; a way of stream winning. When thinking in the best ways, middle way practice can allow you to retain worldly happiness.

Practicing Dhamma for ordinary practitioners to gain Nibbana requires training the mind to reduce clinging to self-view by understanding beyond the ordinary ways of thinking and doing within daily life. For example, when someone experiences a low mood, it is useful to bring back mindfulness and make some effort to reflect on the Tathagata's Dhamma that remind us the universally applicable truth based on life experience; how ups and downs are part of life, as that is the nature of life for all of us. Similarly, when one feels upset or worried, it is useful to bring back mindfulness to reflect that context can be anything, so that feelings and thoughts, good times and bad times are normal things to expect in life, and everything is subject to change universally applicable to all beings. Applying such a dhamma perspective into analyzing real-life experience is a helpful practice to maintain peace of mind. To practice middle-way towards gaining Nibbana requires moving beyond ordinary meditation practices to apply the Dhamma perspective into daily life. This explains why it is useful to train the mind in the "middle-way" in daily life, as this practice allows not with- holding autonomous functioning of thoughts but reducing getting attached to the autonomous functioning of thoughts or reducing identifying the mind as belonging to a stable "self".

When you have a limited vision, you don't see what lies beyond. When you look back on your past, you might notice that there were occasions when you did not see things and that your vision was limited. Just because you don't see does not necessarily mean that there are things beyond your vision. When your vision is stuck in conventions, you tend to forget universal ways of functioning. Yet, what your eyes cannot see, you can see with wisdom. In this way, wisdom can be developed by developing merits.

By integrating Triple Gem, receiving guidance and merits from those who do not undermine your potential for gaining Nibbana but those who treat you with immense respect despite your conventional background, you can develop the Noble Path that will allow you to discover self, freedom from conventional life experience.

"So I have heard. At one time the Buddha was staying near Sāvatthī in Jeta's Grove, Anāthapiṇḍika's monastery.

Now at that time a person called Sāti who was living a monastic life from a conventional perspective, the fisherman's son, had the following harmful misconception: "As I understand the Buddha's teaching, it is this very same consciousness that roams and transmigrates, not another."

Several companions heard about this. They went up to Sāti and said to him, "Is it really true, friend Sāti, that you have such a harmful misconception: 'As I understand the Buddha's teaching, it is this very same consciousness that roams and transmigrates, not another'?"

"Absolutely, friends. As I understand the Buddha's teaching, it is this very same consciousness that roams and transmigrates, not another."

Then, wishing to dissuade Sāti from his view, the companions pursued, pressed, and grilled him, "Don't say that, Sāti! Don't misrepresent the Buddha, for misrepresentation of the Buddha is not good. And the Buddha would not say that. In many ways the Buddha has said that consciousness is dependently originated, since without a cause, consciousness does not come to be."

But even though they pressed him in this way, Sāti obstinately stuck to his misconception and insisted on it.

When they weren't able to dissuade Sāti from his view, the companions went to the Buddha, bowed, sat down to one side, and told him what had happened.

So the Buddha addressed one of the followers, "Please, friend, in my name tell Sāti that the teacher summons him."

"Yes, sir," that companion replied. He went to Sāti and said to him, "Friend Sāti, the teacher summons you."

"Yes, friend," Sāti replied. He went to the Buddha, bowed, and sat down to one side. The Buddha said to him, "Is it really true, Sāti, that you have such a harmful misconception: 'As I understand the Buddha's teaching, it is this very same consciousness that roams and transmigrates, not another'?"

"Absolutely, sir. As I understand the Buddha's teaching, it is this very same consciousness that roams and transmigrates, not another."

"Sāti, what is that consciousness?"

"Sir, he is the speaker, the knower who experiences the results of good and bad deeds in all the different realms."

"Futile man, who on earth have you ever known me to teach in that way? Haven't I said in many ways that consciousness is dependently originated, since consciousness does not arise without a cause? But still you misrepresent me by your wrong grasp, harm yourself, and create much wickedness. This will be for your lasting harm and suffering."

Then the Buddha said to the companions, "What do you think, companions? Has this person Sāti kindled even a spark of ardor in this teaching and training?"

"How could that be, sir? No, sir." When this was said, Sāti sat silent, dismayed, shoulders drooping, downcast, depressed, with nothing to say.

Knowing this, the Buddha said, "Futile man, you will be known by your own harmful misconception. I'll question the mendicants about this."

Then the Buddha said to the companions, "Friends, do you understand my teachings as Sāti does, when he misrepresents me by his wrong grasp, harms himself, and creates much wickedness?"

"No, sir. For in many ways the Buddha has told us that consciousness is dependently originated, since without a cause, consciousness does not come to be."

"Good, good, friends! It's good that you understand my teaching like this. For in many ways I have told you that consciousness is dependently originated, since without a cause, consciousness does not come to be. But still this Sāti misrepresents me by his wrong grasp, harms himself, and creates much wickedness. This will be for his lasting harm and suffering.

Consciousness is reckoned according to the very same condition dependent upon which it arises. Consciousness that arises dependent on the eye and sights is reckoned as eye consciousness. Consciousness that arises dependent on the ear and sounds is reckoned as ear consciousness. Consciousness that arises dependent on the nose and smells is reckoned as nose consciousness. Consciousness that arises dependent on the tongue and tastes is reckoned as tongue consciousness.

Consciousness that arises dependent on the body and touches is reckoned as body consciousness. Consciousness that arises dependent on the mind and ideas is reckoned as mind consciousness.

It's like fire, which is reckoned according to the very same condition dependent upon which it burns. A fire that burns dependent on logs is reckoned as a log fire.

A fire that burns dependent on twigs is reckoned as a twig fire. A fire that burns dependent on grass is reckoned as a grass fire. A fire that burns dependent on cow-dung is reckoned as a cow-dung fire. A fire that burns dependent on husks is reckoned as a husk fire. A fire that burns dependent on rubbish is reckoned as a rubbish fire.

In the same way, consciousness is reckoned according to the very same condition dependent upon which it arises. …

Friends, do you see that this has come to be?"

"Yes, sir."

"Do you see that it originated with that as fuel?"

"Yes, sir."

"Do you see that when that fuel ceases, what has come to be is liable to cease?"

"Yes, sir."

"Does doubt arise when you're uncertain whether or not this has come to be?"

"Yes, sir."

"Does doubt arise when you're uncertain whether or not this has originated with that as fuel?"

"Yes, sir."

"Does doubt arise when you're uncertain whether or not when that fuel ceases, what has come to be is liable to cease?"

"Yes, sir."

"Is doubt given up in someone who truly sees with right understanding that this has come to be?"

"Yes, sir."

"Is doubt given up in someone who truly sees with right understanding that this has originated with that as fuel?"

"Yes, sir."

"Is doubt given up in someone who truly sees with right understanding that when that fuel ceases, what has come to be is liable to cease?"

"Yes, sir."

"Are you free of doubt as to whether this has come to be?"

"Yes, sir."

"Are you free of doubt as to whether this has originated with that as fuel?"

"Yes, sir."

"Are you free of doubt as to whether when that fuel ceases, what has come to be is liable to cease?"

"Yes, sir."

"Have you truly seen clearly with right understanding that this has come to be?"

"Yes, sir."

"Have you truly seen clearly with right understanding that this has originated with that as fuel?"

"Yes, sir."

"Have you truly seen clearly with right understanding that when that fuel ceases, what has come to be is liable to cease?"

"Yes, sir."

"Pure and bright as this view is, companions, if you cherish it, fancy it, treasure it, and treat it as your own, would you be understanding my simile of the teaching as a raft: for crossing over, not for holding on?"

"No, sir."

"Pure and bright as this view is, companions, if you don't cherish it, fancy it, treasure it, and treat it as your own, would you be understanding my simile of the teaching as a raft: for crossing over, not for holding on?"

"Yes, sir."

"Companions, there are these four fuels. They maintain sentient beings that have been born and help those that are about to be born. What four? Solid food, whether solid or subtle; contact is the second, mental intention the third, and consciousness the fourth.

What is the source, origin, birthplace, and inception of these four fuels? Craving.

And what is the source of craving? Feeling.

And what is the source of feeling? Contact.

And what is the source of contact? The six sense fields.

And what is the source of the six sense fields? Name and form.

And what is the source of name and form? Consciousness.

And what is the source of consciousness? Choices.

And what is the source of choices? Ignorance.

So, ignorance is a condition for choices. Choices are a condition for consciousness. Consciousness is a condition for name and form. Name and form are conditions for the six sense fields. The six sense fields are conditions for contact. Contact is a condition for feeling. Feeling is a condition for craving. Craving is a condition for grasping. Grasping is a condition for continued existence.

Continued existence is a condition for rebirth. Rebirth is a condition for old age and death, sorrow, lamentation, pain, sadness, and distress to come to be. That is how this entire mass of suffering originates.

'Rebirth is a condition for old age and death.' That's what I said. Is that how you see this or not?"

"That's how we see it."

"'Continued existence is a condition for rebirth.' …

'Ignorance is a condition for choices.' That's what I said. Is that how you see this or not?"

"That's how we see it."

"Good, companions! So both you and I say this. When this exists, that is; due to the arising of this, that arises. That is: Ignorance is a condition for choices. Choices are a condition for consciousness. Consciousness is a condition for name and form. Name and form are conditions for the six sense fields.

The six sense fields are conditions for contact. Contact is a condition for feeling. Feeling is a condition for craving. Craving is a condition for grasping. Grasping is a condition for continued existence. Continued existence is a condition for rebirth. Rebirth is a condition for old age and death, sorrow, lamentation, pain, sadness, and distress to come to be. That is how this entire mass of suffering originates.

When ignorance fades away and ceases with nothing left over, choices cease. When choices cease, consciousness ceases. When consciousness ceases, name and form cease. When name and form cease, the six sense fields cease. When the six sense fields cease, contact ceases. When contact ceases, feeling ceases. When feeling ceases, craving ceases. When craving ceases, grasping ceases. When grasping ceases, continued existence ceases. When continued existence ceases, rebirth ceases. When rebirth ceases, old age and death, sorrow, lamentation, pain, sadness, and distress cease. That is how this entire mass of suffering ceases.

'When rebirth ceases, old age and death cease.' That's what I said. Is that how you see this or not?"

"That's how we see it."

'When continued existence ceases, rebirth ceases.' …

'When ignorance ceases, choices cease.' That's what I said. Is that how you see this or not?"

"That's how we see it."

"Good, friends! So both you and I say this. When this doesn't exist, that is not; due to the cessation of this, that ceases. That is: When ignorance ceases, choices cease. When choices cease, consciousness ceases. When consciousness ceases, name and form cease. When name and form cease, the six sense fields cease. When the six sense fields cease, contact ceases. When contact ceases, feeling ceases. When feeling ceases, craving ceases. When craving ceases, grasping ceases. When grasping ceases, continued existence ceases. When continued existence ceases, rebirth ceases. When rebirth ceases, old age and death, sorrow, lamentation, pain, sadness, and distress cease. That is how this entire mass of suffering ceases.

Knowing and seeing in this way, friends, would you turn back to the past, thinking, 'Did we exist in the past? Did we not exist in the past? What were we in the past? How were we in the past? After being what, what did we become in the past?'?"

"No, sir."

"Knowing and seeing in this way, companions, would you turn forward to the future, thinking, 'Will we exist in the future? Will we not exist in the future? What will we be in the future? How will we be in the future? After being what, what will we become in the future?'?"

"No, sir."

"Knowing and seeing in this way, companions, would you be undecided about the present, thinking, 'Am I? Am I not? What am I? How am I? This sentient being—where did it come from? And where will it go?'?"

"No, sir."

"Knowing and seeing in this way, would you say, 'Our teacher is respected. We speak like this out of respect for our teacher'?"

"No, sir."

"Knowing and seeing in this way, would you say, 'Our ascetic says this. We speak like this because it is what he says'?"

"No, sir."

"Knowing and seeing in this way, would you dedicate yourself to another teacher?"

"No, sir."

"Knowing and seeing in this way, would you believe that the observances and boisterous, superstitious rites of the various ascetics and brahmins are essential?"

"No, sir."

"Aren't you speaking only of what you have known and seen and realized for yourselves?"

"Yes, sir."

"Good, companions! You have been guided by me with this teaching that's apparent in the present life, immediately effective, inviting inspection, relevant, so that sensible people can know it for themselves. For when I said that this teaching is apparent in the present life, immediately effective, inviting inspection, relevant, so that sensible people can know it for themselves, this is what I was referring to.

Companions, when three things come together an embryo is conceived. In a case where the mother and father come together, but the mother is not in the fertile phase of her menstrual cycle, and the virile spirit is not ready, the embryo is not conceived. In a case where the mother and father come together, the mother is in the fertile phase of her menstrual cycle, but the virile spirit is not ready, the embryo is not conceived. But when these three things come together—the mother and father come together, the mother is in the fertile phase of her menstrual cycle, and the virile spirit is ready—an embryo is conceived.

The mother nurtures the embryo in her womb for nine or ten months at great risk to her heavy burden. When nine or ten months have passed, the mother gives birth at great risk to her heavy burden. When the infant is born she nourishes it with her own blood. For mother's milk is regarded as blood in the training of the Noble One.

That boy grows up and his faculties mature. He accordingly plays childish games such as toy plows, tipcat, somersaults, pinwheels, toy measures, toy carts, and toy bows.

That boy grows up and his faculties mature further. He accordingly amuses himself, supplied and provided with the five kinds of sensual stimulation. Sights known by the eye, which are likable, desirable, agreeable, pleasant, sensual, and arousing.

Sounds known by the ear …

Smells known by the nose …

Tastes known by the tongue …

Touches known by the body, which are likable, desirable, agreeable, pleasant, sensual, and arousing.

When they see a sight with their eyes, if it's pleasant they desire it, but if it's unpleasant they dislike it. They live with mindfulness of the body unestablished and their heart restricted. And they don't truly understand the freedom of heart and freedom by wisdom where those arisen bad, unskillful qualities cease without anything left over.

Being so full of favoring and opposing, when they experience any kind of feeling—pleasant, unpleasant, or neutral—they approve, welcome, and keep clinging to it. This gives rise to relishing. Relishing feelings is grasping. Their grasping is a condition for continued existence. Continued existence is a condition for rebirth. Rebirth is a condition for old age and death, sorrow, lamentation, pain, sadness, and distress to come to be. That is how this entire mass of suffering originates.

When they hear a sound with their ears …

When they smell an odor with their nose …

When they taste a flavor with their tongue …

When they feel a touch with their body …

When they know an idea with their mind, if it's pleasant they desire it, but if it's unpleasant they dislike it. They live with mindfulness of the body unestablished and their heart restricted. And they don't truly understand the freedom of heart and freedom by wisdom where those arisen bad, unskillful qualities cease without anything left over.

Being so full of favoring and opposing, when they experience any kind of feeling—pleasant, unpleasant, or neutral—they approve, welcome, and keep clinging to it. This gives rise to relishing. Relishing feelings is grasping. Their grasping is a condition for continued existence. Continued existence is a condition for rebirth. Rebirth is a condition for old age and death, sorrow, lamentation, pain, sadness, and distress to come to be. That is how this entire mass of suffering originates.

But consider when a Realized One arises in the world, perfected, a fully awakened Buddha, accomplished in knowledge and conduct, holy, knower of the world, supreme guide for those who wish to train, teacher of gods and humans, awakened, blessed. He has realized with his own insight this world—with its gods, Māras, and divinities, this population with its ascetics and brahmins, gods and humans—and he makes it known to others. He proclaims a teaching that is good in the beginning (Sotapanna), good in the middle (Anagami), and good in the end (Arahant), meaningful and well-phrased. He reveals an entirely full and pure spiritual life.

An ordinary person hears that teaching, an ordinary person's child, or someone reborn in a good family. They gain faith in the Realized One and reflect, 'Ordinary life is cramped and dirty, spiritual life is wide open. It's not easy for me to live in a normal household and practice the universal noble path utterly full and pure, like a polished shell. For me, it's probably easier to practice the noble path in a monastic setting. Why don't I join a monastery to live a spiritual life?' After some time, they give up a large or small fortune and a large or small family circle. They dress up as monastic and start practicing a spiritual life in a monastic setting.

Once they've started a spiritual practice, as ordinary practitioners, ideally, they should try taking up the training and livelihood of the noble ones.

They should give up killing living creatures, renouncing the rod and the sword. They should be scrupulous and kind, living full of sympathy for all living beings (A Sotapanna does not require taking the precepts, but a Sotapanna naturally has this quality due to the right view).

As ordinary practitioners, ideally, they should give up stealing. They should take only what's given and expect only what's given. They should keep themselves clean by not thieving (A Sotapanna does not…)

As ordinary practitioners, ideally, they should give up unchastity. They should become celibate, set apart, avoiding the vulgar act of sex (An Anagami naturally gives up such acts due to the right view without having to take precepts).

As ordinary practitioners, ideally, they should give up lying. They should speak the truth and stick to the truth. They should be honest and dependable and don't trick the world with their words (A Sotapanna naturally gives up such acts due to the right view without having to take precepts).

As ordinary practitioners, ideally, they should give up divisive speech. They should not repeat in one place what they heard in another so as to divide people against each other. Instead, they should reconcile those who are divided, supporting unity, delighting in harmony, loving harmony, and speaking words that promote harmony. An Anagami naturally gives up such acts due to the right view without having to take precepts.

As ordinary practitioners, ideally, they should give up harsh speech. They should speak in a way that's mellow, pleasing to the ear, lovely, going to the heart, polite, likable, and agreeable to the people. An Anagami naturally gives up such acts due to the right view without having to take precepts.

As ordinary practitioners, ideally, they should give up talking nonsense. Their words should be timely, true, and meaningful, in line with the teaching and training[21]. They should say things at the right time that are valuable, reasonable, succinct, and beneficial.

As ordinary practitioners, ideally, they should refrain from injuring plants and seeds. They should reduce desire (likes, dislikes) through conscious efforts (Upon gaining Anagami state, a person naturally acts of not harming trees, plants and seeds etc.).

An ordinary person (as a monastic) should put conscious efforts to reduce desire for food and eat one part of the day similar to the noble ones. Anagamis and Arahants naturally have less desires (Arahants have no desires), and Anagamis and Arahants naturally eat in one part of the day, abstaining from eating at night and food at the wrong time.

An ordinary person should put conscious efforts to reduce desire (likes, dislikes) for seeing shows of dancing, singing, and music. Anagamis and Arahants in any setting; monastic or non-monastic from a conventional perspective, they have no desires for seeing shows of dancing, singing, and music.

Ordinary practitioners, in a monastic setting, should try and reduce the desire to beautify and adorn themselves with garlands, fragrance, and makeup through conscious efforts. Upon gaining Anagami or Arahant state, a person who lives in any setting; monastic or non-monastic from a conventional perspective, they naturally have no desires for such things.

---

[21] Teaching and training = Sotapanna and the practice leading to Sotapanna and above

An ordinary person should put conscious efforts to reduce desire (likes, dislikes) for luxury beddings. Anagamis or Arahants in any setting; monastic or non-monastic from a conventional perspective, they naturally have no desires for such things.

An ordinary person should put conscious efforts to reduce mental attachment and desire (likes, dislikes) for gains and losses (i.e. gold and currency, raw grains, raw meat, women and girls, male and female bondservants, goats and sheep, chickens and pigs, elephants, cows, horses, and mares, and fields and land etc.). Anagamis or Arahants in any setting; monastic or non-monastic from a conventional perspective, they naturally have no desires for such things.

An ordinary person should put conscious efforts to reduce mental attachment and desire (likes, dislikes) for making a wrong living; running errands and messages; falsifying weights, metals, or measures; bribery, fraud, cheating, and duplicity; mutilation, murder, abduction, banditry, plunder, and violence. Anagamis or Arahants in any setting; monastic or non-monastic from a conventional perspective, they naturally have no desires for such things.

An ordinary person should put conscious efforts to reduce mental attachment and desire (likes, dislikes) for clothing and food. Someone who has completed four-fold nibbana (Arahant) is content with whatever robes to look after the body and food to look after the belly.

Arahants, wherever they go, they set out taking only these things. They're free as a bird: wherever it flies, wings are its only burden. In the same way, they are content with whatever robes to look after the body and whatever food to look after the belly. Wherever they go, they are free of attachment. When they have this entire spectrum of noble ethics, they experience a blameless happiness inside themselves. When they see a sight with their eyes, they don't get caught up in the features and details. If the faculty of sight were left with desires, bad unskillful qualities of covetousness and displeasure would become overwhelming. Yet they have no desires, as a consequence, they are naturally restrained, not getting caught up in the faculty of sight, and achieving the end of craving. When they hear a sound with their ears … When they smell an odor with their nose … When they taste a flavor with their tongue … When they feel a touch with their body … When they know an idea with their mind, they don't get caught up in the features and details.

If the faculty of mind were left with desires, bad unskillful qualities of covetousness and displeasure would become overwhelming. Yet they have no desires, as a consequence, they are naturally restrained, not getting caught up in the faculty of mind, and achieving its restraint. When they have this noble way of restraint, they experience an unsullied bliss inside themselves.

They act with situational awareness when going out and coming back; when looking ahead and aside; when bending and extending the limbs; when bearing the clothing and carrying everyday items; when eating, drinking, chewing, and tasting; when urinating and defecating; when walking, standing, sitting, sleeping, waking, speaking, and keeping silent.

When they have this entire spectrum of noble ethics, this noble contentment, this noble restraint, and this noble mindfulness and situational awareness, they remain unattached from others wherever they stay- a city, a house, a temple, a forest (wilderness, the root of a tree, a hill, a ravine, a mountain cave, a charnel ground, a forest, the open air, a heap of straw etc.).

After daily activities and the meal, they return to their resting places and maintain noble mindfulness at all postures at any time. Having given up covetousness for the world, they possess a heart rid of covetousness, cleansing the mind of covetousness. Having given up ill will and malevolence, their mind is free from ill will, full of sympathy for all living beings, cleansing the mind of ill will. Having given up dullness and drowsiness, their mind overcomes dullness and drowsiness, perceiving light, mindful and aware, cleansing the mind of dullness and drowsiness. Having given up restlessness and remorse, their mind overcomes restlessness and remorse. Having given up doubt, their minds having gone beyond doubt, not undecided about skillful qualities, cleansing the mind of doubt.

Arahants, they've given up these five hindrances, corruptions of the heart that weaken wisdom.

Anagami gives up given up these five hindrances, corruptions of the heart that weaken wisdom. Then, on the path to Anagami, quite secluded from sensual pleasures, secluded from unskillful qualities, they enter and remain in the first absorption, which has the rapture and bliss born of seclusion, while placing the mind and keeping it connected. Furthermore, as the placing of the mind and keeping it connected are stilled, a person enters and remains in the second absorption ... third absorption ... fourth absorption (An ordinary practitioner should try and gain four-fold nibbana and abandon hindrances across stages so they can give up these five hindrances...).

Arahants, when they see a sight with their eyes, if it's pleasant they don't desire it, and if it's unpleasant they don't dislike it. They live with mindfulness of the body established and a limitless heart. And they truly understand the freedom of heart and freedom by wisdom where those arisen bad, unskillful qualities cease without anything left over (An ordinary practitioner should try gaining four-fold nibban, they should try reducing desires when they see a sight...)

Having given up favoring and opposing, when they experience any kind of feeling—pleasant, unpleasant, or neutral—they don't approve, welcome, or keep clinging to it. As a result, the relishing of feelings ceases. When their relishing ceases, grasping ceases. When grasping ceases, continued existence ceases. When continued existence ceases, rebirth ceases. When rebirth ceases, old age and death, sorrow, lamentation, pain, sadness, and distress cease. That is how this entire mass of suffering ceases.

When they hear a sound with their ears …

When they smell an odor with their nose …

When they taste a flavor with their tongue …

When they feel a touch with their body …

When they know an idea with their mind, if it's pleasant they don't like it, and if it's unpleasant they don't dislike it. They live with mindfulness of the body established and a limitless heart. And they truly understand the freedom of heart and freedom by wisdom where those arisen bad, unskillful qualities cease without anything left over (An ordinary practitioner should try gaining four-fold nibbana, they should try reducing desires, when they know an idea with their mind …)

Having given up favoring and opposing, when they experience any kind of feeling—pleasant, unpleasant, or neutral—they don't approve, welcome, or keep clinging to it. As a result, relishing of feelings ceases. When their relishing ceases, grasping ceases. When grasping ceases, continued existence ceases. When continued existence ceases, rebirth ceases. When rebirth ceases, old age and death, sorrow, lamentation, pain, sadness, and distress cease. That is how this entire mass of suffering ceases.

Companions, you should memorize this brief statement on freedom through the ending of craving. But friend Sāti, the fisherman's son, is caught in a vast net of craving, a tangle of craving."

That is what the Buddha said. Satisfied, the companions approved what the Buddha said."

Chapter 41

Middle Discourses 39: Mahāassapurasutta

The Longer Discourse at Assapura

This discourse records the Buddha saying that if someone claims to be a disciple of Buddha, they should have completed the four-fold Nibbana as people tend to think they are a disciple of Buddha when they practice Dhamma. When asked, "What are you?" they claim that they are a disciple of Buddha. Given they claim they are a disciple of Buddha, may they train to become a true disciple of Buddha, at least becoming a Sotapanna, so that what they say is what they are. When there is no mismatch between what you say and what you are, as you come to maintain integrity, you can grow in universal Dhamma.

The purpose of the noble Sangha order is to provide higher merits and wisdom leading to four-fold Nibbana. This becomes a personal understanding for Sotapanna (and above). For ordinary companions, they may hear it and accept it to a reasonable level. For a Sotapanna (and above), understanding that wisdom and karma contribute to Nibbana becomes personal knowledge and understanding, which one gains, without a doubt, through experience. By fulfilling the training to gain four-fold Nibbana, you become what you claim to be and aid another person in developing wisdom and shaping their karma by supporting you or/and your living, food, accommodation, medicine, etc. In doing so, they gain an opportunity to end their sufferings.

The purpose of Buddha's Dhamma is to attain cessation, and how can a person attain sainthood?
Sainthood in Buddha's path is a state of wisdom. When true Arahants express wise words, they express words without grasping flesh (personal stories etc.), without expectations, likes or dislikes, and simply sharing the teachings.

You may initially practice precepts and training rules and gain some Dhamma knowledge by familiarizing yourself with what the Buddha taught based on conventions. Thereafter, you may apply knowledge of Dhamma in your daily life (you may chant, you may reduce pride, anger, likes, dislikes etc.). You may think that's enough; there's nothing more to do. However, you have lots more to do. Don't abandon the goal of spiritual practice: experiencing four-fold Nibbana.

There are two possibilities. If you apply Dhamma within, your sufferings will cease. If you don't apply Dhamma within, your sufferings will not cease. Depending on the extent to which you apply Dhamma within and your intentional actions, the consequences will be upon you. By engaging in ten wholesome deeds, especially by developing the right view, you may reach a Sotapanna. Noble virtues a person possesses allow a person to have purity in mind day and night. Purity in mind is reflected in your intentional actions and verbal and bodily actions. You may think that's enough, that's nothing more to do. However, you have lots more to do. Don't abandon the goal of spiritual practice; experiencing four-fold Nibbana.

Therefore, by abandoning sensual desires and ill will, you may reach the Angami state. By reaching it, your mind will remain in the "brahma vihara" state while walking, standing, sitting and lying. Thereafter, abandon further desires, doubt, and higher fetters, and you may reach Arahantship. It is difficult to expect benefits of a Dhamma practice without reasoning, and the first reasoning should be that, unless one gains Nibbana, it is reasonable to expect that one will be unable to explain the training path that leads to Nibbana. Second, Buddha's path requires following Buddha's ways. Buddha never kept secrets; instead, the path leading to Nibbana was made available to others. Thus, following Buddha's ways, Dhamma should be made transparent and shared with others, with reasoning and not without reasoning by those who have already gained a full understanding of four-fold Nibbana. In this way, fellow practitioners will have an opportunity to hear Dhamma leading to Nibbana and end suffering for themselves if they wish to.

"So I have heard. At one time the Buddha was staying in the land of the Aṅgas, near the Aṅgan town named Assapura. There the Buddha addressed the companions, "Companions!"

"Venerable sir," they replied. The Buddha said this:

"Companions, people label you as ascetic. And when they ask you what you are, you claim to be ascetics.

Given this label and this claim, you should train like this: 'We will undertake and follow the things that make one a noble disciple and an Arahant. That way our label will be accurate, and our claim correct. Any donations (clothing, food, lodgings, medicines, etc.) that we use will be very fruitful and beneficial for the donor. And our purpose of practicing dhamma to gain four-fold nibbana will not be wasted but will be fruitful and fertile.'

And what are the things that make one an ascetic and a brahmin? You should train like this: 'We will have conscience and prudence.' Now, companions, you might think, 'We have conscience and prudence. This is sufficient; enough has been done. We have achieved the goal of life as an ascetic. There is nothing more to do.' And you might rest content with just that much. I declare this to you, companions, I announce this to you: 'You who seek to be true ascetics, do not lose sight of the goal of the ascetic life while there is still more to do.'

What more is there to do? You should train like this: 'Our bodily behavior will be pure, clear, open, neither inconsistent nor secretive. And we won't glorify ourselves or put others down on account of our pure bodily behavior.' Now, companions, you might think, 'We have conscience and prudence, and our bodily behavior is pure. This is sufficient …' I declare this to you, companions, I announce this to you: 'You who seek to be true ascetics, do not lose sight of the goal of the ascetic life while there is still more to do.'

What more is there to do? You should train like this: 'Our verbal behavior … mental behavior … livelihood will be pure, clear, open, neither inconsistent nor secretive. And we won't glorify ourselves or put others down on account of our pure livelihood.' Now, companions, you might think, 'We have conscience and prudence, our bodily, verbal, and mental behavior is pure, and our livelihood is pure. This is sufficient; enough has been done. We have achieved the goal of life as an ascetic. There is nothing more to do.' And you might rest content with just that much. I declare this to you, companions, I announce this to you: 'You who seek to be true ascetics, do not lose sight of the goal of the spiritual life while there is still more to do.'

What more is there to do? You should train yourselves like this: 'We will restrain our sense doors. When we see a sight with our eyes, we won't get caught up in the features and details. If the faculty of sight were left unrestrained, bad unskillful qualities of covetousness and displeasure would become overwhelming. For this reason, we will practice restraint, we will protect the faculty of sight, and we will achieve its restraint. When we hear a sound with our ears … When we smell an odor with our nose … When we taste a flavor with our tongue … When we feel a touch with our body … When we know an idea with our mind, we won't get caught up in the features and details. If the faculty of mind were left unrestrained, bad unskillful qualities of covetousness and displeasure would become overwhelming. For this reason, we will practice restraint, we will protect the faculty of mind, and we will achieve its restraint.' Now, companions, you might think, 'We have conscience and prudence, our bodily, verbal, and mental behavior is pure, our livelihood is pure, and our sense doors are restrained. This is sufficient …'

What more is there to do? You should train yourselves like this: 'We will not eat too much. We will only eat after reflecting rationally on our food. We will eat not for fun, indulgence, adornment, or decoration, but only to sustain this body, to avoid harm, and to support spiritual practice. In this way, we shall put an end to old discomfort and not give rise to new discomfort, and we will have the means to keep going, blamelessness, and a comfortable abiding.' Now, companions, you might think, 'We have conscience and prudence, our bodily, verbal, and mental behavior is pure, our livelihood is pure, our sense doors are restrained, and we don't eat too much. This is sufficient …'

What more is there to do? You should train yourselves like this: 'We will be dedicated to wakefulness. Reflecting day and night in any posture, we will purify our mind from obstacles, grasping conventions. In the first watch of the night, we will continue to develop or maintain noble mindfulness. In the middle watch, we will lie down in the lion's posture—on the right side, placing one foot on top of the other— we will continue to develop or maintain noble mindfulness, and focused on the time of getting up. In the last watch, we will continue to develop or maintain noble mindfulness, purifying our mind from obstacles.' Now, companions, you might think, 'We have conscience and prudence, our bodily, verbal, and mental behavior is pure, our livelihood is pure, our sense doors are restrained, we don't eat too much, and we are dedicated to wakefulness. This is sufficient …'

What more is there to do? You should train yourselves like this: 'We will have situational awareness and mindfulness. We will act with situational awareness when going out and coming back; when looking ahead and aside; when bending and extending the limbs; when bearing the outer robe, bowl and robes; when eating, drinking, chewing, and tasting; when urinating and defecating; when walking, standing, sitting, sleeping, waking, speaking, and keeping silent.' Now, companions, you might think, 'We have conscience and prudence, our bodily, verbal, and mental behavior is pure, our livelihood is pure, our sense doors are restrained, we don't eat too much, we are dedicated to wakefulness, and we have mindfulness and situational awareness. This is sufficient …'

What more is there to do? Take a person who develops a practice of mental attachment, and wherever they stay—a city, a building (house or temple), a forest (wilderness, the root of a tree, a hill, a ravine, a mountain cave, a charnel ground, the open air, a heap of straw, etc.). After the activities and meal, they return to their place of resting, as ordinary practitioners, they should strive to progress in their practice and to develop noble mindfulness (Those who experience four-fold Nibbana, naturally have noble mindfulness). Giving up covetousness for the world, they should reflect with a heart rid of covetousness, cleansing the mind of covetousness. Giving up ill will and malevolence, they should gain Anagami state with a mind rid of ill will, full of sympathy for all living beings, cleansing the mind of ill will. Giving up dullness and drowsiness, they should get rid of dullness and drowsiness, percipient of light, be mindful and aware, cleansing the mind of dullness and drowsiness. Giving up restlessness and remorse, they should reflect without restlessness, their mind peaceful inside, cleansing the mind of restlessness and remorse. Giving up doubt, they should reflect on their thoughts having gone beyond doubt, not undecided about skillful qualities, cleansing the mind of doubt (Naturally the Arahants have these qualities). Suppose a man who has gotten into debt were to apply himself to work, and his efforts proved successful. He would pay off the original loan and have enough left over to support his partner. Thinking about this, he'd be filled with joy and happiness.

Suppose a person was sick, suffering, and gravely ill. They'd lose their appetite and get physically weak. But after some time they'd recover from that illness, and regain their appetite and their strength. Thinking about this, they'd be filled with joy and happiness.

Suppose a person was imprisoned in a jail. But after some time they were released from jail, safe and sound, with no loss of wealth. Thinking about this, they'd be filled with joy and happiness.

Suppose a person was a bondservant. They would not be their own master, but indentured to another, unable to go where they wish. But after some time they'd be freed from servitude. They would be their own master, not indentured to another, an emancipated individual able to go where they wish. Thinking about this, they'd be filled with joy and happiness.

Suppose there was a person with wealth and property who was traveling along a desert road. But after some time they crossed over the desert, safe and sound, with no loss of wealth. Thinking about this, they'd be filled with joy and happiness.

In the same way, as long as these five hindrances are not given up inside themselves, a person regards them as a debt, a disease, a prison, slavery, and a desert crossing. But when these five hindrances are given up inside themselves, a companion regards this as freedom from debt, good health, release from prison, emancipation, and a place of sanctuary at last.

They give up these five hindrances, corruptions of the heart that weaken wisdom. Then, quite secluded from sensual pleasures, secluded from unskillful qualities, they enter and remain in the first absorption, which has the rapture and bliss born of seclusion, while placing the mind and keeping it connected. They drench, steep, fill, and spread their body with rapture and bliss born of seclusion. There's no part of the body that's not spread with rapture and bliss born of seclusion. It's like when a deft bathroom attendant or their apprentice pours bath powder into a bronze dish, sprinkling it little by little with water. They knead it until the ball of bath powder is soaked and saturated with moisture, spread through inside and out; yet no moisture oozes out.

In the same way, a person drenches, steeps, fills, and spreads their body with rapture and bliss born of seclusion. There's no part of the body that's not spread with rapture and bliss born of seclusion.

Furthermore, as the placing of the mind and keeping it connected are stilled, a person enters and remains in the second absorption, which has the rapture and bliss born of immersion, with internal clarity and mind at one, without placing the mind and keeping it connected. They drench, steep, fill, and spread their body with rapture and bliss born of immersion. There's no part of the body that's not spread with rapture and bliss born of immersion. It's like a deep lake fed by spring water. There's no inlet to the east, west, north, or south, and the heavens would not properly bestow showers from time to time. But the stream of cool water welling up in the lake drenches, steeps, fills, and spreads throughout the lake. There's no part of the lake that's not spread through with cool water.

In the same way, a person drenches, steeps, fills, and spreads their body with rapture and bliss born of immersion. There's no part of the body that's not spread with rapture and bliss born of immersion.

Furthermore, with the fading away of rapture, a person enters and remains in the third absorption, where they reflect with equanimity, mindful and aware, personally experiencing the bliss of which the noble ones declare, 'Equanimous and mindful, one experiences bliss.' They drench, steep, fill, and spread their body with bliss free of rapture. There's no part of the body that's not spread with bliss free of rapture. It's like a pool with blue water lilies, or pink or white lotuses. Some of them sprout and grow in the water without rising above it, thriving underwater. From the tip to the root they're drenched, steeped, filled, and soaked with cool water. There's no part of them that's not soaked with cool water.

In the same way, a person drenches, steeps, fills, and spreads their body with bliss free of rapture. There's no part of the body that's not spread with bliss free of rapture.

Furthermore, giving up pleasure and pain, and ending former happiness and sadness, a person enters and remains in the fourth absorption, without pleasure or pain, with pure equanimity and mindfulness. They sit spreading their body through with pure bright mind. There's no part of the body that's not spread with pure bright mind. It's like someone sitting wrapped from head to foot with white cloth. There's no part of the body that's not spread over with white cloth.

In the same way, they sit spreading their body through with pure bright mind. There's no part of the body that's not spread with pure bright mind.

When their mind has become immersed in noble concentration like this—purified, bright, flawless, rid of corruptions, pliable, workable, steady, and imperturbable—they extend it toward recollection of past lives. They recollect many kinds of past lives, with features and details. Suppose a person was to leave their home village and go to another village. From that village they'd go to yet another village. And from that village they'd return to their home village. They'd think: 'I went from my home village to another village. There I stood like this, sat like that, spoke like this, or kept silent like that. From that village I went to yet another village. There too I stood like this, sat like that, spoke like this, or kept silent like that. And from that village I returned to my home village.'

In the same way, a person recollects their many kinds of past lives, with features and details.

When their mind has become immersed in noble concentration like this—purified, bright, flawless, rid of corruptions, pliable, workable, steady, and imperturbable—they extend it toward knowledge of the death and rebirth of sentient beings. With clairvoyance that is purified and superhuman, they see sentient beings passing away and being reborn—inferior and superior, beautiful and ugly, in a good place or a bad place. They understand how sentient beings are reborn according to their deeds. Suppose there were two houses with doors. A person with clear eyes standing in between them would see people entering and leaving a house and wandering to and fro.

In the same way, with clairvoyance that is purified and superhuman, they see sentient beings passing away and being reborn—inferior and superior, beautiful and ugly, in a good place or a bad place. They understand how sentient beings are reborn according to their deeds.

Upon gaining Arahantship, when their mind has become immersed in noble concentration like this—purified, bright, flawless, rid of corruptions, pliable, workable, steady, and imperturbable—they extend it toward knowledge of the ending of defilements. They truly understand: 'This is suffering' … 'This is the origin of suffering' … 'This is the cessation of suffering' … 'This is the practice that leads to the cessation of suffering.' They truly understand: 'These are defilements' … 'This is the origin of defilements' … 'This is the cessation of defilements' … 'This is the practice that leads to the cessation of defilements.' Knowing and seeing like this, their mind is freed from the defilements of sensuality, desire to be reborn, and ignorance. When they're freed, they know they're freed. They understand: 'Rebirth is ended, the spiritual journey has been completed, what had to be done has been done, there is nothing further for this place.'

Suppose that in a mountain glen there was a lake that was transparent, clear, and unclouded. A person with clear eyes standing on the bank would see the clams and mussels, and pebbles and gravel, and schools of fish swimming about or staying still. They'd think: 'This lake is transparent, clear, and unclouded. And here are the clams and mussels, and pebbles and gravel, and schools of fish swimming about or staying still.'

In the same way, an Arahant, truly understands: 'This is suffering' … 'This is the origin of suffering' … 'This is the cessation of suffering' … 'This is the practice that leads to the cessation of suffering.' They understand: '… there is nothing further for this place.'

This companion is one who is called an 'ascetic', a 'brahmin', a 'bathed initiate', a 'knowledge master', a 'scholar', a 'noble one', and also a 'perfected one'.

And how is a person an ascetic? They have assuaged the bad, unskillful qualities; grasping self-view and conventions that are corrupting, leading to future lives, hurtful, resulting in suffering and future rebirth, old age, and death. That's how a person is an ascetic (Sotapanna to Arahant).

And how is a person a brahmin? They have banished the bad, unskillful qualities, grasping self-view and conventions and other fetters. That's how a person is a brahmin (Sotapanna to Arahant).

And how is a person a bathed initiate? They have bathed off the bad, unskillful qualities, grasping self-view and conventions and other fetters. That's how a person is a bathed initiate (Sotapanna to Arahant).

And how is a person a knowledge master? They have known the bad, unskillful qualities; grasping self-view and conventions and other fetters. That's how a person is a knowledge master (Sotapanna to Arahant).

And how is a person a scholar? They have scoured off the bad, unskillful qualities, grasping self-view and conventions and other fetters. That's how a person is a scholar (Sotapanna to Arahant).

And how is a person a noble one? They have nobbled their foes, the bad, unskillful qualities, grasping self-view and conventions and other fetters. That's how a person is a noble one (Sotapanna to Arahant).

And how is a person a perfected one, Arahant? They are impeccably remote from the bad, unskillful qualities; ten fetters that are corrupting, leading to future lives, hurtful, resulting in suffering and future rebirth, old age, and death. That's how a person is a perfected one (Arahant)."

That is what the Buddha said. Satisfied, the companions approved what the Buddha said.

Chapter 42

Middle Discourses 40: Cūḷaassapurasutta

The Shorter Discourse at Assapura

When people ask you, what are you? A person claims to be a physician, but the person who claims to be a physician has not completed any relevant training. Therefore, a person who pretends to be a physician puts the patient's life at risk. If someone claims to be a physician, a scientist, an engineer, an IT professional, a plumber, or a carpenter, that person should have completed the relevant training so those who attend to them should fulfill the goal for what they attend. Similarly, in Buddha's path, a person who shares Dhamma (Dhamma means four-fold Nibbana) should have completed the relevant training, so those who attend them should fulfill the goal for what they attend. Without completing the relevant training, training related to reducing deluded understanding (expectations come due to self being a permanent self), and reducing greed (likes, dislikes), and hate, a person cannot instruct another to give up too many likes (greed), too many dislikes (hate) and delusions, and to complete training. Training is about reducing fetters: self-view and grasping conventions and giving up the mental attachment that occurs due to a deluded understanding of worldly experiences across stages.

Reducing fetters requires thinking with superior wisdom[22] and wisdom-based concentration, not merely concentration without wisdom. To a greater extent, wisdom means the right view.

Self knows all about self, and when there is a disparity between what the person is thinking and what the person is saying or doing and pretending to be someone who they are not, what is conventionally described as "Two-faced" or "Multi-faced", such a person will only grow in self-view. Similary, due to dishonesty and a lack of integrity and ethics, when people make up Dhamma, a

---

[22] Buddhahood is a state of wisdom. When someone says something, wisdom expressed in words, you can only understand it within your wisdom. Wise people will comprehend wise words (See, for example, Dhp 11 &12 : *"The two Chief Disciples then related to the Buddha how they went to the Giragga festival, the meeting with Thera Assaji and their attainment of Sotapatti Fruition. They also told the Buddha about their former teacher Sanjaya, who refused to accompany them. Sanjaya had said, "Having been a teacher to so many pupils, for me to become his pupil would be like a jar turning into a drinking cup. Besides, only few people are wise and the majority are foolish; let the wise go to the wise Gotama, the foolish would still come to me. Go your way, my pupils."*).

version of some kind of practice and what they label as Buddha's Dhamma, four-fold Nibbana (the noble Dhamma) taught by the Buddha who is perfect in honesty, perfect in integrity and perfect in wisdom, and ethics has been clearly open for many people to see over centuries. As a consequence, people who genuinely seek Nibbana are unable to comprehend what the Buddha taught and what he did not. It is simply for the benefit of those who genuinely seek Buddha's Dhamma; there is a need to open up the right vision, revealing the hidden, the good and the bad, the truth, the Noble Path leading to deathless Nibbana as taught by the Buddha, known only by the noble ones who have completed four-fold Nibbana.

You may want to question yourself and discover what you want. Do you want to be happy? Do you want to continue suffering and experience mental pain? You may make your choice and work on your choices. A person's freedom to make choices should always be respected, a matter related to ethics. Those who make up the choice to end mental pain and experience bliss in four-fold Nibbana may want to hear the wise words of Buddhahood (hear about the practice) and apply the practice (Dhamma) day and night to end their sufferings.

When asked if you claim you are a disciple of Buddha, you should try to become a genuine disciple of Buddha. Without attaining four-fold Nibbana, one cannot train another. Without declaring one's attainment, another person cannot know whether or not the person who shares Dhamma knowledge has completed the training (four-fold Nibbana).

How can one become a disciple of Buddha? By completing the four-fold Nibbana, a person becomes a disciple of Buddha. Until then, one is simply training to become a disciple of the Buddha but is not a disciple of the Buddha.

One who does not complete the four-fold Nibbana and practices the Dhamma is simply touching a double-edged sword. This is because unless one gains Nibbana, one's suffering will not cease. By understanding that, a person who aspires to one's own good may practice the Dhamma in a way that leads to abandoning their own mental pain and samsara.

Practicing Dhamma requires an ordinary person to learn not to boast of self. Those who aspire to train others to Nibbana may fulfill the qualities of noble ones, noble virtues (Sotapanna), noble concentration (Anagami), and noble wisdom (Arahant). May they fulfill the training that benefits those who attend to them for hearing higher Dhamma (Sotapanna to Arahant) and gain merits by supporting them in their living (for clothing, food, accommodation, and medicine, etc.). So, those who seek Nibbana, their intention of practicing the Dhamma to gain four-fold Nibbana is not wasted.

"So I have heard. At one time the Buddha was staying in the land of the Aṅgas, near the Aṅgan town named Assapura. There the Buddha addressed the companions, "Companions!"

"Venerable sir," they replied. The Buddha said this:

"Companions, people label you as the disciples of Buddha. And when they ask you what you are, you claim to be the disciples of Buddha.

Given this label and this claim, you should train like this: 'We will practice in the way that is proper for a disciple of Buddha. That way our label will be accurate, and our claim correct. Any donations you receive (for food, clothing, lodgings, and medicines etc.) will be very fruitful and beneficial for the donor. And your spiritual practice will not be wasted but will be fruitful and fertile.'

And how does a companion not practice in the way that is proper for a disciple of Buddha?

Any person who has not given up covetousness, ill will, irritability, acrimony, disdain, contempt, jealousy, stinginess, deviousness, deceit, corrupt wishes, and wrong view is not practicing in the way that is proper for a disciple of Buddha, I say. And that is due to not giving up these stains, defects, and dregs of an ascetic, these grounds for rebirth in places of loss, to be experienced in bad places.

I say that such a companion's spiritual practice may be compared to the kind of weapon called 'deadborn'—double-edged, whetted with yellow arsenic—that has been covered and wrapped in an outer robe.

I say that you don't deserve the label 'outer robe wearer' just because you wear an outer robe. You don't deserve the label 'naked ascetic' just because you go naked. You don't deserve the label 'dust and dirt wearer' just because you're caked in dust and dirt.

You don't deserve the label 'water immerser' just because you immerse yourself in water. You don't deserve the label 'tree root dweller' just because you stay at the root of a tree. You don't deserve the label 'open air dweller' just because you stay in the open air. You don't deserve the label 'stander' just because you continually stand. You don't deserve the label 'interval eater' just because you eat food at set intervals. You don't deserve the label 'reciter' just because you recite hymns. You don't deserve the label 'matted-hair ascetic' just because you have matted hair.

Imagine that just by wearing an outer robe someone with covetousness, ill will, irritability, acrimony, disdain, contempt, jealousy, stinginess, deviousness, deceit, corrupt wishes, and wrong view could give up these things.

If that were the case, your friends and colleagues, relatives and kin would make you an outer robe wearer as soon as you were born. They'd encourage you: 'Please, dearest, wear an outer robe! By doing so you will give up covetousness, ill will, irritability, acrimony, disdain, contempt, jealousy, stinginess, deviousness, deceit, corrupt wishes, and wrong view.' But sometimes I see someone with these bad qualities who is an outer robe wearer. That's why I say that you don't deserve the label 'outer robe wearer' just because you wear an outer robe.

Imagine that just by going naked … wearing dust and dirt … immersing in water … staying at the root of a tree … staying in the open air … standing continually … eating at set intervals … reciting hymns … having matted hair someone with covetousness, ill will, irritability, acrimony, disdain, contempt, jealousy, stinginess, deviousness, deceit, corrupt wishes, and wrong view could give up these things. If that were the case, your friends and colleagues, relatives and kin would make you a matted-hair ascetic as soon as you were born.

They'd encourage you: 'Please, dearest, become a matted-hair ascetic! By doing so you will give up covetousness, ill will, irritability, hostility, disdain, contempt, jealousy, stinginess, deviousness, deceit, corrupt wishes, and wrong view.' But sometimes I see someone with these bad qualities who is a matted-hair ascetic. That's why I say that you don't deserve the label 'matted-hair ascetic' just because you have matted hair.

And how does a person practice in the way that is proper for a disciple of Buddha?

Any person who has given up covetousness, ill will, irritability, acrimony, disdain, contempt, jealousy, stinginess, deviousness, deceit, corrupt wishes, and wrong view is practicing in the way that is proper for an ascetic, I say. And that is due to giving up these stains, defects, and dregs of an ascetic, these grounds for rebirth in places of loss, to be experienced in bad places.

Upon gaining Sotapanna and Sakadagami, they see themselves purified from all these bad, unskillful qualities. Seeing this, joy springs up. Being joyful, rapture springs up. When the mind is full of rapture, the body becomes tranquil. When the body is tranquil, they feel bliss. And when blissful, the mind becomes immersed in noble concentration leading to Anagami.

They have a heart full of love to one direction, and to the second, and to the third, and to the fourth. In the same way above, below, across, everywhere, all around, they spread a heart full of love to the whole world—abundant, expansive, limitless, free of enmity and ill will.

They have a heart full of compassion …

They have a heart full of rejoicing …

They have a heart full of equanimity to one direction, and to the second, and to the third, and to the fourth. In the same way above, below, across, everywhere, all around, they spread a heart full of equanimity to the whole world—abundant, expansive, limitless, free of enmity and ill will.

Suppose there was a lotus pond with clear, sweet, cool water, clean, with smooth banks, delightful. Then along comes a person—whether from the east, west, north, or south—struggling in the oppressive heat, weary, thirsty, and parched. No matter what direction they come from, when they arrive at that lotus pond they would alleviate their thirst and heat exhaustion.

In the same way, suppose someone has commenced a spiritual practice—whether from a family of aristocrats, brahmins, peasants, or menials—and has arrived at the teaching (path to Arahantship) and training proclaimed by a Realized One. Having developed love, compassion, rejoicing, and equanimity in this way they gain inner peace. Because of that inner peace they are practicing the way proper for a disciple of Buddha, I say.

And suppose someone has commenced a spiritual practice—irrespective of a person's conventional background, whether from a family of aristocrats, brahmins, peasants, or workers—and they realize the undefiled freedom of heart and freedom by wisdom in this very life (Arahantship). And they live having realized it with their own insight due to the ending of defilements. They're a disciple of Buddha because of the ending of defilements."

That is what the Buddha said. Satisfied, the companions approved what the Buddha said.

Chapter 43

Middle Discourses 41: Sāleyyakasutta

The People of Sālā

The discourse explains why some people are reborn in comfortable places (heavenly worlds) and some are reborn in uncomfortable places (hellish worlds), based on the list of the ten kinds of wholesome conduct. At the beginning of one's practice, before reaching a mind state of a Stream-enterer, one may take precepts or monastic rules, gain a theoretical knowledge of Dhamma, listen to Dhamma from Arahants, associate with noble people, develop concentration, live in a suitable location, engage in a suitable education and business activities, engage in wholesome activities and create merits by attending to Triple Gem, become a good person; respect others, maintain loving kindness towards others, look after friends and family and others, discuss Dhamma on due occasions and apply Dhamma in daily life, avoid unwholesome activities, and thereafter gradually develop a higher understanding of Dhamma across four stages.

There is a unified training path to all, which is universally applicable to entering into Stream Entry and which is based on developing the right view and gaining a deep understanding. Before reaching a state of Stream-entry, subject to individual differences, one may possess identities and may give too much value to such views. Abandoning clinging to such identities requires progressive training in the mind.

Practicing Dhamma is reducing too many desires in the middle way (desire meaning touching the worldly experiences in mind; in other words, it means reducing too many likes, dislikes and expectations that come from too many likes and dislikes) for worldly things; possessions, materials, honor, friendships/relationships and similar things by understanding it is meaningless to grasp into worldly experiences, as they eventually change anyway within one's daily life.

Such conduct is not in accordance with the Dhamma, by reason of such unrighteous conduct that some beings here on the dissolution of the body, after death, reappear in states of deprivation, in an unhappy destination, in perdition, even in hell.

Reducing ill will is practicing Dhamma, wishing what belongs to another be mine is developing greediness. May something bad happen to another is developing ill will. Just saying, may these beings be free from enmity, affliction and anxiety but dividing people (i.e. maintaining the hierarchy in monastic institutions etc.), and causing harm or distress to any being is non-dhamma!

Developing the right view:

The right view for an ordinary person is understanding universal ways of functioning and karma. Undistorted vision, thus: "There is what is given and what is offered and what is sacrificed; there is fruit and the results of good and bad actions. There is this world and the other world; there is mother and father; there are beings who are reborn spontaneously; there are good and noble ones and Arahants in the world who have themselves realized by direct knowledge and declare this world and the other world". If a person who observes conduct in accordance with the Dhamma, righteous conduct, should wish: 'Oh, that on the dissolution of the body, after death, I might reappear in the company of well-to-do nobles!' it is possible that, on the dissolution of the body, after death, one will reappear in the company of well-to-do nobles. Why is that? Because one observes conduct (*intentional actions*) that is in accordance with the Dhamma, which is righteous conduct.

"So I have heard. At one time the Buddha was wandering in the land of the Kosalans together with a large group of community members, Saṅgha when he arrived at a village of the Kosalan brahmins named Sālā.

The people from various castes, ordinary people of Sālā heard, "It seems the ascetic Gotama—a Sakyan, spiritual teacher from a Sakyan family—while wandering in the land of the Kosalans has arrived at Sālā, together with a large group of his followers, Saṅgha.

He has this good reputation: 'That Blessed One is perfected, a fully awakened Buddha, accomplished in knowledge and conduct, holy, knower of the world, supreme guide for those who wish to train, teacher of gods and humans, awakened, blessed.' He has realized with his own insight this world—with its gods, Māras, and divinities, this population with its ascetics and brahmins, gods and humans—and he makes it known to others. He proclaims a teaching that is good in the beginning, good in the middle, and good in the end, meaningful and well-phrased. He reveals an entirely full and pure spiritual life. It's good to see such perfected ones."

Then the people from various castes, ordinary people of Sālā went up to the Buddha. Before sitting down to one side, some bowed, some exchanged greetings and polite conversation, some held up their joined palms toward the Buddha, some announced their name and clan, while some kept silent. Seated to one side they said to the Buddha:

"What is the cause, Mister Gotama, what is the reason why some sentient beings, when their body breaks up, after death, are reborn in a place of loss, a bad place, the underworld, hell? And what is the cause, Mister Gotama, what is the reason why some sentient beings, when their body breaks up, after death, are reborn in a good place, a heavenly realm?"

"Unprincipled and immoral conduct is the reason why some sentient beings, when their body breaks up, after death, are reborn in a place of loss, a bad place, the underworld, hell. Principled and moral conduct is the reason why some sentient beings, when their body breaks up, after death, are reborn in a good place, a heavenly realm."

"We don't understand the detailed meaning of Mister Gotama's brief statement. Mister Gotama, please teach us this matter in detail so we can understand the meaning."

"Well then, listen and apply your mind well, I will speak."

"Yes, sir," they replied. The Buddha said this:

"Commoners, unprincipled and immoral conduct is threefold by way of body, fourfold by way of speech, and threefold by way of mind.

And how is unprincipled and immoral conduct threefold by way of body? It's when a certain person kills living creatures. They're violent, bloody-handed, a hardened killer, merciless to living beings.

They steal. With the intention to commit theft, they take the wealth or belongings of others from village or wilderness.

They commit sexual misconduct. They have sexual relations with women who have their mother, father, both mother and father, brother, sister, relatives, or clan as guardian. They have sexual relations with a woman who is protected on principle, or who has a husband, or whose violation is punishable by law, or even one who has been garlanded as a token of betrothal. This is how unprincipled and immoral conduct is threefold by way of body.

And how is unprincipled and immoral conduct fourfold by way of speech?

It's when a certain person lies. They're summoned to a council, an assembly, a family meeting, a guild, or to the royal court, and asked to bear witness: 'Please, mister, say what you know.' Not knowing, they say 'I know.' Knowing, they say 'I don't know.' Not seeing, they say 'I see.' And seeing, they say 'I don't see.' So they deliberately lie for the sake of themselves or another, or for some trivial worldly reason.

They speak divisively. They repeat in one place what they heard in another so as to divide people against each other. And so they divide those who are harmonious, supporting division, delighting in division, loving division, speaking words that promote division.

They speak harshly. They use the kinds of words that are cruel, nasty, hurtful, offensive, bordering on anger, not leading to immersion.

They talk nonsense. Their speech is untimely, and is neither factual nor beneficial. It has nothing to do with the teaching or the training. Their words have no value, and are untimely, unreasonable, rambling, and pointless. This is how unprincipled and immoral conduct is fourfold by way of speech.

And how is unprincipled and immoral conduct threefold by way of mind? It's when a certain person is covetous. They covet the wealth and belongings of others: 'Oh, if only their belongings were mine!'

They have ill will and malicious intentions: 'May these sentient beings be killed, slaughtered, slain, destroyed, or annihilated!'

They have the wrong view. Their perspective is distorted (they do not understand the universal way of functioning through wisdom): 'There's no meaning in giving, sacrifice, or offerings. There's no fruit or result of good and bad deeds. There's no afterlife. There's no such thing as mother and father, or beings that are reborn spontaneously. And there's no noble ones or Arahants who is rightly comported and rightly practiced, and who describes the afterlife after realizing it with their own insight.' This is how unprincipled and immoral conduct is threefold by way of mind.

That's how unprincipled and immoral conduct is the reason why some sentient beings, when their body breaks up, after death, are reborn in a place of loss, a bad place, the underworld, hell.

Householders, principled and moral conduct is threefold by way of body, fourfold by way of speech, and threefold by way of mind.

And how is principled and moral conduct threefold by way of body? It's when a certain person gives up killing living creatures. They renounce the rod and the sword. They're scrupulous and kind, living full of sympathy for all living beings.

They give up stealing. They don't, with the intention to commit theft, take the wealth or belongings of others from village or wilderness.

They give up sexual misconduct. They don't have sexual relations with women who have their mother, father, both mother and father, brother, sister, relatives, or clan as guardian. They don't have sexual relations with a woman who is protected on principle, or who has a husband, or whose violation is punishable by law, or even one who has been garlanded as a token of betrothal. This is how principled and moral conduct is threefold by way of body.

And how is principled and moral conduct fourfold by way of speech? It's when a certain person gives up lying. They're summoned to a council, an assembly, a family meeting, a guild, or to the royal court, and asked to bear witness: 'Please, mister, say what you know.' Not knowing, they say 'I don't know.' Knowing, they say 'I know.' Not seeing, they say 'I don't see.' And seeing, they say 'I see.' So they don't deliberately lie for the sake of themselves or another, or for some trivial worldly reason.

They give up divisive speech. They don't repeat in one place what they heard in another so as to divide people against each other. Instead, they reconcile those who are divided, supporting unity, delighting in harmony, loving harmony, speaking words that promote harmony.

They give up harsh speech. They speak in a way that's mellow, pleasing to the ear, lovely, going to the heart, polite, likable, and agreeable to the people.

They give up talking nonsense. Their words are timely, true, and meaningful, in line with the teaching and training. They say things at the right time which are valuable, reasonable, succinct, and beneficial. This is how principled and moral conduct is fourfold by way of speech.

And how is principled and moral conduct threefold by way of mind? It's when a certain person is not covetous. They don't covet the wealth and belongings of others: 'Oh, if only their belongings were mine!'

They have a kind heart and loving intentions: 'May these sentient beings live free of enmity and ill will, untroubled and happy!'

They have the right view, an undistorted perspective (they understand the universal way of functioning through their wisdom): 'There is meaning in giving, sacrifice, and offerings. There are fruits and results of good and bad deeds. There is an afterlife. There are such things as mother and father, and beings that are reborn spontaneously. And there are noble ones or arahants who are rightly comported and rightly practiced, and who describe the afterlife after realizing it with their own insight.' This is how principled and moral conduct is threefold by way of mind.

This is how principled and moral conduct is the reason why some sentient beings, when their body breaks up, after death, are reborn in a good place, a heavenly realm.

A person of principled and moral thoughts, intentional conduct might wish: 'If only, when my body breaks up, after death, I would be reborn in the company of well-to-do aristocrats!' It's possible that this might happen. Why is that? Because they have principled and moral conduct.

A person of principled and moral thoughts, intentional conduct might wish: 'If only, when my body breaks up, after death, I would be reborn in the company of well-to-do brahmins ... well-to-do householders ... the gods of the four great kings ... the gods of the thirty-three ... the gods of Yama ... the joyful gods ... the gods who love to imagine ... the gods who control what is imagined by others ... the gods of the Divinity's host ... the radiant gods ... the gods of limited radiance ... the gods of limitless radiance ... the gods of streaming radiance ... the gods of limited beauty ... the gods of limitless beauty ... the gods of universal beauty ... the gods of abundant fruit ... the gods of Aviha ... the gods of Atappa ... the gods fair to see ... the fair seeing gods ... the gods of Akaniṭṭha ... the gods of the dimension of infinite space ... the gods of the dimension of infinite consciousness ... the gods of the dimension of nothingness ... the gods of the dimension of neither perception nor non-perception.' It's possible that this might happen. Why is that? Because they have principled and moral conduct.

A person of principled and moral thoughts; intentional conduct might wish: 'If only I might realize the undefiled freedom of heart and freedom by wisdom in this very life, and live having realized it with my own insight due to the ending of defilements.' It's possible that this might happen. Why is that? Because they have principled and moral conduct."

When he had spoken, the people from various castes, ordinary people of of Sālā said to the Buddha, "Excellent, Mister Gotama! Excellent! As if he were righting the overturned, or revealing the hidden, or pointing out the path to the lost, or lighting a lamp in the dark so people with clear eyes can see what's there, Mister Gotama has made the teaching clear in many ways. We go for refuge to Mister Gotama, to the teaching; four-fold nibbana, and to the universal (Savaka) Saṅgha. From this day forth, may Mister Gotama remember us as commoners (ordinary people) who have gone for refuge for life."

Chapter 44

Middle Discourses 42: Verañjakasutta

The People of Verañjā

This discourse records the Buddha explaining the conduct leading to rebirth and Nibbana. What is commonly known is taking precepts. What is needed to bridge the gap between an ordinary state and Sotapanna is shaping one's view. That is the right view.

The practice leading to Nibbana is the right view. The right view is that life is an interaction between the universe and conventions. People are born into random paces at random times. The universe functions in such a way that, when a person is born, birth brings death. Illnesses, losses, gains, falls and rises are part of life, the way of life. Once born, people can do many things and make certain choices that helps them to refine the quality of living, improve lives and their karma.

Life is an interaction between the universe and conventions. What is commonly agreed by the society is not the agreement by universal functioning, Nibbana, rather each and every individual come to experience consequences of their own karma. Each being is responsible for one's own karma, and life experience is individually experienced by teach, so as Nibbana is a personal experience for each.

Everything is a convention. There are only a few things that people can't do through conventions or collective agreements across societies. They cannot retain conventions with stability, decide on certain birth related aspects, where they will be born, etc. The sun shines as the function of the universe. The birth brings death to all in line with universal functioning. The universe functions in such a way that conventions can function only within the universe.

An ordinary person can understand Dhamma within ordinary understanding. Subject to individual differences, an ordinary person may think that Buddha's Dhamma is a life style. Subject to individual differences, an ordinary person not knowing four-fold Nibbana may speak of Dhamma that they haven't realized for themselves by dividing the teachings of the Buddha. Instead of giving priority to Buddha and Buddha's Dhamma, they may give priority to themselves and to other ordinary Sangha members, and they may talk about personal stories and others subject matters during the time that is allocated for their Dhamma discussions pretending to be disciples of Buddha, but they are not disciples of Buddha. In this manner, the path that leads to Buddha's perfect Dhamma; Sotapanna to Arahant may seem to have not visible (and disappear) in the absence of Arahants. Typically, when Arahants and noble ones (trainees) appear, they appear in the same period of time.

As said earlier, the practice leading to Nibbana is the right view. Right view for an ordinary person is understanding that life is an interaction between the universe and conventions, and the universal ways of functioning, karma to a reasonable level. An ordinary person cannot see samsara due to attachment to limited vision. When your vision is stuck in conventions, you tend to forget universal ways of functioning. Yet, what your eyes cannot see, you can see with wisdom. In this way, wisdom can be developed by developing merits, shaping karma and putting efforts to practicing Dhamma in a way leading to four-fold Nibbana.

What makes people reborn in samsara? It is karma that makes people reborn in samsara.

What is karma? Intentional actions are karma. Actions without intentions free one from making new karma, which is the universal way of functioning. You may live in any city, any country, or any place of accommodation. You may wear any dress and speak any language. If you want to practice universal Dhamma in a way leading to four-fold Nibbana, you have to practice in the same way: reduce greediness (too many likes), hatred (too many dislikes), and delusion (expectations) by giving up grasping to fetters across four-fold Nibbana.

Greed, hate and delusion can burn you within. By understanding, you can let go of such burns.

When you have a limited vision, you don't see what lies beyond. When you look back on your past, you might notice that there were occasions when you did not see things and that your vision was limited. Attachment to mind and body makes someone stuck in mind and body, unable to see beyond mind and body.

Non-attachment to mind and body across four-fold Nibbana makes it possible for a person to surpass mind and body to see beyond; previous births, birth and death of beings, understanding attainment of Nibbana through wisdom.

One way to recognise a Sotapanna is that they don't divide the universal teachings. One way to recognize an Arahant is to say that they know Buddha is the knower of all through personal experience:

"So I have heard. At one time the Buddha was staying near Sāvatthī in Jeta's Grove, Anāthapiṇḍika's monastery.

Now at that time, the people from various castes, ordinary people of Verañjā were residing in Sāvatthī on some business. The people from various castes, ordinary people of Verañjā heard:

"It seems the ascetic Gotama—a Sakyan, gone forth from a Sakyan family—is staying near Sāvatthī in Jeta's Grove, Anāthapiṇḍika's monastery. He has this good reputation … It's good to see such perfected ones."

… They said to the Buddha: "What is the cause, Mister Gotama, what is the reason why some sentient beings, when their body breaks up, after death, are reborn in a place of loss, a bad place, the underworld, hell? And what is the cause, Mister Gotama, what is the reason why some sentient beings, when their body breaks up, after death, are reborn in a good place, a heavenly realm?"

"Unprincipled and immoral conduct is the reason why some sentient beings, when their body breaks up, after death, are reborn in a place of loss, a bad place, the underworld, hell. Principled and moral conduct is the reason why some sentient beings, when their body breaks up, after death, are reborn in a good place, a heavenly realm."

"We don't understand the detailed meaning of Mister Gotama's brief statement. …"

"Commoner friends, a person of unprincipled and immoral conduct is threefold by way of body, fourfold by way of speech, and threefold by way of mind. …" …

Chapter 45

Middle Discourses 43: Mahāvedallasutta

The Great Elaboration

This discourse records a conversation between Arahnt Sariputta and ordinary monk Mahākoṭṭhita who appear to not have yet gained Nibbana for he questions about four-fold Nibbana. It presents series of questions. His first question is what is a wise person and what is an unwise person? Wise person refers to someone who has gained four-fold Nibbana. This is because Nibbana is a wisdom and karma-based path.

Buddhahood, in its three routes (Supreme Buddha, Paceka Buddha, Savaka Buddha), is a state of wisdom. This discourse talks about four-fold Nibbana and its fetters and giving up greed, hate and delusion across stages. An ordinary person who has not seen noble ones is unlikely to be able to develop wisdom, not developing wisdom, they are likely to continue experiencing mental suffering in daily life. Wisdom can be gained through meritorious activities[23] and blending with universal ways.

When a person experiences worldly experiences through sensory information, a person's experiences are interpreted as "I experience pleasure", "displeasure" and so forth based on conventions. When a person experiences worldly experiences through sensory information, a person's experiences are interpreted as perceptions: colors, numbers, and so on, based on conventions. Interpreting feelings, perceptions, and consciousness based on conventions (words etc.) are related, not separate. A person requires developing wisdom to let go of attachment to feelings, perceptions and so on across four-fold Nibbana.

After completing the Anagami state, the mind goes into jhanas (space, infinite, etc.) at a random time. Upon becoming an Arahant, one becomes free from grasping conventions.

---

[23] Wisdom to see beyond the ordinary ways can be developed through both universal (creating merits etc.) and conventional ways (putting efforts etc.).

Seeing beyond conventions can be understood by developing wisdom. Wisdom can be developed by blending with the universal rhythm.

In how many existences can a person's rebirth take place? A person's rebirth can take place in sensual realms, fine-material realms, and immaterial realms.

The arising of right view, happens under two conditions. Hearing the words of Dhamma from Arahants, and paying proper attention. When you gain the right view, you can experience freedom from sufferings across four-fold Nibbana.

A person's birth is a combination of mind and body (heat or the body's temperature, living being; vitality that is a combination of material form and psychological form). Death makes a person's physical and mental abilities and warmth vanish; vitality is spent. Cessation temporarily suspends physical and mental abilities and retains heat and vitality, a person's physical and mental abilities remain clear but abandon grasping to the relevant fetters, end of samsara, and grasping "self" based on conventions.

After gaining Sakadagami, a person experiences joy when reflecting or thinking about the Triple Gem. When the mind feels joy, the mind goes into jhana and rupture (first jhana), a feeling of extreme joy that is felt in body and mind takes place at a random time. Rupture leads to a concentrated mind state that arises when unification takes place (second jhana). The unified mind brings equanimity, which is felt across the mind-body (third jhana). Thereafter, with the mind singularly focused upon itself, the mind enters a state of "neither-painful-nor-pleasurable" (fourth jhana). These four jhanas are the path to Anagami state. Upon completion of these jhanas, the knowledge of abandoning fetters takes place and a person abandons ill will and sensuality.

After the Anagami state, a person may experience various states of mind, specifically five kinds of jhanas as below, one after another happening at random times while walking, sitting, lying down, and so forth leading to Arahantship.
- fifth jhāna: infinite space
- Sixth jhāna: infinite consciousness
- Seventh jhāna: infinite nothingness
- Eighth jhāna: neither perception nor non-perception

Beyond the dimension of neither perception nor non-perception lies "nirodha samāpatti", the "cessation of perception, feelings and consciousness" temporary suppression of consciousness and its concomitant mental factors, knowledge regarding the completion of Arahantship arises. Freedom from greed, hate, and delusion is reached, and a person completes the four-fold Nibbāna.

At the Anagami state, one comes to realize that one is free from ill will and sensual pleasures. Thereafter, at the Arahant stage, one comes to realize that one does not like or dislike things. Reflecting on 32 parts is a suitable technique for a Sotapanna to reach the Anagami state.

"So I have heard. At one time the Buddha was staying near Sāvatthī in Jeta's Grove, Anāthapiṇḍika's monastery.

Then in the late afternoon, Mahākoṭṭhita came out of retreat, went to Arahant Sāriputta, and exchanged greetings with him. When the greetings and polite conversation were over, he sat down to one side and said to Arahant Sāriputta:

"Venerable sir, they speak of 'a witless person'. How is a witless person defined?"

"Respected friend, they're called witless because they don't understand. And what don't they understand? They don't understand: 'This is suffering' … 'This is the origin of suffering' … 'This is the cessation of suffering' … 'This is the practice that leads to the cessation of suffering.' They're called witless because they don't understand."

Saying "Good, venerable sir," Mahākoṭṭhita approved and agreed with what Arahant Sāriputta said. Then he asked another question:

"They speak of 'a wise person'. How is a wise person defined?"

"They're called wise because they understand. And what do they understand? They understand: 'This is suffering' … 'This is the origin of suffering' … 'This is the cessation of suffering' … 'This is the practice that leads to the cessation of suffering.' They're called wise because they understand."

"They speak of 'consciousness'. How is consciousness defined?"

"It's called consciousness because it cognizes. And what does it cognize? It cognizes 'pleasure' and 'pain' and 'neutral'. It's called consciousness because it cognizes."

"Wisdom and consciousness—are these things mixed or separate? And can we completely disentangle them so as to describe the difference between them?"

"Wisdom and consciousness—these things are mixed, not separate. And you can never completely disentangle them so as to describe the difference between them. For you understand what you cognize, and you cognize what you understand. That's why these things are mixed, not separate. And you can never completely disentangle them so as to describe the difference between them."

"Wisdom and consciousness—what is the difference between these things that are mixed, not separate?"

"The difference between these things is that wisdom should be developed, while consciousness should be completely understood."

"They speak of this thing called 'feeling'. How is feeling defined?"

"It's called feeling because it feels. And what does it feel? It feels pleasure, pain, and neutral. It's called feeling because it feels."

"They speak of this thing called 'perception'. How is perception defined?"

"It's called perception because it perceives. And what does it perceive? It perceives blue, yellow, red, and white. It's called perception because it perceives."

"Feeling, perception, and consciousness—are these things mixed or separate? And can we completely disentangle them so as to describe the difference between them?"

"Feeling, perception, and consciousness—these things are mixed, not separate. And you can never completely disentangle them so as to describe the difference between them. For you perceive what you feel, and you cognize what you perceive. That's why these things are mixed, not separate. And you can never completely disentangle them so as to describe the difference between them."

"What can be known by purified mind consciousness released from the five senses?"

"Aware that 'space is infinite' it can know the dimension of infinite space. Aware that 'consciousness is infinite' it can know the dimension of infinite consciousness. Aware that 'there is nothing at all' it can know the dimension of nothingness."

"How do you understand something that can be known?"

"You understand something that can be known with the eye of wisdom."

"What is the purpose of wisdom?"

"The purpose of wisdom is direct knowledge, complete understanding, and giving up."

"How many conditions are there for the arising of right view?"

"There are two conditions for the arising of right view: the voice of another and rational application of mind. These are the two conditions for the arising of right view."

"When right view is supported by how many factors does it have freedom of heart and freedom by wisdom as its fruit and benefit?"

"When right view is supported by five factors it has freedom of heart and freedom by wisdom as its fruit and benefit. It's when right view is supported by ethics, learning, discussion, serenity, and discernment. When right view is supported by these five factors it has freedom of heart and freedom by wisdom as its fruit and benefit."

"How many states of existence are there?"

"Respected friend, there are these three states of existence. Existence in the sensual realm, the realm of luminous form, and the formless realm."

"But how is there rebirth into a new state of existence in the future?"

"It's because of sentient beings—shrouded by ignorance and fettered by craving—taking pleasure wherever they land. That's how there is rebirth into a new state of existence in the future."

"But how is there no rebirth into a new state of existence in the future?"

"It's when ignorance fades away, knowledge arises, and craving ceases. That's how there is no rebirth into a new state of existence in the future."

"But what, respected sir, is the first absorption?"

"Respected friend, it's when a person (A Sakadagami), quite secluded from sensual pleasures, secluded from unskillful qualities, enters and remains in the first absorption, which has the rapture and bliss born of seclusion, while placing the mind and keeping it connected. This is called the first absorption."

"But how many factors does the first absorption have?"

"The first absorption has five factors. When a person has entered the first absorption, placing the mind, keeping it connected, rapture, bliss, and unification of mind are present. That's how the first absorption has five factors."

"But how many factors has the first absorption given up and how many does it possess?"

"The first absorption has given up five factors and possesses five factors. When a mendicant has entered the first absorption, sensual desire, ill will, dullness and drowsiness, restlessness and remorse, and doubt are given up. Placing the mind, keeping it connected, rapture, bliss, and unification of mind are present. That's how the first absorption has given up five factors and possesses five factors."

"Respected sir, these five faculties have different scopes and different ranges, and don't experience each others' scope and range. That is, the faculties of the eye, ear, nose, tongue, and body. What do these five faculties, with their different scopes and ranges, have recourse to? What experiences their scopes and ranges?"

"These five faculties, with their different scopes and ranges, have recourse to the mind. And the mind experiences their scopes and ranges."

"These five faculties depend on what to continue?"

"These five faculties depend on vitality to continue."

"But what does vitality depend on to continue?"

"Vitality depends on warmth to continue."

"But what does warmth depend on to continue?"

"Warmth depends on vitality to continue."

"Just now I understood you to say: 'Vitality depends on warmth to continue.' But I also understood you to say: 'Warmth depends on vitality to continue.' How then should we see the meaning of this statement?"

"Well then, respected sir, I shall give you a simile. For by means of a simile some sensible people understand the meaning of what is said. Suppose there was an oil lamp burning. The light appears dependent on the flame, and the flame appears dependent on the light. In the same way, vitality depends on warmth to continue, and warmth depends on vitality to continue."

"Are the vital forces the same things as the phenomena that are felt? Or are they different things?"

"The vital forces are not the same things as the phenomena that are felt. For if the vital forces and the phenomena that are felt were the same things, a person who had attained the cessation of perception and feeling would not emerge from it. But because the vital forces and the phenomena that are felt are different things, a person who has attained the cessation of perception and feeling can emerge from it."

"How many things must this body lose before it lies forsaken, tossed aside like an insentient log?"

"This body must lose three things before it lies forsaken, tossed aside like an insentient log: vitality, warmth, and consciousness."

"What's the difference between someone who has passed away and a person who has attained the cessation of perception and feeling?"

"When someone dies, their physical, verbal, and mental processes have ceased and stilled; their vitality is spent; their warmth is dissipated; and their faculties have disintegrated. When a person has attained the cessation of perception and feeling, their physical, verbal, and mental processes have ceased and stilled. But their vitality is not spent; their warmth is not dissipated; and their faculties are very clear. That's the difference between someone who has passed away and a mendicant who has attained the cessation of perception and feeling."

"How many conditions are necessary to attain the neutral release of the heart?"

"Four conditions are necessary to attain the neutral release of the heart. Giving up pleasure and pain, and ending former happiness and sadness, a person enters and remains in the fourth absorption, without pleasure or pain, with pure equanimity and mindfulness. These four conditions are necessary to attain the neutral release of the heart."

"How many conditions are necessary to attain the signless release of the heart?"

"Two conditions are necessary to attain the signless release of the heart: not focusing on any signs, and focusing on the signless. These two conditions are necessary to attain the signless release of the heart."

"How many conditions are necessary to remain in the signless release of the heart?"

"Three conditions are necessary to remain in the signless release of the heart: not focusing on any signs, focusing on the signless, and a previous determination. These three conditions are necessary to remain in the signless release of the heart."

"How many conditions are necessary to emerge from the signless release of the heart?"

"Two conditions are necessary to emerge from the signless release of the heart: focusing on all signs, and not focusing on the signless. These two conditions are necessary to emerge from the signless release of the heart."

"The limitless release of the heart, and the release of the heart through nothingness, and the release of the heart through emptiness, and the signless release of the heart: do these things differ in both meaning and phrasing? Or do they mean the same thing, and differ only in the phrasing?"

"There is a way in which these things differ in both meaning and phrasing. But there's also a way in which they mean the same thing, and differ only in the phrasing.

And what's the way in which these things differ in both meaning and phrasing?

Firstly, a person possess a heart full of love to one direction, and to the second, and to the third, and to the fourth. In the same way above, below, across, everywhere, all around, they spread a heart full of love to the whole world—abundant, expansive, limitless, free of enmity and ill will. They have a heart full of compassion …

They reflect on life experience spreading a heart full of rejoicing … They reflect on life experience spreading a heart full of equanimity to one direction, and to the second, and to the third, and to the fourth.

In the same way above, below, across, everywhere, all around, they spread a heart full of equanimity to the whole world—abundant, expansive, limitless, free of enmity and ill will. This is called the limitless release of the heart experienced by an Anagami.

And what is the release of the heart through nothingness? It's when a person, going totally beyond the dimension of infinite consciousness, aware that 'there is nothing at all', enters and remains in the dimension of nothingness. This is called the heart's release through nothingness.

And what is the release of the heart through emptiness? It's when a person has gone to a wilderness, or to the root of a tree, or to an empty hut, and reflects like this: 'This is empty of a self or what belongs to a self.' This is called the release of the heart through emptiness.

And what is the signless release of the heart? It's when a person, not focusing on any signs, enters and remains in the signless immersion of the heart. This is called the signless release of the heart.

This is the way in which these things differ in both meaning and phrasing.

And what's the way in which they mean the same thing, and differ only in the phrasing?

Greed, hate, and delusion are makers of limits. A person who has ended the defilements has given these up, cut them off at the root, made them like a palm stump, and obliterated them, so they are unable to arise in the future. The unshakable release of the heart is said to be the best kind of limitless release of the heart. That unshakable release of the heart is empty of greed, hate, and delusion.

Greed is something, hate is something, and delusion is something. A person who has ended the defilements has given these up, cut them off at the root, made them like a palm stump, and obliterated them, so they are unable to arise in the future. The unshakable release of the heart is said to be the best kind of release of the heart through nothingness. That unshakable release of the heart is empty of greed, hate, and delusion.

Greed, hate, and delusion are makers of signs. A person who has ended the defilements has given these up, cut them off at the root, made them like a palm stump, and obliterated them, so they are unable to arise in the future. The unshakable release of the heart is said to be the best kind of signless release of the heart. That unshakable release of the heart is empty of greed, hate, and delusion.

This is the way in which they mean the same thing, and differ only in the phrasing."

This is what Arahant Sāriputta said. Satisfied, Mahākoṭṭhita approved what Arahant Sāriputta said.

Chapter 46

Middle Discourses 44: Cūḷavedallasutta

The Shorter Elaboration

This discourse records a conversation between two spiritual companions: Visaka, an Anagami[24] and Dhammadinna, an Arahant. An ordinary person does not know what it is like to be experiencing lower and higher stages of Nibbana and the practice. An Anagami does not know what it like to experience Arahantship. Therefore, the questions related to four-fold Nibbana are being raised by an Anagami, Visaka and answered by Arahant Dhammadinna.

Desires and cravings are related to continuous attachment to worldly experiences, to a world that is created within a person. An ordinary person tends to possess an underlying tendency to grasp into self-view, body, feeling, perception, intentional action, and consciousness as belonging to me. On the other hand, a noble one does not to grasp into self-view, body, feeling, perception, intentional action, and consciousness as belonging to me.

One who attains cessation does not grasp into or make conscious efforts to experience cessation. 'I will attain the cessation of perception and feeling,' or 'I am attaining the cessation of perception and feeling,' or 'I have attained the cessation of perception and feeling.' Rather, it is a natural happening. They have previously completed former training (completed merits required for the purpose), so their mind reaches such a state without having to concentrate through conscious efforts. The practice is developed so that Nibbana happens at a random time.

---

[24] Visākha, he was a merchant by profession, and he was the former husband of Arahant Dhammadinna.

The middle way; not grasping is the noble way. Taking worldly experiences as belonging to me with an underlying tendency to believe I can retain self or other things is grasping conventions. Not grasping conventions is a noble way. The mind reaches a jhana state without a conscious attempt after completion of the Sotapanna and Sakadagami states. Giving up the underlying tendency to grasp into conventions, some fetters are given up by a Sotapanna. Thereafter, as a Sotapanna progresses across stages, the root cause of suffering (i.e. desire; likes, dislikes, expectations) is given up, and desires are given up naturally at the Arahant stage in mind.

When people who are ill seek treatment and ask a person who appears to be a physician merely because of their appearance (they look like a physician based on common people's assumptions), the physician's qualifications are not checked. Then, if that person without the appropriate training treats a patient, the patient's life may be at risk. Similarly, if a person seeking to end sufferings in this life and samsara approaches a person who looks like a noble saint merely through an assumed appearance, yet the qualifications of the trainer are not checked as to whether they completed four-fold Nibbana because unless one gains Nibbana for oneself, one would not know how to train another. The person's mental sufferings in this life will not end, and the danger of continuing in samsara stands out. Therefore, those who teach Dhamma and those who are learners may grow in their wisdom and integrity, which allows them to acknowledge they have not gained Nibbana and are unable to clarify the four-fold Nibbana in full but are sharing only the basics by keeping space to discover self and discover nibbana.

The training path leading to Nibbana can be developed by developing one's understanding to gain an understanding of a Stream Winner. By understanding what Dhamma and non-dhamma are, understanding who Buddha and non-Buddha is, understanding who noble Sangha and non-noble Sangha, and understanding Triple Gem, one can abandon fetters, and, by abandoning fetters, one can understand Triple Gem. Triple Gem and fetters are linked. Dhamma means Triple Gem and Triple Gem means Dhamma. By eradicating doubts and gaining a clear comprehension, those who wish to aspire to Nibbana may fulfill their wishes.

"So I have heard. At one time the Buddha was staying near Rājagaha, in the Bamboo Grove, the squirrels' feeding ground.

Then Anagami, Visākha went to see Arahant Dhammadinnā, bowed, sat down to one side, and said to her:

"Noble lady, they speak of this thing called 'substantial reality'. What is this substantial reality that the Buddha spoke of?"

"Sir Visākha, the Buddha said that these five grasping aggregates are substantial reality. That is, the grasping aggregates of form, feeling, perception, choices, and consciousness. The Buddha said that these five grasping aggregates are substantial reality."

Saying "Good," Visākha approved and agreed with what Arahant Dhammadinnā said. Then she asked another question:

"Noble lady, they speak of this thing called 'the origin of substantial reality'. What is the origin of substantial reality that the Buddha spoke of?"

"Sir Visākha, it's the craving that leads to future lives, mixed up with relishing and greed, taking pleasure wherever it lands. That is, craving for sensual pleasures, craving to continue existence, and craving to end existence. The Buddha said that this is the origin of substantial reality."

"Noble lady, they speak of this thing called 'the cessation of substantial reality'. What is the cessation of substantial reality that the Buddha spoke of?"

"Sir Visākha, it's the fading away and cessation of that very same craving with nothing left over; giving it away, letting it go, releasing it, and not clinging to it. The Buddha said that this is the cessation of substantial reality."

"Noble lady, they speak of the practice that leads to the cessation of substantial reality. What is the practice that leads to the cessation of substantial reality that the Buddha spoke of?"

"Noble Sir, the practice that leads to the cessation of substantial reality that the Buddha spoke of is simply this noble eightfold path, that is: right view, right thought, right speech, right action, right livelihood, right effort, right mindfulness, and right immersion."

"But Noble lady, is that grasping the exact same thing as the five grasping aggregates? Or is grasping one thing and the five grasping aggregates another?"

"That grasping is not the exact same thing as the five grasping aggregates. Nor is grasping one thing and the five grasping aggregates another. The desire and greed for the five grasping aggregates is the grasping there."

"Noble lady, how does substantialist view come about?"

"Here, an uneducated commoner – one who does not see noble ones, has not mastered the teachings of noble ones. They've not seen true persons, and are neither skilled nor trained in the teaching of the true persons. They regard form as self, self as having form, form in self, or self in form. They regard feeling ... perception ... choices ... consciousness as self, self as having consciousness, consciousness in self, or self in consciousness. That's how substantialist view comes about."

"But how does substantialist view not come about?"

"Here, an educated disciple of noble ones-one who sees the noble ones, and is skilled and trained in the teaching of the noble ones. They've seen true persons, and are skilled and trained in the teaching of the true persons. They don't regard form as self, self as having form, form in self, or self in form. They don't regard feeling ... perception ... choices ... consciousness as self, self as having consciousness, consciousness in self, or self in consciousness. That's how substantialist view does not come about."

"But Noble lady, what is the noble eightfold path?"

"Noble Sir, it is simply this noble eightfold path, that is: right view, right thought, right speech, right action, right livelihood, right effort, right mindfulness, and right immersion."

"Noble lady, is the noble eightfold path conditioned or unconditioned?"

"The noble eightfold path is conditioned."

"Are the three spectrums of practice included in the noble eightfold path? Or is the noble eightfold path included in the three practice categories?"

"The three spectrums of practice are not included in the noble eightfold path. Rather, the noble eightfold path is included in the three practice categories. Right speech, right action, and right livelihood: these things are included in the spectrum of ethics. Right effort, right mindfulness, and right immersion: these things are included in the spectrum of immersion. Right view and right thought: these things are included in the spectrum of wisdom."

"Noble lady, what is immersion? What things are the bases of immersion? What things are the prerequisites for immersion? What is the development of immersion?"

"Unification of the mind is immersion. The four kinds of mindfulness meditation are the bases for immersion. The four right efforts are the prerequisites for immersion. The cultivation, development, and making much of these very same things is the development of immersion."

"How many processes are there?"

"There are these three processes. Physical, verbal, and mental processes."

"Noble lady, what is the physical process? What's the verbal process? What's the mental process?"

"Noble Sir, breathing is a physical process. Placing the mind and keeping it connected are verbal processes. Perception and feeling are mental processes."

"Noble lady, why is breathing a physical process? Why are placing the mind and keeping it connected verbal processes? Why are perception and feeling mental processes?"

"Sir Visākha, breathing is physical. It's tied up with the body, that's why breathing is a physical process. First you place the mind and keep it connected, then you break into speech. That's why placing the mind and keeping it connected are verbal processes. Perception and feeling are mental. They're tied up with the mind, that's why perception and feeling are mental processes."

"But ma'am, how does someone attain the cessation of perception and feeling?"

"A person who is entering such an attainment does not think: 'I will enter the cessation of perception and feeling' or 'I am entering the cessation of perception and feeling' or 'I have entered the cessation of perception and feeling.' Rather, their mind has been previously developed so as to lead to such a state."

"Noble lady, which process ceases first for a person who is entering the cessation of perception and feeling: physical, verbal, or mental?"

"Noble Sir, the verbal process ceases first, then physical, then mental."

"Noble lady, how does someone emerge from the cessation of perception and feeling?"

"A person who is emerging from such an attainment does not think: 'I will emerge from the cessation of perception and feeling' or 'I am emerging from the cessation of perception and feeling' or 'I have emerged from the cessation of perception and feeling.' Rather, their mind has been previously developed so as to lead to such a state."

"Noble lady, which process arises first for a person who is emerging from the cessation of perception and feeling: physical, verbal, or mental?"

"Sir Visākha, the mental process arises first, then physical, then verbal."

"Noble lady, when a person has emerged from the attainment of the cessation of perception and feeling, how many kinds of contact do they experience?"

"Noble Sir, they experience three kinds of contact: emptiness, signless, and undirected contacts."

"Noble lady, when a person has emerged from the attainment of the cessation of perception and feeling, what does their mind slant, slope, and incline to?"

"Noble Sir, their mind slants, slopes, and inclines to seclusion."

"Noble lady, how many feelings are there?"

"There are three feelings: pleasant, painful, and neutral feeling."

"What are these three feelings?"

"Anything felt physically or mentally as pleasant or enjoyable. This is pleasant feeling. Anything felt physically or mentally as painful or unpleasant. This is painful feeling. Anything felt physically or mentally as neither pleasurable nor painful. This is neutral feeling."

"What is pleasant and what is painful regarding each of the three feelings?"

"Pleasant feeling is pleasant when it remains and painful when it perishes. Painful feeling is painful when it remains and pleasant when it perishes. Neutral feeling is pleasant in the presence of knowledge, and painful in the presence of ignorance."

"What underlying tendencies underlie each of the three feelings?"

"The underlying tendency for greed underlies pleasant feeling. The underlying tendency for repulsion underlies painful feeling. The underlying tendency for ignorance underlies neutral feeling."

"Do these underlying tendencies always underlie these feelings?"

"No, they do not."

"What should be given up in regard to each of these three feelings?"

"The underlying tendency to greed should be given up when it comes to pleasant feeling. The underlying tendency to repulsion should be given up when it comes to painful feeling. The underlying tendency to ignorance should be given up when it comes to neutral feeling."

"Should these underlying tendencies be given up regarding all instances of these feelings?"

"No, not in all instances. Take a person who, quite secluded from sensual pleasures, secluded from unskillful qualities, enters and remains in the first absorption, which has the rapture and bliss born of seclusion, while placing the mind and keeping it connected. With this they give up greed, and the underlying tendency to greed does not lie within that. And take a person who reflects: 'Oh, when will I enter and remain in the same dimension that the noble ones enter and remain in today?' Nursing such a longing for the supreme liberations gives rise to sadness due to longing. With this they give up repulsion, and the underlying tendency to repulsion does not lie within that.[25] Take a person who, giving up pleasure and pain, and ending former happiness and sadness, enters and remains in the fourth absorption, without pleasure or pain, with pure equanimity and mindfulness. With this they give up ignorance, and the underlying tendency to ignorance does not lie within that."

"Noble lady, what is the counterpart of pleasant feeling?"

"Noble Sir, painful feeling."

"What is the counterpart of painful feeling?"

"Pleasant feeling."

"What is the counterpart of neutral feeling?"

"Ignorance."

"What is the counterpart of ignorance?"

"Knowledge."

"What is the counterpart of knowledge?"

"Freedom."

"What is the counterpart of freedom?"

"Extinguishment."

"What is the counterpart of extinguishment?"

"Your question goes too far, Sir Visākha. You couldn't figure out the limit of questions. For extinguishment is the culmination, destination, and end of the spiritual life. If you wish, go to the Buddha and ask him this question. You should remember it in line with his answer."

And then Anagami, Visākha approved and agreed with what Arahant Dhammadinnā said. He got up from his seat, bowed, and respectfully circled her, keeping her on his right. Then he went up to the Buddha, bowed, sat down to one side, and informed the Buddha of all they had discussed.

When he had spoken, the Buddha said to him, "Arahant Dhammadinnā is astute, Visākha, she has great wisdom. If you came to me and asked this question, I would answer it in exactly the same way as Arahant Dhammadinnā. That is what it means, and that's how you should remember it."

That is what the Buddha said. Satisfied, Anagami, Visākha approved what the Buddha said.

---

[25] An ordinary person experiences sorrow. Once this sorrow has been used as a basis for giving rise to the discernment that leads to Sotapanna, Sakadagami and Anagami (non-returning), the mind has no further resistance-obsession with painful feeling.

Chapter 47

Middle Discourses 45: Cūḷadhammasamādānasutta

The Shorter Discourse on Taking Up Practices

There are four ways of practice. Some people can take on a practice of pleasant now and pain in the future. Some take a practice of pain now and in the future. Some take a practice of painful now and pleasant in the future. Some take a practice of pleasant now and result in future pleasure.

Those who go to extreme ways to satisfy worldly experiences with unwholesome intentions and sensual pleasures coming from sensory experiences might enjoy pleasure now. After their body breaks up, they may bear the consequences of karma and be reborn in suffocated places like hell.

Those who go to extreme ways to not satisfy worldly experiences, eat no meals, wear no slippers, walk in hard sufferance, bear cold weather and endure extreme sufferings experience suffering now. After their bodies break, they will be born in bad places. They will suffer then.

Those who possess extreme desires (greed, hate, delusion) for sensual pleasures coming from sensory experiences, engage in unwholesome things (eat excessive amounts of food, consume excessive amounts of alcohol, steal other's belongings, divide people for the benefit of self, kill living beings, etc.), merely to satisfy extreme desires, they might enjoy pleasure now. After their bodies break up, they may bear the consequences of karma and be reborn in suffocated places like hell.

When someone ordinary collects meritorious deeds and engages in wholesome activities while practicing Dhamma, they are unable to attain Nibbana in this birth due to lack of meritorious deeds, they won't attain Nibbana. Similarly, when someone ordinary collects meritorious deeds and engages in wholesome activities while practicing Dhamma, if they possess greed, hate, and delusion that is insufficient to meet the entry-level noble standards, they won't attain Nibbana. They may be reborn in good places despite experiencing suffering now (desires;

greed, hate, and delusion make a person burn within) and they will enjoy future pleasures that are subject to change.

When a trainee noble one (Sotapanna, Sakadagami, Anagami) collects meritorious deeds and engages in wholesome activities while practicing Dhamma, they experience Nibbana and progress in the path leading to higher stages of Nibbana in this birth due to sufficient meritorious deeds, they experience pleasures (blissful Nibbana). When someone noble now experiences pleasures, and if they don't gain Arahantship, they may be born in good places. They practice in a way that makes it possible for them to experience pleasures now and pleasures in the future (Arahantship extinguishes fires that burn within a mind).

The middle-way practice abandons fetters progressively. At first, one abandons excessive greed, hate, and delusion by giving up grasping self-view, conventions, and doubts. Then, sensual desires are given at the Anagami state.

"So I have heard. At one time the Buddha was staying near Sāvatthī in Jeta's Grove, Anāthapiṇḍika's monastery. There the Buddha addressed the companions, "Companions!"

"Venerable sir," they replied. The Buddha said this:

"Companions, there are these four ways of taking up practices. What four? There is a way of taking up practices that is pleasant now but results in future pain. There is a way of taking up practices that is painful now and results in future pain. There is a way of taking up practices that is painful now but results in future pleasure. There is a way of taking up practices that is pleasant now and results in future pleasure.

And what is the way of taking up practices that is pleasant now but results in future pain?

There are some ascetics and brahmins who have this doctrine and view: 'There's nothing wrong with sensual pleasures.' They throw themselves into sensual pleasures, cavorting with female wanderers with jeweled bands in their hair. They say, 'What future danger do those ascetics and brahmins see in sensual pleasures that they speak of giving up sensual pleasures, and advocate the complete understanding of sensual pleasures? Pleasant is the touch of this female wanderer's arm, tender, soft, and downy!' And they throw themselves into sensual pleasures.

When their body breaks up, after death, they're reborn in a place of loss, a bad place, the underworld, hell. And there they feel painful, sharp, severe, acute feelings. They say, 'This is that future danger that those ascetics and brahmins saw. For it is because of sensual pleasures that I'm feeling painful, sharp, severe, acute feelings.'

Suppose that in the last month of summer a camel's foot creeper pod were to burst open and a seed were to fall at the root of a sal tree. Then the deity haunting that sal tree would become apprehensive and nervous. But their friends and colleagues, relatives and kin—deities of the parks, forests, trees, and those who haunt the herbs, grass, and big trees—would come together to reassure them, 'Do not fear, sir, do not fear! Hopefully that seed will be swallowed by a peacock, or eaten by a deer, or burnt by a forest fire, or picked up by a lumberjack, or eaten by termites, or it may not even be fertile.' But none of these things happened.

And the seed was fertile, so that when the monsoon clouds soaked it with rain, it sprouted. And the creeper wound its tender, soft, and downy tendrils around that sal tree. Then the deity thought, 'What future danger did my friends see when they said: "Do not fear, sir, do not fear! Hopefully that seed will be swallowed by a peacock, or eaten by a deer, or burnt by a forest fire, or picked up by a lumberjack, or eaten by termites, or it may not even be fertile." Pleasant is the touch of this creeper's tender, soft, and downy tendrils.' Then the creeper enfolded the sal tree, made a canopy over it, draped a curtain around it, and split apart all the main branches.

Then the deity thought, 'This is the future danger that my friends saw! It's because of that camel's foot creeper seed that I'm feeling painful, sharp, severe, acute feelings.'

In the same way, there are some ascetics and brahmins who have this doctrine and view: 'There's nothing wrong with sensual pleasures' ... This is called the way of taking up practices that is pleasant now but results in future pain.

And what is the way of taking up practices that is painful now and results in future pain? It's when someone goes naked, ignoring conventions. They lick their hands, and don't come or wait when called.

They don't consent to food brought to them, or food prepared on their behalf, or an invitation for a meal.

They don't receive anything from a pot or bowl; or from someone who keeps sheep, or who has a weapon or a shovel in their home; or where a couple is eating; or where there is a woman who is pregnant, breastfeeding, or who has a man in her home; or where there's a dog waiting or flies buzzing. They accept no fish or meat or liquor or wine, and drink no beer.

They go to just one house for alms, taking just one mouthful, or two houses and two mouthfuls, up to seven houses and seven mouthfuls. They feed on one saucer a day, two saucers a day, up to seven saucers a day.

They eat once a day, once every second day, up to once a week, and so on, even up to once a fortnight. They live committed to the practice of eating food at set intervals.

They eat herbs, millet, wild rice, poor rice, water lettuce, rice bran, scum from boiling rice, sesame flour, grass, or cow dung. They survive on forest roots and fruits, or eating fallen fruit.

They wear robes of sunn hemp, mixed hemp, corpse-wrapping cloth, rags, lodh tree bark, antelope hide (whole or in strips), kusa grass, bark, wood-chips, human hair, horse-tail hair, or owls' wings. They tear out their hair and beard, committed to this practice.

They constantly stand, refusing seats. They squat, committed to persisting in the squatting position. They lie on a mat of thorns, making a mat of thorns their bed. They're devoted to ritual bathing three times a day, including the evening.

And so they live committed to practicing these various ways of mortifying and tormenting the body. When their body breaks up, after death, they're reborn in a place of loss, a bad place, the underworld, hell. This is called the way of taking up practices that is painful now and results in future pain.

And what is the way of taking up practices that is painful now but results in future pleasure? It's when someone is ordinarily full of acute greed, hate, and delusion.

They often feel the pain and sadness that greed, hate, and delusion bring.

They lead the full and pure spiritual life in pain and sadness, weeping, with tearful faces. When their body breaks up, after death, they're reborn in a good place, a heavenly realm. This is called the way of taking up practices that is painful now but results in future pleasure.

And what is the way of taking up practices that is pleasant now and results in future pleasure? It's when someone is not ordinarily full of acute greed, hate, and delusion (at least a Sotapanna).

They rarely feel the pain and sadness that greed, hate, and delusion bring. Quite secluded from sensual pleasures (path to Anagami), secluded from unskillful qualities, they enter and remain in the first absorption … second absorption … third absorption … fourth absorption.

When their body breaks up, after death, they're reborn in a good place, a heavenly realm. This is called the way of taking up practices that is pleasant now and results in future pleasure. These are the four ways of taking up practices."

That is what the Buddha said. Satisfied, the companions approved what the Buddha said."

Chapter 48

Middle Discourses 46: Mahādhammasamādānasutta

The Great Discourse on Taking Up Practices

Nibbana is a wisdom-based path. Wisdom can be developed by conventional and universal ways. There are four ways of practice. This discourse records Buddha speaks about four kinds of commitments, divided by whether they are pleasant now or not, and whether they bring good future results or not.

Some people can take on a practice of pleasant now and pain in the future (e.g., someone takes pleasure in killing living creatures, and so on). Some take a practice of pain now and in the future (e.g., someone in pain and sadness kills living creatures, and so on). Some take a practice of being painful now and pleasant in the future (e.g., when someone in pain and sadness doesn't kill living creatures and so on). Some take a practice of pleasant now and result in future pleasure (e.g., someone who experiences blissful Sotapanna doesn't kill living creatures, and so on).

Although real life experience will show that both ups and downs are part of life for people, mind-made understanding of a person's world can be different from that of real-life experience. When faced with unpleasant events, an ordinary person is likely to suffer too much distress, particularly when the person's mind is in the habit of hiding certain aspects of life if they are not a part of life. Instead, by reducing thinking erroneously with bias and becoming free from a limited understanding of life and the mind, a person can develop the right understanding of life and mind. The right view/correct understanding of life will allow a person to extend happiness gained through worldly experience (cutting off worldly experiences by cutting off sensory experiences is not practical, as worldly experiences are processed through sensory information in each person) while living with conventions.

Not understanding the truth can produce mental pain. Understanding truth allows a person to experience worldly life without regret. Understanding that change is the nature for all of us, instead of just watching how things unfold, and without getting too worried over things that we cannot control or change, letting go of things that are gone, taking a reasonable course of action to do things that must be done, engaging to resolve things that can be resolved, and making the most of what is available, living life to the fullest is a wise thing to do. When a person understands with wisdom that certain things in the universe cannot be changed, that not everything can be gained, and that the person should therefore let go of things that cannot be changed but attend to doing the things that can be done without regret, this is a wise thing to do; it is a way of developing the middle mind training to abandoning self-view and to achieving the noble way of living. Instead of too much dependence on others and on society for approval or denial and expecting from others and society, a person chooses to do good and avoid doing bad and is true to one's heart, one can find inner peace within despite what other people think and say. In this manner, a person can remain satisfied and unaffected in the very presence of others and the world, not hurting oneself and not hurting others, and that is a way of developing the middle path.

The noble way of thinking is not grasping identities that are socially created in mind, because it is meaningless to cling to identities that are changing anyway. Identity views *("I am young", "I am old", "I am a monk", "I am a householder"*) and social divisions are socially created constructs. What is socially constructed is subject to change. Noble ways of thinking do not divide the earth by grasping (meaning not giving too much value to such things in mind; "*I am from this country*" … "*I am better*"…) and grasping to self-view in many ways. For someone who thinks that there is no stability in self (self-view), instability in self is unlikely to bring too much mental pain.

To go beyond commonly practiced virtues to gain Sotapanna, practicing noble precepts (abstain from killing living beings, stealing, sexual misconduct, false speech, backbiting, harsh or abusive speech, useless or meaningless conversation, wrong means of livelihood), becoming a good person who looks after others as applicable to oneself (it may be looking after friends, family, an employer or employees, ascetics and so forth), and becoming an ethical person who genuinely cares for others and avoids discriminating against others on any grounds is the practice that is helpful in developing noble virtues, a factor of Stream-entry. To practice a noble way of thinking, you have to surpass the majority way of thinking and doing. To gain Sotapanna, one should develop noble virtues, confirmed confidence in the Triple Gem, and give up grasping conventions (i.e self-view, etc.). Thereafter, one should develop higher wisdom and inner qualities similar to Buddha, therefore, not treating others differently is essential for developing noble virtues beyond precepts and progress in the Noble Path.

"So I have heard. At one time the Buddha was staying near Sāvatthī in Jeta's Grove, Anāthapiṇḍika's monastery. There the Buddha addressed the companions, "Companions!"

"Venerable sir," they replied. The Buddha said this:

"Companions, sentient beings typically have the wish, desire, and hope: 'Oh, if only unlikable, undesirable, and disagreeable things would decrease, and likable, desirable, and agreeable things would increase!' But exactly the opposite happens to them. What do you take to be the reason for this?"

"Our teachings are rooted in the Buddha. He is our guide and our refuge. Sir, may the Buddha himself please clarify the meaning of this. The companions will listen and remember it."

"Well then, companions, listen and apply your mind well, I will speak."

"Yes, sir," they replied. The Buddha said this:

"Take an unlearned ordinary person who has not seen the noble ones, and is neither skilled nor trained in the teaching of the noble ones. They've not seen true persons, and are neither skilled nor trained in the teaching of the true persons. They don't know what practices they should cultivate and foster, and what practices they shouldn't cultivate and foster. So they cultivate and foster practices they shouldn't, and don't cultivate and foster practices they should. When they do so, unlikable, undesirable, and disagreeable things increase, and likable, desirable, and agreeable things decrease. Why is that? Because that's what it's like for someone who doesn't know.

But a learned noble disciple has seen the noble ones, and is skilled and trained in the teaching of the noble ones. They've seen true persons, and are skilled and trained in the teaching of the true persons.

They know what practices they should cultivate and foster, and what practices they shouldn't cultivate and foster. So they cultivate and foster practices they should, and don't cultivate and foster practices they shouldn't. When they do so, unlikable, undesirable, and disagreeable things decrease, and likable, desirable, and agreeable things increase. Why is that? Because that's what it's like for someone who knows.

Companions, there are these four ways of taking up practices. What four? There is a way of taking up practices that is painful now and results in future pain. There is a way of taking up practices that is pleasant now but results in future pain.

There is a way of taking up practices that is painful now but results in future pleasure. There is a way of taking up practices that is pleasant now and results in future pleasure.

When it comes to the way of taking up practices that is painful now and results in future pain, an ignoramus, without knowing this, doesn't truly understand: 'This is the way of taking up practices that is painful now and results in future pain.' So instead of avoiding that practice, they cultivate it. When they do so, unlikable, undesirable, and disagreeable things increase, and likable, desirable, and agreeable things decrease. Why is that? Because that's what it's like for someone who doesn't know.

When it comes to the way of taking up practices that is pleasant now and results in future pain, an ignoramus … cultivates it … and disagreeable things increase …

When it comes to the way of taking up practices that is painful now and results in future pleasure, an ignoramus … doesn't cultivate it … and disagreeable things increase …

When it comes to the way of taking up practices that is pleasant now and results in future pleasure, an ignoramus … doesn't cultivate it … and disagreeable things increase … Why is that? Because that's what it's like for someone who doesn't know.

When it comes to the way of taking up practices that is painful now and results in future pain, a wise person, knowing this, truly understands: 'This is the way of taking up practices that is painful now and results in future pain.' So instead of cultivating that practice, they avoid it.

When they do so, unlikable, undesirable, and disagreeable things decrease, and likable, desirable, and agreeable things increase. Why is that? Because that's what it's like for someone who knows.

When it comes to the way of taking up practices that is pleasant now and results in future pain, a wise person … doesn't cultivate it … and agreeable things increase …

When it comes to the way of taking up practices that is painful now and results in future pleasure, a wise person … cultivates it … and agreeable things increase …

When it comes to the way of taking up practices that is pleasant now and results in future pleasure, a wise person, knowing this, truly understands: 'This is the way of taking up practices that is pleasant now and results in future pleasure.'

So instead of avoiding that practice, they cultivate it. When they do so, unlikable, undesirable, and disagreeable things decrease, and likable, desirable, and agreeable things increase. Why is that? Because that's what it's like for someone who knows.

And what is the way of taking up practices that is painful now and results in future pain? It's when someone in pain and sadness kills living creatures, steals, and commits sexual misconduct. They use speech that's false, divisive, harsh, or nonsensical. And they're covetous, malicious, with wrong view. Because of these things they experience pain and sadness. And when their body breaks up, after death, they're reborn in a place of loss, a bad place, the underworld, hell. This is called the way of taking up practices that is painful now and results in future pain.

And what is the way of taking up practices that is pleasant now but results in future pain? It's when someone with pleasure and happiness kills living creatures, steals, and commits sexual misconduct. They use speech that's false, divisive, harsh, or nonsensical. And they're covetous, malicious, with wrong view.

Because of these things they experience pleasure and happiness. But when their body breaks up, after death, they're reborn in a place of loss, a bad place, the underworld, hell. This is called the way of taking up practices that is pleasant now but results in future pain.

And what is the way of taking up practices that is painful now but results in future pleasure? It's when someone in pain and sadness doesn't kill living creatures, steal, or commit sexual misconduct. They don't use speech that's false, divisive, harsh, or nonsensical. And they're contented, kind-hearted, with right view.

Because of these things they experience pain and sadness. But when their body breaks up, after death, they're reborn in a good place, a heavenly realm. This is called the way of taking up practices that is painful now but results in future pleasure.

And what is the way of taking up practices that is pleasant now and results in future pleasure? It's when someone with pleasure and happiness doesn't kill living creatures, steal, or commit sexual misconduct. They don't use speech that's false, divisive, harsh, or nonsensical. And they're contented, kind-hearted, with right view (right view means a Sotapanna).

Because of these things they experience pleasure and happiness. And when their body breaks up, after death, they're reborn in a good place, a heavenly realm. This is called the way of taking up practices that is pleasant now and results in future pleasure. These are the four ways of taking up practices.

Suppose there was some bitter gourd mixed with poison. Then a man would come along who wants to live and doesn't want to die, who wants to be happy and recoils from pain.

They'd say to him: 'Here, mister, this is bitter gourd mixed with poison. Drink it if you like. If you drink it, the color, aroma, and flavor will be unappetizing, and it will result in death or deadly pain.' He wouldn't reject it.

Without reflection, he'd drink it. The color, aroma, and flavor would be unappetizing, and it would result in death or deadly pain. This is comparable to the way of taking up practices that is painful now and results in future pain, I say.

Suppose there was a bronze goblet of beverage that had a nice color, aroma, and flavor. But it was mixed with poison. Then a man would come along who wants to live and doesn't want to die, who wants to be happy and recoils from pain.

They'd say to him: 'Here, mister, this bronze goblet of beverage has a nice color, aroma, and flavor. But it's mixed with poison. Drink it if you like. If you drink it, the color, aroma, and flavor will be appetizing, but it will result in death or deadly pain.' He wouldn't reject it.

Without reflection, he'd drink it. The color, aroma, and flavor would be appetizing, but it would result in death or deadly pain. This is comparable to the way of taking up practices that is pleasant now and results in future pain, I say.

Suppose there was some rancid urine mixed with different medicines. Then a man with jaundice would come along. They'd say to him: 'Here, mister, this is rancid urine mixed with different medicines. Drink it if you like. If you drink it, the color, aroma, and flavor will be unappetizing, but after drinking it you will be happy.' He wouldn't reject it.

After appraisal, he'd drink it. The color, aroma, and flavor would be unappetizing, but after drinking it he would be happy. This is comparable to the way of taking up practices that is painful now and results in future pleasure, I say.

Suppose there was some curds, honey, ghee, and molasses all mixed together. Then a man with bloody dysentery would come along. They'd say to him: 'Here, mister, this is curds, honey, ghee, and molasses all mixed together. Drink it if you like.

If you drink it, the color, aroma, and flavor will be appetizing, and after drinking it you will be happy.' He wouldn't reject it. After appraisal, he'd drink it.

The color, aroma, and flavor would be appetizing, and after drinking it he would be happy. This is comparable to the way of taking up practices that is pleasant now and results in future pleasure, I say.

It's like the last month of the rainy season, in autumn, when the heavens are clear and cloudless. And as the sun is rising to the firmament, having dispelled all the darkness of space, it shines and glows and radiates.

In the same way, this way of taking up practices that is pleasant now and results in future pleasure dispels the doctrines of the various other ascetics and brahmins as it shines and glows and radiates."

That is what the Buddha said. Satisfied, the companions approved what the Buddha said".

Chapter 49

Middle Discourses 47: Vīmaṁsakasutta

The Inquirer

What is relevant for Dhamma is your mind state. The state of mind can be seen through someone's words. When someone declares they have gained Nibbana, an ordinary person who is unable to read another's mind should investigate whether a person who declares this shows the signs of grasping the conventional lifestyle. If they describe the practice of Dhamma as a conventional lifestyle, it means they have not gained what they declared. Instead, if they describe Dhamma as universally applicable training in the mind irrespective of a conventional lifestyle, that is an indication of true Dhamma appearance. It is an indication that they have gained the right view for themselves.

When someone declares they have gained Nibbana, an ordinary person who is unable to read another's mind should investigate whether a person who declares this shows the signs of grasping the social practices, and conventions. If they describe a Dhamma as a ritual, tradition or division, it means they have not gained what they declared. Instead, if they describe Dhamma as universally applicable, that is an indication of true Dhamma appearance. It is an indication that they have gained the right view for themselves.

When someone declares they have gained Nibbana, an ordinary person who is unable to read another's mind should investigate whether a person who declares this shows the signs of grasping worldly experiences[26]. A person's mind state can be expressed in words, and grasping can be observed in words. For example, if they compare one another, glorify themselves, and put others down, they praise one way of a lifestyle, tradition, and so on, that is a sign of grasping. Instead, if they don't compare, if they do not glorify themselves or put others down on that account that is a sign of not grasping. Instead of praising one and degrading another, if they show how a person from any conventional background can reach four-fold Nibbana, Sotapanna and beyond, that is an indication of true Dhamma appearance.

---

[26] Too many likes, dislikes, and expectations toward the worldly experiences.

When someone declares they have gained Nibbana, an ordinary person who is unable to read another's mind should investigate whether a person who declares this shows the signs of grasping to self-view; engage in meaningless conversation and boasting, compare one another, divide people, divide Dhamma and so forth. These are some of the signs of grasping a self-view.

When someone declares they have gained Nibbana, an ordinary person who is unable to read another's mind should investigate whether a person who declares this does not engage in sensuality as a routine part of certain sila and wanting to end samsara, or as a matter of freedom from sensuality due to abandoning the fetters.

When someone declares they have gained Nibbana, an ordinary person who is unable to read another's mind should investigate whether a person who declares this does not engage in sensuality as a matter of fear of Samsara or as a matter of non-fear of Samsara due to abandoning the fetters.

Walking on the Noble Path is a journey you travel yourself, a practice of giving too much importance to conventions. Understanding that the universe functions beyond conventions is the first step to establishing the right view. Understanding that conventions are subject to change and what is changing brings suffering is the second step to establishing the right view. To escape suffering, learning to give up the habits of getting attached to conventions, social pressures, and practices by giving priority to universal Dhamma (blending with universal ways of functioning), is a third step to establishing the right view. In this manner, a person who was unsure of the universal Dhamma can develop a better vision to get a step closer to four-fold Nibbana. Nibbana is a universal happening but not a lifestyle-based practice or meditation-based path. Nibbana is a "Kusal" (and merit) and wisdom-based path.

Evidence based four-fold Nibbana involve testing life experience with evidence (based on worldly experience through sensory information). Testing life experience involves figuring out life is an interaction between the universe and conventions. The purpose is to let go of mental pain, and if you continue to reduce desires, you may initially understand the idea that desires create mental pain, and if you reduce desires, your actual experience relevant to your life would indicate your suffering has reduced (the evidence). You can use evidence-based life experience to make progress in four-fold Nibbana.

How can one give up grasping conventions?

One can give up grasping conventions by understanding conventions are subject to change (right view), understanding that grasping conventions leads to mental pain, understanding that there is a universal training path to reduce grasping conventions, and understanding that the universal path is about shaping one's wisdom, wisdom developed through merits. One thing to remember is that attaining holiness in Dhamma means giving up grasping conventions, which include self-view, religion, tradition, and division and so on. Reducing grasping conventions as a Sotapanna can be developed further to reduce grasping to sensual pleasures coming through sensory information at an Anagami state. Thus, those who truly want to reach Nibbana would benefit from giving up focusing too much on outside matters and others (e.g., political matters, economic matters etc.) Instead, focus on self, investigate self, think of what self can do to benefit others, and engage in wholesome thoughts and actions.

The reason that people grasp conventions is because they think conventions are great. Conventions don't stand alone but stand within the universe. The universe is bigger than conventions, and you can get support from the universe. That support from the universe can help you in conventional life and after. Thus, by understanding what benefits you, you can develop the Noble Path to let go of grasping conventions in the middle way.

Conventional Sangha who have not gained Nibbana can have various doubts about Nibbana, which is reasonable as unless you gain Nibbana, you wouldn't know, yet doubts lead to creating doubt in another and doubts among conventional Sangha make them entangled in circles of doubts, unable to find the practice leading to Nibbana, with the right vision leading to Nibbana. Instead, by not developing an ignoble vision but developing a wise vision by applying reasoning, a wise, ordinary person can develop a practice.

Before Sotapanna, one may believe in karma, and the Triple Gem. Belief indicates the likelihood of certainty but not certainty, and belief can be true or false. After gaining Sotapanna, one may be surprised to know that Dhamma is true, a turning point of understanding. Yet, Sotapanna does not know of the Sakadagami, Anagami, and Arahant stages and has no clue what it means to experience such things. It is only after the Arahant stage that one concludes that Buddha is the knower of all the world. Arahants don't say that merely based on books but say it because they know it for themselves. Therefore, one way to recognize an Arahant is to say that they know Buddha is the knower of all.

Developing the right vision means understanding that life is an experience between the universe and conventions and giving up mental attachment to the fetters, self-view, social practices, and conventions. Society encourages one to look Dhamma in appearance or certain places. Among practitioners, some people can feel delighted or scared (or ignored) when they see the appearance of a conventional Sangha and someone dressed up as a monk. Society teaches you to understand Dhamma through an appearance or a dress. Yet, universal Dhamma can be found beyond socially accepted ways in unexpected people.

Nibbana is not a conscious effect, a natural happening (Four-fold Nibbana happens to a person at a random time) while sitting, walking, or lying down and so forth at a random time. People who don't have a reasonable acceptance of karma can still meditate for years without the right vision. The right view means understanding the universal ways of Dhamma and the practices of Dhamma because, without a right vision, it makes their practice fruitless.

Not understanding the universal ways of functioning, some people tend to make wishes. They may wish, "May I experience bliss, may I not experience loss in my life", yet, just by wishing alone, a person can't gain Nibbana or avoid certain worldly experiences. A person may gain certain control over worldly things. This may be due to multiple factors, such as hard work, receiving support, etc. Yet, certain things, such as birth or certain illnesses like a terminal illness, are beyond a person's control and conventions. There are things that a person can do and things that a person cannot do. Understand what can be done and focus on what's possible to do, let go of what is not possibly a wise thing to do. Wisdom can be developed by producing wholesome intentional actions, and wholesome intentional actions can be developed by engaging in wholesome things.

Blending with the universal rhythm is practicing Dhamma. By attending to fertile soil, you can get fertile fruition. By not dividing Dhamma, you can let go of grasping conventions. Being grateful to those who provided you with care when you needed it, such as your parents, friends, and others, is a wholesome thing. By providing for those in need, you can aid their well-being. Attending to those who have given up their fetters, you can gain detachment from fetters. By engaging in noble precepts, you can shape and produce wholesome intentions.

"So I have heard. At one time the Buddha was staying near Sāvatthī in Jeta's Grove, Anāthapiṇḍika's monastery. There the Buddha addressed the companions, "Companions!"

"Venerable sir," they replied. The Buddha said this:

"Companions, an ordinary person should be an inquirer of four-fold nibbana, unable to comprehend another's mind, examine the thought processes of another person who declare Arahantship to see whether he is a fully awakened Buddha (gained Buddhahood state through either Supreme Buddha route or Arahantship) or not."

"Our teachings are rooted in the Buddha. He is our guide and our refuge. Sir, may the Buddha himself please clarify the meaning of this. The companions will listen and remember it."

"Well then, listen and apply your mind well, I will speak."

"Yes, venerable sir," they replied. The Buddha said this:

"Companions, a companion should be a seeker of universal Dhamma, an inquirer of universal Sangha, unable to comprehend another's mind, should scrutinize the Realized One for two things—things that can be seen and heard: 'Can anything corrupt (i.e., grasping to conventional lifestyle) be seen or heard in the Realized One or not?' Scrutinizing him/her they find that nothing corrupt can be seen or heard in the Realized One.

They scrutinize further: 'Can anything mixed (i.e., clinging to conventions; ritual, tradition, etc.) be seen or heard in the Realized One or not?' Scrutinizing him they find that nothing mixed can be seen or heard in the Realized One.

They scrutinize further: 'Can anything clean be seen or heard (i.e. likes, dislikes, expectations for worldly experiences; clinging to the past, sharing personal stories etc.) in the Realized One or not?' Scrutinizing him they find that clean things can be seen and heard in the Realized One.

They scrutinize further: 'Did the venerable attain this skillful state a long time ago, or just recently?' Scrutinizing him they find that the venerable attained this skillful state a long time ago, not just recently.

They scrutinize further: 'Are certain dangers (i.e. grasping conventions and are they mentally attached to fame, honor, possessions, friends, supporters, etc.) found in that person who claims to gain Arahantship who has achieved fame and renown?'

For, companions, so long as a person has not achieved fame and renown, certain dangers are not found in them. But when they achieve fame and renown, those dangers appear.

Scrutinizing him they find that those dangers are not found in that venerable individual who has achieved fame and renown.

They scrutinize further: 'Is this venerable securely stilled or insecurely stilled (i.e., do they refrain from sensuality as a practice, a part of sila or due to abandoning the relevant fetter)? Is the reason they don't indulge in sensual pleasures that they're free of greed because greed has ended?' Scrutinizing him they find that that venerable is securely stilled, not insecurely stilled stilled (i.e., do they refrain from sensuality due to fear of samsara or due to fearlessness of samsara and abandoning the relevant fetter)? The reason they don't indulge in sensual pleasures is that they're free of greed because greed has ended.

If others should ask that companion, 'But what reason and evidence does the venerable have for saying this?' Answering rightly, the companion should say, 'Because, whether that venerable is staying in a community or alone, some people there are in a good state or a sorry state, some instruct a group, and some are seen among pleasures of the flesh while others remain unsullied.
Yet that venerable doesn't look down on them for that (a person does not compare one another and put down others, for example, they don't say monastic rules are superior to householder rules or householders can enjoy better than monastics etc.).

Also, I have heard and learned this in the presence of the Buddha: "I am securely stilled, not insecurely stilled. The reason I don't indulge in sensual pleasures is that I'm free of greed because greed has ended."'
Next, they should ask the Realized One himself about this, 'Can anything corrupt be seen or heard in the Realized One or not?' The Realized One would answer, 'Nothing corrupt can be seen or heard in the Realized One.'

'Can anything mixed be seen or heard in the Realized One or not?' The Realized One would answer, 'Nothing mixed can be seen or heard in the Realized One.'

'Can anything clean be seen or heard in the Realized One or not?' The Realized One would answer, 'Clean things can be seen and heard in the Realized One. I am the range and the territory of that, but I am not determined by that.'

A disciple ought to approach a teacher who has completed four-fold nibbana in order to listen to the teaching. The teacher explains Dhamma with its higher and higher stages, with its better and better stages, with its dark and bright sides.
When they directly know a certain principle of those teachings, in accordance with how they were taught, the person comes to a conclusion about the teachings. They have confidence in the Buddha: 'The Blessed One is a fully awakened Buddha! The universal

teaching (four-fold nibbana) is well explained! The universal (Savaka) Saṅgha is practicing well!"

If others should ask that companion, 'But what reason and evidence does the venerable have for saying this?' Answering rightly, the companion should say, 'Reverends, I approached the Buddha (or Arahants) to listen to the teaching. He (or they) explained Dhamma with its higher and higher stages, with its better and better stages, with its dark and bright sides.

When I directly knew a certain principle of those teachings, in accordance with how I was taught, I came to a conclusion about the teachings. I had confidence in the Supreme Buddha:
"The Blessed One is a fully awakened universal Buddha!
The universal teaching (four-fold nibbana) is well explained!
The universal (Savaka) Saṅgha is practicing well!"

When someone's confidence is confirmed, rooted, and planted in the Realized One based on evidence based on life experience in this manner, with these words and phrases, it's said to be grounded confidence that's based on evidence. It is strong and cannot be shifted by any ascetic or brahmin or god or Māra or divinity or by anyone in the world.

That is how there is legitimate scrutiny of the Realized One, and that is how the Realized One is legitimately well-scrutinized."

That is what the Buddha said. Satisfied, the companions approved what the Buddha said.

Chapter 50

Middle Discourses 48: Kosambiyasutta

The Mendicants of Kosambī

An incident, "The Quarrel at Kosambi," is an ongoing dispute between two groups of ordinary monks. In this discourse, the Buddha explains to those ordinary monks six kinds of conduct that they should develop and possess to maintain community harmony, especially among ordinary spiritual practitioners. He then moves on to explain that universal Savaka Sangha naturally possess good qualities and that they should strive to develop noble qualities of Savaka Sangha, Sotapanna to Arahant.

Practicing Dhamma means learning to respect other people's choices. Functioning within the frame of nobility means respecting other people, carrying humanity in the heart and not hurting oneself or others. Some ordinary people who grasp views and get attached to their own views may find it hard to respect the choices of others, and they may divide people and struggle to treat everyone with care and kindness, irrespective of differences. Getting attached to one's own view can hurt self and others. Thus, ordinary practitioners would benefit if they observed their minds and reduce the grasp into their views so that they do not feel the need to suppress others' choices and rights. Instead, they respect their choices and rights. Developing the Noble Path requires focusing on self and reducing the focus on others while giving priority to engaging in doing beneficial things for self and others, not hurting self or others, not dividing Dhamma and not dividing people.

Six factors are typically found in noble disciples/communities that help contribute to harmony among spiritual practitioners. Among noble ones, the noble view aids them in maintaining wholesome intentions: thoughts, words, and bodily actions towards all beings. Thus, they don't hurt self and others at any time. They possess noble virtues/qualities; they maintain loving kindness for spiritual companions at all times, and expressing an opinion or suggestion is simply for aiding an ordinary person to link ordinary Dhamma to the Noble Path, higher Dhamma. When higher Dhamma is shared, some ordinary practitioners might understand such Dhamma, and some might not understand. This is because understanding is subjective. When someone says something, you can only understand it within your own understanding and wisdom. You may grow your wisdom to understand higher Dhamma. This can be explained below. When you look at an object, light passes through the lens at the front of your eye and hits the retina. Photoreceptors — cells inside your retina that react to light — change light energy into an electrical signal. This signal travels through your optic nerve and into your brain to become the picture of the world you see. In this manner, you can only see the external world within you. You can only understand what another person says and their mind within your own understanding. The external world is created within one's thoughts. Similarly, freedom from the world can be gained within thoughts, not externally.

Besides, what is noble is sharing whatever you have with fellow spiritual practitioners: material, non-material, knowledge, skills etc. What is noble is living with the noble virtues of a Sotapanna and gaining a view of a Sotapanna. Among these six qualities, the Noble view is the chief view, which allows for the shaping of a person's actions (doing) and words (saying). The noble perspective, grounded in evidence based on life experience, can aid you in developing the Noble Path. When you become a Sotapanna, you may develop further.

Anagami will end sensual desires and ill will. Dullness and drowsiness, restlessness, remorse and doubt (fetters) in the mind will be given up at the Arahant stage. Those who attain four-fold Nibbana will understand Buddha's path is unique. Cessation (Nibbana) is not something common. It is not shared by spiritual practitioners of other paths, including conventional Dhamma practitioners. This is because Nibbana lies beyond conventions, a universal happening.

Those who gain Nibbana (Sotapanna etc.) they possess certain qualities as below;
1. They understand that they have gained Nibbana.
2. They understand that their fetters are abandoned.
3. They understand that Buddha's path is unique, and no one outside Buddha's path has a training leading to cessation, four-fold Nibbana.
4. When noble disciples happen to do any mistake, they instantly apologies.
5. They are constantly interested in progressing in Noble Path despite engage in various duties/responsibilities for others.
6. When higher Dhamma is taught (Sotapanna to Arahant), one listens to the Dhamma carefully, attentively, and wholeheartedly.
7. When hearing Dhamma, and when meeting Triple Gem, they gain joy and develop further constantly.

"Thus have I heard. On one occasion the Blessed One was dwelling at Kosambi, in Ghosita's Park. On this occasion, the monks at Kosambi were engaged in disputes, arguments, and contention; they were verbally assaulting each other. They could not persuade each other, and they were not persuaded by each other; they could not convince each other, and they were not convinced by each other.

"Then a certain ordinary person who lives a conventional monk life style approached the Blessed One, venerated him, and sat to one side. When he was seated to one side, that person said to the Blessed One, "Here, venerable sir, the ordinary people who lives as conventional monks at Kosambi are engaged in disputes, arguments, and contention; they are verbally assaulting each other.

They can not persuade each other, and they are not persuaded by each other; they can not convince each other, and they are not convinced by each other."

Then the Blessed One addressed a certain ordinary person who is a conventional monk: "Friend, go and please call those monks with my words: 'The Teacher calls you.'"

"Yes, venerable sir," that ordinary person, monk replied to the Blessed One. He approached the ordinary monks and said to them, "The Teacher calls you."

"Yes, friend," those ordinary people, conventional monks replied to that monk. They approached the Blessed One, venerated him, and sat to one side. When they were seated to one side, the Blessed One said to those monks, "Friends, is it true that you are engaged in disputes, arguments, contention, and mutual verbal assault? Is it true that you can not persuade each other, and are not persuaded by each other; that you can not convince each other, and are not convinced by each other?"

"Yes, venerable sir."

"Friends, what do you think? When you are engaged in disputes, arguments, contention, and mutual verbal assault, have physical actions… verbal actions… and mental actions based on loving-friendliness been established in regards to your co-practitioners, both publicly and privately?"

"Certainly not, venerable sir."

"Thus, commoner friends, it is apparent that when you are engaged in disputes, arguments, contention, and mutual verbal assault, then physical actions… verbal actions… and mental actions based on loving-friendliness have not been established in regards to your community (Sangha), both publicly and privately.

Foolish men, what could you possibly know or see that leads you to engage in disputes, arguments, contention, and mutual verbal assault, such that you can not persuade each other, and are not persuaded by each other; that you can not convince each other, and are not convinced by each other? Foolish men, this will lead to your long-lasting detriment and suffering."

The Six Factors of Communal Harmony

Then the Blessed One addressed the companions: "Commoner monks, these six things are polite, create affection and respect, and lead to inclusiveness, non-contention, harmony, and unity. What six?

"Here, a commoner monk should establish physical actions based on loving-friendliness towards one's community (Sangha), both publicly and privately. This is one thing that is polite, creates affection and respect, and leads to inclusiveness, non-contention, harmony, and unity.

"Companions, this is another one: A commoner monk should establish verbal actions based on loving-friendliness towards one's community, both publicly and privately. This is another thing that is polite, creates affection and respect, and leads to inclusiveness, non-contention, harmony, and unity.

"Companions, this is another one: A commoner monk should establish mental actions based on loving-friendliness towards one's community, both publicly and privately. This is another thing that is polite, creates affection and respect, and leads to inclusiveness, non-contention, harmony, and unity.

"Companions, this is another one: A commoner monk should unreservedly share with one's community any possessions one has acquired properly – even the food from one's plate. This is another thing that is polite, creates affection and respect, and leads to inclusiveness, non-contention, harmony, and unity.

"Companions, this is another one: When living with one's community, a commoner monk should try to engage both publicly and privately in virtuous behaviors, develop noble virtues that are unbroken, undamaged, unstained, unblemished, liberating, praised by the wise, free of grasping, and conducive to noble concentration.

"Companions, this is another one: When living with one's community, a commoner monk should try to maintain both publicly and privately a perspective which is noble, salvific, and correctly leads the maintainer of that perspective to the elimination of suffering.

"Companions, these are six things that are polite, create affection and respect, and lead to inclusiveness, non-contention, harmony, and unity. Companions, of these six polite things, this is the best one, the all-inclusive one, the unifying one: the perspective which is noble, salvific, and correctly leads its maintainer to the elimination of suffering.

The Seven Factors of Stream-Entry

"Ordinary friends, what is the perspective, which is noble, salvific, and correctly leads its maintainer to the elimination of suffering? Here, an ordinary person has gone to the forest, to the base of a tree, or to an empty building, and considers in this way: 'Do I have an obsession which has not been abandoned, which can obsess my mind such that I will be unable to accurately know and see?' Companions, if a person is obsessed with sensual passion, then his mind is obsessed. Companions, if a person is obsessed with aversion, then his mind is obsessed. Companions, if a person is obsessed with lethargy and languor, then his mind is obsessed.

Companions, if an ordinary person is obsessed with restlessness and remorse, then his mind is obsessed. Companions, if an ordinary person is obsessed with doubt, then his mind is obsessed. Companions, if an ordinary person is intent upon this world, then his mind is obsessed. Companions, if an ordinary person is intent upon the next world, then his mind is obsessed. Companions, if an ordinary person is engaged in disputes, arguments, contention, and mutual verbal assault, then his mind is obsessed.

One understands: 'There is no obsession in me which has not been abandoned, which could obsess my mind such that I would be unable to accurately know and see. My mind is well-directed for awakening to the truth.' This is the first knowledge that one has attained which is noble, transcendent, and not in common with ordinary people.

"Ordinary friends, this is another one: A noble disciple considers in this way: 'When I pursue, develop, and commit to this perspective, do I personally acquire tranquility and peacefulness?' One understands: 'When I pursue, develop, and commit to this perspective, I personally acquire tranquility and peacefulness.' This is the second knowledge that one has attained which is noble, transcendent, and not in common with ordinary people.

"Ordinary friends, this is another one: A noble disciple considers in this way: 'Are there contemplatives and spiritual practitioners outside of this teaching who have the same kind of direct experience based on life as I do?' One understands: 'There are no contemplatives and spiritual saints outside of this teaching who have the same kind of experience as I do.' This is the third knowledge that one has attained which is noble, transcendent, and not in common with ordinary people.

"Ordinary friends, this is another one: A noble disciple considers in this way: 'Do I have the disposition of a person who has attained right perspective?' And friends, what is the disposition of a person who has attained right perspective? Friends, this is the disposition of a person who has attained right perspective: If one commits an offense for which rehabilitation is possible, then one quickly tells, discloses, and clarifies it to the Buddha, or to the community; and after telling, disclosing, and clarifying it, one is restrained in the future.

Friends, just as a young, undeveloped infant that touches a hot coal with its hand or foot quickly withdraws, in the same way, this is the disposition of a person who has attained right perspective: If one commits an offense... one is restrained in the future. One understands: 'I have the disposition of a person who has attained right perspective.' This is the fourth knowledge that one has attained which is noble, transcendent, and not in common with ordinary people.

"Ordinary friends, this is another one: A noble disciple considers in this way: 'Do I have the disposition of a person who has attained right perspective?' And, what is the disposition of a person who has attained right perspective? Friends, this is the disposition of a person who has attained right perspective (Sotapanna): One makes an effort to do whatever needs to be done for one's community, while still having a strong commitment to training oneself in heightened virtue, heightened mentality, and heightened wisdom (Arahant).

Just as a cow with a young calf watches the calf while grazing, in the same way, this is the disposition of a person who has attained right perspective: One makes an effort to do whatever needs to be done for one's community, while still having a strong commitment to training himself in heightened virtue, heightened mentality, and heightened wisdom. One understands: 'I have the disposition of a person who has attained right perspective.' This is the fifth knowledge that one has attained which is noble, transcendent, and not in common with ordinary people.

"Ordinary friends, this is another one: A noble disciple considers in this way: 'Do I have the strength of a person who has attained right perspective?'

And friends, what is the strength of a person who has attained right perspective?

This is the strength of a person who has attained right perspective: When the Dhamma-Vinaya (i.e. Sotapanna to Arahant) which has been declared by the Tathāgata is being taught, one listens to the Dhamma carefully, attentively, and wholeheartedly[3]. One understands: 'I have the strength of a person who has attained right perspective.' This is the sixth knowledge that he has attained which is noble, transcendent, and not in common with ordinary people.

"Ordinary friends, this is another one: A noble disciple considers in this way: 'Do I have the strength of a person who has attained right perspective?'

And, what is the strength of a person who has attained right perspective? This is the strength of a person who has attained right perspective: When the Dhamma-Vinaya (i.e Sotapanna to Arahant) which has been declared by the Tathāgata is being taught, one acquires the correct interpretation, one acquires an understanding of the Dhamma (Sotapanna to Arahant), and one acquires joy connected with the Dhamma. One understands: 'I have the strength of a person who has attained right perspective.' This is the seventh knowledge that one has attained which is noble, transcendent, and not in common with ordinary people.

"Ordinary friends, when a noble disciple has these seven characteristics, one has sought out[5] well the disposition that leads to realizing the attainment of stream-entry[6].

Friends, when a noble disciple has these seven characteristics, one has attained stream-entry."

This is what the Blessed One said. Satisfied, those ordinary monks delighted in the Blessed One's speech.

Chapter 51

Middle Discourses 49: Brahmanimantanikasutta

On the Invitation of Divinity

The Buddha engages in a conversation with Baka, a brahma who believes that his brahma-attainment is the highest attainment there is; fallen into the delusion that he was eternal and all-powerful. When Buddha attempts to discuss further, Māra took possession of a member of the retinue of Divinity, says to Buddha not to go beyond the words of Baka because various others (spiritual practitioners) who attempted to discuss with Baka either ended up reborn in bad places or good places depending on what they said. To which Buddha replied rebirth is not applicable to him, as he has given up attachment, and he knows better than Baka; he knows the realms of births and Nibbana. The lack of validation from others can have no impact on Buddha; Buddhahood does not change whether another person realizes it or not. Although previous practitioners claim they're awakened ones, they are not truly awakened ones because they have not given up fetters. However, Buddha has given up the relevant fetters. The Buddha asserts the benefits he has of his noble wisdom and noble conduct in two major fashions: through a description of his awakened knowledge and through a display of psychic powers.

"So I have heard. At one time the Buddha was staying near Sāvatthī in Jeta's Grove, Anāthapiṇḍika's monastery. There the Buddha addressed the companions, "Companions!"

"Venerable sir," they replied. The Buddha said this:

"This one time, companions, I was staying near Ukkaṭṭhā, in the Subhaga Forest at the root of a magnificent sal tree. Now at that time Baka the Divinity had the following harmful misconception: 'This is permanent, this is everlasting, this is eternal, this is whole, this is not liable to pass away. For this is where there's no being born, growing old, dying, passing away, or being reborn. And there's no other escape beyond this.'

Then I knew what Baka the Divinity was thinking. As easily as a strong person would extend or contract their arm, I vanished from the Subhaga Forest and reappeared in that realm of divinity.

Baka saw me coming off in the distance and said, 'Come, good sir! Welcome, good sir! It's been a long time since you took the opportunity to come here. For this is permanent, this is everlasting, this is eternal, this is complete, this is not liable to pass away. For this is where there's no being born, growing old, dying, passing away, or being reborn. And there's no other escape beyond this.'

When he had spoken, I said to him, 'Alas, Baka the Divinity is lost in ignorance! Alas, Baka the Divinity is lost in ignorance! Because what is actually impermanent, not lasting, transient, incomplete, and liable to pass away, he says is permanent, everlasting, eternal, complete, and not liable to pass away. And where there is being born, growing old, dying, passing away, and being reborn, he says that there's no being born, growing old, dying, passing away, or being reborn. And although there is another escape beyond this, he says that there's no other escape beyond this.'

Then Māra the Wicked took possession of a member of the retinue of Divinity and said this to me, 'Mendicant, mendicant! Don't attack this one! Don't attack this one! For this is the Divinity, the Great Divinity, the Vanquisher, the Unvanquished, the Universal Seer, the Wielder of Power, God Almighty, the Maker, the Creator, the First, the Begetter, the Controller, the Father of those who have been born and those yet to be born.

There have been ascetics and brahmins before you, mendicant who criticized and loathed earth, water, fire, air, creatures, gods, the Progenitor, and the Divinity. When their bodies broke up and their breath was cut off they were reborn in a lower realm.

There have been ascetics and brahmins before you, mendicant, who praised and approved earth, water, fire, air, creatures, gods, the Progenitor, and the Divinity. When their bodies broke up and their breath was cut off they were reborn in a higher realm.

So, companions, I tell you this: please, good sir, do exactly what the Divinity says. Don't go beyond the word of the Divinity. If you do, then you'll end up like a person who, when approached by Lady Luck, would ward her off with a staff; or who, as they are falling over a cliff, would lose grip of the ground with their hands and feet. Please, dear sir, do exactly what the Divinity says. Don't go beyond the word of the Divinity. Do you not see the assembly of the Divinity gathered here?'

And so Māra the Wicked presented the assembly of the Divinity to me.

When he had spoken, I said to Māra, 'I know you, Wicked One. Do not think, "He does not know me." You are Māra the Wicked. And the Divinity, the Divinity's assembly, and the retinue of Divinity have all fallen into your hands; they're under your sway. And you think, "Maybe this one, too, has fallen into my hands; maybe he's under my sway!" But I haven't fallen into your hands; I'm not under your sway.'

When I had spoken, Baka the Divinity said to me, 'But, good sir, what I say is permanent, everlasting, eternal, complete, and not liable to pass away is in fact permanent, everlasting, eternal, complete, and not liable to pass away. And where I say there's no being born, growing old, dying, passing away, or being reborn there is in fact no being born, growing old, dying, passing away, or being reborn.

And when I say there's no other escape beyond this there is in fact no other escape beyond this. There have been ascetics and brahmins in the world before you, mendicant, whose deeds of fervent mortification lasted as long as your entire life. When there was another escape beyond this they knew it, and when there was no other escape beyond this, they knew it.

So, mendicant, I tell you this: you will never find another escape beyond this, and you will eventually get weary and frustrated. If you attach to earth, you will lie close to me, in my domain, subject to my will, and expendable. If you attach to water … fire … air … creatures … gods … the Progenitor … the Divinity, you will lie close to me, in my domain, subject to my will, and expendable.'

'the Divinity, I too know that if I attach to earth, I will lie close to you, in your domain, subject to your will, and expendable. If I attach to water … fire … air … creatures … gods … the Progenitor … the Divinity, I will lie close to you, in your domain, subject to your will, and expendable. And in addition, Divinity, I understand your range and your light: "That's how powerful is Baka the Divinity, how illustrious and mighty."'

'But in what way do you understand my range and my light?'

'A galaxy extends a thousand times as far as the moon and sun revolve and the shining ones light up the quarters. And there you wield your power.

You know the high and low, the passionate and dispassionate, and the coming and going of sentient beings from this realm to another.

That's how I understand your range and your light.

But there are three other realms that you don't know or see, but which I know and see. There is the realm named after the gods of streaming radiance. You passed away from there and were reborn here. You've dwelt here so long that you've forgotten about that, so you don't know it or see it. But I know it and see it. So Divinity, I am not your equal in knowledge, let alone your inferior. Rather, I know more than you.

There is the realm named after the gods of universal beauty … There is the realm named after the gods of abundant fruit, which you don't know or see. But I know it and see it. So Divinity, I am not your equal in knowledge, let alone your inferior. Rather, I know more than you.

Since directly knowing earth as earth, and since directly knowing that which does not fall within the scope of experience characterized by earth, I have not become earth, I have not become in earth, I have not become as earth, I have not become one who thinks 'earth is mine', I have not affirmed earth. So Divinity, I am not your equal in knowledge, let alone your inferior. Rather, I know more than you.

Since directly knowing water … fire … air … creatures … gods … the Progenitor … the Divinity … the gods of streaming radiance … the gods of universal beauty … the gods of abundant fruit … the Vanquisher … Since directly knowing all as all, and since directly knowing that which does not fall within the scope of experience characterized by all, I have not become all, I have not become in all, I have not become as all, I have not become one who thinks 'all is mine', I have not affirmed all. So Divinity, I am not your equal in knowledge, let alone your inferior. Rather, I know more than you.'

'Well, good sir, if you have directly known that which does not fall within the scope of experience characterized by all, may that not be vacuous and hollow for you!

Consciousness where nothing appears, infinite, luminous all-round.

That is what does not fall within the scope of experience characterized by earth, water, fire, air, creatures, gods, the Progenitor, the Divinity, the gods of streaming radiance, the gods of universal beauty, the gods of abundant fruit, the Vanquisher, and the all.

Well look now, good sir, I will vanish from you!'

'All right, then, Divinity, vanish from me—if you can.'

Then Baka the Divinity said, 'I will vanish from the ascetic Gotama! I will vanish from the ascetic Gotama!' But he was unable to vanish from me.

So I said to him, 'Well now, Divinity, I will vanish from you!'

'All right, then, good sir, vanish from me—if you can.'

Then I used my psychic power to will that my voice would extend so that Divinity, his assembly, and his retinue would hear me, but they would not see me. And while vanished I recited this verse:

'Seeing the danger in continued existence—that life in any existence will cease to be—I didn't affirm any kind of existence, and didn't grasp at relishing.'

Then the Divinity, his assembly, and his retinue, their minds full of wonder and amazement, thought, 'Oh, how incredible, how amazing! The ascetic Gotama has such psychic power and might! We've never before seen or heard of any other ascetic or brahmin with psychic power and might like the ascetic Gotama, who has gone forth from the Sakyan clan. Though people enjoy continued existence, loving it so much, he has extracted it, root and all.'

Then Māra the Wicked took possession of a member of the retinue of Divinity and said this to me, 'If such is your understanding, good sir, do not present it to your disciples or those gone forth! Do not teach this Dhamma to your disciples or those gone forth! Do not wish this for your disciples or those who practice a spiritual path!

There have been ascetics and brahmins before you, mendicant, who claimed to be perfected ones, fully awakened Buddhas. They presented, taught, and wished this for their disciples and those gone forth. When their bodies broke up and their breath was cut off they were reborn in a lower realm.

But there have also been other ascetics and brahmins before you, mendicant, who claimed to be perfected ones, fully awakened Buddhas. They did not present, teach, or wish this for their disciples and those gone forth. When their bodies broke up and their breath was cut off they were reborn in a higher realm.

So, companion, I tell you this: please, good sir, remain passive, dwelling in blissful meditation in the present life, for this is better left unsaid. Good sir, do not instruct others.'

When he had spoken, I said to Māra, 'I know you, Wicked One. Do not think, "He doesn't know me." You are Māra the Wicked. You don't speak to me like this out of sympathy, but with no sympathy. For you think, "Those who the ascetic Gotama teaches will go beyond my reach."

Those who formerly claimed to be fully awakened Buddhas were not in fact fully awakened Buddhas. But I am. The Realized One remains as such whether or not he teaches disciples. The Realized One remains as such whether or not he presents the teaching to disciples. Why is that? Because the Realized One has given up the defilements that are corrupting, leading to future lives, hurtful, resulting in suffering and future rebirth, old age, and death. He has cut them off at the root, made them like a palm stump, obliterated them so they are unable to arise in the future. Just as a palm tree with its crown cut off is incapable of further growth, the Realized One has given up the defilements that are corrupting, leading to future lives, hurtful, resulting in suffering and future rebirth, old age, and death. He has cut them off at the root, made them like a palm stump, obliterated them so they are unable to arise in the future.'"

And so, because of the silencing of Māra, and because of the invitation of the Divinity, the name of this discussion is "On the Invitation of Divinity".

Chapter 52

Middle Discourses 50: Māratajjanīyasutta

The Condemnation of Māra

Māra, a being with wicked intentions, has a conversation with Arahant Moggallāna. Arahant Maha Moggallana relates an incident of the distant past to remind Mara of the dangers of creating trouble for a direct disciple of the Buddha. Arahant Moggalana says that in the past, he acted as an evil being, causing suffering for the noble disciples of Buddha Kakusanda. As a result, he suffered a lot in hell. He was reminded and suggested it was unwise to create trouble for the Savaka disciples of Buddha.

"So I have heard. At one time Arahant Mahāmoggallāna was staying in the land of the Bhaggas at Crocodile Hill, in the deer park at Bhesakaḷā's Wood.

At that time Arahant Moggallāna was walking mindfully in the open air.

Now at that time Māra the Wicked had got inside Arahant Moggallāna's belly. Moggallāna thought, "Why now is my belly so very heavy, like I've just eaten a load of beans?" Then he stepped down from the walking path, entered his dwelling, sat down on the seat spread out, and investigated inside himself.

He saw that Māra the Wicked had got inside his belly. So he said to Māra, "Come out, Wicked One, come out! Do not harass the Realized One or his disciple. Don't create lasting harm and suffering for yourself!"

Then Māra thought, "This ascetic doesn't really know me or see me when he tells me to come out. Not even the Teacher could recognize me so quickly, so how could a disciple?"

Then Arahant Moggallāna said to Māra, "I know you even when you're like this, Wicked One. Do not think, 'He doesn't know me.' You are Māra the Wicked. And you think, 'This ascetic doesn't really know me or see me when he tells me to come out. Not even the Teacher could recognize me so quickly, so how could a disciple?'"

Then Māra thought, "This ascetic really does know me and see me when he tells me to come out."

Then Māra came up out of Arahant Moggallāna's mouth and stood against the door. Arahanat Moggallāna saw him there and said, "I see you even there, Wicked One. Do not think, 'He doesn't see me.' That's you, Wicked One, standing against the door.

Once upon a time, Wicked One, I was a Māra named Dūsī, and I had a sister named Kāḷī. You were her son, which made you my nephew.

At that time Buddha Kakusandha, the Blessed One, the perfected one, the fully awakened Buddha arose in the world. Kakusandha Buddha had a fine pair of chief disciples named Arahant Vidhura and Arahant Sañjīva. Of all the disciples of the Buddha Kakusandha, none were the equal of Arahant Vidhura in teaching Dhamma. And that's how he came to be known as Arahant Vidhura.

But when Arahant Sañjīva had gone to a wilderness, or to the root of a tree, or to an empty hut, he easily attained the cessation of perception and feeling. Once upon a time, Arahant Sañjīva was sitting at the root of a certain tree having attained the cessation of perception and feeling. Some cowherds, shepherds, farmers, and passers-by saw him sitting there and said, 'Oh, how incredible, how amazing! This ascetic passed away while seated. We should cremate him.' They collected grass, wood, and cow-dung, heaped it all on Sañjīva's body, set it on fire, and left.

Then, when the night had passed, Arahant Sañjīva emerged from that attainment, shook out his robes, and, since it was morning, he robed up and entered the village for alms. Those cowherds, shepherds, farmers, and passers-by saw him wandering for alms and said, 'Oh, how incredible, how amazing! This ascetic passed away while seated, and now he has come back to life!' And that's how he came to be known as Arahant Sañjīva.

Then it occurred to Māra Dūsī, 'I don't know the course of rebirth of these ethical mendicants of good character. Why don't I take possession of these brahmins and householders and say, "Come, all of you, abuse, attack, harass, and trouble the ethical mendicants of good character. Hopefully by doing this we can upset their minds so that Māra Dūsī can find a vulnerability."' And that's exactly what he did.

Then those common people from various castes abused, attacked, harassed, and troubled the ethical mendicants of good character: 'These shavelings, fake ascetics, primitives, black spawn from the feet of our kinsman, say, "We practice absorption meditation! We practice absorption meditation!" Shoulders drooping, downcast, and dopey, they meditate and concentrate and contemplate and ruminate. They're just like an owl on a branch, which meditates and concentrates and contemplates and ruminates as it hunts a mouse. They're just like a jackal on a river-bank, which meditates and concentrates and contemplates and ruminates as it hunts a fish. They're just like a cat by an alley or a drain or a dustbin, which meditates and concentrates and contemplates and ruminates as it hunts a mouse. They're just like an unladen donkey by an alley or a drain or a dustbin, which meditates and concentrates and contemplates and ruminates. In the same way, these shavelings, fake ascetics, primitives, black spawn from the feet of our kinsman, say, "We practice absorption meditation! We practice absorption meditation!" Shoulders drooping, downcast, and dopey, they meditate and concentrate and contemplate and ruminate.'

Most of the people who died at that time—when their body broke up, after death—were reborn in a place of loss, a bad place, the underworld, hell.

Then Kakusandha the Blessed One, the perfected one, the fully awakened Buddha, addressed the companions: 'Companions, the brahmins and householders have been possessed by Māra Dūsī. He told them to abuse you in the hope of upsetting your minds so that he can find a vulnerability. Come, all of you companions, maintain a heart full of love to one direction, and to the second, and to the third, and to the fourth. In the same way above, below, across, everywhere, all around, spread a heart full of love to the whole world—abundant, expansive, limitless, free of enmity and ill will. Maintain a heart full of compassion … Maintain a heart full of rejoicing … Maintain a heart full of equanimity to one direction, and to the second, and to the third, and to the fourth. In the same way above, below, across, everywhere, all around, spread a heart full of equanimity to the whole world—abundant, expansive, limitless, free of enmity and ill will.'

When those companions (spiritual practitioners) were instructed and advised by the Buddha Kakusandha in this way, they went to a wilderness, or to the root of a tree, or to an empty hut, where they maintained and developed spreading a heart full of love … compassion … rejoicing … equanimity (anagami).

Then it occurred to Māra Dūsī, 'Even when I do this I don't know the course of rebirth of these ethical mendicants of good character. Why don't I take possession of these brahmins and householders and say, "Come, all of you, honor, respect, esteem, and venerate the ethical mendicants of good character. Hopefully by doing this we can upset their minds so that Māra Dūsī can find a vulnerability."'

And that's exactly what he did. Then those brahmins and householders honored, respected, esteemed, and venerated the ethical mendicants of good character.

Most of the people who died at that time—when their body broke up, after death—were reborn in a good place, a heavenly realm.

Then Kakusandha the Blessed One, the perfected one, the fully awakened Buddha, addressed the companions: 'Companions, the ascetics and commoners have been possessed by Māra Dūsī. He told them to venerate you in the hope of upsetting your minds so that he can find a vulnerability. Come, all you friends, since you have completely cut off the first three fetters, reflect the ugliness of the body, perceive the repulsiveness of food, perceive dissatisfaction with the whole world, and observe the impermanence of all conditions (If you have not yet cut off the first three fetters, try and cut off such fetters and then reflect the ugliness …)'

When those companions were instructed and advised by the Buddha Kakusandha in this way, they went to isolated places (a wilderness, or to the root of a tree, or an empty hut or building) where they reflected mindfully the ugliness of the body, perceiving the repulsiveness of food, perceiving dissatisfaction with the whole world, and observing the impermanence of all conditions.

Then the Buddha Kakusandha robed up in the morning and, taking this bowl and robe, entered the village for alms with Arahant Vidhura as his second monk.

Then Māra Dūsī took possession of a certain boy, picked up a rock, and hit Arahant Vidhura on the head, cracking it open. Then Arahant Vidhura, with blood pouring from his cracked skull, still followed behind the Buddha Kakusandha. Then the Buddha Kakusandha turned to gaze back, the way that elephants do, saying, 'This Māra Dūsī knows no bounds.' And as he was gazing, Māra Dūsī fell from that place and was reborn in the Great Hell.

Now that Great Hell is known by three names: 'Related to the Six Fields of Contact' and also 'The Impaling With Spikes' and also 'Individually Painful'. Then the wardens of hell came to me and said, 'When spike meets spike in your heart, you will know that you've been roasting in hell for a thousand years.'

I roasted for many years, many centuries, many millennia in that Great Hell. For ten thousand years I roasted in the annex of that Great Hell, experiencing the pain called 'this is emergence'. My body was in human form, but I had the head of a fish.

What kind of hell was that, where Dūsī was roasted after attacking the disciple Vidhura along with the brahmin Kakusandha?

There were 100 iron spikes, each one individually painful. That's the kind of hell where Dūsī was roasted after attacking the disciple Vidhura along with the brahmin Kakusandha.

Dark One, if you attack a person who directly knows this, a disciple of the Buddha, you'll fall into suffering.

There are mansions that last an eon standing in the middle of a lake. Sapphire-colored, brilliant, they sparkle and shine. Dancing there are nymphs shining in all different colors.

Dark One, if you attack a person who directly knows this, a disciple of the Buddha, you'll fall into suffering.

I'm the one who, urged by the Buddha, shook the stilt longhouse of Migāra's mother with his big toe as the Saṅgha of mendicants watched.

Dark One, if you attack a person who directly knows this, a disciple of the Buddha, you'll fall into suffering.

I'm the one who shook the Palace of Victory with his big toe owing to psychic power, inspiring deities to awe.

Dark One, if you attack a person who directly knows this, a disciple of the Buddha, you'll fall into suffering.

I'm the one who asked Sakka in the Palace of Victory: 'Vāsava, I hope you recall the one who is freed through the ending of craving?' And I'm the one to whom Sakka admitted the truth when asked.

Dark One, if you attack a person who directly knows this, a disciple of the Buddha, you'll fall into suffering.

I'm the one who asked the Divinity in the Hall of Justice before the assembly: 'Reverend, do you still have the same view that you had in the past? Or do you see the radiance transcending the realm of divinity?'

And I'm the one to whom the Divinity truthfully admitted his progress: 'Good sir, I don't have that view that I had in the past.

I see the radiance transcending the realm of divinity. So how could I say today that I am permanent and eternal?'

Dark One, if you attack a person who directly knows this, a disciple of the Buddha, you'll fall into suffering.

I'm the one who touched the peak of Mount Meru using the power of meditative liberation. I've visited the forests of the people who dwell in the Eastern Continent.

Dark One, if you attack a person who directly knows this, a disciple of the Buddha, you'll fall into suffering.

Though a fire doesn't think, 'I'll burn the fool!' Still the fool who attacks the fire gets burnt.

In the same way, Māra, in attacking the Realized One, you'll only burn yourself, like a fool touching the flames.

Māra's done a bad thing in attacking the Realized One. Wicked One, do you imagine that your wickedness won't bear fruit?

Your deeds heap up wickedness that will last a long time, terminator! Give up on the Buddha, Māra! And hold no hope for the mendicants!"

That is how, in the Bhesekaḷā grove, the companion condemned Māra. That spirit, downcast, disappeared right there".

Chapter 53

Middle Discourses 51: Kandarakasutta

With Kandaraka

This discourse speaks about all four stages of Nibbana. Pessa comes to meet Buddha and says that it's amazing that Buddha Gautama, supreme and the blessed one, teaches Dhamma to others so that they can gain four-fold Nibbana and experience Nibbana that is experienced by the Buddha. Those who will be Buddhas in the future will do the same. In response, Buddha says yes, that's indeed correct, those Buddhas of the past and future will also the taches Dhamma to others so that they can gain four-fold Nibbana and experience Nibbana that is experienced by the Buddha similar to that of Gautama Buddha.

Among noble disciples, there are Arahants who have abandoned all ten fetters. There are Anagamis who abandon sensual desire and ill will through practicing satipattana: four kinds of mindfulness.

Pessa says it's amazing, and those who live in any setting (non-monastic settings or monastic and so on), including himself, also gain Anagami through the same techniques of mindfulness four-fold (after Sotapanna). Then, Buddha says there are four kinds of people. Those who hurt self and practice hurting self. Those who hurt others and are engaging in hurting others. Those who neither torment others nor are devoted to hurting others. Those who don't hurt self or others and don't engage in practices hurting self and others. Buddha asks Pessa; who do you prefer among these four kinds of people?

Pessa says he prefers the fourth kind of people because they don't hurt self or others. This means one who follows Dhamma across four-fold Nibbana by giving up grasping three fetters at the first stage and 10 fetters at Arahantship. After the conversation, Pessa went away. Buddha said to the community of practitioners; friends, if Pessa had waited to listen to the rest of the discourse, he might have benefited by gaining Arahantship. Yet even now, as an Anagami, he is good.

People can suffocate themselves; a person who eats nothing or much less by choice, walks without shoes on hard surfaces, and walks without clothes in cold weather conditions is touched by the ups and downs of worldly conditions too much. In engaging in extreme ways to hurt self, a person suffocates themselves. A person suffocates another by killing, stealing, insulting, and so forth, and engages in a practice that suffocates others.

People can suffocate themselves and others; a person who engages in extreme practices, may be living a spiritual life that causes mental suffering to self or others, engages in things that cause harm to self and others; not fulfilling responsibilities, having ill will, encouraging divisions in conventions and mistreating self and others etc.

Sotapanna to Arahant makes a person give up desires (and grasping ten fetters). A person who does not harm self and others (Sotapanna to Arahant) maintains qualities similar to that of the Supreme Buddha. A Sotapanna has noble virtues. They do not need to take precepts because they naturally have noble virtues. Anagami gives up desires (likes, dislikes) for sensual pleasures: luxury beds, perfumes, flower glands, eating meals before noon, and similar ways. Arahant is content with whatever food, clothes, etc.

Hindrances are abandoned at higher stages of Nibbana. A person experiences four arupa or "formless" jhanas on the path leading to Arahantship after completing the Anagami state. After completing Arahantship, some Arahants gain the ability to see past lives. Certain Arahants gain triple knowledge: seeing past lives, seeing the birth of beings shaped by karma, and understanding one's attainment of Nibbana.

"So I have heard. At one time the Buddha was staying near Campā on the banks of the Gaggarā Lotus Pond together with a large group of community, Saṅgha.

Then Pessa the elephant driver's son and Kandaraka the wanderer went to see the Buddha. When they had approached, Pessa bowed and sat down to one side.

But the wanderer Kandaraka exchanged greetings with the Buddha and stood to one side. He looked around the community of Saṅgha, who were so very silent, and said to the Buddha:

"It's incredible, Mister Gotama, it's amazing! How the community of Saṅgha has been led to practice properly by Mister Gotama! All the perfected ones, the fully awakened Buddhas in the past or the future who lead the community of Saṅgha to practice properly will at best do so like Mister Gotama does in the present."

"That's so true, Kandaraka! That's so true! All the perfected ones, the fully awakened Buddhas in the past or the future who lead the community of Saṅgha to practice properly will at best do so like I do in the present.

For in this community of Saṅgha there are Arahants, who have ended the defilements (ten fetters), completed the spiritual journey, done what had to be done, laid down the burden, achieved their own goal, utterly ended the fetter of continued existence, and are rightly freed through enlightenment. And in this community of Saṅgha there are trainee companions (Sotapanna to Anagami) who are consistently ethical, living consistently, alert, living alertly. They reflect regularly in the four kinds of mindfulness practices. What four?

It's when a person reflects on an aspect of the body—keen, aware, and mindful, rid of covetousness and displeasure for the world. They reflect on their feelings—keen, aware, and mindful, rid of covetousness and displeasure for the world. They reflect observing an aspect of the mind—keen, aware, and mindful, rid of covetousness and displeasure for the world. They reflect observing an aspect of principles—keen, aware, and mindful, rid of covetousness and displeasure for the world."

When he had spoken, Pessa said to the Buddha:

"It's incredible, sir, it's amazing! How well described by the Buddha are the four kinds of mindfulness practices! They are in order to purify sentient beings, to get past sorrow and crying, to make an end of pain and sadness, to discover the system, and to realize extinguishment. For we, those who live in various settings can adopt the same practice to experience Anagami state. We reflect on four kinds of mindfulness practices after we gain Sotapanna and completed Sakadagami state. We reflect on observing an aspect of the body ... feelings ... mind ... principles—keen, aware, and mindful, rid of covetousness and displeasure for the world.

It's incredible, sir, it's amazing! How the Buddha knows what's best for sentient beings, even though people continue to be so shady, rotten, and tricky. For human beings are shady, sir, while the animal is obvious. For I can drive an elephant in training, and while going back and forth in Campā it'll try all the tricks, bluffs, ruses, and feints that it can. But my bondservants, servants, and workers behave one way by body, another by speech, and their minds another. It's incredible, sir, it's amazing! How the Buddha knows what's best for sentient beings, even though people continue to be so shady, rotten, and tricky. For human beings are shady, sir, while the animal is obvious."

"That's so true, Pessa! That's so true! For human beings are shady, while the animal is obvious. Pessa, these four people are found in the world. What four?

1. One person mortifies themselves, committed to the practice of mortifying themselves.

2. One person mortifies others, committed to the practice of mortifying others.
3. One person mortifies themselves and others, committed to the practice of mortifying themselves and others.
4. One person doesn't mortify either themselves or others, committed to the practice of not mortifying themselves or others. They live without wishes in the present life, quenched, cooled, experiencing bliss, with self-become divine.

Which one of these four people do you like the sound of?"

"Sir, I don't like the sound of the first three people. I only like the sound of the last person, who doesn't mortify either themselves or others."

"But why don't you like the sound of those three people?"

"Sir, the person who mortifies themselves does so even though they want to be happy and recoil from pain. That's why I don't like the sound of that person. The person who mortifies others does so even though others want to be happy and recoil from pain. That's why I don't like the sound of that person. The person who mortifies themselves and others does so even though both themselves and others want to be happy and recoil from pain. That's why I don't like the sound of that person.

The person who doesn't mortify either themselves or others—living without wishes, quenched, cooled, experiencing bliss, with self become divine—does not torment themselves or others, both of whom want to be happy and recoil from pain. That's why I like the sound of that person. Well, now, sir, I must go. I have many duties, and much to do."

"Please, Pessa, go at your convenience." And then Pessa the elephant driver's son approved and agreed with what the Buddha said. He got up from his seat, bowed, and respectfully circled the Buddha, keeping him on his right, before leaving. Then, not long after he had left, the Buddha addressed the spiritual companions: "Friends, Pessa the elephant driver's son is astute. He has great wisdom. If he had sat here an hour so that I could have analyzed these four people in detail, he would have greatly benefited. Still, even with this much he has already greatly benefited."

"Now is the time, Blessed One! Now is the time, Holy One! May the Buddha analyze these four people in detail. The mendicants will listen and remember it."

"Well then, companions, listen and apply your mind well, I will speak."

"Yes, sir," they replied. The Buddha said this:

"And what person mortifies themselves, committed to the practice of mortifying themselves? It's when a person goes naked, ignoring conventions. They lick their hands, and don't come or wait when called. They don't consent to food brought to them, or food prepared for them, or an invitation for a meal.

They don't receive anything from a pot or bowl; or from someone who keeps sheep, or who has a weapon or a shovel in their home; or where a couple is eating; or where there is a woman who is pregnant, breastfeeding, or who has a man in her home; or where there's a dog waiting or flies buzzing. They accept no fish or meat or liquor or wine, and drink no beer.

They go to just one house for alms, taking just one mouthful, or two houses and two mouthfuls, up to seven houses and seven mouthfuls. They feed on one saucer a day, two saucers a day, up to seven saucers a day. They eat once a day, once every second day, up to once a week, and so on, even up to once a fortnight. They live committed to the practice of eating food at set intervals.

They eat herbs, millet, wild rice, poor rice, water lettuce, rice bran, scum from boiling rice, sesame flour, grass, or cow dung. They survive on forest roots and fruits, or eating fallen fruit.

They wear robes of sunn hemp, mixed hemp, corpse-wrapping cloth, rags, lodh tree bark, antelope hide (whole or in strips), kusa grass, bark, wood-chips, human hair, horse-tail hair, or owls' wings. They tear out their hair and beard, committed to this practice. They constantly stand, refusing seats.

They squat, committed to the endeavor of squatting. They lie on a mat of thorns, making a mat of thorns their bed. They're devoted to ritual bathing three times a day, including the evening. And so they live committed to practicing these various ways of mortifying and tormenting the body. This is called a person who mortifies themselves, being committed to the practice of mortifying themselves.

And what person mortifies others, committed to the practice of mortifying others? It's when a person is a slaughterer of sheep, pigs, or poultry, a hunter or trapper, a fisher, a bandit, an executioner, a butcher, a jailer, or someone with some other kind of cruel livelihood. This is called a person who mortifies others, being committed to the practice of mortifying others.

And what person mortifies themselves and others, being committed to the practice of mortifying themselves and others? It's when a person is an anointed aristocratic king or a well-to-do brahmin. He has a new ceremonial hall built to the east of the citadel. He shaves off his hair and beard, dresses in a rough antelope hide, and smears his body with ghee and oil. Scratching his back with antlers, he enters the hall with his chief queen and the brahmin high priest. There he lies on the bare ground strewn with grass. The king feeds on the milk from one teat of a cow that has a calf of the same color. The chief queen feeds on the milk from the second teat.

The brahmin high priest feeds on the milk from the third teat. The milk from the fourth teat is served to the sacred flame. The calf feeds on the remainder.

He says: 'Slaughter this many bulls, bullocks, heifers, goats, rams, and horses for the sacrifice! Fell this many trees and reap this much grass for the sacrificial equipment!' His bondservants, servants, and workers do their jobs under threat of punishment and danger, weeping with tearful faces. This is called a person who mortifies themselves and others, being committed to the practice of mortifying themselves and others.

And what person doesn't mortify either themselves or others, but lives without wishes, quenched, cooled, experiencing bliss, with self become divine?

It's when a Realized One arises in the world, perfected, a fully awakened Buddha, accomplished in knowledge and conduct, holy, knower of the world, supreme guide for those who wish to train, teacher of gods and humans, awakened, blessed.

He has realized with his own insight this world—with its gods, Māras, and divinities, this population with its various kinds of people, gods and humans—and he makes it known to others. He proclaims a teaching that is good in the beginning (Sotapanna), good in the middle (Anagami), and good in the end (Arahant), meaningful and well-phrased. And he reveals a spiritual practice that's entirely full and pure.

An ordinary person hears that teaching, an ordinary person's child, or someone reborn in a good family. They gain faith in the Realized One and reflect, 'Ordinary life is cramped and dirty, spiritual life is wide open. It's not easy for me to live in a normal household and practice the universal noble path utterly full and pure, like a polished shell. For me, it's probably easier to practice the noble path in a monastic setting and my circumstances favour that. Why don't I join a monastery to commence a spiritual life?' After some time, they give up a large or small fortune and a large or small family circle. They dress up as monastic and start practicing a spiritual life in a monastic setting.

Once they've started a spiritual practice, as ordinary practitioners, ideally, they should try following up on the training and livelihood of the noble ones.

They should give up killing living creatures and renounce the rod and the sword. They should be scrupulous and kind, living full of sympathy for all living beings (A Sotapanna does not need to take the precepts, this is because they naturally have this quality due to the right view).

As ordinary practitioners, ideally, they should give up stealing. They should take only what's given and expect only what's given. They should keep themselves clean by not thieving (A Sotapanna does not…).

As ordinary practitioners, ideally, they should give up unchastity. They should become celibate, set apart, avoiding the vulgar act of sex (Anagamis or Arahants who live in any setting; monastic or non-monastic from a conventional perspective, don't take precepts. They naturally have this quality due to the right view).

As ordinary practitioners, ideally, they should give up lying. They should speak the truth and stick to the truth. They should be honest and dependable and not trick the world with their words (A Sotapanna naturally has this quality due to the right view).

As ordinary practitioners, ideally, they should give up divisive speech. They should not repeat in one place what they heard in another so as to divide people against each other. Instead, they should reconcile those who are divided, supporting unity, delighting in harmony, loving harmony, and speaking words that promote harmony (Anagamis or Arahants who live in any setting…).

As ordinary practitioners, ideally, they should give up harsh speech. They should speak in a way that's mellow, pleasing to the ear, lovely, going to the heart, polite, likable, and agreeable to the people (Anagamis or Arahants…).

As ordinary practitioners, ideally, they should give up talking nonsense. Their words should be timely, true, and meaningful, in line with the teaching and training[27]. They should say things at the right time that are valuable, reasonable, succinct, and beneficial. (Anagamis and Arahants, they naturally …)

As ordinary practitioners, ideally, they should refrain from injuring plants and seeds. Upon gaining the Anagami state, a person naturally reduces desires for acts of harming trees, plants and seeds, etc.

An ordinary person should make a conscious effort to reduce the desire for food and eat one part of the day reflecting the qualities of the noble ones who have given up the higher fetters (i.e. Anagami and Arahants). Anagamis and Arahants don't take precepts. They are naturally abstained from eating at night and food at the wrong time.

An ordinary person should make a conscious effort to reduce the desire (likes, dislikes) for seeing shows of dancing, singing, and music. Anagamis and Arahants naturally have no desire for seeing shows of dancing, singing, and music.

---

[27] Teaching and training refer to Sotapanna and the practice leading to Sotapanna (and above).

Ordinary practitioners, in a monastic setting, should attempt to reduce the desire to beautify and adorn themselves with garlands, fragrance, and makeup through conscious efforts. Anagamis or Arahants naturally have no desire to beautify and adorn themselves with garlands, fragrance, and makeup.

An ordinary person should make conscious efforts to reduce desire (likes, dislikes) for luxury bedding. Anagamis or Arahants don't take precepts. They naturally have no desire for luxury bedding.

An ordinary person should make conscious efforts to reduce desire (likes, dislikes) and mental attachment for gains and losses (i.e. gold and currency, raw grains, raw meat, women and girls, male and female bondservants, goats and sheep, chickens and pigs, elephants, cows, horses, and mares, and fields and land, etc.). Anagamis and Arahants take precepts. They naturally have no desire for such things.

An ordinary person should make conscious efforts to reduce desire (likes, dislikes) for making a wrong living; running errands and messages; falsifying weights, metals, or measures; bribery, fraud, cheating, and duplicity; mutilation, murder, abduction, banditry, plunder, and violence. Anagamis or Arahants don't take precepts. They naturally have no desire for such things.

An ordinary person should make conscious efforts to reduce mental attachment and desire (likes, dislikes) for clothing and food. Arahant is content with whatever robes to look after the body and food to look after the belly.

Arahants, wherever they go, they go without mental attachment. They're free like a bird: wherever it flies, wings are its only burden. In the same way, Arahant is content with whatever robes to look after the body and whatever food to look after the belly. Wherever they go, they go without mental attachment. When they have this entire spectrum of noble ethics, they experience a blameless happiness inside themselves (Ideally, an ordinary person should try and become content with whatever the robes they have ....).

Arahants, when they see a sight with their eyes, they do not get caught up in the features and details. If the faculty of sight were left unrestrained (meaning left full of desires), bad unskillful qualities of covetousness and displeasure would become overwhelming. Yet, Arahants have given up desires, protecting the faculty of sight, seeing is merely seen without an attachment. When they hear a sound with their ears ... When they smell an odor with their nose ... When they taste a flavor with their tongue ... When they feel a touch with their body ... When they know an idea with their mind, they don't get caught up in the features and details. [28]

---

[28] Ideally, an ordinary person should try developing similar qualities.

If the faculty of mind were left unrestrained due to desires, bad unskillful qualities of covetousness and displeasure would become overwhelming. Yet, Arahants have no desire, for this reason, they naturally have restraint, protecting the faculty of mind, and achieving its restraint. When they naturally have this noble sense of restraint, they experience an unsullied bliss inside themselves.

Arahants naturally have situational awareness when going out and coming back; when looking ahead and aside; when bending and extending the limbs; when bearing the clothing, other requisites, and similar things; when eating, drinking, chewing, and tasting; when urinating and defecating; when walking, standing, sitting, sleeping, waking, speaking, and keeping silent (An ordinary person should try and develop similar qualities..).

When they have this entire spectrum of noble ethics, this noble contentment, this noble sense of restraint, and this noble mindfulness and situational awareness, they are not fond of company, and they live isolated in the presence or absence of others wherever they live—in a house, a temple, a city, a village, a forest (wilderness, the root of a tree, a hill, a ravine, a mountain cave, a charnel ground, the open air, a heap of straw), etc. (An ordinary person should try and develop similar qualities..).

After daily activities and the meal, they return to their resting places and maintain noble mindfulness at all postures at any time. Giving up covetousness for the world, they possess a heart rid of covetousness, cleansing the mind of covetousness.

Since they have given up ill will and malevolence, their mind is free from ill will, full of sympathy for all living beings, cleansing the mind of ill will.

Since they have given up dullness and drowsiness, their mind has no dullness and drowsiness, perceiving light, mindful and aware, the mind is free from the stains of dullness and drowsiness. Giving up restlessness and remorse, their mind overcomes restlessness and remorse. Giving up doubt, their minds having gone beyond doubt, not undecided about skillful qualities, cleansing the mind of doubt (Ideally, an ordinary person should try and maintain mindfulness…).

Arahants have given up these five hindrances, corruptions of the heart that weaken wisdom. Anagamis should develop further (Ideally, an ordinary person should develop four-fold Nibbana to give up hindrances…).

While walking the path to higher stages of four-fold nibbana, a Sakadagami quite secluded from sensual pleasures, secluded from unskillful qualities, they enter and remain in the first absorption, which has the rapture and bliss born of seclusion, while placing the mind and keeping it connected.

As the placing of the mind and keeping it connected are stilled, they enter and remain in the second absorption, which has the rapture and bliss born of immersion, with internal clarity and mind at one, without placing the mind and keeping it connected.

And with the fading away of rapture, they enter and remain in the third absorption, where they experience equanimity, mindfulness and awareness, personally experiencing the bliss of which the noble ones declare, 'Equanimous and mindful, one experiences bliss.'

Giving up pleasure and pain, and ending former happiness and sadness, they enter and remain in the fourth absorption, without pleasure or pain, with pure equanimity and mindfulness. Thereafter, they experience higher jhanas (path to Arahant).

When their mind has become immersed in noble mindfulness like this—purified, bright, flawless, rid of corruptions, pliable, workable, steady, and imperturbable—they extend it toward recollection of past lives.

They recollect many kinds of past lives, that is, one, two, three, four, five, ten, twenty, thirty, forty, fifty, a hundred, a thousand, a hundred thousand rebirths; many eons of the world contracting, many eons of the world expanding, many eons of the world contracting and expanding. They remember: 'There, I was named this, my clan was that, I looked like this, and that was my food. This was how I felt pleasure and pain, and that was how my life ended. When I passed away from that place I was reborn somewhere else. There, too, I was named this, my clan was that, I looked like this, and that was my food. This was how I felt pleasure and pain, and that was how my life ended. When I passed away from that place I was reborn here.' And so they recollect their many kinds of past lives, with features and details.

When their mind has become immersed in noble mindfulness like this—purified, bright, flawless, rid of corruptions, pliable, workable, steady, and imperturbable—they extend it toward knowledge of the death and rebirth of sentient beings.

With clairvoyance that is purified and superhuman, they see sentient beings passing away and being reborn—inferior and superior, beautiful and ugly, in a good place or a bad place. They understand how sentient beings are reborn according to their deeds: 'These dear beings did bad things by way of body, speech, and mind. They spoke ill of the noble ones; they had wrong view; and they chose to act out of that wrong view. When their body breaks up, after death, they're reborn in a place of loss, a bad place, the underworld, hell.

These dear beings, however, did good things by way of body, speech, and mind.

They never spoke ill of the noble ones; they had right view; and they chose to act out of that right view. When their body breaks up, after death, they're reborn in a good place, a heavenly realm.' And so, with clairvoyance that is purified and superhuman, they see sentient beings passing away and being reborn—inferior and superior, beautiful and ugly, in a good place or a bad place. They understand how sentient beings are reborn according to their deeds.

When their mind has become immersed in noble mindfulness like this—purified, bright, flawless, rid of corruptions, pliable, workable, steady, and imperturbable—they extend it toward knowledge of the ending of defilements. They truly understand: 'This is suffering' ... 'This is the origin of suffering' ... 'This is the cessation of suffering' ... 'This is the practice that leads to the cessation of suffering'.

They truly understand: 'These are defilements' ... 'This is the origin of defilements' ... 'This is the cessation of defilements' ... 'This is the practice that leads to the cessation of defilements'.

Knowing and seeing like this, their mind is freed from the defilements of sensuality, desire to be reborn, and ignorance. When they're freed, they know they're freed.

They understand: 'Rebirth is ended, the spiritual journey has been completed, what had to be done has been done, there is nothing further for this place.'

This is called a person who neither mortifies themselves or others, being committed to the practice of not mortifying themselves or others.

They live without wishes in the present life, quenched, cooled, experiencing bliss, with self-become divine."

That is what the Buddha said. Satisfied, the companions approved what the Buddha said".

Chapter 54

Concluding Remarks

Below is the summary of the key issues.

♦ Nibbana is a universal happening. Nibbana is a universal happening just like birth, and just like birth happens at random time without control or will of a person, Nibbana happens at a random time to a random person who has fulfilled the requisites for Nibbana; wisdom and merits.

♦ Conventions lose its credibility at the universal level, and all conventions are subject to change. Nibbana is not a socially accepted truth, or truth that is collectively agreed by society.

♦ Noble path can be developed to reducing grasping to conventions. End of birth and death over samsara, the path leading to Nibbana is shaped by one's karma and merits.

♦ Karma and merits have a way of functioning, not all karma come to effect in the same manner, and certain sila can shape karma to a lesser degree, and attending to Triple Gem generates higher degree of merits. Thus, a Sotapanna may have broken the precepts (say drinking alcohol), that are minor karma in the Noble Path, yet, Sotapanna will not divide the teachings of the Supreme Buddha or misinterpret Dhamma that are major karma blocking the Noble Path (Besides, Sotapanna will not grasp into conventions or think self can retain with stability within the universal functioning). In this manner, among those who aspire Nibbana, whoever disrespect the Triple Gem or prevent others progressing to Noble path bears consequences of such actions, they are unable to gain Nibbana. Those who take sila such as some conventional Bhikkhus may not drink alcohol, yet they can divide universal teachings of the Buddha creating major Karma; division in ordinary Sangha. Creating division in ordinary Sangha prevent Nibbana for conventional bhikkhus, such as Devadatta. This is not to say one way of a life style is better than another but to clarify diversity of karma.

◆Triple Gem refers to universal Buddha, universal Dhamma (four-fold Nibbana), and universal Sangha.

◆Vinaya and Sasana refers to Sotapanna to Arahant.

◆Vipassana refers to Sotapanna to Arahant.

◆Nibbana is achieved through four progressive stages (Sotapanna, Sakadagami, Anagami and Arahant).

◆Nibbana is a natural process just like the birth of beings; it happens on its own time shaped by karmic influence.

◆Jhana practice among ordinary people and the practice of jhana by an Anagami in the training path of four-fold Nibbana differs.

◆In Noble Path, jhanas are not developed as consciously developed meditation practice, rather jhanas come to establish naturally in the mind of a practitioner at a random instance once after one completed Anagami state followed by insight of non-self-view gained at the Sotapanna level.

◆What is commonly agreed by the society is not the agreement by universal functioning, rather each and every individual come to experience consequences of their own karma. Each being is responsible for one's own karma, and life experience is individually experienced by each, so as Nibbana is a personal experience for each.

◆What is mutually agreed upon among the people across societies and the conventional Dhamma can have various presentations; traditions, divisions rituals, lifestyles based on conventions, etc. If Nibbana were a convention, that would be subject to change. Rather, Nibbana brings an end to changing conventions, birth and death, and samsara.

◆A person who knows what's in textbooks may know as a scholar, someone who has Dhamma knowledge. A person who teaches what's in textbooks may know as a Dhamma teacher, someone who teaches what's in books. A person who teaches meditation practices may know as a meditation teacher, someone who teach meditation practices. A person who's mind is grasping to conventions; either as a monk or householder, based on rituals, standard practices may know as a ritualistic monk or householder. A person who attains Nibbana may know as a Sotapanna to Arahant irrespective of conventions; caste, age, gender, lifestyle, external appearance, country, nationality, languages spoken etc.

♦ Stream-entry (Sotapanna) is not a consciously produced state but a natural process that happens in a random instance just like birth for beings. That moment allows a being to be born in the noble linage and brings stable change. Stream Entry (and other stages of four-fold Nibbana) causes sudden change in a being so that a person who was before Stream-entry will not be the one after Stream Entry and so on. A person who becomes a Stream Winner comes to possess good inner qualities in an instant.

♦ Nibbana is a training in mind.

♦ To train to cessation or Nibbana, giving up in mind refers to giving up getting attached to one's thoughts that make up the presence of materials, the world, self-view, and others in one's mind. In other words, whatever material things that are physically present and whatever the world is physically present should not interfere with one's mind.

♦ Progress in the Dhamma path is not measured by somebody's appearance or years of a meditation practice but by the extent to which mental attachment to fetters is reduced.

♦ How can a person recognize another person's reduction in attachment to the fetters? Often, thoughts are expressed in words. By analysing their words, those who compare one another and those who divide universal Dhamma are still grasping the fetters.

♦ One who does not complete the four-fold Nibbana and practices the Dhamma is simply touching a double-edged sword. This is because unless one gains Nibbana, one's suffering will not cease. By understanding that, a person who aspires to one's own good may practice the Dhamma in a way that leads to abandoning their own mental pain and samsara.

♦Finding the Triple Gem through an appearance or an action alone can be a difficult task for another person, especially because an ordinary person cannot read another person's intentional actions. Instead, ordinary people may comprehend the Triple Gem through words of wisdom. The subject matter and the content related to four-fold Nibbana should be explained as universally applicable Dhamma that happens at a random occasion shaped by one's karma and merits by whoever explains.

♦Throughout history, you can find many occasions when bhikkhus misinterpreted Dhamma. *The Path of Purification* suggests that a person takes a meditation practice, a method called *kasina,* in which one stares at an external object until the image of the object is imprinted in one's mind. This image then gives rise to a countersign that is said to indicate the attainment of threshold concentration, a necessary prelude to jhāna. When you develop the idea of impermanence through concentration, when you lose concentration, you will likely lose the idea of impermanence. Besides, impermanence is not merely an idea that you imprint through effort but a life experience. When you understand impermanence through imprint, such an understanding can only be short-lived with an underlying tendency to grasp worldly experiences. Instead, when you understand impermanence through life experience, understanding can only be replaced by higher understanding, Sotapanna to Arahant.

♦ Assuming that you understand emptiness as a concept, to reduce mental pain and to experience less of it as an ordinary person, you need to reduce excessive liking, disliking, and expectations based on a deluded understanding that all that you expect can be fulfilled. This can be applied within daily life while doing regular activities.

♦ Assuming that you understand interbeing as a concept, yet if you experience mental pain alone in your own mind, to experience less mental pain as an ordinary person, you need to reduce excessive liking, disliking and expectations based on the deluded understanding that all that you expect can be fulfilled. This can be applied within daily life while doing regular activities.

♦ If you prefer compassion, you should apply compassion to yourself and reduce your mental pain by reducing likes, dislikes, and expectations of worldly experiences. If you want to care about the wellbeing of others, you can become compassionate being by reducing mental pain for yourself and avoid causing pain to others by reducing too much likes (greediness), dislikes (hatred), and expectations (delusion) that you have for them. Thus, practice leading to higher Dhamma (Sotapanna to Arahnat) remain the same for all, universally applicable for all.

♦ What is the point of asking "whether I exist or not"? Merely from a view point, there is clear evidence that a person born into the world experiences good and bad in their mind. When your life experience provides you the evidence that life has good and bad, and if you still experience sadness, disappointment and the like, that is sufficient evidence that you experience mental pain in your daily life. The purpose of Cessation, Nibbana is not to merely discuss viewpoints but to let go of mental pain; reduce desires and end mental pain through cessation; four-fold Nibbana.

♦The universe functions in such a way that, when a person is born, birth brings death, illnesses, losses, gains, falls and rises are part of life, the way of life. Life is an experience where a person is faced to meet with conventions that functions within the universe.

♦Evidence based science involve testing ideas with evidence from the natural world. Scientific arguments typically involve three components: the idea (a hypothesis or theory), the expectations generated by that idea (frequently called predictions), and the actual observations relevant to those expectations (the evidence). Evidence based four-fold Nibbana involve testing life experience with evidence (based on worldly experience through sensory information).

♦When asked if you claim you are a disciple of Buddha, you should try to become a genuine disciple of Buddha. Without attaining four-fold Nibbana, one cannot train another. Without declaring one's attainment, another person cannot know whether or not the person who shares Dhamma knowledge has completed the training (four-fold Nibbana).

♦How can one become a disciple of Buddha? By completing the four-fold Nibbana, a person becomes a disciple of Buddha. Until then, one is simply training to become a disciple of the Buddha but is not a disciple of the Buddha.

♦What things should an ordinary person seeking the Triple Gem look for? They should investigate if the person who claims an Arahant explains Dhammas as a universal happening. The person who delivers higher Dhamma as universal Dhamma should also carry Dhamma within and should reveal the signs of nobility through speech (words), actions, and thoughts. They should investigate if the person who claims an Arahant expects materials, honour and similar things in return for sharing the higher Dhamma. This can be easily understood, if those who claim Arahants charge you a fee for sharing the Dhamma (attending courses, subscription fees justifying the need it for their survival), these are some indications that they are grasping for worldly things (materials, honour etc.) and are not renouncing.

♦ Practicing leading to Nibbana at the entry level (or Stream-entry stage) requires within daily life maintaining the mind in the middle; becoming a good person in all areas of life; and not discriminating against self or others based on social divisions, reflecting the qualities of the Triple Gem in thoughts and engaging in wholesome activities as much as possible in daily life.

♦ In sum, if you want to experience four-fold Nibbana, you may pay homage to the supremely enlightened Buddha in your thoughts day and night!
After that, four-fold Nibbana (universal Dhamma) and universal (Savaka) Sangha! Include noble virtues[29] into your practice of Dhamma and engage in ten wholesome activities, especially work on developing the right view (i.e. give up grasping self-view and conventions). This is a summary of the practice leading to Sotapanna. The practice remains the same for all.

---

[29] Fourth factor of Stream Entry refers to developing noble virtues; noble virtues can be developed by treating others in the manner one would like to be treated, maintain noble precepts (abstain from killing living beings, stealing, sexual misconduct, false speech, backbiting, harsh or abusive speech, useless or meaningless conversation, wrong means of livelihood), becoming a good person who looks after others as applicable to oneself (it may be looking after friends, family, an employer or employees, ascetics and so forth), and becoming an ethical person who genuinely cares for others and avoids discriminating against others on any grounds is the practice that is helpful in developing noble virtues, a factor of stream entry.

Sources

Ajahn Cha, The Collected Teachings of Ajahn Chah - Single Volume (2011): https://www.abhayagiri.org/media/books/Chah_The_Collected_Teachings_of_Ajahn_Chah.pdf

Ajahn Chah. A Taste of Freedom", Access to Insight (BCBS Edition), 30 November 2013, http://www.accesstoinsight.org/lib/thai/chah/atasteof.html

Bhadantacariya Buddhagosa, The Path of Purification (Visuddhinana- katha) translated by Nanamoli Thera (2011): https://www.accesstoinsight.org/lib/authors/nanamoli/PathofPurification_2011.pdf

Bhikkhu Nanamoli and Bhikkhu Bodhi (Translated from the Pali by Bikku Nanamoli and Edited and Revised by Bhikku Bodhi) (1995), Culakammavibhanga Sutta, MN 135, A new Translation of the Majjima Nikaya, Buddhist Publication Society, Kandy. *http://lirs.ru/lib/sutra/The_Middle_Length_Discourses(Majjhima_Nikaya),Nanamoli,Bodhi,1995.pdf*

David Tuffley, (2011), Santideva's, The Bodhicaryaratara, (A Guide to the Bodhisattva Way of Life, Santideva), Retold by David Tuffley Smashwords Edition.

Daw Mya Tin, M. A. (1986). The Dhammapada: Verses and Stories, (1986), Edited by Editorial Committee, Burma Tipitaka, Association Rangoon, Burma, (Courtesy of Nibbana.com). https://tienvnguyen.net/images/file/kx6TZFiS0ggQAEMp/dhammapada- versesandstories-a.pdf

Mark Siderits, (Nagarjuna's Middle Way: The Mulamadhyamakakarika (Classics of Indian Buddhism): The Mulamadhyamakakarikas, Wisdom Publication, Boston.

Other Web Sources:

Buddhist Publication Society
https://www.bps.lk

Dhammatalks.org.
https://www.dhammatalks.org

Pali Text Society
https://ancient-buddhist-texts.net

SuttaCentral.net.
https://suttacentral.net

Images
Angkana6395/shutterstock.com
sarayut_syShutterstock.com
Barashkova+Natalia/shutterstock.com

May all beings be well and happy!

www.ingramcontent.com/pod-product-compliance
Lightning Source LLC
LaVergne TN
LVHW070521070526
838199LV00072B/6669